VISIONS OF FINANCIAL ORDER

Princeton Studies in Global and Comparative Sociology

Andreas Wimmer, *Series Editor*

Visions of Financial Order

National Institutions and the Development of Banking Regulation

Kim Pernell

PRINCETON UNIVERSITY PRESS
PRINCETON AND OXFORD

Published by Princeton University Press
41 William Street, Princeton, New Jersey 08540
99 Banbury Road, Oxford OX2 6JX

press.princeton.edu

Library of Congress Cataloging-in-Publication Data

Names: Pernell, Kim, 1985– author.
Title: Visions of financial order : national institutions and the development of
    banking regulation / Kim Pernell.
Description: Princeton : Princeton University Press, [2024] | Series: Princeton studies
    in global and comparative sociology | Includes bibliographical references and index.
Identifiers: LCCN 2024005098 (print) | LCCN 2024005099 (ebook) |
    ISBN 9780691255422 (hardback) | ISBN 9780691255439 (paperback) |
    ISBN 9780691255446 (ebook)
Subjects: LCSH: Banks and banking—State supervision—United States. | Banks and
    banking—State supervision—Canada. | Banks and banking—State supervision—
    Spain. | Global Financial Crisis, 2008–2009. | BISAC: SOCIAL SCIENCE /
    Sociology / General | POLITICAL SCIENCE / Political Economy
Classification: LCC HG1725 .P476 2024 (print) | LCC HG1725 (ebook) |
    DDC 346/.082—dc23/eng/20240324
LC record available at https://lccn.loc.gov/2024005098
LC ebook record available at https://lccn.loc.gov/2024005099

British Library Cataloging-in-Publication Data is available

Editorial: Meagan Levinson and Erik Beranek
Production Editorial: Natalie Baan
Cover Design: Katie Osborne
Production: Lauren Reese
Publicity: William Pagdatoon
Copyeditor: Kathleen Kageff

Cover Image: anatolir / Adobe Stock

This book has been composed in Adobe Text and Gotham

10 9 8 7 6 5 4 3 2 1

For my parents

CONTENTS

Figures

Tables

VISIONS OF FINANCIAL ORDER

1

Introduction

The story of the global financial crisis of the late 2000s is by now a familiar one. A minor decline in US housing prices sparked a crisis in the mortgage market that ignited a disaster that threatened to bring down the global financial system. As interest rates rose and property values started to drop in 2006, overextended borrowers struggled to refinance or keep up with their mortgage payments, and a wave of foreclosures followed. This unexpected increase in failed mortgages was bad enough, since financial institutions always struggle when more borrowers than expected fail to repay their loans. Yet recent developments in the financial system amplified the problem.

In the decades leading up to the crisis, banks had leaned hard into creating, trading, and holding new financial instruments derived from mortgages or other kinds of debt. As mortgage defaults rose, the value of financial instruments that used mortgage assets as their building blocks plummeted. These dynamics stoked panic. The complexity of the new financial instruments made it hard for investors to determine if they were worth anything. Their opaque structure also made it difficult for market participants to determine exactly how much exposure an individual financial institution had to the underlying risks. Nervous investors scrambled to offload all but the most transparent investments during the crisis, depressing the value of even complex and opaque financial instruments that incorporated few or no mortgage assets. Banks that held these securities suffered big losses. Investors responded by withdrawing their funds from banks, while banks stopped lending to one another. This set off a vicious cycle in which a rising tide of bank losses encouraged investors to further restrict the flow of resources to banks, which only amplified their financial distress.

As the housing crisis transformed into a banking crisis, deep interconnections between banks also transformed what was initially a crisis limited to the United States into a truly global event. Since banks borrow from other banks around the world, market disruptions in one country can easily spark a global liquidity crunch. And since banks also compete in an increasingly global marketplace, bankers face strong pressures to follow their international peers into innovative and risky (but potentially lucrative) strategies. Indeed, in the decade leading up to the crisis, banks from many of the world's other major financial capitals followed their American counterparts in making heavier use of complex and opaque financial instruments, including new forms of asset securitization and financial derivatives. Sometimes, these banks created, traded, or held securities that used US mortgages as their building blocks. Other times, these securities incorporated assets generated closer to home. Both strategies led to losses for banks when the global markets for these financial instruments collapsed in 2007 and 2008. To resolve the severe financial crisis that followed, governments were forced to intervene in financial markets on an unprecedented scale. Many countries, borrowers, and households have yet to recover from the economic blows they experienced in this period.[1]

Given the devastating economic and social impacts of the global financial crisis, it is no surprise that this event has attracted a great deal of scholarly interest. Scholars continue to debate the relative impact of factors that contributed to the emergence of an asset price bubble in the US housing market, including historically low interest rates, global trade imbalances, lax lending practices, government support to housing, and the rising popularity of mortgage securitization.[2] A large body of research has also examined the causes and consequences of the uptake of the complex financial innovations that exponentially increased bank exposure to mortgage performance.[3] More recently, scholars have linked many of the risky behaviors that featured in the crisis to changes in bank corporate governance arrangements, showing how the rise of a new model of management, the shareholder value model, gave bank executives new incentives to seek out riskier strategies and trim reserves to the bare minimum.[4]

Given the powerful competitive pressures banks faced in this period, then, it is no mystery why so many of them ended up getting in over their heads with high-risk, potentially high-reward strategies. The real question—and one that existing scholarship has yet to adequately answer—is why the regulators charged with keeping the financial system safe and stable failed to stop them. In each of the countries where the crisis unfolded, banks operated under the auspices of a well-established regulatory system. But as the experiences of the late 2000s revealed, regulators often fell far short of the goal of protecting the financial system. When we consider that these regulatory failures also arrived on the heels of nearly two decades of development of the international regulatory architecture, the puzzle only deepens. The regulatory failures of this period were also more pronounced in certain countries than in others.

While no country was immune from the effects of the crisis, regulators in some countries (like Canada, France, and Spain) managed to avoid some of the major regulatory missteps that led to serious losses for banks in other countries (like the United States, the United Kingdom, and Germany).[5] Banking regulation may have failed at the global level, in other words, but it also failed more spectacularly in some places than others. In this book, I leverage this cross-national variation to offer new insights into the question of where more or less effective regulatory systems come from.

My central argument is that the systems of financial regulation that defined this era were deeply influenced by the different *principles of order* embedded in national regulatory and political institutions. Or, to state the same point in a different way, regulators in different countries subscribed to different understandings of the causes of prosperity and stability in the economy, which suggested different ideas about how best to regulate finance to promote order. I will show that these divergent principles of order shaped the policy choices of banking regulators at multiple critical junctures, giving rise to regulatory differences with direct implications for how banks in different countries experienced the crisis.

My perspective on regulation (and where it comes from) departs from the conventional wisdom on this subject. When most scholars discuss financial regulation, they tend to treat it as rational—as something that emerges from economic imperatives that *demand* a certain kind of response. Some political scientists and sociologists have challenged this view by underscoring the political roots of regulation. From this perspective, the content of regulation more often reflects the power of certain interest groups (especially the regulated industry) to "capture" regulators, compelling policy makers to introduce policies that serve industry interests. It has been much less common, however, to think about financial regulation as something cultural—as something that emerges from different shared beliefs about efficacy or order among regulators themselves. Recently, scholars have become increasingly open to seeing cultural influences in the development of social policy, like education or social welfare policy, but this perspective has rarely been extended to economic policy making.

This book is an attempt to change that. Even when it came to the fine-grained technical details of banking regulation—one of the most rational of all policy domains—I find that meaning still mattered. In the chapters to come, I show how the broad principles of order embedded in national political and regulatory institutions shaped the way that experts approached their regulatory tasks. As we will see, this approach provides the key to understanding how financial regulation came to be so different across countries, even at a time when regulators around the world had agreed to enforce the same international rules.

Standard Accounts of Regulatory Failure in the 2008 Financial Crisis

Before getting into the details of this argument, it's important to consider how far standard accounts of regulatory success and failure get us toward understanding the regulatory patterns that contributed to the 2008 crisis. Three explanations currently dominate the limited scholarship on this topic. The first explanation emphasizes international influences, with a focus on the weaknesses and limitations of the transnational regulatory framework (the Basel Capital Accord) that governed all internationally active banks after 1988. The second explanation emphasizes the rise of shadow banking, a change within financial markets that made it harder for regulators to understand and effectively govern dynamics in these markets. And the third explanation emphasizes the growing power and influence of the regulated industry, which increased pressures on regulators to relax their standards. These factors are part of this story, but they are not the whole story. Below, I explain why.

REGULATORY FAILURE AT THE INTERNATIONAL LEVEL

In 1988, central bankers from the G-10 countries agreed to enforce the same transnational regulatory agreement, the Basel Capital Accord, which established common minimum standards for bank capital. As highly leveraged institutions, banks operate with very thin financial margins, and unexpected losses can easily drive them into ruin. To protect against this possibility, banks keep resources on hand (capital) to absorb losses before they can impact day-to-day operations. The rise of new requirements for bank capital at the international level was the key shift that redefined the regulatory landscape in the 1990s and 2000s; accordingly, it makes sense that scholars interested in understanding the regulatory failures that featured in the 2008 crisis might start their investigations here.

A sizeable body of research now examines the deficiencies of the Basel Capital Accord. Some of this scholarship focuses on explaining why these international rules failed to restrain risky bank behavior, while other studies go a step further by explaining how these new rules directly encouraged banks to engage in imprudent strategies.[6] Yet attention to these international considerations does not get us very far toward understanding the other part of the puzzle: why regulatory standards in certain countries ended up being so much better than those in other countries in the late 2000s. Even across countries that all complied with the Basel Capital Accord, banking regulation continued to vary considerably, and in ways that mattered for how banks experienced the crisis.

In the chapters that follow, I focus on explaining the divergent development of banking regulation across three countries that were all parties to the

Basel Capital Accord—the United States, Canada, and Spain—yet continued to make different regulatory choices in crucial areas. I chose the United States as the primary case of interest because regulatory choices here carried an outsized impact for the rest of the global financial system.[7] Canada represents a "most similar" case. Although Canadian regulatory standards did depart from American regulatory standards in a few key respects, the regulatory systems of these countries were much more alike than different in global perspective— and these extensive similarities make it easier to identify the factors that led to differences across them. Spain represents a "most different" case. Even by the standards of other European countries, the Spanish bank regulatory system was uniquely strict and interventionist. This case allows us to see whether lessons learned from the close US-Canada comparison continue to apply in a very different context.

The major differences in banking regulation that distinguished these countries can be summarized as follows. In comparative perspective, the US banking regulators did relatively little to prevent banks from gaining exposure to the risks of assets they had *securitized* (e.g., repackaged and sold to financial markets in the form of debt securities). They also failed to encourage banks to set aside significant reserves against these new risks.[8] Additionally, US banking regulators supported excluding banks' financial subsidiaries or affiliates from stricter Basel-style regulation and also endorsed hands-off regulatory treatment for novel innovations like financial derivatives. Each choice carried direct implications for the financial difficulties American banks experienced when the crisis hit.[9]

In Canada, regulatory standards mirrored US regulatory standards in many respects, but they also tended to be stricter in areas that concerned the size or quality of the reserves banks set aside against their risks. Canadian banks faced tighter restrictions on exposures to asset-backed commercial paper programs (a form of securitization), a stronger push to maintain substantial reserves against potential losses from bad loans, and a supervisory framework that encompassed banks *and* their financial affiliates. Each regulatory choice contributed to Canadian banks' ability to weather events that devastated their counterparts in the United States.[10]

In Spain, regulators chose to adopt even more restrictive requirements in many of these same areas. They placed uniquely tight limits on banks' abilities to remove securitized assets from the balance sheet, introduced new regulations that required bankers to increase reserves against bad loans during periods of economic prosperity, and insisted on supervising banks and their financial affiliates as a single, collective unit. While this strict regulatory regime did not prevent the crisis from eventually arriving in Spain, bank outcomes here would have been much worse if Spanish regulators had chosen to copy their US counterparts.[11]

These cross-national differences in banking regulation were not the only things that mattered for bank performance during the crisis, but they did matter. Fully understanding the regulatory failures that gave rise to the crisis, then, requires understanding two patterns at once: why the substantial efforts to strengthen banking regulation at the international level failed to bear fruit *and* why regulators in certain countries used the discretion they enjoyed under these international rules to pursue more or less dangerous regulatory paths. While we already know quite a bit about why the Basel framework failed to keep the global financial system safe, we know almost nothing about why regulatory standards in certain Basel member countries ended up being so much better (or worse) than those in others.

THE RISE OF SHADOW BANKING

One feature that distinguished the 2008 financial crisis from those that preceded it was the heavy involvement of "shadow banks"—financial institutions that, like banks, focus on converting short-term borrowings (i.e., deposits, funds raised in money markets) into long-term assets (e.g., loans, securities), but are not subject to the same regulatory standards as banks. Shadow banks played an active role in the crisis by fueling the origination and securitization of home mortgages, by contributing to the liquidity crunch in funding markets, and by contributing to the lack of market transparency that scared away so many investors in banks and other financial institutions.[12] Some scholars have linked the rising prevalence of shadow banks to the regulatory failures that featured in the crisis by arguing that the transfer of risk from regulated banks to shadow banks prevented regulators from noticing problems until it was too late.

There is no doubt that banking regulators around the world were caught flat-footed by the extent to which credit and liquidity risk built up within the shadow banking system. But this account of regulatory failure, too, struggles to explain the observed regulatory differences across countries. As we will see, there is abundant evidence that regulators around the world were well aware that some risk was shifting outside of the regulated financial system after the 1990s. But they varied in the extent to which they viewed this trend in a positive or negative light. As one example, US banking regulators repeatedly argued that the rise of shadow banking was a positive development that made the financial system safer by enhancing the intensity of market discipline within it. Spanish regulators, by contrast, argued that the same shift presented a serious threat to order in the financial system. These different regulatory views directly informed the different policy choices regulators made in this area. The regulatory failures of this era, then, were not just products of regulatory naïveté in the face of a changing financial market structure. It also mattered how these changes were perceived.

INDUSTRY PRESSURE

A third explanation for the regulatory failures of this period underscores the role of financial industry pressure in encouraging banking regulators to relax their standards. At first glance, this explanation would seem to account for some of the variation we see across countries. The decades after 1980 were defined by rapid growth in the size, profitability, and political power of financial institutions around the world, and these trends were even more pronounced in some countries than in others.

In the United States in particular, financial-sector profits increased sixfold between 1980 and 2009, with commercial banks experiencing particularly large gains. In 1978, the collective assets of US commercial banks totaled around $1.2 trillion, equivalent to 53 percent of GDP; by 2007, they had risen to around $11.8 trillion, equivalent to 84 percent of GDP.[13] The gains of this period were also unevenly shared. In the 1980s and 1990s, the resource share of regional and national banks rapidly increased, while that of smaller, community-oriented banks declined.[14] The total share of industry assets controlled by the five largest US banks increased from around 30 percent in 1997 to just over 44 percent in 2007, while the numbers of banks in operation also declined. In the mid-1980s, there were more than fourteen thousand independent banks in operation in the United States, a number that had dropped below eighty-five hundred by the start of the new millennium.[15]

Many scholars have linked these changes in the structure of the US banking system to the regulatory developments that followed.[16] Starting from the assumption that all regulators are for sale, and that regulation is a commodity purchased by the business groups most interested in and able to buy it, regulatory capture theorists assume that permissive, industry-friendly regulation will become more common as the regulated industry grows more powerful.[17] These scholars argue that regulated firms are especially well positioned to coerce regulators in industries with lower barriers to collective action, as when industries feature fewer individual players to coordinate or where industry resources concentrate in fewer hands.[18] Thus, as the US banking system grew increasingly *consolidated, concentrated*, and *resource rich* after the early 1980s, regulatory capture theorists have argued, American banks also became better positioned to secure regulation that aligned with industry interests.[19]

While historical trends in the development of US banking regulation do seem to align with these predictions, placing the US case in comparative perspective tells a different story. In the 1990s and 2000s, the United States did adopt one of the world's most laissez-faire, market-oriented systems of financial regulation. Given this trend, we might have also expected the industry conditions (consolidation, concentration) known to lead to greater power and influence for regulated firms to be especially pronounced in the US context. Instead, we

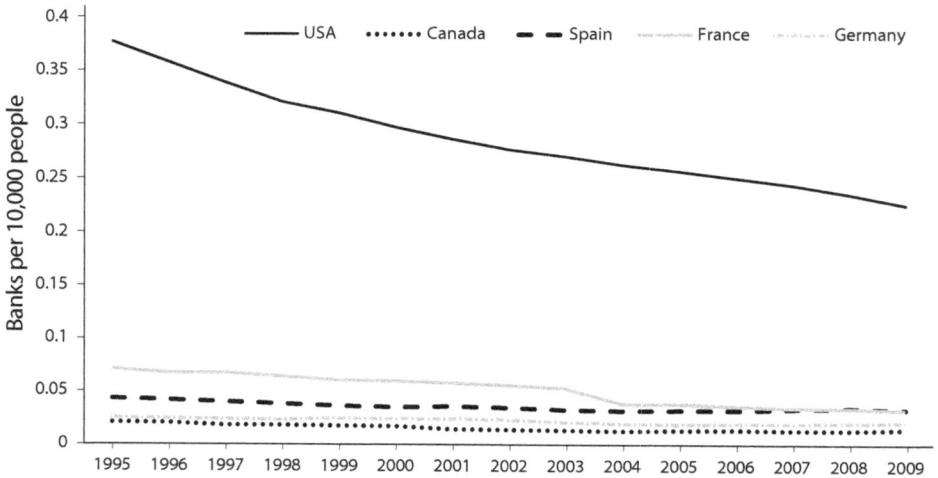

FIGURE 1.1. Banks per capita in the United States, Canada, Spain, France, and Germany. *Sources*: Number of banks: OECD (2014), "Structure of the Financial System," OECD Banking Statistics (database), https://doi.org/10.1787/data-00271-en (accessed September 22, 2014). Population of country: OECD (2015) "Demography and Population," https://stats.oecd.org/Index.aspx?DataSetCode=HISTPOP# (accessed January 12, 2015).

find the opposite pattern. Even as the US banking system grew increasingly consolidated and concentrated over time, it remained far less consolidated and concentrated than the banking system of virtually every other peer country.

To illustrate this point, figure 1.1 compares trends in the number of banks per capita in the United States, Canada, Spain, France, and Germany between 1995 and 2009. As we see, even as the numbers of US banks dropped precipitously over time, the overall level of industry consolidation here remained much lower than in countries with more restrictive regulatory regimes in place. In 2007, there were still about 24 independent banks per million residents of the United States, compared to 3.4 independent banks per million residents of Spain and only 1.3 independent banks per million residents of Canada.

Trends in industry concentration tell a similar story. Using the same five countries, figure 1.2 compares trends in the five-bank asset concentration index, a common measure of industry concentration that reports the proportion of assets that are held by the country's five largest banks as a share of total banking system assets (a higher value on the index suggests a more concentrated industry). Once again, the US banking system did grow substantially more concentrated over time. However, the overall level of banking system concentration in the United States remained much lower than that of virtually every other peer country.

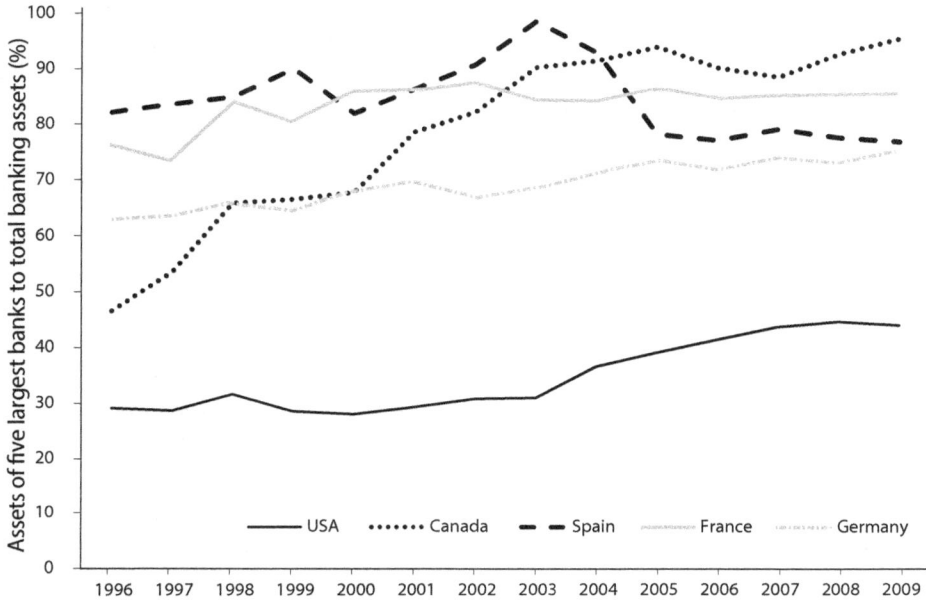

FIGURE 1.2. Top five bank asset concentration index in the United States, Canada, Spain, France, and Germany. *Source*: World Bank, Global Financial Development Database, June 2017 version, https://www.worldbank.org/en/publication/gfdr/gfdr -2016/data/global-financial-development-database (accessed February 1, 2018).

Industry consolidation and concentration are the structural features that have captured the greatest attention from scholars of regulatory capture, because they are thought to be directly linked to the capacity of industry participants to engage in collective action and exert influence over regulators.[20] It is also possible, however, that an industry's capacity for influence could stem from the absolute value of resources its largest members control. In 2005, four of the world's top twenty largest banks were headquartered in the United States, with one of these banks (Citigroup) inhabiting the second-place position. Four French banks and three UK banks were also among the top twenty in this period, as was one Spanish bank and one German bank, but zero Canadian banks.[21] These comparative trends in the mid-2000s, however, are very different from those observed a decade earlier, when only a single US bank held a position among the world's twenty largest banks (Chase Manhattan, at number sixteen) in 1996.[22] While the rising absolute scale of resources controlled by the largest US banks may have very well favored a movement toward more permissive regulation, the timing of this shift implies that this was not its only cause. American policy makers fully embraced a radically more permissive, market-friendly approach to financial regulation in the late 1980s—long before American banks experienced the rapid growth that propelled them into higher positions in the global size ranking. It seems more likely that this turn toward regulatory permissiveness sparked these changes in industry structure, rather than the other way around.

To be very clear: I am *not* arguing that the rising power and influence of the banking industry had zero impact on the development of national regulatory systems, either in the United States or elsewhere. This was almost certainly not the case. In fact, a close look at regulatory policy making in the 1990s and 2000s provides abundant evidence that banking regulators in the United States (and in other countries) were highly attuned to industry interests and kept up a constant dialogue with the firms they regulated. It is also possible that other, less easily measured dimensions of industry power and influence could explain some of these comparative regulatory trends. For instance, the United States could have had a more active "revolving door" between financial institutions and regulatory agencies, which might have given American regulators a greater personal stake in serving industry interests, or, alternatively, paved the way for more subtle "cultural capture" by the regulated industry. For reasons that I will discuss later, I am also skeptical of these explanations. However, in the absence of systematic cross-national data on the career trajectories of banking regulators, it is hard to definitively discount (or confirm) possibilities like these.

These caveats aside, the observation that comparative trends in the structural conditions known to favor regulatory capture did not align with comparative trends in bank-friendly regulation should give us serious pause. At minimum, it implies that scholars of regulation would do well to at least consider alternative explanations for the rise of more or less effective regulatory regimes across countries, instead of assuming that these patterns invariably reduce to trends in industry influence.

Principles of Order Matter

This book offers a fresh perspective on regulation by arguing that different principles of order contributed to divergent approaches to banking regulation in the decades leading up to the 2008 crisis. At first glance, the argument that banking regulators subscribed to different understandings about economic order, which shaped their policy choices, might not seem controversial. Of course, banking regulators (like the rest of us) have their own ways of viewing the world and their place within it, and it is hardly a stretch to imagine that these perspectives might inform the way these actors approached their tasks. Yet serious, sustained attention to the influence of the worldviews and perceptions of banking regulators is surprisingly absent from the scholarship on the crisis, and indeed, from most of the scholarship on regulation itself. In endlessly relitigating whether regulatory policies serve the interests of the general public or those of the regulated industry, scholars of regulation have paid too little attention to the implications of how regulators conceptualize the public interest in the first place.

I suggest that banking regulators from different countries—the United States, Canada, and Spain—made different policy choices in the 1990s and 2000s because they subscribed to fundamentally different understandings about the roots of economic stability and prosperity. In the United States, I find that regulators at the Federal Reserve were heavily influenced by the principle of *competition*, which presented safety and prosperity as deriving from the same source. Competitive market forces, left to their own devices, were expected to automatically select for the most effective strategies, promoting prosperity. Yet these same market forces were also seen as the optimal regulators of undesirable bank behavior, and thus as ideal mechanisms for ensuring financial stability. Automatic and impartial discipline from market actors (like a bank's depositors, shareholders, or creditors) was regarded as the first and best line of defense against excessive risk taking—and American banking regulators sought to preserve this discipline at all costs. As the following quote from a 1997 speech by Federal Reserve Chairman Alan Greenspan suggests, this regulatory commitment to strengthening market discipline was often accompanied by deep skepticism about the benefits of government regulation:

> It is critically important to recognize that no market is ever truly unregulated. The self-interest of market participants generates private market regulation. Thus, the real question is not whether a market should be regulated. Rather, the real question is whether government intervention strengthens or weakens private regulation. If . . . private market regulation is effective, then government regulation is at best unnecessary. At worst, the introduction of government regulation may actually weaken the effectiveness of regulation if government regulation is itself ineffective or undermines incentives for private market regulation.[23]

I will show that this goal of "enhancing market discipline" shaped American regulatory practice by encouraging regulators to mimic market forces as much as possible, to scale back all forms of government intervention into markets (and avoid creating new ones), and to push for the enhanced disclosure of information to market participants. These objectives informed the decisions of US banking regulators in key areas, including the regulation of bank participation in the securitization process and the practice of banks setting aside reserves against potential bad loans.

In Canada, regulators were influenced by the principle of *public rights*, which presented safety and prosperity as deriving from different sources. Here too, regulators assumed that prosperity would emerge most readily in contexts where the state did not interfere with the autonomy of bank managers or directors to freely select desired lines of action. But maintaining economic stability in Canada was thought to require more than market mechanisms alone. Canadian regulators believed that they also had a responsibility to protect the basic rights of vulnerable depositors and other users of banking services by ensuring that banks held adequate safeguards or "cushions" against potential losses. As the following quote from Office of the Superintendent of Financial Institutions (OSFI) Superintendent John Palmer implies, this commitment to striking the right balance between consumer protection and competitive considerations was always at the forefront of regulators' minds:

> The financial sector is key to our current and future economic success. We need a financial sector that offers a competitive array of products and services to Canadians and we need to ensure there is room for competitive, successful Canadian-based financial institutions. . . . While we need to maintain prudential walls around our institutions, those walls can't be higher than those which we see in our major trading partners. . . . OSFI's mandate continues to be the protection of your deposits and insurance policies in federal institutions, but we're trying to do this in a balanced way that recognizes international developments and facilitates a competitive financial system.[24]

This goal of "striking the right balance" shaped Canadian regulatory practice by encouraging regulators to place relatively few limits on banks' abilities to engage in desired activities (including complex financial innovations) while simultaneously insisting that banks hold adequate reserves to counterbalance the risks that they were taking. Regulators also avidly pursued international regulatory harmonization and embraced a "principles-based" regulatory approach with the same goal in mind. These objectives informed Canadian regulatory decision making in crucial areas, including those already discussed above in the US case.

In Spain, regulators were influenced by the principle of *state sovereignty*, which presented centralized administrative oversight and direction as key to both safety and prosperity. Order was thought to emerge most readily in contexts where a single administrator took charge of overseeing, organizing, and directing private initiative in ways designed to promote the greater good. This perspective cast market participants, like bank managers, depositors, or shareholders, as fundamentally shortsighted and incapable of looking beyond their own particularistic interests. State experts, by contrast, had the requisite public-minded motives, centralized viewpoint, and long-term perspective needed to steer private initiative toward an optimal course. As the former official mandate of the Bank of Spain implies, centralized administrative oversight and direction were not just seen as key to maintaining safety and stability—these factors also promoted economic prosperity by facilitating the smooth and harmonious functioning of the financial system:

> The Banco de España supervises credit institutions in a special way. Firstly, a specific regulation has been created to preserve the correct functioning of financial institutions, to strengthen their capacity to deal with adverse events and to harmonise the interests of all parties involved (banks, savers and investors) with general interests, and secondly, they are closely supervised to ensure compliance with banking rules, and in particular, with regulations governing accounting procedures, their solvency, customer protection and market transparency.[25]

This goal of "enhancing state oversight and direction" shaped Spanish regulatory practice by encouraging regulators to focus on keeping bank risk exposures highly visible, to insist on high capital and reserve holdings, and to proactively seek to attenuate disruptive market forces. These objectives, too, directly informed Spanish regulatory decision making in crucial areas.

To understand how principles of order shaped regulatory policy making leading up to the global financial crisis, the metaphor of a card game is useful. Banking regulators in the United States, in Canada, and in Spain were dealt fundamentally different hands in the 1990s and 2000s. By this point, each country had a very different financial system structure, featured different divisions of regulatory authority, and faced different political demands associated with different political systems. These structural features also contributed to the process of divergent regulatory policy making in each country, sometimes in important ways. Yet even amid these structural and political differences, I find that the American, Canadian, and Spanish banking regulators still engaged in discernable "styles of play" that cut across regulatory domains and political contexts. To illustrate this point, the last two chapters of the book take a deep dive into the finer details of regulatory policy making in two domains where regulators faced roughly similar choice opportunities: the regulation of securitization and the regulation of loan loss provisioning. These case studies help to illustrate the process by which these distinctive "styles of play"—or principles of order—gave rise to distinctive regulatory strategies within countries. To fully understand how we ended up with the mess of the 2008 crisis, and to prevent similar events moving forward, I argue that we must devote more serious attention to how banking regulators see the world and what they are hoping to achieve.

Principles of Order and Regulatory Change

Where did these distinctive regulatory worldviews come from? For answers, I look to the political and regulatory institutions that defined each of these countries. An abundant body of scholarship shows how institutions—formal and informal rules, conventions, and arrangements—inform the policy-making process by shaping the kinds of resources, opportunities, and constraints that are available to political actors. Typically, the focus is on the structural or *material* implications of these institutional arrangements: their role in shaping the capacity of governments to legislate or implement policies, the balance of power across various political groups, or even the kinds of players that make it to the bargaining table.[26] But institutions can have cultural effects as well. The same arrangements that shape how power is distributed also come with meanings attached, which can independently affect policy making through their effects on what appears "doable, sayable, or thinkable" to policy makers and other interest groups.[27]

America's notoriously fragmented and administratively weak political institutions, in other words, do not just create roadblocks for advocates of policy change or encourage policy makers to focus on serving narrow geographic constituencies (though they do this too). They also leave the policy makers who inhabit these institutions primed to see benefits in unrestrained competition, dangers in centralized or concentrated power, and harmony in systems that prioritize local control.[28] And these broad principles of order, embedded in the institutions of the polity, also serve as organizational templates or blueprints that actors can apply to the creation of new institutions in other domains of social life. Sociologist Frank Dobbin, for example, explains how nineteenth-century policy makers in the United States, Britain, and France drew from familiar models of organizing political life when designing new economic institutions to organize and govern railroads. Similarly, sociologist Marion Fourcade explains how distinctive political cultures in each of these three countries also facilitated different approaches to organizing the economics profession (and variants of economic knowledge).[29]

My own argument follows in a similar vein by arguing that cultural dimensions of political and economic institutions also shaped the divergent development of banking regulation in the United States, Canada, and Spain in the decades leading up to the 2008 crisis, primarily by making certain principles of order more readily available and salient to regulators in each country. The implication here is that banking regulators are not just members of industry or professional communities. They are also members of national societies, and subject to all the structural and cultural baggage that this institutional membership entails. This argument, however, also features an important twist that distinguishes it from past institutional explanations. Most institutional accounts of regulation—structural and cultural variants alike—focus on explaining how stable institutions facilitate the creation of new regulatory policies that look like a lot like old ones. It is precisely because institutions play such a powerful role in shaping the range of options open to policy makers, in other words, that countries tend to get locked into stable policy patterns that persist for many years. But this style of institutional explanation runs into a problem when it comes to explaining features of the case at hand. When it comes to the recent history of financial regulation, the defining pattern was *not* remarkable stability in the content of national regulatory approaches. It was remarkable change.

To be clear, *recent* regulatory trends—that is, comparative trends in the models of financial regulation that dominated in each country in the 1990s and 2000s—do appear to align with the predictions of a standard institutional account. The United States, for example, is often described as the world's "paradigmatic neoliberal economy," with a long history of eschewing state intervention in the political and economic realms and of creating institutions that celebrate the benefits of market rule.[30] Given this institutional precedent, it is not surprising that US banking regulators would be more receptive to a relatively market-friendly, hands-off regulatory approach. Similarly, Canada is often described as the slightly less market-friendly cousin to the United States, with liberal political and economic institutions that still reflect a preference for the benefits of "peace, order, and good government" over the risk-hungry, revolutionary mentality that prevails to the south.[31] With this precedent, it is not unexpected that Canadian regulators would embrace a slightly more conservative (but still quite market-friendly) regulatory regime. Spain, too, is often described as a country that is more amenable to state participation in both political and economic life, especially when compared to the more liberal regimes of the United States or Canada. Once again, it makes sense that Spanish banking regulators might be more open to a stricter, more interventionist regulatory approach.

But shifting the analytic lens back only a few decades—to the 1960s and 1970s—reveals a very different comparative pattern that challenges the predictions of a standard institutional account. In the 1960s, the United States was not the world leader in laissez-faire banking regulation. Instead, the United States entered that decade with one of the world's *strictest* bank regulatory systems in place, with multiple restrictions on bank structures and activities that other countries did not share. Over the decades that followed, US policy makers were also unusually *slow* to begin dismantling these regulatory restrictions, a pattern that stands in sharp contrast to the common depiction of the United States as the harbinger of neoliberalism. The appendix shows that this pattern applies to nearly every event that is commonly cited as a defining feature of US financial deregulation—from the 1980 deregulation of interest rate ceilings for banks, to the 1982 relaxation of restrictions on thrift activities, to the 1994 repeal of bank branching restrictions, to the 1999 removal of barriers between investment and commercial banking. In each case, these deregulatory events were comparatively *late* to arrive in global perspective.[32] This pattern is important not just because it departs from what institutionalists have come to expect from economic policy makers in the United States. It also departs substantially from the regulatory patterns that would take hold in the same country less than two decades later, suggesting a potential discontinuity in institutional effects.

These unexpected regulatory trends were not limited to the US case. Canadian policy makers may have been lauded for their relatively conservative approach to banking regulation leading up to the 2008 crisis, but banking regulation in Canada took a very different form in the 1960s and 1970s. Canada entered the 1960s with a regulatory system that was exceptionally hands-off and permissive in comparative perspective, defined by comparatively few formal restrictions on bank structures or activities and a well-established tradition of allowing the financial industry to regulate itself. Additionally, Canadian policy makers were relatively quick to repeal the few regulatory restrictions they had in place, dismantling key restrictions (like interest rate ceilings for banks) well over a decade before policy makers in the United States took a similar step.

In Spain as well, the orientation of banking regulation underwent a dramatic reversal between the 1960s and the 1980s. In the early 1960s, Spanish policy makers adopted a highly interventionist regulatory regime that gave the state unprecedented influence in directing credit allocation. Yet by the early 1970s, Spanish regulation seemed to be heading down an entirely different path, as regulators thoroughly embraced the project of financial deregulation. One effect was that by the time that US policy makers finally started to dismantle key regulatory restrictions on banks in the early 1980s, Spanish policy makers were already well down the road toward financial liberalization.

If these unexpected patterns or radical breaks with established institutional traditions had occurred in just one of the countries considered here, we might have been able to explain them away as a fluke or historical anomaly. Yet they happened in all three of them. The discovery of these historical and comparative trends adds important nuance to the puzzle that motivates this book and implies the task of accounting for the emergence of more or less effective bank regulatory systems may be more complicated than it initially seemed. We not only need a theory that can explain why regulatory policies looked so persistently different across countries in the 1990s and 2000s. We also need one that can accommodate the dramatic changes in regulation that occurred *within* these same countries after the 1960s, a process that eventually culminated in the emergence of the regulatory regimes of the immediate precrisis era. This book takes up both issues at once, because, as we will see, our understanding of one will inform our understanding of the other.

Crisis and Conflict among Principles of Order

If institutional legacies within countries are so powerful, then how is radical change possible? This is a question that has intrigued many scholars, who have sketched two major ways that established institutional arrangements can evolve and crumble. Existing policy regimes can collapse rapidly, as when crises upend the status quo and create opportunities for challenger groups to push through new visions, or they can evolve more gradually and endogenously, as when groups with vested stakes in established institutions slowly adapt these institutions to better fit group interests.[33] In the case of financial regulation, crisis seemed to be the primary cause of dramatic shifts in regulatory orientation—including during the puzzling regulatory reversals that occurred in each country between the 1960s and the 1990s. In each country, I find that financial crisis encouraged regulatory change by undercutting the dominance of incumbent groups (those who supported the regulatory status quo), allowing challengers (those who did not) to successfully promote new regulatory models.

While this basic story will be familiar to many scholars of policy change, what will seem less familiar is my account of where these new regulatory models within countries came from. Building on previous scholarship that finds that policy makers often return to discarded past policy experiments and arrangements when searching for new solutions, I show that American, Canadian, and Spanish financial policy makers returned to familiar principles of order when diagnosing and responding to crises.[34] Yet these were not always the principles currently institutionalized in the design of the existing financial regulatory system.

To understand this argument, it is important to first recognize that national institutions like "the state," "the political system," and the "regulatory system" actually comprise *multiple* principles of order. The organization of the American polity, for example, does not just emphasize the merits of using *competitive forces* to organize economic and political life. It also affirms the *sovereignty of the local community* in political and economic affairs and underscores the benefits of combatting dangerous concentrations or centralizations of power.[35] While sociologists have recognized this multifaceted character of institutions, they have also tended to focus on how these multiple principles "hang together" in elective affinities, reinforcing one another to reproduce stable policy patterns over long stretches of time. In the United States, for example, the commitment to a deconcentrated and fragmentated system structure is often depicted as going hand in hand with the commitment to maintaining free competition as the mechanism governing political and economic life. In the words of Theodore Lowi, this American emphasis on "free enterprise" has long "made a happy fit with the native American fear of political power."[36]

But these principles of order are also distinct, which means that they can come into conflict. Consider how attempts to support free enterprise can interfere with attempts to reinforce a deconcentrated system structure when unchecked competitive forces favor the success and growth of larger, resource-rich actors. Similarly, attempts to reinforce community sovereignty can interfere with competitive forces if interventions designed to keep actors small, independent, or locally oriented constrain the full expression of competitive mechanisms.

Closer attention to this *conflict* between principles of order, I argue, provides the key to understanding otherwise puzzling trends in the evolution of national systems of financial regulation—including the dramatic regulatory reversals of the 1980s. Policy makers around the world faced severe and costly financial crises in the 1980s that opened up political opportunities for dramatic reform. Yet policy makers within countries also came to diagnose the causes of these crises in roughly predictable ways. To explain the failures of the regulatory status quo, reform advocates tended to return to principles of order that were *latent* within each country's bank regulatory system—but were still readily available within the broader national institutional context.

Specifically, to explain the troubling financial crises of the 1980s, reformers in the United States drew from the principle of *competition*, which emphasized the benefits of emergent market mechanisms and the dangers of interfering with the process of competitive destruction. They appealed to this principle to explain why a regulatory system previously organized around the principle of *community sovereignty*, which emphasized the benefits of a locally oriented and deconcentrated system structure, had failed to prevent the crisis. This was not the first time that these principles had come into conflict in American debates over financial regulatory reform. The same pattern of conflict also marked debates between Alexander Hamilton and Thomas Jefferson in the early 1800s; the clash between Carter Glass and Henry Steagall over appropriate regulatory responses to the Great Depression in the 1930s; and battles over the desirability of financial deregulation in the 1970s. In the 1980s, this same institutionalized conflict reappeared to guide debates over regulatory reform, with important implications for the kinds of new regulatory arrangements that took hold in the 1990s.

Similarly persistent patterns of conflict also defined historical debates over financial regulation in Canada and Spain. In Canada, conflict over regulation tended to feature tension between the principle of *elite autonomy*, with its emphasis on respect for the freedom of elite individuals to select desired lines of action, and the principle of *public rights*, with its emphasis on the need to protect the basic rights of individuals from exploitation by powerful others. This distinctive pattern of conflict was present in the very first debates Canadians held over the creation and regulation of banks; as in the United States, it also reappeared to shape many other debates, including those in the aftermath of the financial crises of the 1980s. In Spain, conflict over regulation centered around tension between the principle of *corporatist harmony*, with its emphasis on respecting established social hierarchy and proactively brokering harmonious relationships between social groups, and the principle of *state sovereignty*, with its emphasis on giving a centralized administrator the ultimate authority to organize and direct activity within political and economic systems. This conflict also shaped key debates over financial regulation throughout Spanish history, including the influential debates that followed in the wake of the crises of the 1980s.

Importantly, the final outcomes of these national conflicts over financial regulation were never predetermined. The political dynamics or economic conditions of the historical moment often shaped the specific ways such conflicts were resolved. Indeed, this indeterminacy within institutions is key to understanding how radically different regulatory regimes could develop within countries across different historical periods—including in the two periods that are most relevant for the present investigation, the 1960s–1970s and the 1990s–2000s. Yet even as we acknowledge the influence of power, politics, and historical contingency in regulatory policy development, it is equally important not to lose sight of the institutional principles of order that were operating in the background. Looking across historical periods in comparative perspective, it becomes clear just how often a narrow range of principles of order shaped the arenas in which key national reform battles took place. My point is that the story of the regulatory failures that gave rise to the global financial crisis can't be told without them.

The Organization of the Book

This book is divided into three parts, each focusing on a specific historical juncture in the development of national bank regulatory systems. The first part opens in the 1780s, when the first modern chartered banks emerged in the United States, Canada, and Spain. To support the central argument of this book, that principles of order shaped the evolution of banking regulation, it is important to show that the relevant principles preceded the first conflicts over bank regulatory policy. Chapter 2 describes the distinctive principles of order, institutionalized in political institutions, that characterized the American, Canadian, and Spanish political systems in the late eighteenth and early nineteenth centuries. A key point is that political institutions represented order in different, sometimes conflicting, ways within countries. Chapter 3 illustrates how the underlying principles of order embedded in these political institutions also informed the way that Americans, Canadians, and Spaniards debated and developed bank regulatory policies between 1780 and 1860. Chapter 4 extends this story into the twentieth century by showing how the same principles of order also informed crucial debates and developments in national bank regulatory systems between 1860 and 1920.

The second part of the book explains how these institutional traditions contributed to the puzzling evolution of the American, Canadian, and Spanish bank regulatory systems over the course of the twentieth century. It focuses on three successive crisis episodes, each of which played an important role in the development of bank regulatory policy in each country. Chapter 5 compares national regulatory responses to the disruptive financial crises of the 1920s and 1930s. It shows how conflict between the same principles of order that featured in the earliest bank chartering and regulatory debates continued to inform the debates that followed these crises. In the United States, advocates of *community sovereignty* faced off against champions of *competition*; in Canada, advocates of *elite autonomy* challenged arguments founded on the principle of *public rights*; in Spain, advocates of *corporatist harmony* battled advocates of *state sovereignty*. In each case, the way that these debates were ultimately resolved carried implications for the relative dominance of a particular principle of order within the financial regulatory regime. The policy choices of this period contributed to the emergence of a bank regulatory system organized around the principle of *community sovereignty* in the United States; the principle of *elite autonomy* in Canada; and the principle of *corporatist harmony* in Spain.

Chapter 6 examines the implications of this process, explaining how these dominant principles of order, institutionalized in the design of the bank regulatory system, shaped national approaches to the problems of rising inflation in the 1960s and 1970s. In each case, policy makers initially responded to these problems by experimenting with financial regulatory reforms that aligned with the principle already embodied in the existing regulatory system. However, by the 1970s, these prevailing regulatory models were already starting to show cracks, as advocates of alternative regulatory approaches emerged to challenge supporters of the regulatory status quo in each country. Attention to this process offers unique insight into some of the most puzzling regulatory trends of this era, when comparative regulatory patterns across countries seemed to depart from common expectations.

Chapter 7 accounts for the dramatic reversals in regulatory orientation that occurred in each country during the turbulent 1980s. Faced with disruptive financial crises that raised serious questions about the sufficiency of existing models of banking regulation, reformers in each country seized the political moment to successfully push through new approaches. Yet even these new models continued to align with long-standing institutional traditions, reflecting the influence of the latent principles that had *lost* in each country during the reform battles of the 1920s and 1930s. Attention to this process of crisis and institutionally influenced reform sheds new light on the roots of the American regulatory compulsion with enhancing market discipline, the Canadian regulatory commitment to proactively protecting vulnerable consumer rights, and the Spanish regulatory obsession with promoting centralized oversight and guidance.

The third part of the book explains how these events contributed to the development of distinctive goals among banking regulators in the United

States, Canada, and Spain in the 1990s and 2000s and details some of the practical effects of these different regulatory perspectives. Chapter 8 describes the broad visions of financial order that guided regulatory policy making at the Federal Reserve (in the United States), OSFI (in Canada), and the Bank of Spain (in Spain) in the two decades leading up to the 2008 crisis. It underscores the connections between these regulatory perspectives and the diagnoses of the crises of the 1980s that were institutionalized in the dramatic legislative reforms described in chapter 7. Cross-national differences in regulatory goals are not reducible to economic or political dynamics, or even to differences in the professional training or backgrounds of regulators. Instead, I argue that widely shared national interpretations of the most recent episode of financial disorder—interpretations shaped by previously latent principles of order— directly informed the kinds of goals and strategies American, Canadian, and Spanish banking regulators pursued in the 1990s and 2000s.

Chapters 9 and 10 illustrate the practical effects of these distinctive goals and strategies. Chapter 9 takes a deep dive into the development of the regulation that governed bank exposure to asset-backed commercial paper (ABCP) programs. The 2007 collapse of the ABCP market is generally understood as a major precipitating event of the 2008 financial crisis and a source of losses for commercial banks around the world. This chapter explains how different priorities among regulators in the United States, Canada, and Spain informed the divergent development of regulation in this crucial area, which was nominally governed by international regulatory standards.[37] The US regulators, focused on enhancing the influence of market discipline in banking, actively encouraged banks to participate in securitization markets (and removed potential impediments to this participation), with disastrous results. Canadian regulators, focused on the need to strike the right balance between prosperity and stability, took a more measured approach, doing very little to prevent banks from pursuing innovative activities, yet taking a hardline stance on the reserves banks held against the risks of these activities. Spanish regulators, focused on enhancing regulatory capacity to oversee and direct activity in the banking system, placed strict limits on bank participation in off-balance-sheet securitization, which they perceived as threatening to regulatory order.

Chapter 10 further illustrates the influence of these different regulatory worldviews by showing how they also shaped the development of regulations governing the loan loss provisioning practices of banks, a domain of regulation under exclusive national control, with important implications for bank performance during the crisis. Collectively, these chapters illustrate how distinctive regulatory goals and worldviews contributed to the divergent development of regulatory policies across countries.

2

Conflicting Principles of Order within Political Institutions

This book sets out to make a simple point: that financial regulation has taken different forms in different countries, both historically and in modern times, because national policy makers subscribe to fundamentally different principles of order, which inform the types of strategies they pursue. From the moment that the first banks emerged in the United States, Canada, and Spain, each country's banking system started to develop along different lines. They quickly came to feature different kinds of organizational arrangements, different types of political coalitions, and different divisions of regulatory authority and responsibility.

For this reason, I start my story even before the first debates over bank chartering and regulation emerged in each country. This approach highlights the broader principles of order that preceded (and directly informed) the development of these early regulatory systems—which were also the same principles that would come to structure later debates. At the moment that national policy makers started to make choices about the first banks, these principles of order were already institutionalized in prominent features of national political systems and in state design.

The purpose of the present chapter is to describe the principles of order that were embodied in the political institutions of nineteenth-century United States, Canada, and Spain, giving special attention to the heterogeneous and multiple elements these institutional arrangements contain. One key point is that national institutions previously categorized underneath a single heading or descriptor, like "state sovereignty" or "federal constitutionalism," can be equally well described as packages or constellations that contain multiple principles of order.[1] Attention to this multifaceted character of institutions—a perspective that also underscores the possibility of *conflict* between the underlying principles of order—provides a foundation for the arguments to come. As we will see, trends in the relative dominance or latency of particular principles of order shaped the evolution of national regulatory systems in ways that explain otherwise puzzling patterns in regulatory development in the three countries under consideration.

To support this argument, I focus on retelling familiar stories about national political institutions in a slightly different way.[2] Drawing from existing scholarly descriptions of the features that defined and distinguished nineteenth-century US, Canadian, and Spanish political institutions, I focus on describing the multiple principles these institutions embodied. Specifically, I show how American political institutions embodied both *community sovereignty*, which affirmed the benefits of local autonomy and the hazards of centralized or concentrated power, and *competition*, which affirmed the benefits of allowing emergent mechanisms to guide political outcomes and underscored the hazards of interfering with this process. Nineteenth-century Canadian political institutions both embodied *elite autonomy*, which affirmed the benefits of allowing elite individuals to freely pursue desired lines of action, and underscored the importance of safeguarding *public rights*. Nineteenth-century Spanish political institutions embodied *state sovereignty*, which affirmed the benefits of centralized leadership, direction, and control, and *corporatist harmony*, which affirmed the benefits of reinforcing established social hierarchies, proactively coordinating relations between elite groups, and use of patronage relationships.

Competition and Community Sovereignty in the United States

Scholars have long recognized that a nation's moment of political emergence makes a lasting imprint on its political culture, and the American case offers no exception. At the time that American revolutionaries were preparing to overthrow British rule, the inhabitants of the thirteen colonies were already telling stories about what they stood for—and what they stood against. The content of these stories reflected the historical experience of life within a network of fragmented colonies in the absence of effective centralized administration.[3] Sociologist Jason Kaufman explains how the British government had granted colonial charters in the seventeenth and eighteenth centuries in a disorganized and haphazard way, producing near-constant struggle and contestation over jurisdictional boundaries and overlapping legal claims in early colonial life.[4] Colonists left to sort out their own problems in the absence of a centralized administrator gradually developed local, home-grown institutions to serve necessary political functions.

This history of resistance to centralized political control continued into the revolutionary era of the 1760s and 1770s, when the members of the thirteen colonies united against the British government's attempts to expand centralized control over taxation and other political affairs. After the colonists emerged victorious from the Revolutionary War, they set about designing new political institutions that would affirm the authority of American citizens to govern themselves.

When French historian and political philosopher Alexis de Tocqueville toured the United States in the 1830s, he discovered a country with a political culture defined both by the celebration of local initiative and community spirit and by a strong resistance to centralized and concentrated forms of political authority. The structure of the nineteenth-century American state, which stood out in comparative perspective in the degree to which it restricted the powers of the federal government and boosted those of state or local governments, embodied these tendencies. The architects of the US Constitution presented these methods of allocating political power as a good fit with human nature, under the assumption that citizens would automatically feel greater loyalty to local governments responsive to local needs than to a more spatially remote, diffuse federal government. In one of the *Federalist* papers, Alexander Hamilton elaborated on this intuition: "It is a known fact in human nature, that its affections are commonly weak in proportion to the distance or diffusiveness of the object. Upon the same principle that a man is more attached to his family than to his neighborhood, to his neighborhood than to the community at large, the people of each State would be apt to feel a stronger bias toward their local governments than toward the government of the Union."[5] An implication was that political order, from an American perspective, was expected to emerge more readily in systems that accommodated these natural tendencies, that is, those that *empowered* the local institutions that were most likely to secure loyalty from the citizens they governed.

The architects of this political system also depicted the strategy of fragmenting political power across regions as a method of safeguarding against dangerous centralized or concentrated power. Nineteenth-century Americans were also distinctive in the degree to which they feared both rule by a powerful centralized administrative state *and* rule by an aristocratic or ecclesiastical elite.[6] When the American colonists chose to rebel against British rule, they were also signaling their opposition to what they perceived as characteristic features of British political life, including the political dominance of traditional elites (e.g., the king and wealthy aristocrats) and the centralization of political authority within a legislature comprising these individuals. Both conditions— rule by the king and rule by aristocrats—were expected to promote political tyranny by increasing the potential for powerful public or private groups to infringe on the natural rights of the sovereign American people. As historian

William J. Novak describes it, these concerns contributed to the development of an "American state (like the American Revolution that produced it) [that was] organized against despotic power. It is obsessive about separating and distributing powers and creating checks, balances, and offsets within the formal constitutional organization of government."[7] Subdividing political powers across many separate local governments was thus expected to limit dangerous concentrations of political power; subdividing political authority across various branches or departments of government (another distinctive feature of the American state) served a similar function.

This latter initiative—diffusing and fragmenting political power across separate departments or units of government—was also touted by its proponents as having an additional benefit. One of the quirks of early US colonial history was that no single colony had successfully managed to impose its will on the rest, despite centuries of constant jurisdictional jockeying and political struggle between colonies.[8] Writing in the eighteenth century, James Madison rearticulated this historical legacy in the form of a positive principle of order, arguing that the broad diffusion of political powers across so many separate units of government also served as an automatic safeguard against the dangers of *majority* rule. In the course of pursuing their own distinctive local interests, the thirteen colonies had managed to collectively check the ambitions of their rivals. Madison argued that the subdivision of the functions and responsibilities of the US government across many various departments or units would serve a similar function. This division of responsibility would equip governance units with the "necessary constitutional means and *personal motives* to resist encroachments of the others" by giving them distinctive interests. In this context, a stable majority was unlikely to form; instead, each unit of government would automatically check and balance the ambitions of others in pursuing its own distinctive objectives. In this way, "the private interest of every individual" (or individual unit of government) would serve as a "sentinel over the public rights"—precluding the need for any kind of potentially dangerous state or elite intervention to protect minority rights.[9]

United States political institutions were also distinctive in their nominal commitment to promoting more equal access to political participation and political leadership. Although the political institutions of the United States and Britain each affirmed the political sovereignty of the individual, the American variant of individualism was much more "rooted in the common person" than was the British variant.[10] In Britain, political participation followed the traditions of the crown and aristocracy: it was determined by status at birth and restricted to the classes that had historically held power. By contrast, early American political institutions provided greater opportunities for participation to those not born into wealth or land ownership, relative not just to Britain but to other European societies as well. By the early nineteenth century, the

US political system was characterized by a comparatively broad voting franchise, in which property ownership was less likely to be a vital prerequisite for political participation, and by the dismantlement of aristocratic institutions like entailment and primogeniture.[11] The design of the representative democratic electoral system itself, in which top government officials are chosen in regular elections (that is, in a public competition for power), reinforced the country's rejection of intrinsic right or privilege.[12]

Let's be clear: this egalitarian principle only extended so far in practice. Women and nonwhite (and especially Black and Native American) citizens continued to face heavy restrictions on political participation well into the twentieth century, and this racist legacy is equally as foundational to the development of the US state as the other developments described above. However, the choice to develop a political system that institutionalized the promotion of open access (in a class-based sense) to the political process—if only for white men—still revealed something important about American political culture, especially in comparative perspective. In everyday practice, political life in the United States has often failed to live up to the egalitarian commitments inscribed in the country's constitution. Yet this ideal still exists as an American social construct—and this has come with important practical consequences.

In summary, the key features that defined and distinguished US political institutions in comparative perspective included the extent to which they subdivided political power and allocated it to the local level. The local community represented the locus of political order, and institutional arrangements sought to reinforce the principle of community self-rule while also restraining dangerous centralized and concentrated authority—of both public and private forms. Maintaining the *deconcentrated* character of both public- and private-sector power was an important goal. Early Americans created multiple institutional safeguards designed to prevent any single group from consistently dominating the political system, primarily by ensuring that this system would always include enough independent players pursuing specialized and distinctive interests. I group these related political-cultural traditions under the heading of the *principle of community sovereignty,* which both affirmed the benefits of local autonomy and underscored the dangers of the centralization or concentration of public *or* private power.

American political institutions were also distinctive in the degree to which they celebrated and affirmed the benefits of open competition as the primary mechanism that produced and maintained political order. The idea was that both resource allocation and political outcomes were optimally executed through an open competitive process, that is, through forces that emerged from below (via democratic or market mechanisms) rather than being imposed from above (via administrative fiat). Maintaining widespread and equal access to the competitive process was also an important goal, with the understanding that

TABLE 2.1. Principles of Order in US Political Institutions

Principle	Explanation
Community Sovereignty	
Establish local sovereignty and community self-rule	Local institutions are best suited to serve local needs, because of their close proximity to local citizens and awareness of their unique and specialized interests and needs.
Restrain centralized authority	Entrusting political decision making to a powerful centralized state is both ineffective (local institutions better serve local needs) and dangerous (conducive to political tyranny).
Maintain deconcentrated power	No individual or group should come to consistently dominate the political system. Systems that feature a multiplicity of players with distinctive interests will naturally find it easier to maintain balance as players check the ambitions of rivals in pursuit of their own interests.
Competition	
Preserve competitive process	Political order emerges from the bottom up—from the emergent collective decisions of the individuals that constitute civil society. External influences (administrative fiat) should not interfere with the emergent mechanisms through which order is produced. Competition between rivals also helps to keep potential abuses of power to a minimum.
Maintain open access	Access to political participation should not be restrained to a subset of society. When all have an equal opportunity to engage in competition for political and economic resources, the best suited rise to the top, and ideal outcomes follow.

competitive processes could select for the most talented or meritorious actors (and optimal outcomes) only if participation was widespread. I group these related political-cultural traditions under the broader heading of the *principle of competition*, which affirmed the benefits of entrusting political outcomes and resource allocation to the collective will of the people, in the form of a competitive contest open broadly to all. Table 2.1 outlines key components of these principles of order.

Elite Autonomy and Public Rights in Canada

If the nineteenth-century United States was defined by its rejection of British institutions, then the nineteenth-century British colonies that would eventually form Canada were defined by their acceptance of these same institutions.[13]

As Seymour Martin Lipset wrote in his influential comparative account of the US and Canadian political systems:

> The United States is a country of the revolution, Canada of the counter-revolution. These very different formative events set indelible marks on the two nations. One celebrates the overthrow of an oppressive state, the triumph of the people, a successful effort to create a type of government never seen before. The other commemorates a defeat and a long struggle to preserve a historical source of legitimacy: a government's deriving its title-to-rule from a monarchy linked to a church establishment.[14]

Nineteenth-century Canadian political institutions, like the British political institutions they were modeled on, were distinctive in the extent to which they entrusted political governance to a wealthy and educated aristocratic elite. Within the European context, the British political system had long been unique for the weakness of its administrative state, or the extent to which the political system delegated power to the wealthy elites making up Parliament while restricting that of the Crown. The tradition emerged with the 1215 signing of the Magna Carta, which prevented the king from levying taxes without the consent of his royal council, and was reinforced by the Glorious Revolution of 1688, when a group of English parliamentarians and the Dutch stadtholder William of Orange successfully overthrew King James II and further expanded Parliament's power relative to the Crown. The introduction of a formal Bill of Rights in the same period further increased aristocrats' sense of security in pursuing their own prerogatives without the fear of royal interference. Over the centuries that followed, the English landholding elite continued to enjoy unprecedented autonomy, power, and political influence. Well into the nineteenth century, British volunteers from the landed gentry still retained control over most local affairs, local governance, and other political functions typically executed by professional civil servants in other European countries.[15]

The design of the Westminster parliamentary model of government further reinforced the political power and authority of the British landed and mercantile elite. Under this model of government, a single centralized body (Parliament), which originally comprised landowners seeking to preserve the power of the aristocracy, dominates the rest of the political system. Unlike the American political system, where legislators face a variety of checks and balances from various levels and branches of government, the Westminster parliamentary system does little to restrain the power of the legislative branch. Writing in 1873, British journalist Walter Bagehot summarized the key distinction between these systems: "The English Constitution, in a word, is framed on the principle of choosing a single sovereign authority and making it good; the American, on the principle of having many sovereign authorities, and hoping that their multitudes may atone for their inferiority."[16] Moreover, this combination of a strong legislature with a weak executive also distinguished the British system from the political systems of France or Spain, in which the sovereign held more political power. Under the British political system, the executive branch derives legitimacy entirely from (and is accountable to) Parliament. The prime minister, as head of government, is a member of the legislature, while the sovereign (as head of state) holds only circumscribed and primarily ceremonial powers.

In short, these institutional arrangements reflected a particular understanding of political order in which aristocrats—relative to both ordinary citizens and the Crown—were assumed to hold certain characteristics, talents, tastes, and interests that left them fundamentally better equipped to rule. In the words of sociologist Marion Fourcade, the British gentleman was believed to carry "a distinction of status, but also of education and manners," that gave him "moral authority . . . vis-à-vis the rest of society."[17] The writings of domestic political philosophers like Edmund Burke also framed rule by aristocrats as a desirable strategy for avoiding the two most pressing threats to individual political liberty: a tyrannical, excessively powerful monarch on the one hand and unchecked majority rule—"dictation of a brutal mob and wicked sect"—on the other.[18] To guard against the latter concern, the British political system relied on aristocrats and landholders (appointed to the House of Lords), who were believed to naturally subscribe to more conservative and public-minded viewpoints, to check the potential excesses of broader society (as embodied in the elected House of Commons).[19] This institutional emphasis on respect for heritage and tradition as the basis for political order stands in sharp contrast to the American celebration of open competition and the self-made man. Although Canadian political institutions were more egalitarian than British political institutions in some respects, especially after a series of rebellions in the 1830s and 1840s ushered in a more representative form of government in the provinces, the design of the Canadian political system (which was modeled directly on the Westminster parliamentary model) and its limited voting franchise reinforced elite control to a much greater degree than comparable institutions in other countries like the United States.[20]

Notably, British political institutions—and the Canadian political institutions modeled on them—were also distinctive in the extent to which they affirmed protection for individual rights. This tradition extended back to the 1689 English Bill of Rights, which affirmed the sovereign political rights of individual citizens in the form of thirteen articles articulating specific freedoms. This document, which also helped to establish a true constitutional monarchy in Britain, also reflected the understanding that political order required some minimal state participation in protecting individual rights from external infringement. Contemporary British philosophers like John Locke elaborated this point by arguing that individuals in political systems with a weak state were "constantly exposed to the invasion of others: for all being kings as much as he, every man his equal, and the greater part no strict observers of equity and justice." These circumstances made a given individual's enjoyment of his property "in this state . . . very unsafe, very unsecure," and it was this threat to individual rights that necessitated a government, in which individuals "unite[d] . . . for the mutual preservation of their lives, liberties and estates."[21]

Indeed, protecting individual rights from external encroachment represented the sole exception to the otherwise dominant tradition of state noninterference in the British political system. By the mid-nineteenth century, this commitment had expanded to protecting the rights of citizens to a basic standard of welfare.[22] As both the ranks and the social needs of the poor expanded with Britain's transition toward industrial capitalism, the British state started to take a more active role in fulfilling moral obligations to the needy and vulnerable that had once been the traditional responsibilities of the aristocracy, including relief against the most extreme forms of poverty. As Marion Fourcade explains, this British commitment to "moral benevolence" was reflected in, among other initiatives, the country's comparatively early adoption of publicly provided education, health care, and poor relief.[23]

Canadian political institutions also reflected this British emphasis on the protection of individual rights and moral benevolence, but they were further marked by an additional commitment to the preservation of group rights. Canadian political history, much more so than British political history, had been a history of extensive compromise, featuring concessions to distinctive groups designed to keep the peace. This tradition extended back to the 1763 Treaty of Paris, when the French colonial holding of New France (which extended from the coast of Labrador past the Great Lakes) was transferred to British control. Faced with the task of governing such a large territory inhabited by a French-speaking majority, the British at first imposed their own political traditions on these new subjects, requiring French-speaking colonists to swear an oath of loyalty to the British Crown and to abandon their Catholic faith, civil law traditions, and other cherished cultural practices. After observing the mounting political unrest in the American colonies, however, the British government adopted a new tactic. The Quebec Act in 1774 reversed course by explicitly affirming the religious freedoms, legal traditions, and cultural rights of French Canadians in an attempt to strengthen their allegiance to the British Crown. After the American revolution, further political compromise was required as a large population of British loyalists emigrated to Canada. These loyal subjects viewed French-style cultural traditions and legal institutions skeptically and were eager to see the restoration of the British political institutions and traditions they were accustomed to. The Constitutional Act of 1791 attempted to assuage these tensions by formally splitting the province of Quebec into two separate provinces, with the western half becoming

Upper Canada, with English law and political institutions, and the eastern half becoming Lower Canada, retaining French civil law and land policies.[24] Collectively, these episodes implied that political order could be secured only through officially tolerating and accommodating the distinctive traditions and rights of multiple interest groups, something that was necessary to earn their political allegiance.[25]

Another notable difference between British and Canadian political institutions that reflected Canada's relatively stronger commitment to group rights lay in the design of the political system.[26] The Canadian political system, unlike the British political system, was organized along federalist lines. Following the passage of the 1867 British North America Act, the four Canadian provinces (Ontario, Quebec, Nova Scotia, and New Brunswick) agreed to be governed as a federation, a model of political organization that departed from Britain's unitary political structure and looked more like the political structure of United States. In comparative perspective, however, this federalist tradition still remained much more pronounced in the United States. The US Constitution, for example, reserved all powers not explicitly granted to the federal government for the individual states, while the Canadian Constitution did the opposite, reserving all powers not explicitly granted to the provinces for the federal government.

Here again, it is important to note that the rights of all individuals and groups have not been treated with equal respect in Canada in practice. The political and cultural rights of indigenous Canadians, for example, while formally enshrined in the Royal Proclamation of 1763, were later sharply circumscribed by repressive and discriminatory legislation (and nonenforcement of key treaty provisions) throughout the nineteenth and twentieth centuries.[27] This troubled legacy of settler colonialism was just as fundamental to the development of the Canadian state as any of the other institutional developments described above, and the Canadian government has often fallen far short of the ideal of protecting individual or group rights, particularly when it came to indigenous communities or citizens. Yet this ideal does exist as a social construct in Canada, and its presence has carried practical consequences.[28]

In summary, one of the key features that defined and distinguished the Canadian political system was a strong commitment to elite individualism and elite autonomy, a political tradition that was inherited alongside Canada's embrace of British political institutions. From this perspective, political and economic leadership was best executed by elite gentlemen, under the idea that wealthy and educated members of civil society were best qualified to lead. As in the United States, political order was expected to emerge most readily when individuals were free to pursue their own prerogatives without external administrative interference. These traditions can be grouped under the broader heading of the principle of *elite autonomy*, which affirms the

TABLE 2.2. Principles of Order in Canadian Political Institutions

Principle	Explanation
Elite Autonomy	
Preserve elite individualism	Political and economic leadership is best executed by elite gentlemen—the wealthy and educated are best qualified, and best equipped, to lead society. Order emerges most readily when these individuals are free to determine and pursue their own prerogatives within their own domains.
Maintain state noninterference	A powerful centralized state is disruptive to order because it is conducive to tyranny. Order emerges most readily when individuals are free to pursue desired lines of action. The state should not interfere with the emergent mechanisms through which order is produced.
Public Rights	
Safeguard individual (and group) rights	The state has a duty to protect the sovereign rights and freedoms of individuals from external infringement. In Canada, protection of group rights was also key.
Demonstrate moral benevolence	Protection of the basic rights of vulnerable groups is an important moral value and a key concern of the state.

benefits of permitting elite individuals to freely pursue their own prerogatives and underscores the hazards of state interference.

Another defining and distinguishing feature of the Canadian political system, and the British political system it was modeled after, was strong commitment to protecting the rights of individual citizens, especially needy and vulnerable citizens, from external infringement. Respect for sovereign individual rights had long been a defining feature of the British political system; respect for group rights was a defining feature of the colonial-era Canadian political system. In line with a long-standing emphasis on the state's moral obligation to provide for the basic welfare of citizens, the rights of the vulnerable received particular attention. These related political-cultural traditions can be grouped under the broader heading of the principle of *public rights*, which affirms the need to safeguard the rights of citizens, especially needy and vulnerable citizens, from infringement.

Table 2.2 outlines the key components of these principles.

Corporatist Harmony and State Sovereignty in Spain

Historians trace the origins of modern Spain back to the fifteenth century, when Isabella of Castile, the heir to the largest of the Spanish kingdoms, married Ferdinand of Aragon, the heir to the next-largest kingdom, and annexed the Kingdom of Navarre. These kingdoms were initially ruled as separate entities, with respect for the autonomy of their separate institutions, laws, and elites. But this pattern ended with the ascendance of a French Bourbon monarch to the Spanish throne in the early eighteenth century.[29] After a thirteen-year war of succession, the Bourbon king Philip V, a grandson of Louis XIV of France, secured the Spanish throne in 1700. Philip V sought to introduce his grandfather's vision of a polity unified by a powerful centralized nation-state to Spain, and this period of absolutist Bourbon rule coincided with Spain's gradual recovery of its former position as a leading power in Europe.[30] During the rule of Philip V (1700–1746), and that of his sons Ferdinand VI (1746–59) and Charles III (1759–88), Spain revitalized its government, strengthened its military might, and increased its wealth via transatlantic commerce.

Neither this prosperity nor the dominance of French-style rule would last. In 1808, Spanish revolutionaries arose in popular rebellion against the Napoleonic French occupation, with the resistance declaring Spain a constitutional monarchy with sovereignty that emanated from the collective will of the people. The war ended in 1813 with the withdrawal of French troops from Spain and the restoration of a Bourbon monarch (Ferdinand VII) to the throne; however, internal conflicts between liberal reformers, who sought to modify or dismantle old feudal bases of power, and advocates of the ancien régime, including proponents of absolutist monarchical control (the Carlists), their allies in the church, and members of the landed aristocracy, persisted. Over the sixty years that followed, political power repeatedly changed hands between these groups, and Spanish political institutions were in a constant state of flux.

Political stability briefly returned to Spain during the era of the *restauración* (1874–1931). In 1874, a coup by General Arsenio Martínez Campos toppled the short-lived First Spanish Republic and restored a Bourbon monarch (Alfonso XII) to the throne. During the restauración, Spain was initially governed as a constitutional monarchy, with a bicameral legislature. The Crown nevertheless continued to hold considerable power within this political system: the king had the exclusive authority to appoint the members of the upper house of the legislature, to revoke laws at will, and to control and command the army.

Even amid the many political changes of the nineteenth century, a few distinctively Spanish institutional traditions remained. One was relatively strong support for a centralized administrative state, which carried through historical periods. Scholars have traced this support for centralized governance in Spain back to the country's long and often positive experience with French-style absolutist rule.

To fully understand the basis of this tradition in Spain, we must first take a brief detour through the emergence (and evolution) of absolutist rule in France. Faced with the task of unifying and holding together a culturally diverse territory with few natural geographic boundaries, Louis XIV of France sought to impose order by centralizing political power within a state bureaucracy accountable to a single ruler.[31] Political power within this system was exercised within a centralized, pyramidal bureaucracy, staffed by civil servants (centrally appointed provincial administrators) with considerable decision-making authority.[32] Political duties that were carried out by the nobility, church, or other social elites in other countries were taken over by centrally appointed *intendents* in France who were directly accountable to the state and dependent on the state for their livelihood. To accomplish this change in the political regime and solidify power within the Crown, Louis XIV restricted the autonomy of local seigneurial authorities within their own territories, forcing them to devote their military and other resources to national purposes instead.[33] This model of political governance provided few opportunities for political participation outside of the state. Scholars of French political institutions have argued that the roots of a political culture affirming the benefits of a powerful state stem from this period of absolutist rule.[34]

This political-cultural tradition also survived the political upheaval of the nineteenth century in France. The ongoing concentration of political power in a single centralized state bureaucracy was one of the few constants of French political life in this period, even as an absolutist state was replaced by a republican one. As Frank Dobbin writes, "while the *purpose* of France's political structure varied as widely as was imaginable [in this era] . . . the institutionalized *means* employed to achieve public purposes varied little."[35] The perceived benefits of a powerful centralized state were only reinforced by the experience of the French Revolution, which affirmed views of civil society as "a locus of unbridled individualism and hence of factionalism and chaos" in need of impartial control.[36] French political philosophers from Descartes to Rosseau to Saint-Simon highlighted the benefits of centralized administrative rule and the dangers of excessive individualism or fragmentation, casting the state as a comparatively impartial, stable, and disinterested arbiter of political life, especially when compared to more mercurial and particularistic social influences.[37] This relative aloofness from particularistic interests gave state actors the capacity to rise above the fray and see the bigger picture, providing the moral authority needed to effectively lead and behave as the "teacher" or director to civil society. The state was representative of the nation, and factors that blocked its capacity to pursue general interests were thus opposed to the national interest. This emphasis on the benefits of state sovereignty was also embodied in the design of other French political institutions, including a political system that restricted the role of the legislature in political governance and failed to subject administrative decisions to judicial or legislative review.

The Spanish political system was also deeply influenced by these French institutional traditions. When Philip V sought to expand his absolute power by introducing a French-style intendant system to Spain in the eighteenth century, he also helped to usher in a French-style commitment to the state-led direction of individual action toward collective goals.[38] The reforms of Charles III, which included the expansion of the intendent system and a series of ambitious, centrally coordinated infrastructure projects, only reinforced this institutional tendency. And, as in the French case, even after Spanish liberal reformers obtained control over the state in the 1830s, the strength and stability of the centralized state bureaucracy created under absolutist rule persisted. Early versions of the Spanish Constitution still granted considerable power to the monarch, including the power to veto legislation and to dissolve Parliament. And during the era of the restauración, leading policy makers tried to further centralize political power within the administrative state by appointing new mayors to villages, allowing the Crown to make all local and provincial official appointments, and removing the evaluation and assessment of property from local hands.[39]

To be sure, the Spanish commitment to centralized administrative control never reached the intensity that it did in France, a point that I will soon discuss at length. However, it is worth noting that many Spanish policy makers and intellectuals in the eighteenth and nineteenth centuries perceived this as a significant problem to be addressed via additional centralizing reforms. As the following comments from eighteenth-century Spanish politician and lawyer Pablo de Olavide imply, at least some Spanish elites attributed the country's many economic and political woes to its relatively fragmented (compared to France) state structure:

> [The Spanish state is] a body composed of other and smaller bodies, separated and in opposition to one another, which oppress and despise each other and are in a continuous state of war. Each province, each religious house, each profession is separated from the rest of the nation and concentrated in itself. . . . Modern Spain can be considered as a . . . monstrous Republic of little republics which confront each other because the particular interest of each is in contradiction with the general interest.[40]

In summary, in Spain as well as France, there was a long-standing, and well-institutionalized, assumption that political order would emerge most readily in systems organized around authoritative, rational administration from a powerful, centralized state.

The design of Spanish political institutions did depart from French political institutions in other crucial respects, however. Elite groups within civil society continued to hold much greater political power in Spain than in France. In France, the ancien régime largely succeeded in destroying autonomous sources of seigneurial and aristocratic power, but its success had been more moderate in Spain.[41] When Philip V sought to increase the centralized administrative power of the Spanish Crown in the early eighteenth century, he faced strong opposition from regional aristocrats and other local authorities. To secure the political allegiance of these actors and convince them to cede their formal government positions to centrally appointed intendents, the Crown agreed to leave many of the fundamental economic and social privileges of these elites intact.[42] Accordingly, local landowners and other societal elites found it easier to maintain political control in Spain than in France.[43]

This historical legacy came with implications for the design of Spanish political institutions. Like the British political system, the Spanish political system affirmed the political sovereignty of elites—but the identity of these elites also varied across the two political systems. Where the British model conceptualized the polity as a collection of sovereign *individuals*, the Spanish model conceptualized the polity as a collection of functionally divided *social groups*. In Spain, individualism was considered naturally subordinate to group identity, a view of society with roots in sixteenth-century Roman Catholic organicist and corporatist traditions.[44] This *corporatist* view depicted society as a human body with multiple functionally interrelated and interdependent parts. The social body's overall health depended on the degree to which each part accomplished its distinctive, necessary, and God-given function, in proper harmonious relation to the other parts.[45] As political scientist Howard Wiarda explains, viewing the corporate group as the building block of society also implies that "there is little room for change in such a conception [of society], or for much overlapping membership, or for much competition or pluralism of ideas. Nor is there supposed to be 'rebellion' against this corporate system. Rather, society is supposed to be tied closely together into an organic whole with all its parts (individual as well as corporate) intermeshed in accord with God's just and harmonious ordering of the universe."[46]

Early Spanish political institutions were also organized along corporatist lines. During the medieval period, the king inhabited the top of Spain's social and political hierarchy, with functionally divided corporate groups (them- selves organized around hierarchies of social rank) falling immediately below the king in this pyramidal system. There were sharp boundaries between corporatist groups with different ascribed functions or statuses (e.g., nobles, warriors, laborers), with certain functions deemed more societally useful than others. Political institutions rewarded corporate groups in accordance with their perceived social value, with the noble and warrior classes receiving more political and social privileges than the laborer class. One of the key mecha- nisms through which the Crown maintained order in this system was through the grant of *fueros*, or special rights and privileges (e.g., freedom from taxa- tion, the ability to exempt family from military service) bestowed on some corporate groups that were unavailable to others. This practice was expected to strengthen corporate group loyalty to the Crown.[47] As Spain transitioned to a money economy, some of these traditional barriers and distinctions began to blur; however, as historian Lyle McAlister notes, the broader "image of a society ordered on the basis of functionally derived social quality" remained a constant in Spain well into the eighteenth and nineteenth centuries.[48]

Nineteenth-century Spanish institutions further preserved and reinforced the power of corporatist associations by formally designating these groups as the sole legitimate representatives of their members' interests and by suppressing the influence of rival organizations.[49] They also established official forums for the state-sanctioned corporate groups to express their interests and work through conflicts, with the state responsible for coordinating this negotiation and bargaining process. This feature of political system design also reflected an understanding of individuals as naturally belonging to social groups; anarchy was expected to follow from deviations from this natural social and hierarchical order. As Antonio Cánovas del Castillo (one of the leading figures of the restauración) argued, excessive individualism in the form of widespread political representation was "fatal to the interest of the state"; instead, the preservation of a good society required a political system defined by *"nuclei of authority,* placed throughout the nation and embodied in parties of opposite tendency."[50]

The corporatist model suggests a different role for the state in bringing order about from the role suggested by the French-style model of *state sovereignty* discussed above. The French model emphasizes the benefits of the state (treated as equivalent to the national interest) imposing its will over a disorderly civil society. The state is the *teacher* and *director* to civil society, which includes aristocrats and other societal elites. By contrast, the corporatist view underscores the benefits of the state negotiating, brokering, or coordinating the interests of rival groups to better allow these groups to arrive at collectively optimal outcomes. The difference is subtle, but important. From the corporatist standpoint, the state is best suited to act as a *partner* to societal elites, not as an instructor or opponent. The state is responsible for brokering relationships *between* established social groups to ensure the smooth functioning of the social body.[51]

Spanish political institutions were also defined by a highly *patrimonial* character. Attempts to secure political order by creating relationships of mutual obligation have a long history in Spain, stretching back to the medieval period when the Crown ruled through the exchange of fueros (political privileges and favors) for military support from nobles and landowners.[52] This patrimonial character persisted through the absolutist and liberal eras of the eighteenth and nineteenth centuries and was perhaps most clearly reflected in the design of the 1885 Pacto de El Pardo, one of the defining political institutions of the restauración. The Pacto de El Pardo was a formal power-sharing agreement between the Liberal and Liberal-Conservative political parties that instituted the practice of *turnismo*, or periodically rotating the political party in power in government. It formalized a long-standing patrimonial tradition whereby the government attempted to prevent groups from leaving the ruling coalition by providing inducements—in this case, a "fair turn . . . at the trough."[53] The same tradition persisted with the emergence of the Spanish liberal state, under which state actors continued to grant favors and privileges to local elites (*caciques*) in exchange for political support.[54]

In summary, strong commitment to corporatism defined and distinguished the Spanish political system and the design of Spanish state structures. Spanish political institutions were organized along corporatist lines, with individuals assigned to social and functional groups that presented different values to society and held correspondingly different social ranks. The state was expected to promote political order indirectly through partnership with elite groups, brokering, negotiating, coordinating, and balancing the interests of these groups to promote harmony. This tradition placed heavy emphasis on patrimonial relationships as the means to cement political order, with the state bestowing rights and privileges on powerful groups within civil society in exchange for political support. I group these related political-cultural traditions under the principle of *corporatist harmony*, which affirms the benefits of respect for the established social hierarchy, state coordination of group interests, and patrimonial exchange.

Another key feature that distinguishes Spanish political institutions was their commitment to preserving the authority and power of the centralized state. Especially compared to the political institutions of the United States, Britain, or Canada, the Spanish (and French) political institutions gave the state a more substantial role in checking the perceived hazards of unchecked individualism or particularism. The state was considered more far seeing, impartial, and public minded than the particularistic interest groups that made up civil society; accordingly, the centralized state was also the appropriate guardian of the greater good and must retain sufficient power and authority to successfully impose its will. I group these related political-cultural traditions under the principle of *state sovereignty*, which affirms the benefits of centralized administration and underscores the hazards of uncontrolled particularism. Table 2.3 outlines the key components of these principles of order.

Conclusion

The United States, Canada, and Spain developed distinctive political institutions in the nineteenth century, which were themselves shaped by each country's distinctive historical experiences. The design of these political systems also embodied multiple distinctive principles of order, or institutionalized understandings about the proper relationship between state and society. This chapter has drawn on established scholarship to describe the characteristics that

TABLE 2.3. Principles of Order in Spanish Political Institutions

Principle	Explanation
Corporatist Harmony	
Reinforce social hierarchy	Political leadership is best executed by societal elites, organized into social groups. To promote political order, the state must respect the established social hierarchy.
Coordinate and harmonize	Order must be proactively imposed (it does not emerge automatically from the unchecked collective actions of civil society). Order is achieved only when the state uses its power to effectively coordinate the interests of social groups, balancing interests to achieve harmony. The state acts as a partner to social groups.
Rely on patrimony	The state is responsible for allocating privileges and rewards to induce groups to serve the greater good. This influence occurs through patrimonial relationships of mutual obligation.
State Sovereignty	
Centralize state authority	The state is more stable and more impartial than social or political influences. A powerful centralized state promotes order by ensuring that its will triumphs over the particularistic interests of subordinate groups or individuals, often by directly steering or directing activity within civil society.
Avoid individualism and fragmentation	When groups within civil society become too numerous to effectively manage, and are free to pursue their own particularistic interests at the expense of the general interest, disorder follows.

distinguished each country's political institutions. National state structures and features of the political system embody multiple principles of order—principles that can conflict with one another.

Specifically, US political institutions embodied a commitment to both the principle of *community sovereignty*, which emphasized the benefits of local autonomy and the hazards of centralized or concentrated power, and the principle of *competition*, which emphasized the need for an impartial and open competitive process to guide the production of political outcomes and the distribution of resources. Canadian political institutions embodied a commitment to both the principle of *elite autonomy*, which emphasized the merits of allowing elite individuals to freely pursue their own prerogatives, and the principle of *public rights*, which emphasized the need to safeguard the basic rights of individuals, especially the vulnerable and needy. Spanish political institutions embodied a commitment to the principle of *state sovereignty*, which empha-sized the benefits of centralized leadership and direction, and the principle of *corporatist harmony*, which emphasized the benefits of preserving the estab-lished social hierarchy, coordinating relations between corporate groups, and relying on patronage relationships to secure political stability and harmony.

While the focus of the present chapter was on introducing potentially conflicting principles of order, the next chapter, chapter 3, will explain how these principles of order dominated the earliest debates and developments in chartered banking in each country. In each country, we will see that these principles of order, institutionalized in the structure of the state and political system, also shaped early discussions over the state's appropriate role in bank-ing. Established principles of order informed the kinds of issues most likely to spark controversy in each country, the range of policy options on the table, and the kinds of arguments that reform advocates and opponents were more likely to mobilize for or against particular policy arrangements.

3

Creating Chartered Banks in the United States, Canada, and Spain

The story of the rise of modern banking starts with the state—or more specifically, with the practice of *corporate chartering*. Chartering was the original public-private partnership. In chartering a corporation, sovereign powers granted specific legal rights or privileges to a private group in exchange for public services. Before the eighteenth century, banking was either an entirely state-owned business or a wholly private one, and banks operated on a much smaller scale. The introduction of chartered banking, which fell between these public and private extremes, transformed the sector by paving the way for the emergence of larger, modern banks.

The first chartered bank, the Bank of England, provided a blueprint for the chartered banks to come. This institution emerged in 1694 as one solution to the mounting financial problems of the state. At this point, the English Treasury was nearly bankrupt. To continue financing its ongoing war with France, the Crown needed to secure a large volume of funds quickly. Raising taxes would not be sufficient, and foreign loans were not forthcoming. Instead, Parliament turned to the domestic private sector for financial support. The private sector met the challenge, but at a high cost. The state granted a corporate charter authorizing a group of eight goldsmiths to organize a joint-stock banking company with limited liability. The new company, the Bank of England, received permission to provide banking services, which included issuing banknotes (paper money) and accepting deposits from both the government and the private sector on a near-monopoly basis. In exchange for these privileges, the Bank of England's shareholders agreed to extend a £1.2 million loan directly to the Treasury.[1] This was, in the words of economist Charles Calomiris, a "equity-for-debt swap of sovereign debt," which benefitted the state by helping "to consolidate other sovereign debts into a single, more liquid sovereign bond."[2]

The Bank of England successfully fulfilled the key function its supporters hoped it would accomplish: placing the government's finances on a more stable footing. At the same time, the arrangement also enriched the bank's shareholders, ultimately giving rise to a new kind of economic institution. After a banking crisis led to the failure of many private banking partnerships in 1825, the British state began to charter new banks that were modeled on similar lines to the Bank of England. Policy makers further expanded the scope of the chartering privilege after 1833.[3] The powers and privileges banks received through state-granted charters paved the way for the banking industry itself to dramatically expand in size and scope. Monopoly power came with crucial economic benefits, including the ability to lend more freely than ever before on the basis of paid-in equity capital.[4] The state's blessing and support increased the value of banks in the eyes of important external audiences, which in turn allowed chartered banks to offer banking services on a scale that fully private competitors could not match.

The political and commercial success of the Bank of England did not go unnoticed beyond the British Isles. By the start of the nineteenth century, many other countries were adopting or considering adopting the practice of chartered banking—including the United States, Canada, and Spain. A century later, chartered banks would dominate the banking systems of all three countries, as well as the majority of others around the world. Yet these early chartered banks also looked and operated quite differently in each individual national context.

This chapter tells the story of the emergence and evolution of different models of chartered banking in United States, Canada, and Spain, focusing on the period between the late eighteenth century and the mid-nineteenth century. Although national chartering and regulatory policies took many twists and turns in this period, a ten-thousand-foot view of their evolution reveals the influence of familiar organizing principles. As organizations that straddled the public and the private realms, chartered banks (and their regulation) also raised deeper questions about the appropriate relationship between the state and society. In what follows, I explain how the different models of chartered banking that developed in each country reflected the imprint of the same principles of order already embedded in national political institutions.

Policy makers in each country confronted a series of roughly similar questions during this period. Should the government get into the business of chartering banks? If so, which arm of government should receive the authority to bestow this privilege, and how diffuse or widespread should access to that privilege be? And what—if anything—did chartered banks owe the state in exchange for the powers they had been granted? How involved should the state be with their ongoing operations? In both banking and politics, Americans were highly attuned to the dangers of centralized government power, the hazards of rule by hereditary aristocratic elites, and the drawbacks of excluding individuals or groups from competing for key economic or political privileges. Canadians were more attuned to the dangers of government interference in economic and political life, with some concerned by the potential danger of allowing important economic and political functions to become too broadly accessible or dispersed. Spaniards were most attentive to the dangers of a weak state in economic and political life, and to the more specific dangers of undue private-sector power or excessive private-sector fragmentation. This institutional backdrop shaped the kinds of problems policy makers were more likely to perceive in the banking system and the kinds of arguments interest groups mobilized for or against particular policy arrangements, with important implications for how regulatory debates and developments unfolded.

These principles of order were never determinative, nor were they the only influences that mattered for the development of bank chartering policies in this period. The precise design of the banking system was never *foretold* by political culture; indeed, each country's chartering regime could have taken a substantially different form if these early debates had been settled in a different way. Yet, just the same, a comparative lens reveals how the presence of particular political-cultural traditions was the common thread that linked a variety of important policy debates and developments within countries. Principles of order shaped the range of options or concerns that American, Canadian, and Spanish policy makers perceived as most readily available and salient at critical junctures; in this way, they also structured the initial development of these banking systems.

Early Bank Chartering Policies in the United States

American policy makers, like those in many other countries, turned to chartered banking to finance a war. At the start of the US Revolutionary War, the Continental Congress did not yet have the authority to tax the members of the thirteen colonies. To finance its mounting military expenses, it experimented with a range of strategies, including printing paper money (notes) backed by the government's promise to repay them, issuing government bonds, and securing loans from European powers. All three strategies soon proved insufficient. The government-backed notes quickly lost their value relative to gold and silver, the bonds failed to attract sufficient investor interest, and international loans were not forthcoming. The government urgently needed more money. It was at this point that Philadelphia merchant Robert Morris, the nation's first superintendent of finance, proposed creating a bank chartered by the nascent federal government, modeled on the Bank of England. The bank would extend a substantial loan directly to the Treasury, presenting a solution to the government's financial problems, while its issuance of notes would have the added benefit of providing the colonies with a more stable form of currency.

Unlike banks today, early chartered banks funded their activities by issuing banknotes (paper money) backed by the capital shareholders had provided in the form of metallic money or *specie*. Notes were generally issued in the course of a bank's lending or discounting activities: providing a borrower with banknotes represented the main method of making a loan in this period. Banks were required to maintain convertibility of their notes, meaning that they could be redeemed for specie by presenting them to a bank's chief cashier. Banknotes were commonly used in trade, being more convenient than coins for this purpose, and also circulated as a medium of exchange—a feature that made it rare for all note holders to seek to redeem their notes at once. The gap between notes issued and notes redeemed presented a profit opportunity for banks: the excess specie could be used to invest in interest-bearing loans or bills. When these investments succeeded, profit followed. When they failed, or when a bank issued more notes than the public believed it could reasonably redeem, trouble (and insolvency) were often close at hand.[5] There was no doubt that chartered banking had its risks. Yet early American policy makers also recognized that the paid-in capital of bank shareholders provided a more secure foundation for a national credit system than a fledgling government's unsecured promises to repay debts.

In 1781, Congress endorsed the establishment of the country's first federally chartered bank, the Bank of North America, which opened its doors to the public in 1782. At the time, it was only the third chartered bank in the world. The bank was authorized to operate as a joint-stock banking company with limited liability and note-issuing powers for thirty years in exchange for extending a large loan directly to the US Treasury. Although the bank was headquartered in Philadelphia, it was also given authority to establish branches in Massachusetts, New York, Rhode Island, and Connecticut.

When viewed in economic terms, the Bank of North America was a clear success. It successfully provided the funds the US Treasury so desperately needed to finance the war. Its activities also propelled the growth of commercial enterprise. The Bank of North America extended credit directly to commercial ventures, fueling their growth; it also created banknotes that served as a more stable form of currency and reduced transaction costs. However, the bank was less successful in political terms. Early Americans weighed the benefits of this institution against the political dangers it presented—and many of these dangers were seen as quite serious. As a corporation created by the federal government that also benefitted from monopoly privileges that its competitors did not enjoy, the Bank of North America tapped into deeply rooted American concerns about the hazards of both centralized government and elite power.

At the time that the Bank of North America was chartered (prior to the ratification of the US Constitution), US policy makers had not yet settled the question of whether the federal government had the authority to offer charters at all. Recognizing that their federal charter stood on potentially shaky legal ground, the shareholders of the Bank of North America immediately sought an additional charter from the Commonwealth of Pennsylvania. The terms of this state charter were initially identical to those of the federal charter, and the bank continued operations under both charters until 1786. That year, the Pennsylvania legislature voted to revoke the bank's state charter. To explain why they had voted to repeal the charter of a bank that had seemed to offer important services and benefits to both economy and government, the bank's Pennsylvanian opponents returned to a familiar line of reasoning. Drawing from the principle of *community sovereignty*, they argued that *any* chartered bank could serve as a dangerous gateway to aristocratic rule.

One of the major advantages of the joint-stock corporate form is that it allows many shareholders to combine capital and share in a firm's rewards. The act of incorporation also gave the firm a legal personality separated from that of its owners, making it easier for the firm to continue in perpetuity. In a political context defined in part by the rejection of hereditary elite rule, both advantages were more likely to appear threatening to political order. The logic was that a practice (chartering) that made it easier to concentrate and pass along wealth also risked recreating a rigid British-style class structure in the New World, in which an established elite maintained its economic and political privileges by passing down inherited wealth. Accordingly, the Pennsylvanian opponents of the Bank of North America opposed the continuation of the bank's charter on the basis that "the wealth and influence of th[is] corporation, and particularly its attribute of perpetual existence, were dangerous to the Government, and destructive of that equality that ought to exist in a free country."[6]

The revocation of its Pennsylvania charter put the bank's shareholders in a difficult position. Technically, the bank could continue to operate under its federal charter alone. But this was a risky strategy in the political climate of the time. If the drafters of the new US Constitution ultimately chose to restrict the chartering powers of the centralized government, the Bank of North America might end up with no charter at all. Unwilling to take this risk, the shareholders begged the Pennsylvania legislature to restore the bank's state charter. After a long debate and multiple false starts, the legislature agreed to extend a new charter to the bank—but on much more restrictive terms. The new state charter restricted exactly those elements of the corporate privilege that opponents had found most threatening: its term was changed from thirty years to fourteen years, limiting the perpetuity of this privilege, and the size of the bank's permitted capital subscription was also reduced, reducing its ability to further concentrate wealth.[7] When the Bank of North America restructured to meet these terms, it was effectively transformed into a purely state-chartered (versus federally chartered) institution.

This episode of the rise and fall of the country's first chartered bank highlights the influence of two principles that would reappear again and again as US policy makers debated issues in bank chartering over the decades to come. First, in a political context organized around the principle of *community sovereignty*, which celebrates the benefits of local rule, state-chartered banking was viewed as more legitimate than federally chartered banking. Second, in a political context that underscored the dangers of allowing political power to concentrate in the hands of established economic elites, policy makers were highly attuned to the perceived political dangers of the chartering privilege itself.

In 1790, American banking entered a new chapter when Alexander Hamilton introduced a proposal to establish a new federally chartered bank, the Bank of the United States. To justify this proposal, Hamilton cited the valuable services the Bank of England had rendered to its government and the economy and argued that achieving a similar level of prosperity in the United States would require Americans to embrace similar economic institutions. The proposed Bank of the United States would lend directly to the Treasury and serve as the government's fiscal agent. It would also promote commercial development by accepting deposits from the public, issuing banknotes on its own security, and making loans to private citizens and businesses.[8] In exchange, the federal government would grant the bank a twenty-year federal charter to operate as a joint-stock banking company with limited liability and note-issuing powers. Although the bank would be headquartered in Philadelphia, it would be free to establish multiple branches in different states. It would not replace the existing state-chartered banks (in addition to the Bank of North America, the Bank of New York and the Bank of Boston had been chartered by their respective state legislatures in the 1780s), but it would directly compete against them.

Hamilton's proposal attracted serious controversy and opposition, which fell along institutionally patterned lines. The most common argument against the chartering of the Bank of the United States was that it was unconstitutional. Since the Constitution did not specifically give the federal government the power to charter banks, its opponents argued that Congress would be overstepping its limited powers by creating such an institution. They saw particular evils in the federally chartered bank's ability to establish branches in different states, which directly infringed on the natural rights of individual states to set terms for institutions operating within their borders.[9] Another, smaller group of opponents objected to the establishment of the privilege the chartering process implied. As Representative James Jackson of Georgia argued, the creation of the Bank of the United States threatened to perpetuate the entrenched wealth-based inequalities Americans had fought so hard to escape: "What was it drove our forefathers to this country? Was it not the ecclesiastical corporations and perpetual monopolies of England and Scotland? Shall we suffer the same evils to exist in this country, instead of taking every possible method to encourage the increase of emigrants to settle among us? For, if we establish the precedent now before us [the Bank of the United States], there is no saying where it shall stop."[10] In the end, however, the advocates of the Bank of the United States triumphed over its opponents, and the bank received a twenty-year charter in February 1791. At the time, the bank was the largest corporation of any type yet created in the United States, with a capitalization of $10 million—with $2 million owned by the government and the remaining $8 million owned by private investors.[11]

Over its twenty-year history, the Bank of the United States successfully rendered important services to the government, collecting tax revenues, securing government funds, lending to the treasury, and paying the government's bills. It promoted commercial and industrial development, extended credit to the private sector, and issued a more stable form of currency. The bank's notes were widely accepted throughout the country—and unlike the notes issued by state-chartered banks, they were also accepted in payment of federal taxes. The bank also exerted an additional stabilizing influence on the economy through a different, and more controversial, channel. In the course of everyday business, the bank accumulated a large volume of notes issued by state-chartered banks, which gave it tremendous power over the expansion of money and credit. Whenever the Bank of the United States threatened to submit its accumulated state banknotes for payment in specie, the state banks were forced to cut back on note issuance to protect their reserves.[12] This arrangement contributed to economic stability by constraining inflation, but it also attracted considerable resentment from state-chartered banks and the state governments that derived revenue from them.

When the charter of the Bank of the United States came up for renewal in 1809, its enemies (which included not just state-chartered banks and state governments, but merchants with an interest in credit expansion and hard-line agrarians who hated all banks) succeeded in destroying the institution. After the bill to extend the bank's charter was narrowly defeated in the Senate in 1811, it was required to cease operations and liquidate. The kinds of arguments that featured in this debate once again reflected the imprint of familiar principles of order. Opponents of rechartering the bank resurrected familiar arguments about the dangers of federal overreach, merits of local sovereignty, and the hazards of elite control, while the bank's supporters highlighted the many beneficial services the institution had already provided to the government and economy.

Yet the character of this debate had also changed to some degree by the early nineteenth century. Many of the agrarians who had strongly opposed the initial charter of the Bank of the United States were now split on the question of whether it should be allowed to continue to operate. The relevant trade-off was no longer between the absence of chartered banking altogether and the establishment of a national bank, as it had appeared to many observers in 1791. Instead, the trade-off was now between the unchecked expansion of state-chartered banks and the tolerance of a federally chartered one. A substantial minority of agrarians, and especially those from southern or western states, saw the national bank as the lesser of two evils. They justified this stance by arguing that the national bank, at least, operated under the watchful eyes of Congress and helped to restrain the speculative excesses of state-chartered banks (and, by extension, the power of the economic elites who controlled them).[13] Senator Pope of Kentucky, a former opponent of the Bank of the United States, described his change of heart on a federally chartered bank in the following terms: "If the object of gentlemen was to eradicate the banking system from the country, I might, in obedience to my former prejudices, be more disposed to join them [in destroying the Bank of the United States]. But this is not even pretended. The sole object, in the death of this, is, to generate more of these *vipers* [state banks]."[14] Thus, agrarian arguments *in favor* of the continuation of the charter of the Bank of the United States in 1809 appealed to the same principle reflected in arguments *against* the continuance of the Pennsylvania charter of the Bank of North America a few decades earlier: that the government had a duty to proactively guard against dangerous concentrations of economic power. With conditions being what they were, some agrarians now believed that it was better to develop institutions that kept powerful economic elites (in this case, state-chartered banks) accountable to a government that represented the collective, democratic will of the American people than to leave these elite actors to their own devices.

In the years that followed the 1811 destruction of the Bank of the United States, both the numbers and the note issuance of state-chartered banks exploded. Freed from the restraining influence of a federal bank, state-chartered banks rushed to meet growing demand for credit from both the public and the private sectors. By 1812, the US federal government was back at war, and the Treasury was back to searching for funds to finance the country's mounting military expenditures. The Treasury encouraged the state-chartered banks to purchase war bonds to raise the money needed, offering very favorable interest rates as an enticement.[15] Industry and commerce were also growing rapidly in the same period, and private-sector demand for credit reached new heights. Many state-chartered banks responded to this period of prosperity by expanding their note issuance beyond prudent limits, contributing to a serious scarcity of specie and to the inflationary proliferation of paper money. These dynamics ultimately led to the emergence of a speculative bubble that produced widespread economic difficulties when it burst a few years later.[16] By 1815, many of the former opponents of federally chartered banking had reconsidered their position.[17] It was clear that the contributions of state-chartered banks alone had been insufficient to meet the financial needs of a government at war; moreover, the unchecked speculative excess of these institutions had only made recent economic troubles worse. Even Representative Henry Clay of Kentucky, once one of the most vehement opponents of the Bank of the United States, responded by advocating for the creation of a new federal bank, noting that if he had "foreseen in 1811 what had since come to pass," he would have "voted for the renewal of the earlier charter."[18]

It was in this context that a bill to establish a Second Bank of the United States, very much like the first Bank of the United States in both form and function, entered onto the policy agenda. This time, opposition came primarily from the Federalist minority (previously a group that had supported federally chartered banking), who wanted neither war with Britain nor a Republican-created bank to finance it.[19] After a long debate, a presidential veto, and numerous false starts, a heavily revised national bank bill was put to a vote in the House in 1816, followed by a vote in the Senate.[20] After successful passage through both chambers of Congress, a charter for the Second Bank of the United States was signed into law by President James Madison in April 1816.

After a somewhat rocky start, the Second Bank of the United States fulfilled its promise of enhancing the financial health of the federal government and bringing greater stability to the volatile American banking system over the decade that followed.[21] Its legitimacy was strengthened by a key 1819 court decision (*McCulloch v. Maryland*) that affirmed the constitutional legality of a federally chartered bank and prevented state governments from taxing its branches. The managers of the Second Bank seized the political opportunity this decision provided by expanding the bank's branch network, establishing twenty-five separate branches across the country. By the mid-1820s, public impressions of the bank were quite favorable, and it seemed as if the renewal of its twenty-year charter (in 1836) would proceed without difficulty.[22]

The election of Andrew Jackson to the presidency in 1828 changed this forecast. Jackson had run on a political platform that promised to restore Jeffersonian principles of limited government and decentralization to the United States—and the Second Bank, as a powerful, centralized financial institution with unusually close connections to the federal government, was an easy political target. Jackson had initially left the bank alone, but as reelection approached in 1832, he seized the political moment and began to attack the institution. The bank's directors, aware that the political winds were shifting, decided to push for an early renewal of its charter (in 1832). In the debates that followed, pro-bank National Republicans faced off against hard-money Jacksonian Democrats. Like most of the advocates of federally chartered banking before them, the Republicans emphasized the many services the bank had faithfully rendered to the government and economy. The antibank Democrats also returned to mostly familiar arguments, following the previous opponents of federally chartered banking by emphasizing the political dangers that such a large, powerful, and *federal* financial institution presented to the political order of the United States. Despite recent court decisions to the contrary, these opponents also contended that a federally chartered bank was inherently unconstitutional and criticized its violations of the sovereignty of individual states.

The opponents of the Second Bank also added an additional and important new twist to these familiar arguments by emphasizing the dangers associated with the *unequal access* to rewards and opportunities. They argued that a major problem with the existing arrangement, in which the Second Bank operated as a private institution, supported by the capital of shareholders, was that it allowed the rewards of the Second Bank's operations to concentrate in the hands of a few "opulent citizens," instead of being dispersed more broadly among the American people. These critics also argued that allowing the Second Bank to act as the government's sole banker and fiscal agent (a provision in its charter) unfairly restricted other groups from entering the competition to provide these services. Jackson himself emphasized the hazards of this latter arrangement, arguing that because the Second Bank's charter "does not permit competition in the purchase of this monopoly," it also prevented actors more willing "to take a charter on terms much more favorable to the Government and country" from competing for the opportunity—at a loss to the American people.[23] In short, many of the Second Bank's opponents defined the central problem not in terms of *whether* the government should be distributing powers and privileges (including corporate privileges) to the private sector, but as *that* those privileges were being distributed *unequally*. As Jackson wrote when he vetoed the Second Bank's charter in 1832, "There are no necessary evils in government. Its evils exist only in its abuses. If it would confine itself to equal protection, and, as Heaven does its rains, shower its favors alike on the high and the low, the rich and the poor, it would be an unqualified blessing."

This new line of reasoning appealed to the principle of *competition*. In a context where political order was assumed to rest on equality of opportunity to compete for political privileges, policy makers were also primed to see dangers in arrangements that allowed only a narrow subset of citizens to benefit from, or compete for, key economic privileges. This framing of the problem to be solved also pointed to new pathways for making bank chartering more politically palatable to the American public. If the issue was that the privilege was too exclusive, then broadening access to it might help mitigate the dangers.

In the three decades that followed the destruction of the Second Bank of the United States, the American banking system consisted entirely of state-chartered banks. Before the 1830s, most US states followed the same method of bank chartering that British policy makers had used to establish the Bank of England. Charters were granted by the state legislature on a case-by-case basis, following a thorough review of the qualifications of a specific applicant or group of applicants. Chartering was thus a *legislative decision*, and success in obtaining a charter was a matter of legislative *discretion*. In the 1830s and 1840s, however, this traditional model of bank chartering came under attack in many states. As one Massachusetts editorialist writing under the pseudonym "Equal Laws" explained, many actors (drawing from a Jacksonian-style commitment to "democratizing" the chartering practice) saw problems in chartering practices that allowed legislators to exclude certain groups from this privilege:

> Does not the State—by the conditions it imposes on us in consequence of its policy of granting to banking corporations the exclusive privilege of issuing notes . . . of limiting at its own discretion the number of such corporations . . . and of receiving to itself the power of deciding who shall be favored with charters, at the same time that it imposes the further conditions that none shall enjoy the privilege or become a corporation other than those it may choose to favor—does it not by these conditions cut off proper and wholesome competition in the trade? . . . We . . . firmly believe that corruption (or partiality, if you please) and tyranny are the *necessary effects.*[24]

Chartering limited by legislative discretion, these critics argued, was not in keeping with either egalitarian traditions or distrust of government authority. It violated the "proper and wholesome competition in the trade" by artificially limiting access to it; it also invited corruption by giving too much power to state legislators.

In the 1840s and 1850s, many states began to experiment with alternative methods of chartering banks. One popular method was *free banking*, which transformed the chartering decision from a legislative one to an administrative one. States that embraced free banking agreed to automatically grant bank charters to any group that met a set of requirements, which included the securement of a minimal capital subscription and the requirement to use a portion of capital to purchase bonds of the state government to back note issuance. Unlike the bespoke charters that had been historically granted by state legislatures, free bank charters were highly standardized and featured identical terms. One effect of the rise of free banking was to make charters much more widely available. Any group that met the common minimum requirements could obtain one, presenting a relatively low barrier to entry into banking. Importantly, free banks were also required to assume a *unit bank* structure: to operate as a stand-alone bank, with a single headquarters and no branch offices.

Free banking made a government-granted privilege (in this case, a bank charter) more palatable to Americans by sidestepping several long-standing political taboos. It originated at the state level, a more legitimate site for political authority in a system organized around respect for *community sovereignty*. The restrictions on the structures of free banks (the unit bank form) also had the practical effect of forcing these institutions to serve the needs of a single local community. Free banking also sidestepped concerns about concentrated economic power by broadening access to the chartering privilege, aligning with a long-standing emphasis on the benefits of open *competition* in allocating political and economic resources. Finally, it further addressed long-standing concerns about the hazards of government control by removing legislative discretion from the chartering equation altogether. These features help to explain why free banking was easily framed (especially by the followers of Andrew Jackson) as a natural next step toward "destroy[ing] the monopoly and mak[ing] banking open to all."[25]

Free banking ultimately became the dominant model of bank chartering in the United States, spreading to the vast majority of states by the end of the 1850s. Banking historian Bray Hammond described the widespread popularity of this chartering model at the state level as one of "the most important event[s] in American history," owing to its lasting legacy for the development of the banking system.[26] States that adopted free banking laws saw an explosion in local banks owned by local capitalists, leading the banking system to increasingly mirror the idealized structure of the American polity, in which political power diffused across hundreds of independent institutions with close ties to a single local community.

Free banking was not, however, the only alternative chartering model state policy makers enacted.[27] Some states, especially in the Midwest, experimented with an alternative model that transformed chartered banking into a state-owned monopoly. Under this model, only a single chartered bank (with multiple branches) was authorized to operate in the state. This bank nominally remained a private institution, but the state government was often its sole or majority shareholder. This model of bank chartering represented another possible solution to the problem that free banking was designed to solve. It sought to democratize chartering by transferring control over chartered banking—a field then dominated by private-sector actors rich or lucky enough to obtain a charter from legislators—to the hands of the American people via their elected representatives. Faced with the choice between allowing economic power to concentrate in the hands of a small number of elites (the legislative chartering method) or entrusting it to the local government (the state-owned banking method), these state policy makers viewed the latter option as less politically dangerous. Although this alternative model of chartered banking never achieved the widespread popularity of free banking, it proved especially popular among groups who still held deep reservations about the merits of chartered banking more generally.

Early Bank Chartering Policies in Canada

Canadian policy makers were comparatively reluctant to charter banks. In 1782, 1808, and again in 1810, influential merchants in Upper and Lower Canada pressured their respective provincial assemblies to establish a chartered bank, but these efforts failed. Canada would not establish its first chartered bank until 1822, forty years after the first chartered banks were established in both the United States and Spain. Much of this delay can be attributed to the fact that the provinces of Upper and Lower Canada were still British colonial holdings in this period, which gave the British Home Government (Parliament) the final say on all chartering decisions. To understand why the Home Government was so reluctant to permit chartered banking in Canada, a brief detour through historical experience with the practice of corporate chartering in Britain is relevant.

The Bank of England was not the only corporation British policy makers chartered in the eighteenth century. Other examples included the East India Company, a joint-stock company formed to trade in the Indian Ocean region, and the South Sea Company, a joint-stock company formed to supply African slaves to South America. While some of these chartered projects proved lucrative for shareholders and the state, others ended in disaster. Rampant speculation in the share price of the South Sea Company, for example, led to the development of a speculative bubble that financially ruined many shareholders when it burst. To account for the origins of this crisis, many contemporary observers blamed the joint-stock corporate form itself, arguing that it had created powerful incentives for mismanagement. Writing fifty years after the collapse of the South Sea Bubble in *The Wealth of Nations*, Adam Smith elaborated on this line of reasoning, explaining how the separation of ownership and management (a defining feature of the joint-stock corporation) favored imprudent behavior by interfering with some of the mechanisms that ordinarily kept such behavior in check: "The directors of [chartered corporations], however, being the managers rather of other people's money than of their own, it cannot well be expected, that they should watch over it with the same anxious vigilance with which the partners in a private co-partnery frequently watch over their own. . . . Negligence and profusion, therefore, must always prevail, more or less, in the management of the affairs of such a company."[28] This line of reasoning is important because it highlighted a perceived danger of chartering that aligned with one of the major dangers British policy makers had long perceived in the political realm. A charter, by definition, represented a form of state interference in the economy. In a political context defined by a long tradition of seeing inefficiency and tyranny in a powerful administrative state, British actors were already primed to see potential problems in economic institutions (like chartering) that departed from the principle of laissez-faire. In keeping with this interpretation, the British corporate chartering regime became much more restrictive after the South Sea debacle. The Bubble Act of 1720 prevented the formation of any new joint-stock companies without explicit royal approval; this stalled the development of this form of business organization for more than a century.[29]

This historical experience likely contributed to the substantial British opposition to chartering Canadian banks in the early nineteenth century. Initial steps toward chartered banking in Canada arrived only after concerns about national economic security became more pressing in the early 1820s. Canadian merchants had historically used either metallic money (specie) or the notes of US banks to pay for American goods, but as trade expanded, these practices had encouraged specie to drain out of the provinces of Upper and Lower Canada and into the vaults of chartered banks in the United States.[30] To stem the flow of British wealth out of the provinces, the British Home Government finally agreed to charter two Canadian banks in 1822: the Bank of Montreal (in Lower Canada) and the Bank of Upper Canada (in Upper Canada). These bank charters were modeled on those of the Bank of England (and that of the First Bank of the United States) and followed their terms in most respects.[31] One key difference, however, was that Canadian chartered banks were not expected, or encouraged, to play a direct role in financing the state. The provincial governments held no shares in the chartered banks, and the banks did not lend directly to the provincial governments. Both banks were connected to the provincial ruling class via informal and business ties, but their formal relationship with the state was minimal.[32] In an institutional context that was already organized around the principles of state noninterference and elite autonomy, Canadian policy makers were primed to see benefits in chartering arrangements that broke the link between the activities of the state and those of the private sector.

Even after local interest in expanding banking services increased in Canada during the boom times of the 1820s and early 1830s, similar patterns repeated. As commercial demand for credit reached new heights, policy makers across political lines pushed for the expansion of banking services but diverged in their interpretations of the best way to do this. Republican reformers seeking to introduce a more representative model of government were eager to reduce the concentrated power of established banks by making bank charters more widely accessible. Their goal was to follow "the general principle, widely advocated in the states to the south, of opening the business of banking under some uniform scheme of safeguards to whomsoever should wish to enter it."[33]

However, the reigning political elite (the Family Compact and Château Clique) in Lower and Upper Canada preferred to keep the banking business closed to all but a few select gentlemen. The establishment enjoyed close professional and personal ties to the managers and shareholders of the existing chartered banks and preferred expansion to occur through increasing the maximum capital subscriptions (resources) of the few existing banks.

The British imperial authorities, once again, saw things differently. They argued that Canada in the 1830s had "only too much reason to anticipate the rapid approach of a period in which the multiplication of ill-secured representatives of coined money [chartered banks] would involve the British-American colonies in the most serious financial difficulties," citing recent experiences with financial crises in the United States. They repeatedly returned proposals to create new chartered banks to the provincial assemblies for further consideration.[34]

Only a single additional chartered bank was established in Canada between the mid-1820s and the early 1840s (in Kingston in 1832), with an existing chartered bank (the Bank of Upper Canada) receiving the authority to double its capital stock in the same legislative session.[35] The local Canadian push for banking expansion was further dampened by the onset of a banking panic in the United States in 1837, with the ease of obtaining banking charters identified as one of its central causes. This comparative reluctance to establish new chartered banks, combined with a relative comfort with expanding the capital subscriptions of existing banks, aligned with a long-standing British/Canadian tradition of delegating key political and economic functions to elite gentlemen. Translated to the banking system, the principle of *elite autonomy* supported the continuation of a chartering regime that restricted the extension of this important privilege to a few highly qualified, well-resourced groups—yet did very little to interfere with the activities of these groups, once established.

A potential turning point in Canadian chartered banking arrived in 1841, when the new governor general of Upper Canada, Lord Charles Sydenham, introduced a proposal for a provincially owned bank of issue. While this proposal was motivated primarily by Sydenham's desire to place the province's finances on firmer ground and secure much-needed revenue for public works, he also believed that it would have the added benefit of "prevent[ing] the introduction of wild-cat American banking schemes" to Canada.[36] After uniting the colonies of Upper and Lower Canada into a single Province of Canada, Sydenham turned to the task of creating a new bank to serve the needs of the province. This provincially owned bank would be given the exclusive authority to issue banknotes—a power that would have presented a serious threat to the survival of the existing chartered banks at a time when note issuance served as the primary source of profit. Sydenham and his supporters saw this as a benefit, arguing it would enhance the overall stability of the banking system by eliminating "all but the soundest [chartered] banks."[37]

Unsurprisingly, in a political system already organized around a tradition of state noninterference, an initiative that gave a government body direct control over a key economic function was extremely controversial. Opponents of the provincially owned bank offered arguments that appealed to key tenets of the principle of *elite autonomy*, highlighting the dangers of infringing on the sovereign privileges of existing chartered banks and the potential for tyranny that a state-owned economic institution presented. They argued that a provincial bank was "too monopolistic in its tendencies" and "fraught with grave political dangers."[38] Existing chartered banks argued that restricting their ability to issue notes would interfere with their "ability to render essential services to their customers."[39] In interfering with the prerogatives of private institutions to pursue desired lines of business as they saw fit, a provincially owned bank would disrupt the foundations of economic order itself. The opponents of Sydenham's plan eventually triumphed over the supporters, and the bill to create the bank was dropped from the legislative agenda in August 1841.[40]

A different experiment in Canadian bank chartering a decade later proved more successful.[41] Demands for banking services increased substantially after the late 1840s, especially among smaller communities west of Toronto. Members of these communities pushed legislators to establish new chartered banks to serve their needs—and to lower capital requirements to make it easier for these banks to be established. While the liberal policy makers then in power were inclined to accommodate these interests, they also worried about the potential consequences for banking system stability.[42]

At this point, proposals to establish an American-style free banking system in Canada returned to the policy agenda. William Hamilton Merritt, an American immigrant and liberal politician, was a leading figure in this push for reform. He argued that the embrace of free banking would give policy makers everything they wanted: more specifically, it would allow smaller banks to be established in growing communities without threatening banking stability. As Merritt explained it, the many restrictions that came with free banking (e.g., unit bank structure, the requirement to back note issuance via the purchase of government securities) would also offer greater protections to the users of banking services. Under the existing bank chartering regime in Canada, banks were forced to meet high minimum capital subscriptions but faced few restrictions on their activities or structures otherwise. Merritt's proposal also pleased Canadian populist reformers, who had been pushing for the adoption of US-style political and economic institutions since the early 1840s, because free banking was expected to reduce the dominance of existing large and concentrated chartered banks.[43]

The opponents of free banking argued their case using familiar arguments that aligned with the principle of *elite autonomy*. They argued that expanding access to the chartering privilege would invariably invite disorder by allowing the wrong sort of actor to enter the banking business. Under the existing regime, charters were only extended to applicants whom the legislature believed had the requisite character and skill to bear this privilege effectively. The superior character, professionalism, and public mindedness of these individuals was expected to keep incentives for mismanagement (which the chartering privilege itself was thought to invariably increase) at bay. To justify this stance, free banking opponents referenced the cautionary tale of the United States, in which a state-sanctioned "multiplication of small local banks" had resulted in "excessive [note] issues, as well as . . . weakness and deficient responsibility shown by such banks in times of stress."[44]

Initially, it looked like the supporters of free banking had won. In June 1850, Canada introduced its first free banking law. However, only six banks were ultimately established under the new free banking laws. Of these banks, two failed relatively quickly, with the rest converting to legislative charters by the 1860s.[45] By 1854, it was clear to most that the Canadian experiment with free banking had failed. To explain this failure, most historians point to the fact that the free banking regime in Canada did not replace the existing bank chartering regime but was layered on top of it. Even after free banking laws were introduced, Canadian banks could still obtain charters through the conventional legislative format, and these legislative charters remained more attractive to most applicants. They required banks to retain less specie, did less to constrain their note issuance, and placed fewer restrictions on the structural forms they could assume.[46] Additional changes to the bank chartering regime in 1854 only further entrenched the control of elite banks. Convinced that more extensive borrowing in Britain was needed to fuel Canada's economic development, liberal policy makers approved large increases in the capital subscriptions of existing chartered banks, a practice that was expected to make it easier for banks to tap into British savings. This increase in incumbent bank resources further stacked the competitive deck against new entrants. By the time that Finance Minister Alexander Tilloch Galt formally repealed free banking in 1860, the model had few defenders in Canada left.

If free banking was the distinctively American model of chartering banks, the model that solidified after Canada's failed experiment with free banking became the distinctively Canadian one. In 1860, Finance Minister Galt recommended that any future expansion in banking services take place by expanding the branch networks or capital subscriptions of existing chartered banks. The banking system that developed in the wake of these policy choices came to look very much like the idealized version of the Canadian polity, with a comparatively narrow group of elite economic institutions (large and powerful branch banks) dominating the sector. The Canadian banking system was also defined by relatively little state interference with these chartered banks: banks faced few restrictions on their organizational structures, operated with minimal government oversight of their activities, and played no role in directly financing the state.

Early Bank Chartering Policies in Spain

Early experiments with chartered banking in Spain had more in common with those in the United States than with those in Canada. Spain also turned to chartered banking to address the state's wartime financial needs. Spain was a participant in the US Revolutionary War, with King Charles III seeing this war as an opportunity to weaken and exact revenge on Britain while also protecting Spain's colonial interests. As the country's military expenses mounted in the 1770s and 1780s, the state came under pressure to locate additional sources of finance. The Spanish Crown initially responded by issuing Treasury bills (*vales reales*) backed by a loan from a syndicate of Spanish, French, and Dutch financiers. However, the value of the bills quickly declined relative to gold, and it became clear that this was not a sustainable solution. As in the United States and Britain, Spanish policy makers responded to this dilemma by turning to a chartered bank.

When French financier François Cabarrus, the syndicate's representative in Madrid, introduced a proposal to create a chartered bank in Spain, it received widespread support. In 1782, Spain established the Banco Nacional de San Carlos, the country's first chartered bank. The bank was tasked with providing a broad array of services to the government in exchange for the privilege of operating as joint-stock banking company with the ability to issue its own notes. Like the Bank of England and the Bank of North America before it, the first act of the newly incorporated Banco Nacional de San Carlos was to extend a large loan directly to the Treasury. It was also charged with managing the redemption of the vales reales, making foreign remittances on the Crown's behalf, and acting as supply contractor for the army and navy.[47]

In short, like American and British policy makers before them, Spanish policy makers chartered a bank to secure a more reliable source of state finance, a goal that was accomplished through extending monopoly privileges to a private-sector group. However, the Spanish model of bank chartering departed from its US and British equivalents in terms of how much the state demanded from the bank in return. Unlike the Bank of North America, which prospered economically but lost its charter for political reasons, the Banco Nacional de San Carlos ran into serious economic troubles only a few short years after it was created. Most of these problems stemmed from the heavy costs of the services the bank provided directly to the state. The costs of provisioning the Spanish army and navy, for example, turned out to be much higher than expected. When the bank submitted the relevant invoices to the state, the Crown refused to pay them in full.[48] At a 1790 shareholder's meeting, the shareholders of the Banco Nacional de San Carlos and the Crown agreed to dissolve this provisioning contract, placing the bank on a sounder financial footing.[49] Yet the bank's financial difficulties did not end here. After Spain entered a new war with France in 1793, and an additional war with Britain in 1796, the chartered bank was pressured once again to offer additional financial support to the state. By 1801, government debt constituted the overwhelming majority of the bank's assets.[50] From the start, then, it appeared that the financial needs of the state were paramount in chartered banking, and something to be prioritized over the needs of the private sector.

This pattern of prioritizing the state's financial needs continued throughout the next three decades of development in Spanish chartered banking. When Spain erupted in rebellion against French rule in 1808, the Treasury turned to the Banco Nacional de San Carlos once again to finance its growing military expenses. As the bank's already bloated portfolio of state debt expanded even further, the situation became untenable, and the bank became effectively insolvent.[51] In 1829, policy makers responded by creating a new chartered bank, the Banco de San Fernando, which assumed some of the debts of the San Carlos and also operated with a larger capital subscription. The shareholders of the San Fernando hoped to build a reputation for stability by operating very conservatively for the first few years of the bank's existence, but this institution soon succumbed to the same state-generated pressures that had ruined the San Carlos. When civil war broke out in 1833, the state turned to the chartered bank for support, and public debt came to constitute the majority of the Banco de San Fernando's assets. By 1840, the bank had essentially stopped lending to the private sector, devoting all its resources to financing the Treasury.[52]

By this point, a clear pattern was emerging in Spanish chartered banking. The state's financial needs came first, and changes to the chartering regime tended to occur only when banks could no longer effectively serve these needs. The earliest chartered banks in Spain were also distinctive in the comparatively broad array of services they rendered to the state. These chartering arrangements aligned with a long-standing emphasis on the merits of centralized state power and guidance in the broader Spanish institutional context.

When the Carlist civil war ended in 1839, Spain entered a brief period of political peace and intense economic growth. In this era many new industrial enterprises were founded that needed access to credit and banking services to expand and reach their full potential. Yet the provision of banking services to the private sector was limited at best. The sole chartered bank, the Banco de San Fernando, was not capable of meeting private-sector demands for credit with its massive portfolio of public debt.[53] The liberal-moderate policy makers then in power responded to this dilemma by creating new chartered banks, establishing two additional Spanish banks of issue (the Banco de Isabel II and the Banco de Barcelona) in 1844.

This change signaled the beginning of another key theme that characterized early Spanish banking history. Bank chartering arrangements in Spain fluctuated with the political party in power. Liberal policy makers, who sought to broaden political participation to groups beyond the traditional landed elite, were more likely to view the diffusion of economic power across multiple banks as a positive development. Their efforts to expand banking services through the provision of additional charters were supported by merchants, industrialists, and other capitalists that stood to benefit from cheaper and more expansive banking services. Conservatives were less likely to see the diffusion of the chartering privilege as a good thing. In this, they were joined by the shareholders of the Banco de San Fernando, who resented the loss of what had formerly been monopoly control over the banking system. The architects of the 1844 legislation that established the two new banks of issue attempted to assuage the concerns of this latter group by also offering additional powers and privileges to the Banco de San Fernando, including a lucrative contract to serve as the nation's tax collector.[54] This was intended to compensate for the loss of the bank's monopoly; the practice also aligned with a long-standing Spanish tradition of using the grant of powers, rewards, and privileges to restore political harmony. Importantly, the goal of this reform was not to undercut the power of an incumbent firm (the Banco de San Fernando) with close financial and political ties to the state, as it had been for American reformers intent on destroying the Bank of the United States and the Second Bank of the United States. Instead, the goal was to expand available banking services—while still keeping established elites happy enough to play along with state-determined goals.

This expanded bank chartering regime in Spain did not last long. In the late 1840s, a major financial crisis originating in London and Paris led to a devastating wave of commercial bankruptcies in Spain, which contributed to the collapse of the Madrid Stock Exchange and a run on the Spanish banking system. The Banco de Isabel II was one casualty of this crisis. The newly established bank was forced to merge with its more established rival, the Banco de San Fernando, after becoming insolvent in 1848. The Isabel II had been the first and only bank to compete against the San Fernando in commercial lending activities. With its absorption by its competitor, any form of serious competition for the Banco de San Fernando also came to an end for at least a decade.

The accounts that Spanish policy makers provided to explain the 1848 crisis are telling. Many blamed the expansion in corporate chartering that had been a feature of the liberal-moderate regime. Although most liberal policy makers in the aftermath of the crisis continued to believe that corporations, when properly regulated, could work to promote economic prosperity by "serving as an element of wealth for individuals and the State," most also agreed that the crisis had revealed the dangers of an excessively lax chartering or regulatory regime. As the minister of finance framed the issue, corporations were naturally inclined to make "seductive promises" to solicit investor interest.[55] The public—which included investors—was framed as inherently gullible, or easily misled by these "private individuals who promote guarantees of success." This line of reasoning implied that unchecked corporate speculation, fueled by excessive optimism among myopic shareholders, had produced the disaster that followed. The problem, in short, was that a weak regulatory and chartering environment had allowed the "particularistic interests" of powerful corporations to "work . . . at cross-purposes" with the public or general interest, violating the principle of *state sovereignty*.

This understanding of the causes of the crisis informed the kinds of policy remedies Spanish policy makers undertook. In 1848, liberal-moderate policy makers introduced legislation that made it much harder for new (nonfinancial) corporations to be established without explicit royal approval and subjected existing firms to additional inspection and accounting requirements in the name of public safety. Although these restrictions initially applied only to nonfinancial corporations, they were extended to chartered banks in 1849.[56] As Spanish banking historian Mercedes Bernal Lloréns explains, the main purpose of these reforms was to "impose *strict administrative order* on companies and thereby protect the shareholders and those contracting with the company."[57] By increasing its direct monitoring of corporations, the state expected to improve its capacity to redirect powerful organizations, forcing them to serve the greater good. Restricting the ranks of chartered corporations, banks included, was also expected to make this domain of the economy easier for the state to manage and control.

Much to the delight of the shareholders of the Banco de San Fernando, no additional Spanish banks were chartered in the seven years that followed the 1849 reform. This episode, taken as a whole, suggests that Spanish policy makers perceived a different kind of problem in chartering banks from that of their American or Canadian counterparts. Unlike American policy makers, Spanish policy makers seemed to devote little attention to the issue of whether the grant of exclusive privileges violated foundational egalitarian principles. And although Canadian policy makers also sought to restrict the expansion of the chartering privilege to new groups, they viewed the danger to be combatted as *too much* state interference (e.g., more chartering threatened to disrupt the emergent mechanisms that kept order intact), while Spanish policy makers focused on the opposite problem of *not enough* state interference. In Spain, the restriction of the chartering privilege was part of a broader package of efforts designed to prevent powerful corporations from interfering with the state's capacity to proactively promote and maintain order.

The bank chartering regime in Spain changed once more when a more progressive branch of the liberal party assumed political leadership in the mid-1850s. These policy makers were eager to break with what they saw as the entrenched corruption of their liberal-moderate predecessors and sought to demonstrate this commitment to "honest government" by executing long-planned major infrastructure projects.[58] Their plans sought to harness the power of the private sector by leaving the actual construction and management of infrastructure to private initiative, while reserving planning, supervision, and stimulus responsibilities for the state. To succeed, this project would require considerable financing—not just for the state, but for the private firms that were expected to take a leading role in executing and implementing the state's vision. With this goal in mind, policy makers introduced two pieces of financial legislation (the Issuing Banks Law and the Credit Companies Law) in 1856. This legislation relaxed the 1849 prohibition on new (commercial) banks of issue and allowed for the unlimited establishment of investment banks (or credit societies). Over the decade that followed, the number of banks of issue in Spain jumped from three to twenty-one, and dozens of new credit societies were established.[59]

At this point, the chartered banking regime in Spain came to look much more like the comparatively liberal bank chartering regime of the United States. Barriers to entry to the banking business were lowered, and private-sector access to banking services increased. Yet even with these reforms, many long-standing Spanish trends continued. One key difference between the Spanish and North American banking systems was that Spanish chartered banks continued to face many restrictions that American or Canadian banks did not, including a requirement to appoint government representatives directly to the bank's board and restrictions on establishing more than one bank in a given location.[60] Another key difference was that the 1856 reforms also extended the exclusive privileges of a powerful incumbent (the Banco de San Fernando) even as they made the chartering privilege more broadly accessible. The San Fernando may have lost its near-monopoly control over note issuance and commercial lending, but it also received many other compensating privileges in exchange, including the authority to increase its already sizeable capital subscription and to establish additional branch offices in the provinces. These were powers that the bank had long desired and that it used to further entrench its market power.[61] As another indicator of its special importance to the state, the 1856 reform also changed the name of the Banco de San Fernando to the Banco de España (Bank of Spain).[62]

Thus the same way the US and Canadian banking systems came to mirror the idealized structures of their polities, the structure of the Spanish banking system as the country entered the 1860s came to mirror its own. Even the reformed banking system continued to be dominated by a single powerful institution with close ties to the state (the Bank of Spain). The Spanish state also continued to exercise relatively large and direct influence over the governance of chartered banks and attempted to reconcile competing interests through the grant of extensive and exclusive powers and privileges.

Conclusion

In making and debating choices about how to create and manage their first chartered banks, policy makers in the United States, Spain, and Canada were preoccupied by different concerns—which mirrored the same kinds of concerns that captured their attention in the political realm. Such institutional legacies help to explain how the structure of each country's banking system at the start of the 1860s came to bear such striking resemblance to its idealized vision of the polity.

In the United States, chartered banks were relatively numerous, small, locally oriented, and governed exclusively by regional (versus federal) levels of government. Under the dominant model of free banking, bank charters were also comparatively easy to obtain, with no need for legislative approval and relatively low up-front capital requirements. In developing the chartering and regulatory institutions that gave rise to this banking system, American policy makers were influenced by an institutional legacy marked by the principle of *community sovereignty*, with its emphasis on the benefits of local self-rule and on the dangers of centralized and concentrated power, and by the principle of *competition*, with its emphasis on the benefits of competitive allocation of privileges and widespread access to opportunity. Early debates over bank chartering were dominated by concerns about the dangers of centralized federal power and concentrated economic power, but these debates later started to center around the potential hazards of *exclusive* access to the chartering privilege and its associated rewards.

In Canada, there were comparatively few chartered banks, but these banks were also relatively large and powerful and were national in scope and operation. Bank charters were hard to obtain in Canada, but once created, chartered banks were largely left to their own devices. In developing the chartering and regulatory institutions that gave rise to this banking system, Canadian policy makers were particularly attuned to the dangers of state interference. They were also comparatively amenable to chartering practices that increased barriers to entry in banking by reserving this privilege for only highly qualified (or connected) individuals. Both trends aligned with the principle of *elite autonomy*, which equated state interference with tyranny and inefficiency and underscored the disadvantages of distributing privileges too broadly to less qualified or established groups.

In Spain, a single powerful private institution with close ties to the state (the Bank of Spain) dominated the banking system. In developing the chartering and regulatory institutions that gave rise to this banking system, policy makers were influenced by an institutional legacy marked by the principle of *state sovereignty*, with its emphasis on the benefits of state primacy and on the hazards of allowing particularistic group interests to interfere with the promotion of the greater good, and by the principle of *corporatist harmony*, with its emphasis on respect for established social hierarchy, state-led coordination, and patrimonial inducements. Spanish policy makers originally developed a bank chartering regime that did comparatively little to serve the needs of the private sector but quite a bit to serve the needs of the state. As this system evolved, policy makers responded to economic crises by attempting to enhance state oversight of, and guidance provided to, chartered banks. Even as liberal-progressive policy makers broadened access to the chartering privilege in the late 1850s, they continued to adhere to corporatist principles, pairing expanded charters with much more substantial powers and privileges for an established, dominant financial institution (in this case, the Bank of Spain) with the closest ties to the state.

The next chapter, chapter 4, picks up where this one leaves off, focusing on the transformations in bank chartering and regulatory policy that occurred during the turbulent period between 1860 and 1920. Focusing on what banking historians have already underscored as especially salient events in the evolution of each country's banking system, chapter 4 explains how the same underlying principles of order carried forward to shape key developments in regulatory and chartering policy at time of rapid growth in banking and the economy.

4

Branching Regulatory Paths into the Twentieth Century

Having created chartered banks, American, Canadian, and Spanish policy makers confronted new questions about how best to govern them in the late nineteenth and early twentieth century. Each country's economy underwent dramatic changes in this period as industrialization firmly took hold. Policy makers were eager to design financial systems that would be more effective in serving the needs of a rapidly changing economy, but that would also avoid disruptive banking crises and other kinds of disorder. This chapter examines how different strategies for addressing these goals developed in each country, focusing on key events in the evolution of bank chartering and regulatory policies between 1860 and 1920.

By the start of the 1860s, the American, Canadian, and Spanish banking systems had already taken very different forms. The US banking system was dominated by hundreds of small, independent, and locally oriented banks, each created by, and accountable to, local state governments rather than the federal government. The Canadian banking system, by contrast, was dominated by a handful of very large, capital-rich branch banks, which operated comparatively free from obligations to, and restrictions from, the government. And although the Spanish banking system had recently witnessed the creation of new banks of issue, it was still dominated by a single powerful private institution with extremely close ties to the state (the Bank of Spain). One implication of these differences is that comparing national banking systems in this period is no longer a matter of comparing apples to apples. Different banking system structures also produced different kinds of policy dilemmas. In practice, late nineteenth and early twentieth century policy makers in the

United States, Canada, and Spain were often focused on completely different issues.

However, the diverse regulatory debates and developments across these three countries still shared a key similarity: they continued to reflect the imprint of long-standing political-cultural traditions. American, Canadian, and Spanish policy makers may have focused on different dilemmas in this period, but the nature of these concerns, and the debates that surrounded them, still reflected the ongoing influence of the principles of order embedded in national political (and early banking) institutions. In the United States, concerns about *community sovereignty* and *competition* shaped the design of a new national banking system in the 1860s, the content of debate over bank branching reform in the late nineteenth century, and the type of arguments that Americans mobilized for and against the establishment of a central bank in the early twentieth century. In Canada, concerns about *elite autonomy* and *public rights* dominated regulatory debates throughout this period, including debates that touched on the appropriate role for the government in issuing paper money and the government regulation of chartered bank activities. In Spain, conflict between the principles of *state sovereignty* and *corporatist harmony* was at the center of repeated and prolonged debate over the monopoly privileges of the Bank of Spain.

In summary, well into the early twentieth century, American, Canadian, and Spanish policy makers were focused on a relatively narrow range of perceived hazards in the banking system—hazards that mirrored the same dangers they had long perceived in the political system. Focusing on regulatory developments that historians have already identified as especially salient for the development of the banking system in each country, this chapter illustrates how long-standing principles of order influenced these developments. To understand why restrictions on the structural form of banks were so controversial in the United States, why debates over the government's role in regulation became especially heated when they touched on issues of consumer protection in Canada, and why debates over monopoly control turned on the issue of state power in Spain, we must attend to the broader institutional arenas in which these conflicts took place.

Decentralization and the Rise of Central Banking in the United States

When Andrew Jackson successfully destroyed the Second Bank of the United States, he also effectively destroyed any form of a national (or federally chartered) banking system for many decades to come. Yet the Civil War of 1861–65 upended established institutional arrangements in the banking system, much as it also upended established American political institutions. One of the central issues in this war concerned the scope of the federal government's authority to govern activities and policies within individual states—particularly those related to slave ownership. And when the war finally ended in a northern victory, the balance of political power also shifted toward the federal government.

During the war, Congress had passed the National Bank Acts of 1863 and 1864, which restored the practice of chartering banks at the federal level. The reintroduction of a national banking system solved multiple problems. All federally chartered banks created under the National Bank Acts were required to purchase federal government securities before beginning operations; this provided a valuable source of funding to the federal government at a time when half of the existing state-chartered banking system was under enemy control. The creation of national banks also helped to bring greater stability to the currency. In 1860, US currency was made up of notes issued by over ten thousand different state banks. With so many different kinds of banknotes in circulation, it was hard for note holders to tell the difference between notes offered by sound and unsound banks. During the state-chartered banking era, unscrupulous bankers had taken advantage of the public's ignorance in this regard and overissued notes. Unsurprisingly, many Americans under these conditions became wary of using banknotes altogether. The National Bank Acts sought to address this problem by making the country's currency more uniform.[1] Federally chartered banks were required to accept notes issued by other federal banks at par value, and to circulate greenbacks (paper money issued directly by Congress during the war) in place of their own notes.[2] This legislation also provided greater security to federal banknote holders by tying a bank's note issuance to the value of its holdings of government securities. Crucially, the National Bank Acts also struck at the foundation of the state-chartered banking system by assigning a heavy tax to the notes of state-chartered banks, which threatened to drive these institutions out of existence.

Although the rise of the new federally chartered banking system clearly signaled the triumph of federal authority over state authority, the way that Congress chose to exercise this new authority is also instructive. The architects of the National Bank Acts essentially recreated free banking, a practice that had become extremely popular at the state level, at the national level. Federal charters were automatically granted to any group of five or more individuals that secured a minimum amount of capital, with no further investigation into their character or qualifications.[3] New banks were also required to structure as unit banks (banks without branches and only a single headquarters) and to purchase government bonds to back note issuance. As the first comptroller of the currency, Hugh McCulloch, took care to explain to the public, this new federal bank chartering regime would depart from its predecessors in its emphasis on diffuse, rather than concentrated, economic power: "The [new] national system of banking . . . is not to be a mammoth corporation with power . . . to control the business and politics of the country. It can have no concentrated political power. . . . It will concentrate in the hands of no privileged persons a monopoly of banking. . . . It is . . . not only a perfectly safe system of banking, but it is one that is eminently adapted to the nature of our political institutions."[4]

This feature of the design of the national banking system was a clear attempt to increase the legitimacy of federally chartered banking. As McCulloch's comments above suggest, the architects of the new US banking system were well aware of the long-standing taboos against concentrated financial power and restrained competition for economic privileges—or, in other words, the need to avoid violating the principle of *community sovereignty* and the principle of *competition.* In this institutional context, a deconcentrated banking system comprising thousands of unit banks was politically legitimate in ways that a centralized, federal branch banking system could never be. Thus the adoption of free banking at the national level represented yet another manifestation of a long-standing American strategy: making government authority more palatable by fragmenting and subdividing it as much as possible.

In the decades that followed the creation of a national banking system in the United States, regulatory debates shifted away from the question of whether federally chartered banks should exist at all and toward the question of how these banks should be regulated and structured. The branching powers of federally chartered banks emerged as a particularly salient and controversial issue. In 1870, prospects for state-chartered banks had seemed quite grim. The National Bank Acts had taxed their primary source of funding out of existence, and most observers expected that it would only be a matter of time before state-chartered banks disappeared altogether. Yet state-chartered banks staged a comeback in the 1880s and 1890s after discovering deposit banking (offering checking or demand deposit accounts). That is, instead of using banknotes to fuel their lending, state banks started to rely on deposits solicited from savers instead. The resurgence of state-chartered banks was also fueled by comparatively lax regulatory standards at the state level. State banks generally faced less stringent regulatory requirements (including lower capital requirements) than national banks, which gave them an important competitive edge in serving small rural communities that lacked sufficient capital to establish their own federally chartered bank. At the time, national banks could not be organized with a less than a $50,000 capital subscription, a requirement that was out of reach for many small agricultural communities. State-chartered banks, in contrast, might encounter capital requirements as low as $10,000.[5] State-chartered banks grew rapidly in the 1880s and 1890s. By the turn of the century, their numbers once again surpassed those of federal banks.

It was in this context that the advocates of the national banking system, which included many academic economists, the federal banking regulators, members of the Grover Cleveland administration, and supporters of the gold standard, began to call for branching restrictions for federally chartered banks to be relaxed.[6] They argued that restrictions on branching for federally chartered banks were preventing the nation's banking system from realizing its full promise. Branch banks were expected to do a better job of serving the country's banking needs. Adopting a branch structure was expected to allow banks to save on resources: it was much easier for an existing bank to establish a new branch in a different community than for a community to secure sufficient capital to establish its own independent bank. For this reason, branch bank advocates expected that the relaxation of government-imposed restrictions on branching would allow the banking system to better serve the needs of smaller, rural, capital-poor communities.[7] Drawing from the principle of *competition*, they argued that dismantling the "present complicated and unscientific system" of state restrictions would enhance the performance of the banking system as a whole by permitting emergent *market forces* (not the government) to determine the proper structural form for banks. This unleashing of market competition, in turn, was expected to "give a vigor to the credit system of this country which has been lacking."[8]

Opponents of branching reform appealed to a very different line of reasoning. Whatever efficiency advantages branch banking allowed, opponents argued that the grave political dangers of this practice outweighed them. Allowing banks to branch was expected to produce a more concentrated and less locally oriented banking system—two structural characteristics long defined as threats to order in the US institutional context. The fact that unit banks were confined to operating a single office in a single location made them highly dependent on the goodwill and economic health of that particular locality. In the words of economist Bernhard Ostrolenk, under unit banking, each bank was fundamentally "a *local* institution, *locally* financed and managed, drawing funds from *local* depositors, and using its financial resources for the development of *local* business enterprises."[9]

Branch bank opponents argued that allowing branch banks to establish alongside unit banks was politically dangerous precisely because it might reduce this local orientation of the banking system. Branch banks (which, unlike unit banks, operated offices across multiple communities) were expected to be less attuned to, and therefore less effective in serving, the particularistic interests and needs of their communities of origin. Viewed through the lens of the principle of *community sovereignty*, which assumes that specialized, local institutions do an inherently better job of serving local needs, such an arrangement seemed ripe for disorder. Branch bank opponents also expected the reform to give rise to larger banks that would drive their smaller, locally oriented competitors out of the marketplace. As Comptroller of the Currency Charles G. Dawes, a strong opponent of branch banking, argued, these dynamics would unleash "economic tendencies adverse to business individualism."[10] By making it easier for banks to accumulate resources, branch banking also threatened "the proper development of the country through small institutions fit to cope with the conditions of their localities, built up as we have built up the great American nation."[11]

Between the 1890s and the 1920s, the question of branch branching reform returned to the US policy agenda again and again. But with only a few minor exceptions, the branching regime for federally chartered banks changed very little over this period. Seeing the writing on the wall, advocates of federally chartered branch banks eventually pursued alternative methods of leveling the competitive playing field with state-chartered banks. One of the most important was a push to reduce minimum capital requirements for federally chartered banks, a reform that was expected to enable federally chartered banks to compete more effectively against state-chartered banks for the business of smaller, resource-strapped rural communities. Unlike branching reform, this effort succeeded in mobilizing sufficient political support. The average capital holdings of federal banks fell by almost half between 1870 and 1914, circumstances that dramatically increased the likelihood that these institutions would experience solvency issues when trouble hit.[12] Thus, faced with a choice between allowing federally chartered banks to change their structural form or allowing them to operate with less shareholder skin in the game, American policy makers opted for the latter. Reducing barriers to entry in banking (one consequence of reducing capital requirements for federally chartered banks)—even as it made the banking system as a whole more economically fragile—simply did not violate long-standing institutional taboos in the same way that branch banking did.

As the industrial economy increased in size and complexity and the geographic scope of trade broadened, American banks started to organize into correspondent and chain networks to circumvent the problem of clearing and settling economic transactions.[13] A handful of large reserve city banks (located in New York, Chicago, and St. Louis) were at the top of this correspondent pyramid, with city banks, located in commercial financial centers, inhabiting the middle. The thousands of country banks (federally chartered banks outside of large commercial financial centers) served as the base. The country banks involved in these interbank networks placed a large share of their reserves in deposit accounts with their city and reserve city banks "correspondents"; these country bank deposits, in turn, served as important funding sources for city and reserve city banks. Reserve city banks also rendered valuable services (like clearing and settling draft payments and checks) to city and country banks across the nation. In practice, these chain and correspondent bank networks led to a heavy concentration of deposits and balances in a few commercial centers—especially New York.[14]

Between the 1870s and the early 1890s, the extremely fragmented and decentralized US banking system weathered three major financial crises that originated in, or were exacerbated by, the financial difficulties of New York reserve city banks. In 1893, suspensions among New York banks plunged the United States into a true nationwide financial crisis and sparked a major recession. In 1907, similar dynamics returned, as a sharp decline in the value of the New York Stock Exchange led to runs on New York bank and trust companies. These bank and trust company failures had a domino effect, spilling over to impact the financial health of thousands of smaller banks around the country that held correspondent relationships with these major financial institutions.[15] These crisis episodes increased public resentment against bankers. Many argued that the crises had been caused by bankers; others resented the fact that bankers had appeared to tend to their own interests over those of their depositors as these crises had unfolded.

During the 1907 crisis, New York financier J. P. Morgan pledged large sums of his own money to support confidence in the banking system and convinced other leading New York bankers to do the same. Although these private-sector attempts to restore order were successful in calming the fears of depositors and temporarily stabilizing the banking system, they only fueled growing public concern about a banking conspiracy centered around the interests of New York banks.[16] That the New York banking elite had been successful in bringing the panic to an end suggested that these actors had extraordinary market power. Many Americans wondered: this time, these actors had used their power for good—but what was preventing them from using it for less benevolent purposes next time?

In the face of five major banking panics over the course of five decades, observers across political lines agreed that the US banking system was in need of serious reform. Yet policy makers from different political camps disagreed on the appropriate nature of these reforms. Debates over this issue intensified after Congress established the National Monetary Commission in 1908, a bipartisan group of experts charged with examining the 1907 crisis and recommending reforms to prevent the return of similar events. The solution that the chairman of the commission, Senator Nelson W. Aldrich (R-RI), endorsed was to establish a new private institution, the National Reserve Association, that would be controlled by a board of powerful bankers. To stabilize the economy and reduce the frequency of crises, this institution would be given the authority to issue the nation's currency and to rediscount the commercial paper of member banks. This initiative essentially proposed to institutionalize what elite bankers like J. P. Morgan were already doing in practice: using their considerable market power to regulate the economy and restrain disruptive banking crises. However, this solution, which was endorsed by most of the New York banking elite, was strongly opposed by most progressive Democrats and bankers outside of New York. These opponents, drawing from long-standing concerns about the hazards of concentrated economic power, argued that the northeastern banking elite already enjoyed too much power and control over the nation's banking system. They were not eager to endorse any institution that might expand that power, regardless of its theorized beneficial effects for stability.

Instead, opponents of the National Reserve System wanted the state to step in to develop a truly *national* reserve system directly accountable to a representative government. For their part, bankers in many midwestern, southern, and western states were quite eager to break their current dependence on the New York banks and saw great promise in the prospect of government-backed regional bank clearinghouses that could provide similar clearing and payment services.[17] In keeping with a familiar commitment to egalitarian principles, these bankers argued that if concentrated financial power had to exist, it was better for it to concentrate in the hands of the common people (in the form of their elected political representatives) than in the hands of a few elite bankers.

After Democrat Woodrow Wilson was elected to the presidency in 1912, the political balance tipped toward the adoption of this democratic plan for a national reserve system. In the months leading up to the election, Wilson appealed to by-now familiar themes in describing the money supply as "the greatest monopoly in this country" and made it clear that he would not tolerate "any plan which concentrates [this] control in the hands of the banks."[18] Yet the final form of the Federal Reserve Act, signed into law in December 1913, reflected a political compromise.[19] This legislation established a Federal Reserve System comprising twelve *privately* controlled regional reserve banks, each of which would hold a portion of member banks' reserves, perform other central banking functions, and issue currency against commercial assets and gold. These regional reserve banks would operate under the watchful eye of a government-controlled, seven-member Federal Reserve Board in Washington.

This was not exactly the government-controlled reserve system the democratic reformers and their allies had envisioned—but it was a step in that direction. The Federal Reserve Act dramatically increased the government's control over the national banking and monetary system, pleasing reformers who sought to reduce the power of the eastern money trust. But this was also government control organized in a very particular way. Central banking, like federally chartered banking before it, ultimately arrived in the United States in a highly decentralized and fragmented form.

Banking without Government Influence in Canada

Canada also underwent considerable political change in the 1860s. On July 1, 1867, the colonies of Canada, Nova Scotia, and New Brunswick united into a single Dominion of Canada, divided into four distinct provinces (Quebec,

Ontario, Nova Scotia, and New Brunswick). Early Canadian policy makers faced the task of designing comprehensive banking legislation to govern the new federation. In the debates over banking policy that followed, many of the issues that sparked so much controversy in the United States, including the identity of the actor that should have the authority to charter banks and what limits (if any) should be placed on the ability of chartered banks to branch, received virtually no attention from Canadian policy makers. The vast majority of those attending the Canadian Constitutional convention of October 1864 agreed that the federal government had exclusive jurisdiction over banking; the existence of branching powers for chartered banks was taken for granted.[20] Instead, the key controversy in Canada centered around the appropriate degree of influence the government should hold over important banking system functions, especially currency issuance.

In the 1860s, Canadian banks encountered considerable difficulties when the country entered into a recession.[21] In the fall of 1866, the Bank of Upper Canada closed its doors because of insolvency and inadequate capital, and the Commercial Bank of the Midland District, another large and powerful bank, followed suit in 1867. The first Canadian minister of finance, Sir John Rose, was eager to place the banking system on a more stable footing, and he introduced a new banking plan with this goal in mind. Echoing Lord Sydenham's earlier proposal for a provincially owned bank of issue, the plan that Rose introduced in May 1869 sought to abolish the note issuance privileges of chartered banks and to transfer control over currency issuance to the federal government.[22] Rose was motivated by his observations of the positive outcomes that had followed the recent American experiment with a new national banking system. It seemed as if taxing the notes of state-chartered banks out of existence had brought order to that country's troubled banking and currency systems: in Rose's words, it put an end to "the extreme inconvenience, not to say disaster, which result[s] from promiscuous circulation of the notes of Banks, established in various localities all over the Union, each of which had a different degree of security to give its note-holders."[23] To achieve a similar outcome in Canada, Rose sought to reserve the note-issuing privilege for the government, rather than delegating it to the chartered banks.

In the same legislation, however, Rose also proposed increasing capital requirements for chartered banks—a distinctly un-American approach to banking reform. If his proposal had succeeded, it would have required all Canadian chartered banks to secure capital of at least one million dollars before opening their doors, with at least 20 percent of this capital already paid in by shareholders. This can be contrasted with the extremely low capital requirements of the United States, where only $50,000 of capital was required to establish a federally chartered bank (and state-chartered banks often required even less). This proposal was also framed as a reform to stabilize the Canadian banking system by forcing individual shareholders to put more of their own funds at stake. The implication was that a safer banking system was also one where key privileges concentrated in only a few, appropriately motivated hands.

Rose's proposal faced opposition from multiple groups. One group, which included members of the Liberal Party, the Canadian Bank of Commerce, the Bank of Toronto, and multiple other banks in Ontario, Quebec, and Halifax, resisted it on the basis that it would further concentrate financial power in Canada. Higher capital requirements might lead to the development of more stable banks, but they would also offer competitive advantages to already capital-rich institutions (particularly the Bank of Montreal). A second, allied group, which also included many bankers and members of the Conservative Party, objected to the potentially disruptive consequences of the state taking over an important function (note issuance) that had historically belonged to the private sector. Tying the note issuance of banks to their holdings of government securities, rather than leaving them free to respond to the demands of the economy, was predicted to artificially restrict the money supply and strangle economic development. The same group objected to the claim that a currency backed by the security of the government would be more stable than a currency backed by the issuance of the private banks, citing the three financial crises that had followed the establishment of government note issuance in the United Kingdom.[24] Ultimately, Rose's bill to reform the banking system failed to pass the legislature, and Rose resigned as finance minister soon after.

Rose's successor, Sir Francis Hincks, introduced a watered-down version of a banking reform proposal that retained many features of Rose's plan but dropped the elements that had proven most controversial. This time, the reform proposal succeeded. Although this legislation, the Banking Law of 1870, did increase capital requirements for banks, it did not do so to the extent that Rose had envisioned. Minimum capital requirements were set at $500,000, with 40 percent of this capital required to be paid up before the bank could open its doors. The law did not abolish the right of the chartered banks to issue their own notes; however, it did restrict chartered banks to issuing notes in denominations of four dollars or more.[25] The federal government assumed responsibility for issuing all smaller-denomination notes.

This latter decision aligned with a long-standing Canadian institutional practice of deviating from the principle of laissez-faire in cases where the rights of individuals—particularly vulnerable individuals—seemed to be threatened. In a political context that placed great value on the safeguarding of basic individual rights, arrangements that threatened to allow powerful actors to exploit the naïveté of the vulnerable or unsophisticated were especially likely to be perceived as threatening to order. As Adam Smith argued in *The Wealth of Nations*, while it was important to uphold the natural liberties of individuals, exceptions to this rule could and should be made in cases where "those exertions of the natural liberty of a few individuals . . . might endanger the security of the whole society." To illustrate this point, Smith actually used the example of banks issuing notes and the potential for this practice to result in exploitation of unsophisticated users of banking services; he described the state regulation of banknote-issuance powers as akin to building party walls for fire prevention. As he argued, both "the obligation of building party walls . . . to prevent the communication of fire" and "regulations of the banking trade" infringed on the natural liberty of private individuals, yet both activities "are, and ought to be, restrained by the law of all governments" since each impinged on the natural liberties of others.[26]

Smith went on to explain more precisely how the ability to issue small notes facilitated bank malfeasance. Most reasonable people, he explained, would agree to accept a very small note without inquiring into the solvency of the bank that had issued it.[27] However, this natural tendency also came with a steep social cost borne primarily by the poor. In Smith's time, vulnerable farmers, members of the working class, and other unsophisticated market actors were also the actors most likely to be paid in the form of small-denomination notes, and therefore most likely to suffer if the value of these notes declined in the event of bank insolvency. By contrast, businesses and other sophisticated market participants, who had the requisite knowledge and power to effectively fend for themselves in a competitive marketplace, were more likely to deal in large-denomination notes. To protect the rights of the former group, Smith argued that the issuance of small-denomination notes must be regulated and constrained. The Banking Law of 1870, which transferred responsibility for small-denomination note issuance to the state, was thus in keeping with a well established British political-cultural tradition of supporting state intervention only in cases where the rights of the vulnerable were understood to be threatened.[28]

These new reforms, while important, were the exception. When viewed in comparative perspective, developments in Canadian banking regulation in the late nineteenth and early twentieth centuries were, on the whole, marked by a strong commitment to the principle of laissez-faire. The essential privileges and freedoms for banks established in the earliest bank charters remained largely unaltered throughout this period.[29] Even after the 1870s brought another wave of bank failures and suspensions to Canada, this comparative lack of state intervention in banking continued uninterrupted.

Minister of Finance Sir Samuel Leonard Tilley's failed proposal to create a government inspector of banks in the early 1880s offers a case in point. Following the experiences of the 1870s, which had shown that some Canadian banks were "grossly neglectful of proper inspection," Tilley proposed creating a government agency to formally inspect and regulate chartered banks.[30] His expressed goal was to promote greater stability and more prudent behavior in the banking system, but his plan quickly attracted strong opposition from the chartered banks. The banks framed their opposition to this initiative in instructive ways. Drawing from the principle of *elite autonomy*, they argued that greater state oversight could not produce a more stable banking system. The reason? Because government supervisors would never be able to match the superior knowledge and expertise of bankers themselves. As banking historian R. M. Breckenridge explained, "The bankers argued that . . . it would be impossible for a government inspector, or an auditor, properly to inspect a Canadian bank. It was far better to rely on the careful organization of the banks, the vigilance of the directors, and the inspection by trained men of its own staff, who, travelling the year round from branch to branch and reporting to the general manager, would have nought to gain by concealing the truth, and everything to lose."[31] This line of reasoning drew from a well-established pattern in British (and Canadian) institutional life, in which the administration of key political and economic functions were entrusted to elite gentlemen instead of the centralized state. The underlying principle was that effective governance depended on the skill and the efforts of individuals overseeing their own domains, not the centralized dictates of a powerful administrative state. In the 1880s, bankers used the same organizing principle to justify the continuation of self-regulation (rather than government regulation) in the banking sphere. Tilley ultimately abandoned the proposal of a government inspectorate, persuaded either by the content of these arguments or by the considerable political power of the established chartered banks.[32]

At this point, the Canadian chartered banks responded to the recent episodes of instability in the banking system with their own industry-led solutions. In 1880, they acceded to a reform that would offer note holders first lien on a bank's assets in the event of bank failure. The purpose was to offer greater legal protection to these vulnerable actors if the bank failed, thereby increasing public confidence (and, by extension, stability) in the banking system overall. In 1891, the chartered banks continued by establishing an industry self-regulatory body and lobbying group, the Canadian Bankers Association (CBA), which took on the responsibilities of establishing clearinghouses for the settlement of bank payments, handling the suspensions of failed banks, and managing the redemption of banknotes.[33] The CBA also developed a Circulation Redemption Fund to redeem the banknotes of failed banks, to which each bank was asked to contribute 5 percent of its total circulation.

In the words of political scientist Louis W. Pauly, now that the banking industry had assumed a more direct role in promoting banking system stability, "the federal government [agreed that it] would remain on the sidelines with respect to day-to-day banking activities."[34] Banks were now mutually responsible for each other's note circulation. Yet control over note circulation was not linked to the state. Many of the functions that became the responsibility of the new Federal Reserve System in the United States (including the development of a national, paper-based clearing and settlement system and a system of regulatory supervision) were officially controlled and overseen by a powerful industry self-regulatory association in Canada. Thus the long-standing Canadian institutional tradition of state noninterference continued into the twentieth century, in the form of this distinctive regulatory architecture.

Next Steps in Spanish Bank Regulatory Policy

Spain in the 1860s was marked by considerable economic and political upheaval. After a decade of relative prosperity, a major international financial crisis in 1864 upended the Spanish economy. Political change followed when a coalition of progressive-liberal reformers deposed Queen Isabella II in September 1868. Isabella was replaced on the throne by Amadeo of Savoy, the son of Italian king Emmanuel I, who took a friendlier view of progressive liberal and republican interests. When Amadeo I abdicated the throne only three years later, Spain was officially proclaimed a constitutional republic. This embrace of liberal-republican principles in the political sphere was also reflected in changes in the banking system. In 1869, the bank chartering regime was liberalized even further. A new company law issued that year allowed for the unlimited creation of new banks of issue, discount banks, agricultural banks, and credit companies, with the goal of enriching both the state and the private sector.[35]

Spain's experiment with extreme banking system liberalization proved brief. This period ended abruptly in 1874, well before political power officially left liberal-republican hands. At this point, the Spanish state was effectively bankrupt. Other leading European powers did not recognize the legitimacy of the new, unelected liberal-republican government and refused to lend to the Spanish Treasury. And at a time when social unrest was brewing, any further increase to taxes to address this deficit did not seem like a viable option. Of course, there was always the familiar option of appealing to chartered banks— but the problem was that only one bank had the scale and resources necessary to extend a loan of the size that the Treasury required.

As the state's financial difficulties increased, leading liberal-republican policy makers felt that they had no choice but to turn to the powerful Bank of Spain for support. Minister of Finance José Echegaray successfully negotiated a massive loan from the bank to the Treasury—but the bank extracted a heavy price. In exchange for financial support to the state, the Bank of Spain requested a total monopoly over note issuance. In other words, it wanted to be the only institution with the power to offer banknotes in Spain, to hold the "monopoly of issue." Spanish policy makers, backed into a corner, took the powerful institution up on this deal.

It is hard to overstate the momentousness of the decision to grant the Bank of Spain these powers. In addition to completely violating liberal economic principles, it was also legally suspect, since it repealed the issue privileges already outlined in the charters of Spain's other fifteen banks of issue.[36] This was a case where "the *raison d'Etat* overrode [these] legal and ethical niceties."[37] Their backs against the wall, liberal-republican policy makers put aside their commitment to liberalization and embraced a familiar strategy for preserving political order in Spain: bestowing rewards and privileges to secure the compliance of powerful private-sector groups. The shareholders of the other chartered banks were given the option to remain independent entities without note-issuing powers or to convert into branches of the Bank of Spain, and most chose this latter option. The size and geographic reach of the Bank of Spain expanded dramatically. From this point onward, this privately owned institution enjoyed near-complete dominance over the Spanish banking system.

The Bank of Spain's monopoly of issue privileges would remain controversial whenever they came up for renewal, as they did in 1891, 1907, and 1921. However, these privileges were never repealed.[38] Throughout this period, the debates over the bank's monopoly of issue were dominated by disagreements over whether the Bank of Spain (as a powerful, privileged private-sector institution) was providing adequate services to the state. Advocates of allowing the Bank of Spain to retain its monopoly privileges argued that the bank was fulfilling the terms of the bargain it had struck with the government. Drawing from the principle of *corporatist harmony*, these actors also argued that assigning exclusive control over currency issuance to this powerful private institution was an efficient and rational method of organizing this important function.[39] Concentrating this key economic privilege in the hands of the leading industry incumbent reflected and affirmed respect for established hierarchy; bestowing privileges and rewards in return for important services to the state affirmed a long-standing tradition of relying on patrimonial relationships to secure political (and now economic) order.

Opponents of the bank's monopoly of issue, by contrast, offered arguments that drew from the principle of *state sovereignty*. They argued that the powerful private Bank of Spain was not giving enough back to the state (especially in terms of profit share from its activities) to justify extending its considerable monopoly privileges.[40] They also underscored the economic woes that they believed had followed from giving a single private institution monopoly control over the banking system: these included the inadequate flow of resources to the agricultural and industrial sectors. From this standpoint, current arrangements in the banking system were serving only the particularistic interests of a powerful private group (in this case, the Bank of Spain) at the expense of the general good. For order to be maintained, this situation could not stand—the state needed to reclaim the powers that properly belonged to it and not the private sector.

To keep both groups happy, Spanish policy makers in the late nineteenth and early twentieth centuries resorted to a familiar strategy for maintaining political and economic order. They worked around the edges of their deal with the Bank of Spain, always keeping the bank's monopoly of issue privilege intact, yet also seeking to placate advocates of expanded banking services in other ways. In this period, additional, state-owned banks were established to support the extension of long-term credit to industry and agriculture.[41] An additional fifty charters (albeit without issue privileges) were also granted to banks located in Madrid and the Basque Country, a strategy to placate those seeking a greater flow of credit to commerce.[42]

This status quo in the banking system persisted even after a series of major centralizing reforms at the turn of the twentieth century. Spain's loss of its colonies to the United States in 1898 came as a severe shock and inspired a broader societal turn toward protectionism, interventionism, and state self-sufficiency in the political system. Yet even as Spanish policy makers focused on giving the centralized state a more powerful role in nearly every other domain of the economy, the established privileges of the Bank of Spain (still a powerful, privately owned institution in this period) remained untouched.[43]

In 1900, the liberal-conservative Spanish minister of finance Raimundo Fernández Villaverde introduced an economic stabilization plan that included tax reform as its centerpiece. For the first time, the Spanish state achieved a balanced budget, which persisted for a decade. From the start, however, Villaverde recognized that maintaining this balance would require more than simply reforming the tax system—it would also require a substantial reduction in public debt.[44] Since government deficits represented the biggest source of banknote expansion in Spain at the time, strict limits on currency issuance were expected to promote fiscal discipline. Accordingly, Villaverde limited banknote circulation by the Bank of Spain, reducing the maximum circulation from 2.5 to 2 billion pesetas.[45]

However, when familiar economic challenges arrived in 1909, the state reverted to old habits in the banking system. Increased military expenditures in Spanish Morocco brought the state's budget back into the red; once again, the state turned to chartered banks to finance its military efforts.[46] In an important change from past practice, however, the Bank of Spain did not shoulder the responsibility of financing the government alone. Over the past two decades, the rest of the Spanish chartered banks had developed to a degree that allowed them to play a more active role in financing the state. All Spanish chartered banks were encouraged to purchase government bonds; to make these bonds sufficiently attractive, the Treasury asked the Bank of Spain (as the dominant player in the banking system) to accept these bonds as collateral at low interest rates and to give them favorable tax treatment.

As banking historians Tortella and García Ruiz explain, this public-private partnership made government bonds very attractive to chartered banks: these securities "guaranteed an acceptable rate of interest and were quite liquid, as they could be pawned at the Bank of Spain at any moment for interest rates that were ordinarily below the bonds' yield."[47] Chartered banks were now automatically eligible to obtain credit from the Bank of Spain up to a value equivalent to 90 percent of their holdings of public debt.[48] This arrangement encouraged the expansion of the Spanish banking system by offering chartered banks virtually unlimited access to credit, and scholars have argued that this easy access to relatively cheap financing also encouraged banks to branch out into riskier, less conventional, and potentially more lucrative financial activities (such as direct promotion of industrial firms and investment in private securities).[49] Political scientist Sofía Pérez describes this practice of Spain underwriting industrial promotion via inflationary public finance—a process mediated by chartered banks—as the "original sin" that would shape the relationship between Spanish banks and industry for many years to come.[50]

For our purposes, what is most important is the extent to which the design of Spain's new model of state finance continued to reflect the imprint of familiar principles of order. It is notable that a powerful private institution that already received considerable state-granted privileges, the Bank of Spain, was also asked to coordinate the activities and privileges of other private-sector firms to promote state goals. The extreme concentration of economic power in a single privately owned bank, especially with the close and mutually supportive relationship between this bank and the state, would have horrified American policy makers. Yet it was entirely in keeping with the principle of *corporatist harmony* and its emphasis on state respect for established social hierarchies (further supporting incumbent groups), state-led "concertation" (proactively working with powerful private-sector actors to smooth coordination and promote harmony within the system), and the benefits of patrimonial exchange to secure desired state goals.

Conclusion

The period between the 1860s and 1920s was one of turmoil and change in the political systems and banking systems of the United States, Spain, and Canada. The economy was changing rapidly in this period, and the organization of banking was changing alongside it. As policy makers in each country confronted different kinds of problems in their respective banking systems, their approaches to debating and resolving these problems continued to reflect familiar institutional legacies.

In the United States, concerns about concentrated and centralized power continued to dominate debates over banking policy and regulation. Concerns about threats to open competition in the banking sector became much more salient in this period as well. This legacy linked the multiple banking reform episodes that defined this turbulent period. Even as the authority of the federal government to govern banking strengthened in the aftermath of the Civil War, the architects of the country's new federally chartered banking system remained mindful of the lessons of the past. They took care to ensure that bank charters under the new system would be widely accessible to all Americans interested in the privilege (in keeping with the principle of *competition*) and that federally chartered banks themselves would take small, independent, and locally oriented unit-bank forms (in keeping with the principle of *community sovereignty*). Similar concerns about the dangers of interference with open competition and the dangers of tolerating concentrated power dominated extended debates over bank branching restrictions, which pitted advocates of unleashing competitive forces against opponents of allowing the numbers or local orientation of banks to decline. Then, in the early twentieth century, the debates that ultimately produced the Federal Reserve System featured similar themes, as groups concerned about the dangers of government interference in the economy faced off against groups concerned about the hazards of concentrated elite power.

In Canada, concerns about the hazards of state interference in the economy continued to dominate debates over banking policy and regulation. Concerns about the potential for powerful banks to exploit vulnerable groups also became more salient in this period. This conflict between the principle of *elite autonomy* and the principle of *public rights* featured in the heated debates over proposals to transfer the power to issue currency to the state; it also helps to account for the content of the policy compromises that followed these debates. Similar themes reappeared in the debates over the creation of a government bank inspectorate in the late nineteenth century. Although most Canadian efforts to expand the state's presence in the banking system ultimately proved unsuccessful, they did inspire the established chartered banks to organize and introduce an alternative system of industry self-regulation.

In Spain, concerns about limiting the state's capacity to rule *and* the dangers of losing powerful group support for state objectives continued to feature in debates over banking regulation. In the 1870s, liberal policy makers compromised some of their economic principles as part of an effort to boost the political authority of the state, striking a bargain with a powerful private-sector group (the Bank of Spain) to secure the financial resources the state needed to effectively govern. Controversy over the terms of this bargain would dominate all Spanish debates over banking policy for the next fifty years. In these debates, advocates of maintaining the bank's monopoly of issue emphasized the benefits of mutual accommodation between societal elites and the state, while opponents highlighted the dangers associated with delegating excessive power to the private sector. Over the decades that followed, Spanish policy makers continually navigated this dilemma by offering interest groups on both sides compensating benefits, maintaining the Bank of Spain's cherished monopoly of issue while extending new forms of support and privilege to new entrants. The uniquely close relationship between the Bank of Spain and the state continued into the early twentieth century, with this powerful private-sector actor continuing to enjoy privileges that allowed it to dominate the rest of the banking system, but also assuming new and important quasi-public coordinating functions. These arrangements were guided by the influence of the principle of *state sovereignty*, with its emphasis on the benefits of centralized oversight and control, and the principle of *corporatist harmony*, with its emphasis on respect for hierarchy and the merits of effective public-private collaborations.

In summary, taking the long view of the evolution of banking policy over the course of the nineteenth and early twentieth century illustrates how often a relatively narrow range of principles of order shaped the development of national regulatory regimes. By the start of the 1920s, the design of each country's bank regulatory system embodied the same principles of order long reflected in the political system. The next chapter, chapter 5, will explain how conflict between these cherished principles also structured the pivotal regulatory debates—and ultimately the policy solutions—that emerged in each country after the devastating banking crises of the 1920s and 1930s. This moment would be a turning point in the development of national regulatory systems.

5

Debating Regulatory Reform
in the 1920s and 1930s

World War I brought unprecedented prosperity to the United States, Canada, and Spain, but all three countries experienced sharp deflationary recessions at the end of the war. Farmers had responded to soaring crop prices during the war by expanding the size of their farms and investing in new technology to maximize agricultural output. But when agricultural commodity prices plummeted after peace was restored, overextended American, Canadian, and Spanish farmers found themselves in trouble. Similarly, manufacturing and industry in all three countries had benefitted from booming export demand during the war but struggled to adjust to the peacetime economy. Many factories were forced to retool operations or shut down, and the civil labor force struggled to absorb millions of returning soldiers.

The effects of this recession, the recession of 1920–21, were severe, but thankfully brief. The decade that followed—the Roaring Twenties—was marked by explosive demand for consumer goods, huge gains in industrial productivity, and unprecedented economic growth in all three countries. But economic troubles made a dramatic return in October 1929, when the collapse of the US stock market sparked a global decline in investment and consumer spending. Certain countries were hit harder than others. While the United States and Canada each experienced massive declines in industrial production and entered into a deep depression, the fallout in Spain was limited by policy choices in the 1920s that had reduced this country's exposure to the global economy.[1]

As they often do, these troubles in the real economy translated into problems in the banking system. American, Canadian, and Spanish regulators each grappled with distinctive problems in this period, but they faced some common dilemmas as well. In all three countries, banks were forced to absorb the costs of rising loan defaults when borrowers struggled to adjust to economic recessions. Persistent deflation left many banks holding assets with declining value, while rising volatility in foreign exchange markets also contributed to losses for banks with international exposures. And in each country, these issues culminated in one or more banking crises of greater or lesser severity at some point in the 1920s or 1930s.

In the United States, the banking crisis of the early 1930s was extreme: over a third of all banks in operation failed or disappeared between 1929 and 1933, with many falling victim to multiple nationwide runs on deposits that ended only with President Roosevelt's declaration of a mandatory four-day "bank holiday" in March 1933. In Canada, no bank failed in the early 1930s, although quite a few came close. However, Canada had experienced its own disruptive local banking crisis in the early 1920s, when the unexpected failure of a major bank, the Home Bank, nearly sparked a systemic financial crisis. Spain also experienced its own widespread banking panic in the early 1920s that originated in the industrial capital of Catalonia but quickly spread to other commercial centers.

Historians generally agree that the 1920s and 1930s represent a crucial turning point in the evolution of national bank regulatory systems. Around the world, the banking crises of this period raised deep questions about the adequacy of existing regulatory standards, and policy makers in multiple countries responded with strategies for regulatory reform. This chapter explains how the same long-standing principles of order that had contributed to the divergent development of national bank regulatory systems over the previous century also shaped the content of American, Canadian, and Spanish regulatory reform battles in the 1920s and 1930s.

In the course of making this argument, I also explore questions others have neglected. Most of the existing historical and social scientific scholarship on the influential regulatory changes of this period asks why, given the policy options on the table, national policy makers chose to adopt certain regulatory remedies while rejecting others.[2] To explain these patterns, scholars have focused either on the objective economic challenges that appeared to make the need for dramatic change more pressing, or on political dynamics that tipped the balance toward particular proposed reforms and away from others.[3] Instead of asking why certain reforms were ultimately selected over others within countries, I instead ask why the kinds of policy options on the table looked so different across countries in the first place. In the 1920s and 1930s, American, Canadian, and Spanish policy makers perceived distinctly different problems in their banking systems, and they entertained different kinds of regulatory solutions. To make sense of this, it is important to understand the different ways national actors viewed the roots of order and disorder in economy and society. As we will see, the influence of these institutionalized understandings is most readily seen in how the advocates *and* opponents of regulatory reform across a broad array of issue areas resorted to a relatively narrow (but by now, familiar to us) array of principles of order in each country.

Debating Regulatory Reform in the United States: Competition and Community

The US banking system at the start of the 1920s comprised nearly twenty-nine thousand independent banks—a massive number of banks, especially in comparative perspective. One-third of the industry operated under the auspices of the Federal Reserve, with the rest operating under individual state banking regulators.[4] When surging farm income during World War I brought large surpluses of deposits to rural banks, many responded by offering more agricultural loans. When both farm income and the value of farmland plummeted in the postwar recession, many of these bankers also found themselves in a bind. Between 1920 and 1929, nearly fifty-eight hundred banks—20 percent of those in operation—became insolvent, with the vast majority of failures occurring among unit banks in the Midwest or South.[5]

Prospects for large banks in urban centers (especially in New York) looked much brighter. During the economic boom of the 1920s, many of these banks saw large gains in assets and deposits and began to pursue new kinds of activities.[6] In the latter half of the 1920s, the US stock market also reached unprecedented heights as the public became more active in securities investment (often using bank credit or advances from stockbrokers to fund these purchases) and businesses became increasingly likely to turn to securities markets (versus banks) to fulfill their financing needs.[7] Flooded with deposits and facing reduced demand for commercial loans, larger banks began to search for new investment opportunities. Some of these opportunities included affiliating with firms that specialized in investment banking, granting installment loans to consumers who wished to purchase securities, engaging in new forms of consumer and mortgage lending, and increasing investments in corporate, utility, and municipal bonds. By 1929, commercial banks and their affiliates were responsible for more than half of new securities issues that reached the market.[8]

When the stock market collapsed in October 1929, many of these commercial banks came in for a reckoning. Even after the Federal Reserve succeeded in stabilizing the troubled securities markets, a series of banking panics followed in the early 1930s, with each panic worse than the last.[9] By March 1933, the situation had grown truly desperate, leading the newly elected President Roosevelt to take the unprecedented step of declaring a national bank holiday only two days after taking office. Banks were forced to close for four days while Congress

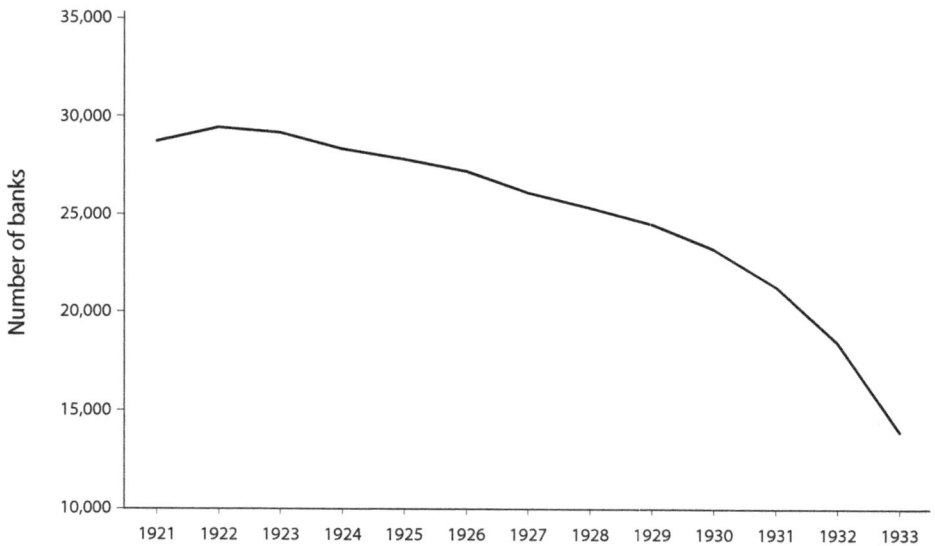

FIGURE 5.1. Total US banks in operation, 1921–33. *Source*: Board of Governors of the Federal Reserve System (US), Number of Banks in the United States (X02NOB), retrieved from FRED, Federal Reserve Bank of St. Louis, https://fred.stlouisfed.org /series/X02NOB (accessed February 1, 2020).

acted to allow the Federal Reserve to issue additional currency on good assets to all reopened banks. Although this bank holiday (and government support) did succeed in ending the widespread banking panic, the damage had been done. After a slow but progressive decline in the total number of independent banks throughout the 1920s, an additional ninety-one hundred banks (nearly a third of the entire banking system) closed their doors between 1930 and 1933 (see figure 5.1). At this point, few Americans were in doubt that the banking system needed significant reform. But how should the problem be fixed?

This question dominated legislative hearings and debates throughout the early 1930s. Banking reform efforts in the House were initially led by Chairman of the House Banking and Currency Committee Louis Thomas McFadden, a Republican from Pennsylvania and a strong opponent of interstate bank branching and the Federal Reserve System. In March 1931, McFadden was replaced by Henry B. Steagall, a Democrat from Alabama with a long history of supporting the interests of unit bankers. In the Senate, the reform effort was led by Senator Carter Glass, a long-serving Democrat from Virginia and a key architect of the Federal Reserve System. After a few aborted attempts at earlier banking reform bills, Glass introduced a comprehensive reform bill in January 1932 that included four key proposals:[10]

1. *Separate commercial and investment banking.* All commercial banks and investment firms would be required to specialize in either commercial banking (e.g., accepting deposits) or securities activities (e.g., dealing in nongovernmental securities for customers, investing in nongovernmental securities, underwriting corporate securities). Commercial banks would be prevented from affiliating with organizations that engaged in securities activities, and vice versa.
2. *Expand branching privileges for national banks.* All federally chartered banks would be permitted to establish branches within their "trade area," regardless of state laws on bank branching. Banks would be free to establish branch offices up to fifty miles into adjacent states if the area was deemed part of the trade area.
3. *Increase regulatory supervision.* More banks, and more kinds of bank activities, would be brought under Federal Reserve supervision. Supervisory and disciplinary powers of the Board of Governors would be increased. The secretary of the Treasury would be removed from the Federal Reserve Board, increasing the political independence of the central bank.
4. *Restrict interest rates on deposits.* A regulatory ceiling would be established on the interest rates banks could offer on time, savings, and demand deposits. Banks would no longer be permitted to offer any interest on demand deposits; interest rates on time and savings deposits would be capped at a rate determined by the Federal Reserve.

Like most of the regulatory reform attempts that had preceded it, this reform bill immediately attracted controversy. The proposed expansion of bank branching privileges was especially controversial and sparked a determined filibuster by branching opponent Senator Huey Long (D-LA) and his supporters.[11] Worried that the branching provisions would kill the bill, Senator Sam G. Bratton (D-NM) introduced an amendment in early 1933 that would allow federally chartered banks to branch only in states that already allowed branching for state-chartered banks. A version of the Glass Bill with the Bratton amendment passed the Senate with an overwhelming majority in late January 1933, but it received a frosty reception in the House, where it was sent to wither away in committee.[12]

In the House, Steagall was in the process of developing his own reform bill. The centerpiece of the House bill was the establishment of a federal deposit insurance system. Steagall proposed to create a government agency, the Federal Deposit Insurance Corporation (FDIC), to oversee a deposit insurance fund backed by the US Treasury. All deposits in US banks would be fully insured by the government up to $10,000.[13] This proposal had its own detractors: it was supported by advocates of unit banking but strongly opposed by most other actors, including Glass, the majority of the Senate, the lame duck president Herbert Hoover, the soon-to-be-president Franklin Delano Roosevelt, the majority of academic economists, and the banking industry itself.[14] The House passed a reform bill that included a deposit insurance component in May 1932, but the bill was poorly received by the Senate.

The stalemate continued until March 1933, when the US banking system hit rock bottom. Policy makers temporarily put the issue of regulatory reform on hold as they rushed to introduce emergency measures. Resolution finally arrived on June 16, 1933, in the form of the Banking Act of 1933. The final legislation was a political compromise that incorporated key features of both the Glass and the Steagall bills. While including most of the reforms Glass had championed, like the enforced separation of commercial and investment banking, expanded supervisory and enforcement powers for the Federal Reserve, and the establishment of regulatory ceilings on deposit rates, it also established a federal deposit insurance system, an initiative Steagall had strongly favored (and Glass had strongly opposed). With the Bratton amendment still intact, national banks also received only very limited branching powers.[15]

In the debates leading up to the passage of the Banking Act of 1933, there seemed to be general agreement on many of the facts. It was generally acknowledged that the vast majority of failures had occurred among unit banks and had been especially common among state-chartered banks that were not members of the Federal Reserve System.[16] It was also well known that the 1929 collapse of the stock market had sparked the crisis, and that banks with heavier exposure to securities or bond markets had suffered extensive losses. Policy makers also agreed that the rising popularity of new models of banking, like group banking and chain banking, had contributed to the contagion of the crisis by encouraging depositors to pull their funds from institutions linked to troubled groups. Official inquiries also revealed evidence of weak management, unsound banking practices, and even outright fraud at many banks—especially smaller banks.[17]

The patterns, then, were clear: the controversy centered around what these patterns *represented*. One account, advanced by members of the financial elite, academic economists, and regulators, among other groups, was that US policy makers had contributed to the crisis by doing *too much*. In imposing and maintaining artificial restrictions on bank structures and activities, this argument went, policy makers had unwittingly interfered with the competitive processes that organically produced beneficial economic outcomes, with crisis as the inevitable result of this interference. A second account, much more popular among agrarians, unit bankers, and their supporters, was that policy makers had not done *enough* to protect the banking system. They contended that the strength of the US banking system lay in its deconcentrated, community-oriented structure, and that the regulatory system of the 1920s, in allowing unchecked competitive pressures to "drive the little fellow out of business," had also created conditions conducive to crisis.[18]

Most arguments in favor of expanded bank branching, against deposit insurance, and against the enforced separation of investment and commercial banking appealed to this first account, which drew from the principle of *competition*. The advocates of expanded branching powers for federally chartered banks were especially attuned to the evils of disrupted market mechanisms. They argued that branching reform was needed to correct for inherent problems in the design of the unit banking system, which they regarded as an outdated and inefficient model of banking. The average unit bank controlled fewer resources, held less diversified assets, and struggled more to attract competent managers than the average branch bank, and branching reform advocates argued that these features had become increasingly serious deficiencies in the new economy of the 1920s and 1930s.[19] Changes in the character of the economy had demanded corresponding changes in the structural form of banks, but long-standing restrictions on branching powers had prevented these market actors from effectively responding to these new imperatives.[20] These commentators, in other words, framed the branch bank as the *market-selected bank*: the organizational form that competitive forces would naturally select for, if allowed to operate freely. Drawing from long-standing assumptions about the benefits of a free and open competitive process, branch banking advocates argued that greater systemic stability and efficiency would be the natural result of allowing market forces to winnow out poor-performing banks and reward their more prudent, high-performing competitors.[21] Bankers responding to market signals, not policy makers, should determine the appropriate structural form for their institutions.

Arguments against a federal deposit insurance system appealed to a similar line of reasoning. To the proponents of branch banking, deposit insurance seemed like a disaster ready to happen. This framework enhances banking system stability in part by removing penalties for market failure, for example, by fully compensating depositors for lost savings if a bank fails. As William S. Elliot, vice president of the Georgia Bankers Association, explained before the House Committee on Banking and Currency, many observers expected this to encourage more imprudent banking; Elliot argued that it would "stimulat[e] a laxity on the part of the officials who run the banks, knowing that their depositors whom they have to look into the face every day on the street, cannot lose anything by their mismanagement of the banks."[22] Thus, instead of reinforcing competitive mechanisms, deposit insurance actively worked to undermine these mechanisms by preventing the losers of the competitive process from actually experiencing loss. It was this distinction that prompted Comptroller of the Currency John Pole to describe a general guaranty of bank deposits as "the very antithesis of branch-banking."[23]

Although arguments against the enforced separation of investment and commercial banking were both less common and less vehement than arguments in favor of branch banking and against deposit insurance, they generally appealed to the same line of reasoning. As Benjamin M. Anderson, economist at Chase National Bank in New York, described the problem: "Before the great chartered banks developed security affiliates, the business of underwriting securities was primarily in the hands of a few great private bankers. . . . To throw the issue of securities back into the hands of private bankers little subject to public authority, as proposed in the Glass bill, could hardly improve the picture."[24] In short, the issue was that restricting banks from *freely competing* for securities business might allow the wrong sort of actors to end up in control of this business.

Most arguments against the relaxation of bank branching restrictions, in favor of deposit insurance, in favor of the enforced separation of investment and commercial banking, and in favor of the introduction of deposit rate ceilings appealed to the second account of the crisis, which drew from the principle of *community sovereignty*. The actors who subscribed to this view, which included most American agrarians, unit bankers, and their allies, saw real dangers in the increasing dominance of large banks in urban capitals and the declining influence of small, locally oriented, and rural institutions. In the 1920s, these actors argued, the banking system had been allowed to depart from the deconcentrated structure that was so key to its strength and success, and predictably negative consequences had followed.

If the branch bank was framed by its advocates as the *market-selected* bank, the unit bank was framed by its advocates as the *community-oriented* bank. Unit banks, which were not permitted to establish branches, specialized in lending to, and accepting deposits from, a single local community by necessity. Branch banking opponents framed the community orientation of these institutions in a positive light. Senator Peter Norbeck (R-SD), for example, described unit banks as the quintessential "American bank" that "came into its full flower and strength during a century of growth in this country; and what country has had any growth like ours? In every community was a bank that had the deposits of the community, the savings of the community, in charge of the leading men of the community, men interested in the progress of every person in the community."[25]

In an institutional context that presented the local community as the building block of political life, this connection between unit banking and community focus was an important one. Opponents of branch banking implied that any threat to the competitive survival of unit banks was also a threat to the American way of life itself, and many contended that the political dangers associated with a departure from unit banking outweighed any perceived economic benefits of this practice. The central worry was that branch banks might crowd smaller, locally oriented unit banks from the marketplace. With a superior capacity to gather resources and withstand economic shocks, branch banks were likely to outcompete their unit bank counterparts. Opponents also argued that the tendency of branch banks to operate offices in multiple communities threatened to "enlarge . . . centralized banking," potentially leading to "a centralization of the control of the credit of the country."[26] This perceived connection to centralized economic power explains why branching opponent Representative Thomas Alan Goldsborough (D-MD) described branching reform as "a matter which involves our whole social and economic system. . . . Give me the control of the credit of a community and I will control every activity in it."[27]

Other branch banking opponents denied the economic benefits of this practice altogether.[28] A branch structure might allow individual banks to accumulate more resources and withstand shocks, but opponents argued that specialized unit bankers were inherently better bankers. As one speaker at a 1929 American Bankers Association conference put the matter, "Only the well-posted unit banker thoroughly identified with his community can solve the problem of furnishing proper credit and avoid excessive loans in an agricultural community—nay more, can assist and develop the worthy individual through an intimate knowledge of his affairs and check the scheme of a rascal."[29] In other words, since branch bankers were distracted by their commitments to multiple communities, they could not match the same in-depth understanding of borrowers and local conditions that unit bankers enjoyed, with negative consequences for the banking system overall.

Advocates of deposit insurance drew from the same line of reasoning to argue in favor of this reform. Greater stability in the banking system was clearly desperately needed, and advocates of deposit insurance argued that this framework represented a way of restoring stability that would not disrupt the banking system's community-oriented structure. If anything, deposit insurance would strengthen the relative power and independence of the unit bank. As Senator Arthur Vandenberg (R-MI) put it in 1933, "there is one purpose more than another which is inherent in . . . [deposit insurance]. . . . It is the purpose to protect the smaller banking institutions."[30] Deposit insurance was expected to promote small bank survival by disrupting one of the key mechanisms through which the nation's savings had come to concentrate in the hands of large banks. Depositors sought to place savings in more stable institutions, and larger banks (with greater resources) were generally perceived as safer. But what if deposit insurance could remove these stability concerns altogether? As banker A. P. Fierson explained, "if we had a law that would guarantee deposits in banks . . . the money that is now daily flowing into the great metropolitan centers of the country, would remain in towns where it originates, where it could be loaned in a banking way for the development of industry and commerce and agriculture of the communities."[31] Although many advocates of deposit insurance also recognized that a government guarantee might amplify incentives for mismanagement (as its critics contended), they were confident that government supervision and an effective system design would prevent this behavior.[32]

Interestingly, arguments in favor of the enforced specialization of investment and commercial banking drew from a similar line of reasoning. This reform (unlike branching reform or deposit insurance) appealed to policy makers across political lines. Advocates of maintaining the system's community-oriented structure appreciated the way it would block yet another mechanism through which deposits concentrated in the hands of large banks. Most of the leading US commercial banks had established securities arms in the 1920s. These had proved lucrative prior to the crisis. This capacity to affiliate with securities firms, which was not a capacity that smaller banks shared, only compounded the competitive advantages of larger banks. Some reformers were eager to prevent banks from affiliating with securities firms at all to give community banks more of a fighting chance.[33]

Other proponents of this reform supported it for a different reason. Americans had long celebrated the benefits of specialized institutional focus, on the grounds that institutions that focused on addressing a narrow range of local needs were also fundamentally better at serving these needs. Many advocates of separating investment and commercial banking drew from this logic, which had previously applied to *geographic* specialization, to push for *functional* specialization as well. These actors, which included Senator Glass, regarded the increasingly diverse constituencies commercial banks served, which now included investors, brokers, and industrial firms as well as local savers and borrowers, as a problem. The need to appeal multiple audiences was thought to create "divided allegiances" within banks, inviting inefficiency and corruption. As Representative Herman P. Kopplemann (D-CT) argued, "The unholy alliance between the brokerage office and the bank . . . has grave dangers. It violates the fundamental principle of the lawyers' code of ethics—that of undivided allegiance. In banking as elsewhere, no man can serve two masters."[34] In other words, bankers that sought to maximize profits in securities markets *and* effectively serve the interests of depositors faced an irreconcilable conflict of interest.[35] As Representative Robert L. Bacon (R-NY) explained to Congress in 1933, requiring bankers to specialize in one activity would better serve the needs of both commerce and industry by imposing familiar American checks and balances: "By divorcing long-term financing from short-term financing the conditions affecting each [to] serve as a check upon the other, and the exaggerated results of the intimate association between the two will be avoided. From this we may expect sounder credit policies from our commercial banks and an investment business more accurately responsive to the needs of industry."[36]

Finally, advocates of limiting the interest rates banks could offer on time, savings, and demand deposits also offered arguments that drew from the principle of *community sovereignty*. Here too, support for this reform cut across political lines. Opponents of concentrated power appreciated the way that it restricted yet another mechanism that promoted the concentration of deposits: the economies of scale that naturally allowed larger banks to offer more attractive interest rates on time and savings deposits. Capping deposit rates for all banks was expected to restore this competitive balance.[37] Other reform advocates, including Senator Glass, appreciated the way that the reform would enhance banking system stability by putting an end to destructive "rate wars" between financial institutions. Many of the banks that failed in the 1920s and 1930s had attempted to obtain scarce resources by offering very high interest rates to depositors, leaving them with no choice but to seek out riskier investments that offered potentially higher returns. It was hoped that regulatory ceilings on deposit rates would put an end to this "mutually destructive" behavior by dampening rate competition.[38]

Long-standing US principles of order, embodied in the design of political and economic institutions, were not the only factors that mattered for the development of bank regulatory reforms in the 1920s and 1930s. Yet accounts that deny the role of these principles in shaping regulatory policy end up going to great lengths to explain the policy positions that some actors took. The case of American farmers, the group whose attitudes toward banking reforms have been most closely studied, is particularly instructive. Existing explanations emphasize material conditions to explain why American farmers rationally preferred unit banking as a mode of organization. These explanations have taken a variety of forms. For example, sociologist Monica Prasad attributes agrarian opposition to branch banking to the preexisting "anti-monopoly fervor" of agrarians, itself a product of the objective (and extreme) scale of monopoly power in the late nineteenth century United States.[39] It was precisely because large US firms had reached such unprecedented scale in the 1880s and 1890s, Prasad suggests, that American farmers became so particularly attuned to the dangers of unchecked monopoly power. Political economists Charles Calomiris and Stephen Haber highlight an even more direct link between the material conditions of farmers and their support for restrictive banking regulation, arguing that farmers prefer unit banks because they rationally value insurance against credit scarcity during times of economic trouble. As the authors put it, "Identifiable economic interests predict support for unit banking in the states where it was popular. Apparently, landowning farmers in prosperous banking districts . . . calculated that they had something to gain from unit banking. A local banker who was not part of a branch network had to lend to them or no one."[40]

The problem is that if we assume that economic actors are motivated purely by these objective material interests, farmers' desire to preserve unit banking makes little sense. Recall that *nearly a third* of the entire US banking industry disappeared between 1920 and 1933, with the vast majority of these failures concentrated among unit banks operating in agricultural areas. Clearly, unit banking did not offer an effective form of insurance against the withdrawal of credit from local communities. Yet even as thousands of American farmers in communities with failed unit banks suddenly found themselves without access to any banking services at all over the course of the 1920s, support for unit banks only increased. Similarly, while the distinctive Progressive Era experiences that Prasad highlights in her account of agrarian interests surely *intensified* agrarian opposition to monopoly power, chapters 3 and 4 of the present book revealed how American opposition to concentration and (geographic) diversification—at least when it came to financial institutions—long predated this period. It is only after considering farmers' deeper concerns about concentrated financial power—concerns with established roots in preexisting American political and economic institutions—that the intensity of farmers' commitment to unit banking starts to make sense.

Recognizing how these principles of order shaped the process of regulatory reform also suggests an additional insight: that the regulatory reforms that finally prevailed in each country also came with *meanings* attached. In the end, US policy makers chose to adopt some of the reforms they considered in the 1930s while forgoing others. These choices—to establish the world's first national deposit insurance system instead of allowing banks to branch, to forcibly separate investment from commercial banking, and to establish regulatory caps on the interest rates banks could offer depositors—did not just embody the triumph of the interests of particular groups over other, less powerful groups. They also embodied the triumph of a specific principle of order (*community sovereignty*) over an alternative (*competition*). As we will see, the relative dominance or latency of these principles, now institutionalized in the structure of the US bank regulatory system, would go on to have crucial implications for the regulatory developments to come.

Debating Regulatory Reform in Canada: Elite Autonomy and Public Rights

Canada entered the 1920s with a banking system that looked very different from the banking system of the United States. In 1920, there were only eighteen independent banks operating in Canada, each with hundreds of branches stretching across the country. This was an extremely concentrated banking system, with the four largest banks holding over 70 percent of the nation's deposits.[41] The effects of any single bank failure were greatly amplified in this system, as Canadians discovered with the failure of the Home Bank, then Canada's third-smallest bank, in August 1923. Although the bank had suffered financial difficulties for some time, the depth of its problems became apparent only in the sharp postwar deflationary recession. Over sixty thousand depositors at seventy branches around the country lost their savings when the bank closed its doors. This event, which sparked a crisis in depositor confidence, led to serious financial strain at three other banks in Ontario and Quebec and prompted a series of government-coordinated mergers to avoid additional failures.[42] By January 1925, only fourteen independent banks were left operating in Canada.

The Home Bank debacle received widespread media coverage and inspired a parliamentary investigation. Although this crisis was ultimately less destructive than the US banking panics of the early 1930s or even the Catalan banking crisis of the early 1920s in Spain, it was extremely politically salient. The bank's August 1923 failure occurred at an especially embarrassing time for the recently formed minority Liberal government, which had successfully fended off a push for significant regulatory reform from the Progressive Party in early 1923.

The Progressive Party, a new political party, had recently upset over fifty years of Liberal or Conservative political dominance in the 1921 federal election. The party represented a coalition between members of provincial United Farmers Parties (which enjoyed strong support in the agriculture-heavy western provinces), Liberals who opposed high tariffs on farm products, and labor advocates. The Progressives ran on a platform of support for small farmers, greater state intervention to promote social progress, and opposition to economic inequality and the entrenched power of big business. Its leaders saw serious problems in how a handful of large banks headquartered in eastern Canada dominated the financial system.[43] When the Bank Act (the legislation governing all chartered banks) came up for renewal in 1923, its members pushed for four major reforms to restrict the power of incumbent banks:

1. Relaxing barriers to entry in banking by reducing the required qualifications (e.g., paid-in capital) needed for groups to obtain a charter
2. Limiting the maximum interest rates banks could charge on loans
3. The creation of a central bank
4. The establishment of a formal government agency to inspect banks.

Liberals and Conservatives successfully thwarted this initial push for reform by appealing to a familiar Canadian institutional theme. Drawing from the principle of *elite autonomy*, they argued that assigning key economic functions to the state would not produce more effective—or safer—results. As one Liberal member of Parliament (MP) from Nova Scotia explained the matter, public servants could never match the superior knowledge and expertise bankers naturally acquired in the course of pursuing their day-to-day business. Thus, public servants were poorly suited to govern or oversee the industry:

I suppose [a bank] is a public service corporation, but I do not think it one which must be controlled in all its operations by the state. . . . Why not put the responsibility upon the directors and the manager? They are following the transactions of the bank daily; they are intimately acquainted with every detail of its operations. . . . It is only those who audit frequently and who become intimately associated with the bank's methods of business who can audit properly.[44]

The failure of the Home Bank that summer changed the debate. Progressives seized this political moment by calling for a formal inquiry into the bank's collapse, which informed a comprehensive reevaluation of the regulatory regime in 1924. When the inquiry uncovered evidence of gross fraud and mismanagement at the Home Bank, as well as evidence that key figures in government had ignored warning signs, the Liberals changed their own stance on the creation of a government bank inspectorate agency, introducing a bill to create such an agency in July 1924. This was an important symbolic step away from Canada's long tradition of financial industry self-regulation, yet it still fell far short of the comprehensive reform the Progressives had hoped to achieve.

In the aftermath of the Home Bank crisis, Progressive reformers pushed for much more aggressive policy changes, which included some of the same initiatives they had supported in 1923 (the creation of a central bank, the transfer of control over currency issuance from banks to the government) as well as new initiatives (the establishment of a federal deposit insurance system). In the regulatory reform debates that centered around these Progressive policy proposals in 1924, two familiar principles of order dominated the discussion. Policy makers across political lines agreed that gross mismanagement, unsound banking practices, and even outright fraud by managers and directors were the most proximate causes of the Home Bank crisis.[45] It was equally clear that the Conservative government had overlooked important warning signs. Directors at the Home Bank's Manitoba office had written to then minister of finance Sir William White in 1916 and 1918 with evidence that the bank was continuing to pay dividends to shareholders from uncollected interest on outstanding loans (a known unsound banking practice). Both times, White called on the Home Bank's internal auditors to investigate its financial situation; each time, the bank passed these internal audits.

The question that dominated the regulatory debates of 1924 was whether the Home Bank episode was a troubling aberration—a regrettable event that was unlikely to be repeated—or a reflection of much deeper structural flaws in the banking system itself. While most Liberal and Conservative policy makers and representatives from the banking industry argued the former point, most Progressives, and the agrarian interests they represented, argued the latter.

Liberal and Conservative arguments against substantial regulatory reform—including those in opposition to a central bank, expanded government control over currency issuance, and the establishment of federal deposit insurance—overwhelmingly appealed to the principle of *elite autonomy*. Arguments against these reforms started from the same basic premise: that the historical strength of the Canadian banking system lay in its development through "natural evolution"—a commitment that must not be abandoned even in light of recent events.[46] The celebration of a banking system that had evolved organically (as expert bankers freely and independently responded to market imperatives) aligned with a long-standing institutional emphasis on the benefits of state noninterference. To these opponents of reform, a system where policy makers took a more active role in shaping its structure and function—that is, a banking system like that of the United States—represented the opposite of Canada's "naturally evolved" banking system. As Thomas Vien, a Liberal MP from Quebec and soon-to-be-chairman of the Banking and Commerce Committee, argued, introducing "drastic" regulatory reforms to the Canadian banking system would be an "error of principle" that risked violating the country's established and beneficial commitment to banker-led natural evolution.[47] Opponents also argued, once again, that the reforms would invite inefficiency by encouraging public servants to assume functions that properly belonged to expert managers and directors.[48] A central bank in particular was expected to introduce an undesirable "human element" into what was supposed to be automatic, impartial, and market-led governance of the economy.[49]

The established Canadian banks and their Liberal and Conservative allies regarded deposit insurance as dangerous for similar reasons. Canadian deposit insurance opponents, like those in the United States, worried that the introduction of a government guarantee would discourage depositors from distinguishing between prudent and imprudent banks, interfering with the processes that automatically kept order intact in systems without a powerful, centralized administrator. As the Department of Finance wrote in a 1924 memo, deposit insurance was expected to "only be a disaster . . . as the public would not be called upon to discriminate between sound institutions, with whom their funds would be safe, and others."[50] Opponents of all three reforms further argued that keeping the government out of the banking system would help to prevent the financial system from turning into an engine of the state.[51] The message was clear: multiple negative consequences would follow if the government became too involved with the business of banking.

In contrast, arguments in favor of these three regulatory reforms overwhelmingly appealed to the principle of *public rights*. Progressive policy makers argued that the Home Bank episode had clearly revealed that the prudence and self-interest of bank managers and directors was not enough to prevent failure and scandal. As William Irvine, an MP from Alberta and a leader in the agrarian Dominion Labour Party, argued, "We had prudent bankers before the failure of the Home Bank and yet their prudence did not save the Home Bank depositors. We had efficient management before that, and that did not prevent this failure.

If we have not been safeguarded by prudent management in the past, how can we feel sure that we will be safeguarded by prudent management in the future? Prudent management is not enough."[52] Restoring order would require more substantial protections for vulnerable depositors, preserving their basic rights to a safe and stable banking system. As Irvine explained the crux of the matter, "Under the current Bank Act . . . gambling by responsible or irresponsible individuals who are regarded under the act as the guardians of the public savings has taken place. The depositors—including widows, orphans, and the aged—are unprotected."[53] In framing depositors as the "ordinary man on the street"—weak and vulnerable actors easily exploited by more powerful and sophisticated bankers—reform advocates also tapped into a long-standing Canadian tradition of seeing benefits in state intervention when vulnerable group or individual rights were threatened. They recognized a formal bank inspectorate agency as an important step in the right direction, but one that did not go far enough.

Overall, progressive arguments in favor of more substantial reform primarily emphasized the benefits for the protection of depositor rights. Greater depositor protection was framed as one of the primary benefits of a central bank, which would protect depositor interests by reducing disruptive ebbs and flows in the business cycle.[54] Depositor safety was also cited as one of the primary benefits of transferring control over currency issuance from chartered banks to the government. Under the existing regime (where banks issued their own notes), note holders had the first claim on the assets of a failed bank, while depositors, as unsecured creditors, were much further back in line. The Progressives emphasized how government control over note issuance would remove the need for note holders to have this first claim on bank assets, thereby benefitting depositors as well.[55] Deposit insurance, too, was primarily framed as a mechanism for protecting depositor rights. Its advocates argued that the state, in creating chartered banks that bore its stamp of approval, also had the responsibility to ensure that the institutions it had created would not exploit the end users of the banking system.[56] Because the existence of a bank's charter implied a state endorsement, it was only natural for depositors to seek some sort of compensation from the state for the losses they had suffered.[57] As Leon Johnson Ladner, a Conservative MP from British Columbia, argued, "Especially in view of the experience of the last few months, [Parliament] should come to the aid of the citizen who avails himself of the banking privileges of the country and give him the protection to which he is entitled [in the form of deposit insurance]. . . . I cannot see how any hon. member can deny the justice, the merit, or the reason of such a proposal."

Canadian reformers also drew from additional principles in arguing for these reforms, including American-style appeals to the benefits of maintaining smaller banks as independent financial institutions.[58] For their part, many

American advocates of deposit insurance had also appealed to the need to protect the rights of vulnerable group or individuals when arguing for reform. Yet there were also differences in the relative salience and frequency of these kinds of arguments across the two countries, as well as in their reception by reform opponents. The opponents of a central bank and deposit insurance in Canada were generally unwilling to entertain the validity of *community sovereignty*-based arguments, with many retorting that the local orientation of the US banking system—something that had developed in response to artificial political restrictions, not market imperatives—had served as a direct cause of the disorder that had continually plagued the financial system of that country, not an inherent strength.[59]

Faced with multiple reform strategies that seemed to offer greater protection to depositors but also invited greater state interference with the activities of chartered banks, Canadian policy makers ultimately rejected most of these reforms. While they did depart from Canada's long tradition of near-complete industry self-rule by establishing the first official government bank supervisory agency, the Office of the Inspector General of Banks (OIGB), in 1924, this agency was relatively weak in comparative perspective and kept with a long-standing British tradition of avoiding direct participation in on-site examinations in favor of external private audits. Canadian policy makers rejected most of the other proposed remedies. The country would not create a central bank for another eleven years, and it was not until 1935 that Canadian banks officially lost the power to issue their own banknotes. Federal deposit insurance would not arrive in Canada until 1967. In this way, the 1924 reforms to the Canadian Bank Act also embodied and reflected the primacy of the principle of *elite autonomy* over the alternative principle of *protecting public rights*.

Less than a decade later, Canada would also suffer a massive economic blow during the Great Depression. Although no Canadian bank failed in this period, many suffered large losses, and the credit contraction that followed devastated many Canadian farmers. The Canadian banking system grew even more concentrated over this period, with only ten independent banks left operating in Canada by 1930.[60] The regulatory debates that followed this crisis episode proceeded along the same lines as those that followed the collapse of the Home Bank a decade earlier. Once again, opponents of substantial regulatory reform mostly appealed to the principle of *elite autonomy* to make their case, arguing that the primary reason Canada had avoided an American-style banking system collapse was that Canadian policy makers had resisted the temptation to tinker with the principle of natural evolution.[61] Advocates of more substantial regulatory reform overwhelmingly appealed to the principle of *public rights*, for example, arguing that the current structure of the banking system had failed to sufficiently protect the rights of vulnerable farmers and other users of the financial system.[62] "The Canadian people," as one reform advocate wrote in *Maclean's* magazine, had not been provided with "their reasonable and just requirements" in a banking system that operated to serve the interests of elites—conditions that merited more substantial regulatory reform.[63]

While Canadian legislators and policy makers considered many additional regulatory remedies during this period, once again, only one significant reform passed. In 1934, Canadian policy makers established the Bank of Canada, the country's first central bank. Much like the creation of a government bank inspectorate agency a decade earlier, this central bank was adopted as a concession to calls for a more substantial overhaul of the bank regulatory system.[64] It was also one of the least interventionist reforms on the table: the Bank of Canada was a relatively weak and toothless central bank, initially structured as an entirely private institution, with no role for the government in its governance or operation.[65] In the 1930s as well as the 1920s, then, conflict over banking regulation in Canada continued to center around the perceived benefits of state noninterference and the perceived need to safeguard public rights. This conflict was ultimately settled in ways that largely affirmed the primacy the principle of *elite autonomy* within the banking system.

Debating Regulatory Reform in Spain: Corporatist Harmony and State Sovereignty

Spanish banks greatly benefitted from the country's neutrality during World War I. Bank profits doubled between 1915 and 1917, largely fueled by expanded lending to, and investment in, industrial firms.[66] Easy access to cheap funding (via the *pignoración automatica*) encouraged banks to embrace a "mixed" mode of banking that combined traditional commercial banking with the riskier (but potentially quite lucrative) direct promotion and financing of industrial firms. During this period of prosperity, many new banks emerged, and existing institutions opened new branches, with bigger banks in industrial areas like Madrid, Catalonia, and the Basque Country seeing the largest gains.

When the wartime boom came to an end, this heavy bank exposure to industrial performance became a point of weakness.[67] The deflation of the 1920s hit Spanish industrial and manufacturing businesses especially hard, and the banks who loaned money to or invested in these firms suffered heavy losses.[68] These dynamics sparked the emergence of a banking panic in the industrial capital of Catalonia in 1920, which eventually spread to Spain's other commercial centers.

The crisis began with the November 1920 collapse of the Bank of Terrassa, a minor Catalan bank that had suffered large losses in volatile foreign currency markets. The bank's failure only increased the growing sense of unease among Spanish depositors, who began to withdraw funds from banks with more extensive international exposures. The venerable Bank of Barcelona, then the leading bank in Catalonia, was the next casualty. As rumors spread that the bank had engaged in excessive speculation in currency markets and gone too far in granting excessive loans to troubled industrial firms, depositors were no longer willing to bet that it would survive the postwar recession. Initially, the Bank of Spain responded to the Bank of Barcelona's distress with a temporary loan, but it withdrew this support as the bank's financial troubles grew more pressing. In January 1921, the Bank of Barcelona suspended operations and permanently closed its doors. The failure of such a prominent bank sparked another crisis in depositor confidence that assumed a national character. Although banks across Spain (especially in Madrid and Bilbao) suffered in the national banking panic that followed, Catalan banks remained the hardest hit.

The regulatory reform debates that followed were heavily influenced by the ideas and actions of a single individual, the charismatic Catalan politician and newly appointed minister of finance Francesc Cambó. Cambó was a leader in the Lliga Regionalista, a new political party that had recently emerged to challenge the entrenched dominance of the Liberal and Liberal-Conservatives who had been alternating in power since 1881. The party's platform, and the political beliefs of Cambó himself, combined two seemingly incompatible objectives. First, it sought greater autonomy and self-governance for Catalonia, including the promotion of uniquely Catalan cultural, political, and economic values and interests. Members of the Lliga Regionalista argued that Spain's many economic and political problems at the start of the twentieth century were products of its predominantly agricultural economy and unrepresentative political system, which was dominated by elite interests in Madrid. To create a better Spain, they sought to restructure the entire country along Catalan lines, both by opening up the existing political system to more Catalan influence and by transforming Spain into a modern industrial economy via heavy infrastructure investment.

But—and here is the tension—Cambó and the Lliga Regionalista were not interested in dismantling the established social status quo. They just wanted to restructure it. The party remained deeply conservative and supported the continuation of the monarchy while restraining democracy. In other words, Lliga Regionalista did not reject the idea that elites (versus the masses) should remain in control of Spanish political and economic life—they just subscribed to a different conception of which groups should constitute this elite.

This combination of transformative and conservative aims confused and frustrated Cambó's critics on both the right and the left. As Liberal Republican Nicelo Alcalá Zamora famously argued on the floor of the Cortes in December 1918, "Autonomy and hegemony are two things that cannot be put together. . . . You cannot be Catalonia's Simon Bolívar and Spain's Bismarck at the same time."[69]

Cambó seized the political opportunity that the Catalan banking crisis provided to push through a series of major reforms to the bank regulatory system
that aligned with his broader aims. These reforms were intended to restructure and modernize the banking system, while simultaneously maintaining the
dominance of traditional elite groups within it, and included the following:

1. *Change the role of the Bank of Spain* (yet keep its key privileges intact).
   The Bank of Spain was to be restructured as a banker's bank. It would
   no longer be allowed to compete directly with other commercial
   banks, but it would continue to enjoy its valuable monopoly of
   currency issue. Cambó proposed extending the bank's monopoly of
   issue for another twenty-five years.
2. *Increase state participation in the governance of the Bank of Spain* by
   increasing the number of government-appointed representatives on
   the board of the Bank of Spain.[70] The total amount of credit supplied
   to the Treasury would also be capped. Both reforms were part of an
   attempt to make the Bank of Spain a true aid to the private sector, not
   just the state's cashier.[71]
3. *Establish a new regulatory body dominated by elite banks.* A new bank
   regulatory and supervisory body, the Consejo Superior Bancario (CSB)
   or "supreme banking council," would be established to serve as "an
   official channel between the private-sector banks and the authorities."[72]
   It would be nominally controlled by a royal commissioner appointed
   by the government, who would oversee a council comprising the
   heads of the country's six largest banks. The CSB would be given
   multiple regulatory and supervisory responsibilities.[73]
4. *Establish special financing relationships.* Banks that chose to register
   with the CSB would receive special benefits, most notably the privilege
   of discounting bills with the Bank of Spain at a subsidized rate. These
   institutions would gain access to ample liquidity at a cheap price.[74]
   Only domestic institutions would be permitted to register with CSB.

Each of the proposed remedies proved unpopular, albeit for different reasons.
The fact that any reform passed at all in this period has surprised banking historians, given the intensity of opposition from both the political right and the
political left.[75] Yet, in the end, the Cortes passed a stripped-down version of
Cambó's original reform proposal in December 1921 that included most of the
major reforms he had proposed: the Bank of Spain assumed central banking
functions and abandoned its presence in commercial banking; its monopoly
of issue was renewed for an additional twenty-five years; the CSB was formally
established; and a special financing relationship was created for banks that
registered with this regulatory body. However, the reform package failed to
add greater government representation to the board of the Bank of Spain.

Spanish policy makers across political lines agreed on the basic facts of the crisis. Many banks had engaged in unsound banking practices during the wartime boom period and were ill equipped to withstand the recession and losses that followed. Exposure to international market fluctuations had worsened the problem for many banks. It was also clear that Bank of Spain's withdrawal of financial support to the Bank of Barcelona in 1920 had contributed to the latter's demise. As in the United States, the contentious issue centered around what this pattern of events suggested.

Cambó and his supporters argued that the true cause of the Catalan banking crisis lay in the incompatibility between the current form of the banking system and the realities of the modern economy. Drawing from the principle of *corporatist harmony*, this group argued that one of the primary causes of the crisis had been the unproductive and excessive fragmentation that had occurred in the banking system. Over the preceding decade, the numbers of new banks had exploded, and the intensity of competition between banks had increased. Cambó pointed to these dynamics as a central cause of a system-wide "race to the bottom" in prudential standards in the banking business, arguing that "the most prudent banks, the most serene banks, [we]re encouraged, inevitably, to follow the path that has been marked by the boldest or the most thoughtless."[76] In other words, the uncoordinated expansion of banking had contributed to "a spirit of exaggerated individualism, one could even say almost anarchy" in the same way that unchecked and uncoordinated democratic participation was anticipated to lead to disorder in the political realm. These similar kinds of problems demanded similar kinds of solutions: the state had the obligation to impose a more rational structure on the organization of banks, which would improve the degree of coordination across banks and allow those best equipped to lead to assume a more influential role.[77]

Cambó and his supporters framed the creation of the CSB as one method of bringing this goal about. The CSB, which gave a handful of elite bankers new powers and privileges, institutionalized and formalized the established social hierarchy within the banking system. As Cambó explained, "With this system [dominated by the CSB], an aristocracy of banks will arise, composed of those banks that have submitted to the imposed order."[78] These elite actors were expected to use their natural authority as industry leaders to bring the rest of the banking system in line, contributing to greater stability. Domestic consolidation was also expected to help strengthen the banking system against potential foreign threats.[79]

The restructuring of the Bank of Spain's role in the financial system was primarily framed as a method of enhancing coordination within the banking system. As Cambó explained in a 1921 speech, one reason the Catalan banking crisis had reached such great heights was that the Bank of Spain had not been properly "coordinated and linked" to the rest of the banking system.[80] Drawing from corporatist themes, he explained that the Bank of Spain and other private banks were "part of the total organization of credit in Spain; each one has a different function." He went on to warn that "if these two functions are not duly coordinated and linked, Spanish economic life will never have at its service the credit organization that other countries have."[81] In other words, the goal was to proactively bring these component elements back into balance and promote enhanced coordination across them. The goal was corporatist harmony.

Cambó and his supporters also argued that their reforms would promote order by offering more effective enticements to the banking system. Cambó argued that to convince the Bank of Spain to assume a more appropriate role in the banking system, it would need (at minimum) to keep its cherished monopoly of issue—otherwise, the powerful institution might not agree to take on its new functions.[82] To justify the establishment of a special financing relationship for banks that registered with the CSB, he appealed to the same line of reasoning. If private banks were to accede to this body's leadership, they too would need to receive something in exchange. Cheaper financing for banks registered with the CSB was thus, in Cambó's words, a privilege "granted to the private banks as a quid pro quo, that is, as a submission to restoring order to the banking system."

Even some opponents of Cambó's plan, especially those on the political right and center-right, offered arguments that appealed to the principle of *corporatist harmony*. For example, opponents on the political right argued against the forced restructuring of the Bank of Spain as a banker's bank because it infringed on the existing rights and privileges of this institution, one of the "essential socioeconomic forums" of the existing political establishment, and violated conservative principles on this basis. As historian Fidel Gomez Ochoa explains, these actors were not eager to "put the privileges [this] institution enjoyed into question" by preventing it from operating as a commercial bank, and they "noted their distaste for the subordination of the Bank to the decisions of the state and the needs of private banking."[83]

Other opponents of Cambó's plan, especially those on the political left, offered antireform arguments that appealed to a different principle—the principle of *state sovereignty*. These actors contended that the root cause of the crisis lay in an imbalance of power between private banks (the Bank of Spain included) and the state. From this view, the most direct cause of the Catalan banking crisis had not been the system's excessively fragmented structure, but rather the outsized power of a handful of chartered banks within this system. They argued that banks had exploited their power by undertaking strategies that served their own narrow interests, without regard to the greater good. Correcting for these conditions would require the state to reassume more of its natural authority in the banking system. It was on this basis that most left-wing policy makers viewed the continuation of the Bank of Spain's monopoly of issue as deeply problematic. Although they welcomed greater government participation in the bank's governance, they worried that Cambó's plan did not go far enough in asserting the state's authority over the powerful bank, and they further argued that the state was not currently deriving sufficient returns from the privileges it had already granted to this institution (e.g., the monopoly of issue).[84]

For similar reasons, many of these same actors strongly objected to the creation of the CSB. As journalist Luis Olariaga wrote in the Madrid newspaper *El Sol*, the CSB was problematic because it allowed "the [leading] banks to run themselves," delegating regulatory powers that properly belonged to the state "to a Superior Banking Council in which the public power will not be represented and the representatives of banks will be in the majority."[85] Left-wing policy maker Emilio Riu echoed these concerns, arguing that ceding the state's legitimate "power to regulate private banking" to elite bankers would only encourage the system to serve the narrow interests of these banks versus those of Spanish society as a whole.[86] As the Bank of Spain transformed into a banker's bank, moreover, it was expected to "undergo a transformation, not for the benefit of the State, not for the benefit of what we could call the consumer, that is, the merchant, but for the benefit of private banking, that is, the intermediary."[87]

One implication is that, when the Banking Law of 1921 finally passed with most of Cambó's proposals intact, it also affirmed the primacy of the principle of *corporatist harmony* over the alternative principle of *state sovereignty*. Most of the reforms that were included in the final legislation were framed by their advocates as methods of reinforcing the established hierarchy within the banking system, of advancing state-led coordination, or of enhancing existing incentives for banks to pursue state-determined goals. The unsuccessful opposition to these initiatives had been based on the perceived threat they presented to state sovereignty.

Finally, as in Canada, the bank regulatory framework in Spain changed very little in the 1930s. Although the global crisis in 1929 also affected Spanish banks, it did not produce the same level of economic devastation seen in the United States or even Canada.[88] Spanish policy makers did adopt a few minor reforms to the bank regulatory system in 1931, but these reforms were a continuation of the basic patterns established by the revolutionary Banking Law of 1921.[89] At the start of the 1930s, Spanish policy makers also had other, more pressing things on their minds—like the looming onset of civil war.

Conclusion

The regulatory debates that followed the banking crises of the 1920s and 1930s were heated and prolonged and produced reforms with lasting implications for the divergent evolution of the banking systems of the United States, Canada, and Spain. The new regulatory framework that took hold in the United States in the 1930s reinforced an unusually deconcentrated, decentralized, and (geographically and functionally) specialized banking system, which operated under tight regulatory restrictions but also benefitted from considerable state support. By contrast, the Canadian regulatory framework that emerged after the Home Bank crisis reinforced a highly concentrated banking system structure that subjected the few banks in operation to minimal regulatory restrictions but offered comparatively little direct government support. In Spain, the revolutionary regulatory reforms of 1921 contributed to a highly concentrated banking system centered around a single powerful, privately owned organization (the Bank of Spain) with extensive and close ties to the state. In short, the regulatory reforms of the 1920s and 1930s came with powerful effects for the kinds of structural forms banks could assume and the range of activities they could pursue in each country, ultimately giving rise to different kinds of financial actors.

This chapter suggests that long-standing institutional arrangements in each country contributed to the development of these divergent regulatory frameworks in important but overlooked ways. In focusing on the content of the regulatory debates that preceded these reforms, we see how the arguments of supporters and opponents of key reforms were organized around familiar themes. American policy makers were preoccupied by a tension between the desirability of ensuring that the banking system remained deconcentrated and specialized, in line with the principle of *community sovereignty*, and the benefits of allowing impartial market processes to govern activity within this system, in line with the principle of *competition*. Canadian debates centered around the tension between ensuring that the state did not interfere with the prerogatives of bank managers and directors, in line with the principle of *elite autonomy*, and the need to protect the rights of vulnerable depositors from potential bank exploitation, in line with the principle of *public rights*. In Spain, the conflict centered around the desirability of respect for established hierarchy, ensuring smooth coordination within the banking system, and offering effective incentives to banks to secure their allegiance, in line with the principle of *corporatist harmony*, and the need to ensure that powerful banks did not interfere with the state's ability to execute its prerogatives, in line with the principle of *state sovereignty*.

Importantly, these regulatory settlements came with cultural implications too. That is, they did not simply reflect the triumph of the desires of particular interest groups over others (although they did do that). When certain regulatory solutions, which had been argued for in particular ways, triumphed over alternative solutions, the associated principle of order also became more dominant or *institutionalized* within the bank regulatory system relative to alternative principles. In the United States, for example, the reforms of the

1920s and 1930s affirmed the primacy of the principle of *community sovereignty* over the rival principle of *competition*. In Canada, they affirmed the primacy of the principle of *elite autonomy* over the competing principle of *public rights*, while in Spain, they affirmed the primacy of the principle of *corporatist harmony* over the principle of *state sovereignty*.

The next two chapters (chapters 6 and 7) explore some of the implications of these developments. Chapter 6 considers another pivotal moment in the development of national bank regulatory systems, when policy makers around the world confronted the menace of rising inflation and the economic and political dilemmas it presented. As the chapter will show, the institutionalization process described above informed the choices of national regulators as they attempted to address these new challenges in the 1960s and 1970s. The following chapter, chapter 7, shows how these developments contributed to the major about-face in regulatory orientation each country experienced during the turbulent 1980s.

6
Responding to New Dilemmas in the 1960s and 1970s

By the end of the 1930s, the United States, Spain, and Canada had settled into regulatory patterns that embodied the dominance of a particular principle of order in each country. In the United States, the design of the bank regulatory system reflected the imprint of the principle of *community sovereignty*, with multiple restrictions on bank structures and activities and forms of government support designed to keep banks independent, deconcentrated, specialized, and locally oriented. In Canada, the design of the bank regulatory system reflected the influence of the principle of *elite autonomy*, featuring comparatively few restrictions on bank structures and activities and few forms of government support, with the goal of leaving industry members free to develop the regulatory institutions that made most sense to them. In Spain, the design of the bank regulatory system reflected the imprint of the principle of *corporatist harmony*, organized around reinforcing the power and influence of leading banks, featuring institutions designed to proactively coordinate activity between banks, and built on a foundation of exchanging key rights and privileges (e.g., special financing arrangements) for bank acquiescence to the regulatory regime.

These bank regulatory systems proved remarkably resilient over the decades that followed, weathering a world war and numerous changes in political leadership (including the rise of a fascist dictatorship in Spain) with surprisingly few changes to their basic elements. However, policy makers in all these countries encountered a regulatory crossroads in the late 1950s and early 1960s, when they faced new political and economic dilemmas that seemed to demand reforms to existing financial regulatory systems. The 1950s and 1960s are usually depicted as the "golden age" of capitalism, when countries around the world experienced rising prosperity and consistent economic growth. But as the standard of living rose within countries, so did the rate of inflation. And while this mild rise in inflation in the late 1950s and early 1960s would pale in comparison to the double-digit inflation of the 1970s and 1980s, it still startled policy makers into action.

Given the serious dilemmas policy makers faced in the 1960s—dilemmas that they believed could be partially addressed through reforms to the financial system—this represents a period in which we might *expect* to find substantial change in national regulatory models. And to be sure, the specifics of banking regulation in each country did change in response to these pressures. However, as we will see, the principles of order underlying each country's financial regulatory systems changed very little in this period, if at all. In the United States, policy makers continued to focus on restrictions designed to keep financial institutions small, locally oriented, and functionally specialized. In Canada, policy makers doubled down on an approach designed to maintain an unfettered and self-regulated financial system. In Spain, policy makers continued to seek to promote better coordination within the financial system while still keeping the most cherished privileges of banks intact. In other words, the regulatory reforms that emerged in each country in the 1960s continued to reflect the same dominant principle of order that was already embodied in the preexisting bank regulatory system.

Why is this important? A closer look at the balance of continuity and change within national regulatory systems in the 1960s also shifts the timeline for bigger changes within the economy. There is general agreement among scholars that the global turn toward neoliberalism, or the embrace of a model of economic organization that highlighted the benefits of unfettered free markets and discouraged most forms of state meddling with the economy, originated with the global crisis of rampant inflation combined with slow growth (stagflation) that arrived on the heels of the oil price shocks of the 1970s and the collapse of the Bretton Woods system. These circumstances created political opportunities for the critics of Keynesian-style economic management to push through an alternative vision of the good economy. These critics successfully argued that what the troubled global economy needed most was greater market rule in the form of increased privatization, deregulation, and a general return to economic laissez-faire—not stronger government or public institutions. This shift in economic ideology and policy has been linked to many of the greatest economic and social transformations of our time, including financialization, rising income and wealth inequality, and welfare state retrenchment.[1]

It is also broadly accepted that the restructuring of national financial regulations represented a crucial stepping-stone in this global march toward neoliberalism. The extensive deregulation of the 1970s and 1980s paved the way for the ascendance of financial capitalism, while laissez-faire approaches to financial regulation in the 1990s and 2000s further fanned the flames by doing little to restrain the abuses this new system generated. Importantly, however, most existing explanations for these influential regulatory changes were developed after only considering events that took place within a single country, especially the United States. These standard explanations—which emphasize the effects of changing economic imperatives in a high-inflation era, shifts in the political power of the regulated industry, the desire of state actors to avoid blame for credit allocation or to resolve pressing budget problems, and changes in dominant academic economic thought[2]—struggle to explain why the content of financial regulatory reform varied across national borders.

For example, countries varied greatly in the relative speed or comprehensiveness with which they deregulated the banking system, and often not in the ways we might expect. Countries also varied in the extent to which they continued to pursue a highly laissez-faire, market-oriented regulatory approach after this initial episode of financial deregulation. One of the key arguments of this book is that national reforms to financial regulation in the 1960s, 1970s, 1980s, and 1990s—and relatedly, national pathways to neoliberalism—were deeply shaped by the presence of particular dominant and latent principles of order incorporated into the institutions that regulated each country's financial system. This institutional influence becomes apparent only when these financial reforms are viewed in comparative perspective.

The next three chapters show how by-now familiar principles of order in the United States, Canada, and Spain informed national policy makers' choices at three critical junctures between 1960 and 1990: initial reforms to financial regulation amid rising inflation in the 1960s; debates over eliminating a crucial regulatory restriction (interest rate ceilings governing deposits or loans or both) in the 1970s; and distinctive interpretations of disruptive banking crises in the 1980s. To fully understand how national banking regulators arrived at the regulatory approaches they did in the 1990s and 2000s, we must consider how long-standing but heterogeneous political-cultural institutions shaped the interpretation of problems in each of these episodes.

The present chapter, chapter 6, opens this story by explaining how different dominant principles of order in each country, institutionalized legacies of the regulatory reforms of the 1920s and 1930s, carried forward to shape the initial reforms to financial regulation national policy makers undertook in the 1960s. Before getting into the details of these regulatory approaches, this chapter first outlines the major economic and political challenges that US, Canadian, and Spanish policy makers faced in the late 1950s and early 1960s. Since these conditions were broadly similar in the United States and Canada, these two cases are discussed together before turning to the specifics of the Spanish case. After describing the regulatory reforms US, Canadian, and Spanish policy makers undertook to resolve the problems they faced in the

1960s, the story diverges. In Canada, where policy makers had ready access to modern tools of monetary policy and banks found it relatively easy to pass along rising costs to consumers, calls for subsequent regulatory reform were muted. In the United States and Spain, however, policy makers continued to face challenges on at least one of these fronts throughout the 1970s, and calls for additional reform were louder. I trace the development of the regulatory reform debates that characterized the 1970s, paying close attention to the kinds of arguments that were mobilized both for and against deregulatory reform.

The Challenge of Rising Inflation

Rising inflation at the end of the 1950s worried monetary policy makers in the United States and Canada. In the United States, Federal Reserve Chairman William McChesney Martin Jr. had long viewed inflation as a disruptive "thief in the night" that threatened the cherished goal of price stability, and he sought to combat emerging signs of inflation with immediate corrective action.[3] To slow the pace of economic expansion and restrain inflation, the Fed used tools like open market operations and adjustments to the discount rate, which manipulated short-term interest rates through different channels. Open market operations influenced the rate at which commercial banks borrowed and lent excess reserves to each other overnight, while adjustments to the discount rate directly affected the price of the loans or advancements the central bank offered to private banks.[4] When evidence of inflationary pressure reappeared in 1958, the Fed under Martin immediately took actions that led to a 3 percent year-over-year increase in the federal funds rate and raised the discount rate to 4 percent. In Canada, similar dynamics were at play. Bank of Canada Governor James Elliott Coyne shared Martin's commitment to preserving price stability as a top priority. In 1959, the Bank of Canada under Coyne responded to indications of rising inflation by raising the bank rate (the Canadian equivalent of the discount rate) to 6 percent, up from only 2 percent a year earlier.

In both cases, these efforts succeeded in reducing the rate of economic expansion, thereby slowing inflation, but the tight money environment that followed generated economic and political problems of its own. A major issue was that banks in both the United States and Canada faced some form of interest rate ceiling: a restriction on the interest rates they were allowed to charge on loans or offer on deposits (or both). Historically, these restrictions had rarely acted as a binding constraint on banks, but the spike in short-term interest rates that had followed the tightening of monetary policy in the late 1950s brought this feature of banking regulation into sharp focus. In the United States, the relevant ceiling was on bank deposit rates, a policy framework known as Regulation Q. Introduced as part of the Banking Act of 1933, Regulation Q provided the federal banking regulators with the authority to set and enforce maximum rates on the interest banks could offer on time or savings deposits. Banks in some US states also faced usury restrictions, or statutory caps on the interest rates charged on loans. In Canada, the relevant ceiling was on bank loans, a policy framework colloquially known as the "6 percent ceiling." While Canadian banks were technically free to offer any interest rate they chose on deposits, they were restricted to charging borrowers interest rates of 6 percent or less on loans. This restriction had a long history: Canadian banks had been limited to charging no more than 7 percent interest on loans in the original 1871 Bank Act, with this threshold lowered to 6 percent in 1950.

Importantly, both kinds of interest rate ceilings produced similar types of market disruptions in practice. As sociologist Greta Krippner has explained in detail, deposit rate ceilings in a context of rising short-term interest rates contributed to disintermediation, or the outflow of savings from formal financial institutions into new kinds of market intermediaries.[5] As market interest rates increased, so did the interest rates savers could receive on alternative investments (like investments in stable government securities). When large depositors like corporations saw that they could obtain higher returns elsewhere, they began to withdraw deposits from banks. Under the terms of Regulation Q, which limited the interest rates they could offer, banks struggled to remain competitive in the market for savings. These shortfalls on the liabilities side of the balance sheet came with implications for a bank's lending and investment activities. With less money available to finance new loans or investments, banks faced difficult choices about where to continue investing and where to cut back.[6] Many responded by diverting their available credit toward larger businesses (who were traditionally banks' best and most reliable customers) while neglecting smaller, riskier borrowers like municipalities, smaller businesses, home builders, or mortgage borrowers. After the late 1950s, many of these smaller borrowers faced increasing difficulty obtaining credit at reasonable rates.[7]

The same process took place in reverse in Canada. As market interest rates approached the 6 percent ceiling, Canadian banks found that it no longer made economic sense to continue lending to smaller borrowers (who were ordinarily charged higher interest rates to compensate for the greater credit risk they presented). Mortgage borrowers in particular suffered from this shift in bank lending practices. Canadian banks had been granted the authority to offer government-insured mortgages only in 1954; however, they had quickly become a dominant force in this market, originating more than a quarter of all new mortgages by 1958. However, in 1959, when market interest rates surpassed 6 percent, banks withdrew from mortgage lending entirely, leaving prospective home buyers in a bind.[8] At the same time, these constraints on the rates banks could charge on loans also carried implications for the rates they could offer savers. Unable to charge competitive market rates on loans,

Canadian banks also struggled to pay depositors "as high returns on their liabilities as they otherwise might [have]."[9] As in the United States, these dynamics favored disintermediation.

In both countries, the inability of regulated banks to keep pace with changing economic circumstances came with serious political implications. The housing sector bore the brunt of these adjustments. With banks reducing credit to smaller borrowers first, potential home buyers were often left unable to obtain adequate financing, sellers struggled to find buyers, and home builders became more hesitant to construct new units. As the higher interest rates persisted into the 1960s, policy makers in both countries came under considerable political pressure to do something about this housing finance problem.

Compounding these pressures, the rising cost and scarcity of housing finance also held negative implications for the budget of the federal government. Focusing on the US case, sociologist Sarah Quinn explains how the disrupted flow of credit to the housing sector served as a major obstacle to Lyndon B. Johnson's ambitious agenda of welfare state expansion.[10] In the United States, a network of housing finance agencies created after the Great Depression was tasked with injecting liquidity into the mortgage market by purchasing loans directly from private-sector lenders. Whenever credit markets were tight, as they were in the late 1950s and early 1960s, the loan purchases of these agencies expanded. However, since the loan purchases were recorded as expenditures on the administrative balance sheet, they also created budget constraints that threatened Johnson's ability to finance his new social programs. Solving the problems in the housing finance market would go a long way toward addressing this issue.

In Canada, Prime Minister Lester B. Pearson faced similar budgetary constraints for similar reasons. Like Johnson, Pearson arrived in office ready to push through an ambitious agenda of welfare state expansion. During his five-year tenure as prime minister, his administration successfully established many of the institutions that now define the modern Canadian welfare state, including universal health insurance and the Canada Pension Plan. Although Canada lacked the same complex architecture of housing finance agencies as the United States, the Canadian government still served as a direct provider of mortgage credit. The Canadian Mortgage and Housing Corporation (CMHC), a government agency, was charged with directly supplying mortgage credit to qualified borrowers whenever credit conditions were tight. By the late 1950s, the CMHC was originating more than a third of all new Canadian mortgages.[11] As in the United States, this form of government support to the housing sector came with a heavy budgetary impact, directly constraining Pearson's ability to fund his political agenda.

Moreover, the episodes of financial disintermediation (and associated sharp contractions in credit provision) that the interest rate ceilings produced also raised deeper concerns about the stability and competitiveness of the banking system. As highly leveraged institutions, banks are extremely vulnerable to sudden economic shocks or losses. Banking regulators in both countries worried about the potential for disintermediation-induced deposit shortfalls to set off a financial crisis. They were also concerned about the competitive implications of maintaining restrictions—like interest rate ceilings—that might threaten bank growth and profitability at a time when international competition was on the rise.[12]

One obvious solution to these dilemmas was to get rid of disruptive interest rate ceilings, which were at the root of all the economic and political problems described above. However, the same consideration potentially stood in the way of this kind of reform in both countries. American and Canadian policy makers recognized that any adjustment to the interest rate ceiling framework (which governed banks) would come at the expense of the competitive viability of a different class of nonbank savings institutions. In the United States, these institutions were known as thrifts (a category that encompassed savings and loan associations and mutual savings banks); in Canada, they were known as near banks (a category that encompassed mortgage loan companies and trust companies). Importantly, both thrifts and near banks were mortgage specialists, or financial institutions that held the vast majority of their assets in the form of long-term mortgages.[13]

Over the course of the 1940s and 1950s, these institutions had captured a growing share of the deposit market from banks, enriched by strong demand for housing finance in the immediate postwar era. However, their highly specialized business model left thrifts and near banks at a competitive disadvantage when interest rates began to climb.[14] Financial institutions at the time made most of their money off the spread (or difference) between borrowing and lending rates, and as interest rates climbed, institutions needed to counterbalance rising borrowing costs with increased rates of return on investments. Those that specialized in long-term lending, like thrifts and near banks, found it much harder to make these necessary adjustments. This was especially true relative to commercial banks, which also participated in more short-term lending activities.

Thrifts and near banks did, however, enjoy an important advantage over commercial banks: they were not subject to the same restrictive regulatory ceilings on loan or deposit rates. Accordingly, any attempt to relax restrictions on loan or deposit rates for banks was expected to come at the expense of the competitive performance of thrifts or near banks, especially given the new challenges these nonbank institutions were facing in a higher interest rate environment. As American and Canadian policy makers entered the 1960s, they faced tough choices about how (and how not) to restructure a feature of banking regulation that currently advantaged thrifts and near banks and disadvantaged banks.

In Spain, rising inflation in the late 1950s presented different challenges. Spain in the 1950s was neither a democracy nor an entirely market-based economy. Since the end of the Spanish Civil War, the country had operated under the control of fascist dictator General Francisco Franco. Throughout the 1940s and 1950s, Franco pursued an extremely inward-looking (autarkic) model of economic development that combined heavy domestic state intervention in the economy with near-complete isolation from global markets. In practice, economic autarky was maintained through extensive price and quality controls on goods and services, heavy tariffs on imports, and strict limits on inflows of foreign capital.[15]

Autarky was not conducive to economic growth: in the 1940s, Spain's economy stagnated, and poverty increased. However, the largest Spanish banks remained surprisingly immune to the troubles of this period.[16] The country's seven largest banks (hereafter the "Big Seven") remained quite profitable throughout this period, largely because they faced very little domestic or international competition. They also greatly benefitted from the cheap liquidity obtained through the special state financing relationship known as the *pignoración automatica*, which allowed banks to automatically secure credit from the Bank of Spain for up to 90 percent of the value of the public debt they purchased. Between 1940 and 1960, the numbers of Spanish banks substantially declined, with most of the associated gains in market share accruing to the Big Seven. By 1957, these large banks collectively held more than 72 percent of all deposits.[17]

The Franco regime repeatedly resorted to bank monetization of the public debt to finance the massive investments in industry and infrastructure that the autarkic model demanded. As a result, the public debt portfolios of the Big Seven swelled throughout the 1940s and 1950s, contributing to rapidly rising inflation. Between 1940 and 1950, consumer prices tripled in Spain. They doubled again between 1950 and 1960.[18] With banks able to easily redeem their bloated public debt portfolios for cheap credit, it was hard for policy makers to control the kinds of expansions in bank lending that contributed to inflation.

High inflation was somewhat manageable so long as Spain remained almost completely isolated from (and therefore undisciplined by) global markets. However, when foreign capital began to flow into the country in the early 1950s, serious economic problems started to emerge. In 1953, Franco struck a historic bargain with the United States to exchange direct financial aid for the establishment of four US military bases on Spanish soil. This event signaled that the Western boycott on trade with Spain might be coming to an end and boosted overall economic confidence, with the Spanish economy growing by an average 5 percent per year between 1953 and 1958.[19] Although this was a generally positive development, it also carried negative implications for the country's balance of payments. As the standard of living increased, so did

Spanish citizens' demand for imported industrial and consumer products. As imports outran domestic production, Spain's foreign exchange reserves turned negative in 1959—right around the time that policy makers were introducing two dramatic wage increases for industrial workers with the goal of reducing growing political unrest.[20] Inflation spiked once again in response, dynamics that led even more businesses to turn to credit from private banks to help them stay afloat, setting off a destructive cycle.[21] Banks responded to the increased credit demand by cashing in their public debt portfolios for credit from the Bank of Spain (via the pignoración automatica), which they used to finance additional lending and investment—and inflation continued to rise.[22]

By June 1959, this situation had become critical. It was obvious that the economic status quo was unsustainable, but the question was what to do about it. Franco responded by reshuffling the economic ministers in his cabinet, replacing champions of economic autarky with a new, influential group of technocrats associated with the powerful Catholic lay organization Opus Dei. The Opus Dei technocrats, joined by leading Spanish economists, argued that resolving the country's economic ills would require greater economic liberalization. Key figures in this new administration included Alberto Ullastres, a Spanish economist who had frequently collaborated with the German ordo-liberal economist Heinrich von Stackelberg, and Laureano López Rodó, an administrative law professor who sought to adopt some of Keynes's ideas to the Spanish context.[23]

In July, these actors unveiled a revolutionary stabilization plan that eliminated most of the autarkic-era industrial price controls, sharply reduced tariffs, devalued the peseta, repealed barriers to inward foreign investment, and—crucially—put an end to the pignoración automatica.[24] This initiative represented a sea change in Spanish economic policy: "a regime dedicated to autarchy turn[ed] outward; a system based on bureaucratic regulation [was] liberalized."[25] It signaled to external audiences that Spain was ready to return to the price mechanism as a basic instrument of economic organization and to rejoin the global economy.[26] However, even as the technocrats rejected the extremely high levels of protectionism that had defined the autarkic era, they continued to see a positive and proactive role for the state in guiding economic development.[27]

The 1959 stabilization plan was a major economic success. In the year after its introduction, official reserves went from almost zero to over $209 million, Spain successfully avoided a possible suspension of payments to foreign creditors holding its currency, and the devaluation of the peseta led to a significant increase in exports and a doubling in the number of tourists, from three million in 1958 to almost six million in 1961.[28] Yet even with the economic triumphs of this period, political discontent with this new model of economic governance began bubbling under the surface. While the stabilization plan addressed some of Spain's most pressing economic challenges (at least temporarily), it also introduced new political issues. Under economic autarky, widespread access to abundant and cheap credit had soothed tensions between rival economic sectors or groups. Maintaining this unlimited access to cheap credit (and the inflation it generated) would clearly no longer be an option if Spain were to rejoin the global economy. But what mechanism could replace it? The existence of the pignoración automatica had also served the interests of the Big Seven banks, which then represented the "sole clearly organized representative of national private capital in Spain."[29] How could these powerful institutions be accommodated?

Thus, the technocrats who had recently assumed positions of power within the Franco regime also faced a formidable challenge at the start of the 1960s. Spain needed a new model of economic governance that would somehow elicit sustainable (among other features, noninflationary) economic growth while also maintaining political support from a variety of powerful, and potentially disruptive, social groups.

Solving the Problems: Financial Regulatory Reform in the 1960s and 1970s

Political and economic dynamics in the United States, Canada, and Spain clearly differed in important respects the late 1950s and early 1960s, but they also shared some important commonalities. In this period, policy makers around the world were forced to grapple with the problem of rising inflation and the side effects of policies adopted to combat this issue. In many countries, the United States, Canada, and Spain included, policy makers sought to reform the existing financial regulatory system to mitigate these pressures. As we shall see, the regulatory solutions that national policy makers arrived at took strikingly different forms—forms that reflected the influence of the dominant principle of order enshrined in each country's existing financial regulatory institutions.

AMERICAN REFORMS: REINFORCING COMMUNITY SOVEREIGNTY

In the United States, short-term market interest rates again surpassed the Regulation Q ceilings on time deposits in 1963, 1964, and 1965. Each time this happened, banks experienced another episode of disintermediation. Regulators at the Federal Reserve initially responded by temporarily increasing the Regulation Q ceiling for banks, to prevent a more substantial exodus of commercial deposits. However, it soon became apparent that these interventions were threatening the competitive viability of thrifts. When small savers discovered that they could earn higher returns by opening deposit accounts with banks (temporarily freed from interest rate ceilings), they increasingly withdrew their savings from thrifts.

When short-term market interest rates surpassed the Regulation Q ceilings once again in the summer of 1966, regulators faced a hard choice. This time, they decided to hold firm and keep the Regulation Q ceiling for banks intact. This event was followed by a major episode of disintermediation, and a credit crunch, as stress on the liabilities side forced many banks to sell off investments or sharply curtail the provision of loans. The impact of this credit crunch was felt most keenly by smaller borrowers, yet even large corporations were not immune. In the last half of August 1966 alone, bank lending to corporations dropped by $668 million, a trend that alarmed the business sector and captured attention from legislators.[30]

In the aftermath of the 1966 credit crunch, the Johnson administration introduced a regulatory reform bill with the goal of restoring order to the financial system and preventing the return of similar events. The administration made it clear that the primary intent was to "restrain . . . excessive competition for savings" between banks and thrifts.[31] As Undersecretary of the Treasury Joseph W. Barr explained during an August 1966 hearing on the credit crunch, the administration believed that rising competition for deposits between banks and thrifts was at the root of the rising cost and declining availability of mortgage credit. As these financial institutions entered into increasingly heated competition for savings, their borrowing costs had also increased, which were then passed along to mortgage borrowers in the form of higher interest rates on loans. Long-term lending (like mortgage lending) also becomes a riskier proposition when borrowing costs are on the rise. Collectively, Barr argued, these factors had disrupted the US credit system.[32]

Barr also suggested that heightened competition between banks and thrifts hadn't just made things harder on potential home buyers—it was starting to threaten financial stability. In the 1930s, proponents of creating the Regulation Q interest rate ceilings for banks had argued that caps on deposit rates would discourage mutually destructive savings "rate wars" between banks and thus limit incentives for these institutions to seek out inappropriately risky investments. In the 1960s, Barr and his colleagues drew from the same logic to defend the expansion of interest rate ceilings to thrifts as well. They argued that history was starting to repeat itself, with greater competition for deposits "encourag[ing] thrift institutions to take an overextended position . . . reach[ing] for higher yielding . . . credits in order to cover their higher rates paid on savings accounts." Thrifts, in other words, currently had no choice but to follow in the destructive footsteps of the unit banks of the 1930s.[33] And like the unit banks that had preceded them, thrifts were worth protecting from competition. Indeed, Barr explicitly referenced the legacy of the Great

Depression to explain why he supported the expansion of bank-style regulatory restrictions to thrifts, noting that "Congress reached a decision in the 1930s . . . that unbridled competition in a situation where we have 14,000 banks and 7,000 thrift institutions in the United States was not in the best interests of the country. . . . We are here recommending today that that authority [to establish interest rate ceilings] be broadened and be extended to the other half of the savings market."[34]

In this period, the US financial regulatory system was already organized around protection of *community sovereignty* as an overarching goal, which left US policy makers primed to see serious hazards in threats to the system's deconcentrated or specialized structure. Depression-era policy makers had already successfully cast unfettered competition between financial institutions as one especially salient threat. This legacy was thus institutionally available to the Johnson administration to tap into when developing and justifying new solutions to the economic and political problems of the 1960s.

Importantly, American policy makers may have supported bringing thrifts under the same general regulatory umbrella as banks, but they continued to see thrifts as institutions that merited special regulatory treatment. In an institutional context where maintaining the independence of small and local institutions was already defined as a top regulatory priority, it was easy to cast the autonomy of thrifts (which were considerably smaller and more locally oriented than the average commercial bank) as something worth preserving. As Representative Wright Patman (D-TX), chairman of the House Banking and Currency Committee, explained in 1966, it was precisely because "the vast majority of [thrifts] are small, independent, locally owned institutions" that "Congress has a particular responsibility to make certain that these thrift institutions continue to effectively meet the housing needs of their communities."[35]

In practice, this "particular responsibility" consisted of a small differential in the rates that banks and thrifts were authorized to offer to depositors under the terms of the new legislation. The Johnson administration reform bill gave thrifts the authority to offer deposit rates .25 percent higher than those offered by banks (this gap between thrift and bank rates was known as the Regulation Q differential). Why offer thrifts this kind of regulatory advantage? In addition to being smaller and more locally oriented, thrifts also had a *specialized focus* on lending to the housing sector. Recall that advocates of separating investment from commercial banking in the 1930s had appealed to the inherent benefits of functional specialization to justify that particular reform. The Johnson administration now drew from the same logic to explain why thrifts needed to maintain regulatory advantages over banks. As *specialized* lenders to the housing sector, thrifts were also assumed to be better equipped to serve the needs and interests of this sector, especially compared to diversified commercial banks.

Representatives from the US home-building industry shared this assumption. In statements at legislative hearings, home builders endorsed special regulatory protections for thrifts and highlighted the perceived benefits of thrifts' specialized focus: "By *specialization* [thrifts] have responded to local needs. They have reduced the cost of financial transactions. And they have brought about lower mortgage interest rates in this country than in most other countries."[36] Commercial banks were not expected to prioritize the housing industry's needs in the same way, as one industry representative explained: "If allowed to compete for . . . savings practically without restraint, commercial banks can take most of it for their own uses—which are not the uses which support homebuilding and other industries based on long-term credit."[37] Even the US banking regulators in the 1960s, who included economists known to favor unfettered market competition in other settings, appeared to subscribe to this view. In their testimony before Congress, these actors endorsed forms of state intervention into the financial system (like interest rate ceilings) that helped to preserve the competitive survival of smaller and specialized thrifts.[38]

Indeed, the most surprising feature of the passage of the Interest Rate Adjustment Act in the fall of 1966 was the degree to which leading American policy makers and interest groups were on the same page. The final version of this reform passed relatively quickly and with minimal controversy: it both expanded the Regulation Q interest rate ceilings to thrifts and included a slight interest rate differential for these institutions over banks. The only serious opposition came from the thrift industry itself, which opposed the extension of any bank-style regulatory restrictions to the thrift industry and did not see the Regulation Q differential as adequate compensation.[39] Otherwise, key interest groups—including home builders, regulators, monetary policy makers, banks themselves, and legislators across political lines—seemed to endorse the basic goals of this reform.

What is most striking in comparative perspective is the initial absence of *any* constituency for the repeal of deposit rate ceilings in the United States. This is especially remarkable when we consider that the complete elimination of similar restrictions was on the table, and actively being debated, in Canada at the exact same time. Overall, the same interest groups that pushed for the elimination of interest rate restrictions in Canada in the 1960s were ready to settle for the expansion of these restrictions to thrifts in the United States. For example, large US banks, like their Canadian counterparts, clearly found these restrictions disruptive, as evidenced by their repeated lobbying of the Federal Reserve to raise the Regulation Q ceiling between 1959 and 1964 and in their development of new financial instruments (like negotiable certificates of deposit) designed to skirt these restrictions.[40] And yet the American Bankers Association declared that it was "in full accord" with the Johnson administration's goal of "prevent[ing] destabilizing interest competition" through the expansion of the Regulation Q framework to thrifts in 1966.[41] To make sense of this puzzling feature of the American reform effort, we must turn to the Canadian case.

CANADIAN REFORMS: REINFORCING ELITE AUTONOMY

In Canada, the regulatory reforms of the 1960s unfolded in a context of high anxiety about Canada's economic security at a time of rising global competition. In 1961, Parliament established an expert commission, chaired by chief justice of Ontario Dana Porter, to evaluate the country's financial system and offer recommendations for improvement. The Porter Commission focused primarily on evaluating the adequacy of monetary policy arrangements, the sufficiency of public safeguards in dealings with the financial sector, and the extent to which financial policies aligned with national economic goals.[42] The commission's final report, published in 1964, sent a clear and unambiguous message: Canada's liberal financial system, which featured comparatively few restrictions on bank structures or activities, a commitment to industry self-regulation, and minimal government interference, was serving the country quite well. However, further improvements could be made if Canada intensified its existing commitments to laissez-faire principles. As former governor of the Bank of Canada Gordon Thiessen explained in a retrospective account: "The [Porter] Commission believed in markets. . . . [It] came out strongly in favour of increased competition and deregulation. It was aware that this might entail some risks, but thought they were worth taking."[43]

In sharp contrast to the dynamics that were unfolding in the United States in the same period, in which policy makers moved to preserve legislative and regulatory restrictions that encouraged financial institutions to specialize by function, the authors of the Porter Commission report wrote that this type of regulatory approach threatened to restrain economic progress: it increased "the risk that in a changing economic environment the financial system will become unduly compartmentalized and will contain pockets of activity which are relatively free of vigorous competition."[44] Instead, they argued that scaling back on state intervention would unleash the natural "spirit of vigorous, restless innovation" that stimulated economic growth and promote Canada's effective adjustment to a changing global economy.[45]

These conclusions deeply informed the content of the financial reform bill that the Lester B. Pearson administration introduced in 1965. The stated purpose of this reform was to "further the objective of greater . . . competition" within the financial system—precisely the opposite of what the Johnson administration had sought to accomplish in the United States in the same period.[46] Crucially, the Pearson administration viewed recent troubles in the financial system (including the rising cost and declining availability of housing credit) as products of *too little* competition between different types of financial institutions. Liberal minister of finance Mitchell Sharp attributed Canada's recent woes in housing finance to the fact that the powerful chartered banks (then governed by the 6 percent ceiling) had been effectively blocked from participating in mortgage lending in the high interest rate environment of the late 1950s. Under these conditions, mortgage borrowers had been left with no choice but to seek credit from alternative lenders like small and specialized near banks, and Sharp and his supporters blamed the actions of these institutions for many of the problems that had followed. In their view, near banks not only struggled to provide adequate credit to the housing sector; they also operated as inefficient and exploitative lenders, charging exorbitantly high interest rates on the loans they did offer.

With this diagnosis in mind, Sharp argued that the obvious solution was to repeal the restrictions that currently insulated near banks from the kind of competition that might lead them to change their ways. In making this argument, Sharp also built on one of the key conclusions of the Porter Commission in singling out the 6 percent ceiling on bank lending as especially problematic. This restriction had played a key role in encouraging banks to exit mortgage markets as interest rates climbed, leaving borrowers with no option but to turn to complacent near banks.[47] To explain why he believed that the 6 percent ceiling must be repealed, Sharp referenced these dynamics:

> [Since the 6 percent ceiling] hampers . . . the ability of the banks to provide a service to riskier borrowers at rates above the ceiling . . . we believe that the banks can serve the many borrowers they are not now serving if they had some freedom to charge more than the ceiling. Those people would then not be in the hands of [near banks]; they could come to the banks and be able to get accommodation at somewhat higher than prime rates but lower than they could borrow at from other parts of the market.[48]

Why did liberal policy makers and economic experts in Canada view this issue so differently than their American counterparts did? While multiple factors may have contributed to these divergent viewpoints, one key consideration relates to the different principles of order then embodied in the design of each country's existing regulatory system. Operating in a system that was already organized around the preservation of *elite autonomy*, Canadian policy makers were primed to see dangers in state interventions that might interfere with the freedom of bank managers and directors to pursue their own prerogatives. In this context, it was relatively easy to cast the 6 percent ceiling as a threat to economic order.

The institutionalized dominance of the principle of *elite autonomy* also helps to explain why other key interest groups, including the Canadian home-building industry, echoed similar arguments in pushing for the repeal of the 6 percent ceiling. Unlike their American counterparts, Canadian home builders dismissed near banks as ineffective and excessively parochial lenders and supported the repeal of regulatory restrictions that were thought to enhance near banks' competitive advantages.[49] Instead, these actors, like organized labor, most chartered banks, and banking regulators and monetary policy makers, welcomed the elimination of the 6 percent ceiling, a change that they expected both to expand the total supply of mortgage credit (by encouraging banks to reenter this sector) and to subject near banks to greater competitive discipline.[50] The point is that this line of argument is much more likely to be persuasive in an institutional context where excessive state interference with the free selection of activities by economic actors is already defined as the most salient threat to order.

Support for the repeal of the 6 percent ceiling, however, was not unanimous in Canada. Unsurprisingly, the near bank industry opposed this reform, which they saw as benefitting banks at their expense.[51] Some western Conservative MPs, most members of the New Democratic Party (NDP), and members of the Social Credit Party also opposed repealing this restriction. Even some leading Liberal politicians, including Walter Gordon, the Liberal minister of finance who preceded Sharp, were strongly opposed to the elimination of the 6 percent ceiling in the early 1960s. In all these cases, opposition to the reform stemmed from the understanding that freeing banks from current regulatory constraints would make it easier for these powerful actors to exploit the rights of vulnerable borrowers. This line of reasoning was grounded in the principle of *public rights*. For example, Minister of Finance Gordon feared that "that the oligopoly position of the banks would allow them to raise their lending rates if the ceiling were lifted," impacting borrowers, and supported "government control over banking operations, including interest rates" on this basis.[52]

Indeed, it was only after Gordon resigned as minister of finance, following a poor showing by the Liberal Party in the federal election of 1965, that the path to financial deregulation in Canada was cleared. Historians have argued that Sharp, Gordon's replacement, was likely selected because of his friendlier stance toward the elimination of the 6 percent ceiling, which helped to secure much-needed political support from powerful chartered banks.[53] On March 21, 1967, revisions to the Canadian Bank Act, which included the immediate elimination of the 6 percent ceiling, were signed into law.[54]

Two things about this episode are particularly notable. First, from a very early point, leading Canadian policy makers and interest groups viewed the problem of the rising cost and declining availability of mortgage finance as one of *too much* state interference with banks' selection of desired activities. This framing aligned with the principle of *elite autonomy*, in which economic order was expected to emerge most readily (and organically) from the aggregated free choices of elite actors. Second, these different political-cultural traditions were not the only features of the institutional environment that likely mattered. The structures of the American and Canadian financial systems also differed in important respects in the early 1960s. At the time, US savings and loan institutions (thrifts) supplied around 45 percent of all mortgage credit, with Canadian mortgage loan and trust companies (near banks) supplying only around 40 percent (Canadian life insurance companies originated the largest share of mortgages in this period).[55] Since Americans already had greater familiarity with small and specialized mortgage lenders, this could also explain some of the extra support thrifts received in this country.

But these structural differences, while notable, do not suffice to explain the different degrees of promise American and Canadian policy makers perceived in commercial banks taking on a larger role in mortgage lending. In the late 1950s, commercial banks controlled an equivalent share of the mortgage market in both countries: banks originated around 25 percent of mortgages both in the United States and in Canada. And yet many Americans, including the home-building industry and policy makers across political lines, saw dangers in allowing commercial banks to expand their relative footprint in mortgage lending. This view makes sense only when viewed through the lens of a long-standing American cultural preoccupation with the inherent benefits of both functional and geographic specialization. In Canada, where this same preoccupation was not institutionalized to the same degree, it is telling that these same actors (including home builders and the majority of policy makers) saw great opportunity in encouraging diversified commercial banks to assume a larger role in this particular market.

SPAIN: REINFORCING CORPORATIST HARMONY

The Opus Dei technocrats who rose to new positions of power within the Franco regime in the late 1950s were eager to introduce a more outward-looking, market-oriented economic approach. Yet they also continued to believe that the state had a proactive role to play in smoothing and coordinating the process of economic development. To resolve the multiple economic and political dilemmas these actors faced in the early 1960s, they turned to a new model of economic development—indicative planning—that borrowed directly from France, where it had been used with great success in the immediate aftermath of the Second World War. Although private-sector initiative served as the primary engine of growth under this model, the state was responsible for coordinating and guiding the resource allocation process to ensure that scarce resources flowed toward the users most vital to the national economy.[56] The goal was to coordinate private and public investment and output plans through the use of forecasts or targets, which were expected to supply economically valuable information to the private sector more efficiently than market mechanisms alone.[57] The model was characterized by the creation of a centralized planning commission, staffed by economic experts, which would generate five-year economic development plans that would anticipate and counteract potential roadblocks to rapid growth. To encourage the private sector to comply with these plans, the state was expected to offer inducements (like subsidies, preferential lending relationships, tax credits, or grants) to targeted actors.

The technocrats who promoted indicative planning saw important parallels between the conditions France had faced in the immediate aftermath of World War II and those that Spain now faced in the early 1960s. Like postwar France, Spain was not a wealthy country and thus "could not afford the luxury of misdirected development."[58] The technocratic planners operated under the view that state-led "concertation" (coordination, organization, and rationalization) of a market-driven growth process would reduce wasteful, unproductive experimentation, offering Spain a more efficient pathway to a sustainable economy. In 1962, the Spanish technocrats established the country's first indicative planning commission. In 1964, this commission, led by Rodó, issued an initial five-year development plan that prioritized public and private investment in transportation, housing, and soil improvement.

A push for substantial financial regulatory reform developed in this general context. Although the technocrats held the power to channel public resources toward users who were deemed especially important for national economic progress, they recognized that true change would require private-sector resource providers to alter their behavior as well. In the early 1960s, Spanish chartered banks supplied more than 70 percent of all credit to business and industry. The success of the indicative planning effort thus depended on getting these powerful actors on board with the state's intentions. To accomplish this, the Spanish technocrats embarked on the most comprehensive overhaul of Spanish banking regulation since the revolutionary Banking Law of 1921.

Spain's Banking Law of 1962 introduced four key changes to the bank regulatory regime.[59] First, it nationalized the Bank of Spain, officially transferring ownership of this institution from private to public hands. Second, it restricted the activities of private banks, requiring all financial institutions to specialize in either industrial or commercial banking.[60] Third, it restructured the division of regulatory control, assigning official authority over the regulation of commercial banks to the Bank of Spain, authority over the *cajas* (regionally focused savings banks that were rough equivalents to US thrifts or Canadian near banks) to a newly created Savings Bank Credit Institute, and authority over medium- to long-term credit institutions to a newly created Medium- to Long-Term Credit Institute. Fourth, it established two channels designed to encourage private-sector resources to flow toward state-prioritized borrowers. The first channel required all private financial institutions to invest a certain percentage of deposits (10 percent for banks, 80 percent for cajas) in public debt, with the proceeds used to finance the state-owned official credit institutions. The second channel involved "special rediscount lines" that enabled banks to redeem loans to state-specified users for credit with the Bank of Spain. This was essentially a reinstantiation of the pignoración automatica, but now applied only to a state-specified subset of loans.

At first glance, many of these reforms, which on paper strengthened the state's control over chartered banks, seem to depart from the principle of *corporatist harmony*. However, as political scientist Sofía Pérez explains, the details of implementation tell a different story. Some advocates of the Banking Law of 1962 may have framed this initiative as a strike against entrenched bank control, but this reform actually did very little to disrupt the existing balance of power in the Spanish financial system. This helps to explain why the leaders of the Big Seven banks never opposed this regulatory reform, and even helped to craft specific elements of it.

Importantly, the provisions of the Banking Law of 1962 that might have seriously threatened bank interests were never enforced, including the provision that allowed foreign banks to enter the Spanish banking system. Other elements of the reform included key loopholes that defanged their potential impact on the Big Seven. For example, the legislation separating industrial and commercial banking never prevented commercial banks from indirectly owning industrial banks. Most of the Big Seven banks took advantage of this by purchasing (and indirectly controlling) the newly created industrial banks—largely reinforcing the banking status quo.[61] Additional features of the 1962 reform—including a provision that tied authorization for branch network expansion to a bank's total capital (further advantaging the largest banks), the continuance of unfavorable tax treatment for capital market financing, and a continued role for the Big-Seven-dominated CSB in regulatory standards setting—continued to reinforce the market dominance of the leading banks.[62]

Finally, while the 1962 reform did give the restructured state-owned, official credit institutions a more important role to play in the financial system, even this aspect of the reform was carefully designed to prevent state-owned credit institutions from offering any form of serious price competition to banks. The official credit institutions did not compete with banks in the market for savings, since they were financed through the compulsory debt ratio (not deposits).[63] This compulsory debt ratio also disproportionately impacted cajas—institutions that did compete with banks for savings. In this way, it also worked to support the existing structure of the financial sector.[64]

Two elements of the 1962 reform package did introduce real change to the structure of the Spanish financial system: the nationalization of the Bank of Spain and the introduction of the special rediscount line framework. Advocates justified both elements as initiatives that advanced *corporatist harmony*. The technocrats argued that if the Bank of Spain was to serve its "lofty mission as the Government's assistant, informant and advisor with regard to monetary and exchange policy and the supervision of private banking," then a change in ownership would be required, with the bank shedding "its original character of a joint-stock company" to become an impartial institution on par with the state itself.[65] Crucially, this newly nationalized bank would not upset the current balance of power within the financial system by seizing market share from the leading banks. Instead, it was expected to give the technocrats more direct access to the necessary tools or "implementing instruments" to more effectively guide or coordinate economic "expansion in such a way as to preserve balance."[66]

The special rediscount line framework was expected to serve a similar function. It was designed to give the private banks a powerful inducement to follow the development plans the technocrats had developed as part of the indicative planning process. While the technocrats were eager to redirect the flow of private-sector resources toward state-specified users, they were not prepared to directly instruct banks on where to lend. Instead, they resorted to a familiar quid pro quo strategy of offering valued privileges and rewards to powerful groups (in this case, abundant access to cheap liquidity for banks) in exchange for desired services to the state (in this case, redirecting credit toward state-sanctioned users).[67]

In short, the Banking Act of 1962 sought to enhance the state-guided coordination of economic activity, in line with objectives associated with the principle of *corporatist harmony*. As the preamble of the new law noted, this reform effort was geared toward ensuring that "the groups of institutions which compose [this financial] system should function in a harmonious and well-coordinated manner, without breakdowns, hitches or deficiencies, so that the formation of savings will be stimulated by adequate measures and the funds saved will be appropriately channeled into investment."[68] This was essentially the logic of indicative planning applied to the financial system itself: the state offered a framework for development and coordinated and smoothed dynamics within the system, while private initiative still served as the engine for change. Importantly, none of these new reforms seriously threatened the most cherished privileges of the leading private banks, particularly the near-complete absence of price competition: the state sought to work with (rather than against) the interests of the established banking hierarchy to better harmonize activity within the financial system, including by making active use of patronage relationships to elicit buy-in from key groups.

Three Countries at a Crossroads: Regulatory Reform Battles in the 1970s

These different regulatory pathways that the United States, Canada, and Spain followed in the 1960s held direct implications for how each country would experience the turbulent 1970s. By the start of the 1970s, it was clear that rising inflation was not a problem of the past. Figure 6.1 shows trends in the rate of

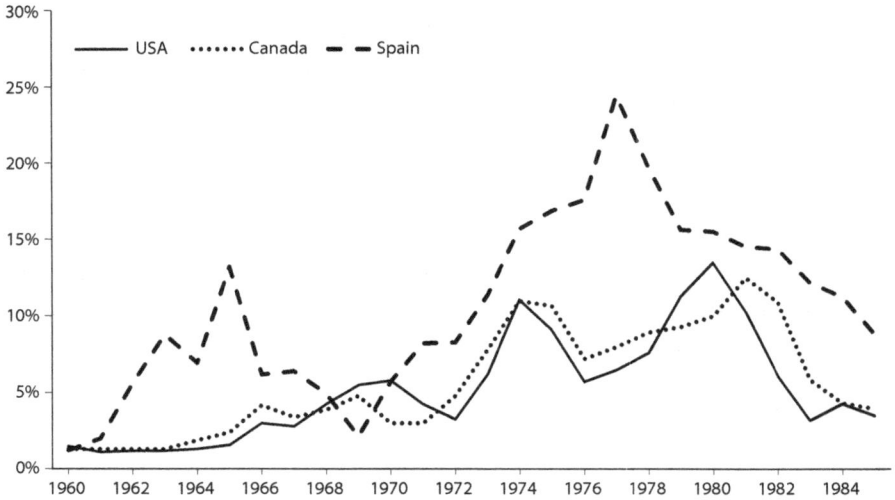

FIGURE 6.1. Trends in inflation (change in the consumer price index) in the United
States, Canada, and Spain (1960–85). *Source*: Steve H. Hanke and Tal Boger,
2018, "Inflation by the Decades Series," https://sites.krieger.jhu.edu/iae/research
-programs/hanke-boger-inflation/ (accessed May 1, 2022).

change in the consumer price index (a common measure of inflation) in the
United States, Canada, and Spain between 1960 and 1985. Spurred on by rising
international oil prices, changes in monetary policy, and other domestic and
global events, each country experienced double-digit inflation at some point
before 1975. These conditions placed heavy pressure on the financial system.
In Spain, inflation remained persistently high throughout the 1970s, while
inflation spiked periodically in the United States and Canada, with especially
severe spikes in the early 1980s. In all three countries, policy makers found
these trends deeply disturbing, especially because they occurred in a context
of rising unemployment and stagnant economic growth. While policy makers
around the world spent much of the 1970s searching for policy solutions to the
problem of inflation, the extent to which this search also encompassed reforms
to financial regulation varied across the three countries.

In the United States, a fierce and prolonged battle over financial deregulation (and particularly the deregulation of interest rate ceilings for banks and
thrifts) dominated the 1970s. By the start of this decade, it was clear that the
bipartisan consensus that had led to the smooth passage of the Interest Rate
Adjustment Act of 1966 had disappeared. Debate over financial regulatory
reform, and especially the possibility of eliminating the Regulation Q framework, would eventually generate thousands of pages of committee hearings,
legislative discussions, and government research reports.

By the start of the 1970s, it was obvious that the regulatory reforms of the mid-1960s had neither solved the problems in housing markets nor effectively addressed unsettling episodes of disintermediation. As market interest rates rose above the Regulation Q ceilings once again in 1969, 1973, and 1974, thrifts and banks alike experienced serious outflows of savings. Market savings vehicles (like money market mutual funds) that were free to offer higher rates were the major beneficiaries of this trend and experienced substantial growth. At the same time, banks also faced heightened competition on the lending side, as markets for alternative forms of corporate finance (like commercial paper, junk bonds, or asset securitization) developed and expanded.[69] Thrifts, with business models centered around long-term lending, struggled to maintain profitability as borrowing costs skyrocketed. It seemed like the long-term sustainability of these financial institutions was now in serious question, and American policy makers came under immense pressure to do something about the problem.[70]

For banks in both Canada and Spain, the situation was less desperate. In Canada, the deregulatory reforms of the mid-1960s had made it much easier for banks to keep pace with rising rates on both the lending and the deposit side. With banks free to offer competitive rates on deposits, Canadian savers did not face the same pressure to shift savings out of formal financial institutions. Banks with ample liquidity also found it easier to remain competitive in loan markets.[71] One implication was that Canadian policy makers faced less intense pressure to undertake substantial reforms to financial regulation in the 1970s.

In Spain, banks prospered for a different reason: they were almost completely insulated from price competition. Even as the Spanish economy suffered in the 1970s, Spanish banks continued to see record profits. Spain's recent experience with economic prosperity came to an abrupt end in 1967, as the country saw a sharp decline in industrial production, increased short-term capital outflows, greater consumer demand for imports, and an even more serious balance of payments problem. In 1968, Spain's current account surplus transformed into a $140 million deficit. The alarmed technocrats used all the fiscal tools at their disposal in an attempt to restore balance to the economy, devaluing the peseta in 1967 and 1968 and reducing government spending. However, these initiatives failed to bring inflation back within reasonable bounds for a reason that will be familiar to the readers of this book: Spanish banks had no intention of cutting back on credit provision during a period of unprecedented credit demand. And their ready access to cheap liquidity (this time, provided through the special rediscount line framework) gave them the capacity to resist most forms of financial discipline.[72] As banks increasingly cashed in their rediscount-eligible loans with the Bank of Spain, inflation continued unabated, and the balance of payments crisis deepened. In short, Spanish banks were doing just fine in this period, but the Spanish economy was in increasingly dire straits. In this context, calls for regulatory reform grew louder.

In what follows, I describe the debates over financial regulatory reform that emerged in the United States and Spain in the turbulent 1970s. As these debates were relatively muted in Canada, I do not discuss them here. The goal is to show how long-standing but heterogeneous institutional traditions within countries informed even the perspectives and arguments of groups that *challenged* an increasingly unstable regulatory status quo.

UNITED STATES: RESURGENCE OF THE PRINCIPLE OF COMPETITION

By 1971, a constituency for the complete repeal of the Regulation Q interest rate ceilings had finally emerged in the United States. After another serious episode of disintermediation in 1969, the newly elected president Richard Nixon established a presidential commission to examine and recommend measures to improve the workings of the US financial system. In December 1971, this commission, chaired by corporate executive Reed Oliver Hunt, issued its final report, which offered reform recommendations that closely aligned with those offered by the Porter Commission in Canada almost a decade earlier.[73]

The Hunt Commission report concluded that the financial system's recent troubles were products of excessive state interference with competitive market forces. Above all, it urged policy makers "to move as far as possible toward freedom of financial markets and equip all institutions with the powers necessary to compete in such markets"—a goal that would require them to dismantle many of the regulatory and legal restrictions that currently governed US financial institutions.[74] Although the report covered many issues, a central focus was the fate of the Regulation Q framework.[75] It advocated for the gradual repeal of this framework, on the grounds that the expansion of interest rate ceilings to thrifts had not been effective in restraining rising interest rates or in providing sufficient protection to troubled thrifts.

The Financial Institutions Act of 1973, the first financial reform bill the Nixon administration introduced, was heavily influenced by these recommendations. Among other proposals, it sought to expand the range of permissible activities for thrifts, allowing them to behave more like banks, and to phase out the Regulation Q ceilings for both banks and thrifts over the course of five and a half years. As the advocates of the reform explained, the underlying motivation was for the government to stop fighting market forces and start working with them, unleashing beneficial competition to organically restore order to an overregulated and rigid financial system.[76] This goal represented a clear departure from the goal of preserving community sovereignty that had guided the development of American financial regulation for decades.

Perhaps unsurprisingly, the 1973 reform bill—and especially its proposal to eliminate Regulation Q—attracted immediate controversy, and the bill died in committee. An additional reform bill in 1975, which also attempted to gradually phase out the Regulation Q ceilings, suffered a similar fate. Although this latter reform bill passed the Senate, the House strongly objected to its proposed repeal of Regulation Q, and the bill once again died in committee.[77] In 1976, the same pattern repeated following the introduction of another financial reform bill. Tellingly, the only significant piece of financial reform legislation to pass in the United States in the 1970s, the Financial Institution Interest Rate Control Act of 1978, did not touch the fate of Regulation Q.

In the end, the United States did not take the first steps toward deregulating interest rate ceilings until the 1980 passage of the Depository Institutions Deregulation and Monetary Control Act (DIDMCA), nearly nine years after the initial publication of the Hunt Commission report. Even this reform arrived only after an explicit deadline from the US Court of Appeals and a direct appeal from President Jimmy Carter.[78] Among other changes, the legislation established a schedule for gradually phasing out interest rate ceilings for banks and thrifts over the course of five years. Interest rate ceilings for American banks and thrifts were not completely eliminated until 1986, nearly twenty years after a similar reform had been undertaken in Canada.

Why was the elimination of the Regulation Q framework so politically controversial in the United States, especially at a moment in which policy makers were actively entertaining deregulatory reforms in many other policy settings? At least part of the answer lies in the degree to which this proposed reform pitted two cherished American principles of order against each other. The regulatory reform debates of this period echoed a familiar historical conflict: reform opponents, who appealed to the principle of *community sovereignty* to justify their opposition, faced off against reform advocates, who appealed to the principle of *competition* to justify their support.

Advocates of repealing Regulation Q, who by 1973 included monetary policy makers, most academic economists, the American Bankers Association, and the federal banking regulators, offered a case for this reform that echoed the case for deregulation that was then being mobilized in other settings as well.[79] They appealed to the principle of *competition* by highlighting the multiple dangers of maintaining "artificial institutional barriers" to free competition between financial institutions.[80] As one banking regulator, the Honorable J. Charles Partee, explained in 1980, the Federal Reserve had come to support the gradual elimination of deposit interest rate ceilings for both banks and thrifts because "we believe that such controls are anticompetitive, inequitable to small savers, and can be disruptive to financial and housing markets. By restricting competition among commercial banks and thrifts, deposit rate ceilings have retarded the adjustment of many of these institutions to a changing market environment."[81] Chairman of the FDIC Frank Wille drew from similar logic to explain his support for eliminating interest rate ceilings in 1973, arguing that "while greater deposit rate competition could have a significant impact on the earnings of banks or thrift institutions, I do not feel that the public is well served by the present policy which insulates banks and thrift institutions from competition to the degree that high earnings are assured even for institutions with questionable management quality."[82] Echoing an argument associated with the Chicago school of economics, these regulators implied that regulatory restraints on price competition invited disorder by insulating financial institutions from the kinds of market pressures that would encourage them to innovate to adapt to the times and by allowing suboptimal financial institutions to continue operating with impunity.

Leading legislators, including Senator William Proxmire (D-WI), chairman of the Senate Banking Committee, and Representative Fernand St Germain (D-RI), chairman of the House Subcommittee on Financial Institutions Supervision, Regulation, and Insurance, also appealed to the principle of *competition* by highlighting the undesirability of the inequitable or uneven impact of Regulation Q. They argued that the effects of this regulatory constraint were felt more keenly by ordinary households than by businesses, because households did not enjoy the same access to alternative savings vehicles that businesses had and were thus more disadvantaged by the credit crunches Regulation Q produced. As Proxmire argued in 1979, the removal of interest rate ceilings was expected to benefit the financial system by leveling this competitive playing field, "end[ing] blatant discrimination against savers. It is unconscionable to continue the present tax on savers so that all types of borrowers can be subsidized."[83]

Yet the opponents of eliminating Regulation Q enjoyed an important advantage in these debates. In a context where the design of the regulatory system already affirmed the merits of preserving a deconcentrated and specialized system, arguments against financial deregulation (a reform that would likely produce more concentrated and diversified financial institutions) were compelling. The thrift industry, unsurprisingly, was the strongest opponent of eliminating the Regulation Q framework. Thrifts had come to see the slight differential they enjoyed under Regulation Q as key to their continued survival and had no interest in seeing this framework change. As Lloyd Bowles, chairman of the US Savings and Loan League, explained in 1977, the industry believed that getting rid of the Regulation Q framework would make it easier for diversified banks to outcompete specialized thrifts, violating the principle of *community sovereignty*:

> There is no way over the long run that a financial institution that specializes in making loans on homes can earn as much as a financial institution which specializes in financing the 500 top corporations in the United States. . . .

Regulation Q . . . helps maintain our present system of financial institutions and helps the smaller institution compete with the big.[84]

The thrift industry also continued to tap into long-standing assumptions about the merits of specialized focus by framing the elimination of Regulation Q as a threat to their ability to remain focused on lending to the housing sector. United States Savings and Loan Association chairman Tom B. Scott warned policy makers that repealing this restriction would lead to the development of a more homogenous financial system: "One of the basic strengths of our financial system today is the uniqueness of each type of financial institution. . . . The implicit advantages available to our nation thanks to the structural differences between savings associations and commercial banks . . . would clearly be lost if [deregulation of Regulation Q] were implemented. . . . The American people want to be assured of ample opportunity to borrow money from specialized institutions established to meet their needs."[85]

Extending the same principle, thrifts framed any strike against their industry as a strike against the housing sector itself. Without the regulatory protections currently offered to thrifts, industry representatives argued, the housing market would likely be in even worse shape than it already was.[86] Representatives from the housing sector and organized labor seemed to subscribe to this view as well, although their support for thrifts began to wane as the troubles of the 1970s dragged on.

Even actors that endorsed the elimination of Regulation Q appeared to accept the premise that repealing interest rate ceilings would hurt the housing sector. For example, while Senator Proxmire supported a 1975 proposal to phase out Regulation Q, he continued to worry about the implications for the thrift industry, and the housing sector by extension.[87] Similarly, Representative St Germain, a strong advocate of financial deregulation, conceded at a 1976 committee hearing that "most people would agree that there are great efficiencies and conveniences" in maintaining thrifts as specialized lenders to housing.[88]

The prolonged American regulatory reform debates of the 1970s thus suggest that Regulation Q could be, and was, viewed in multiple ways. On the one hand, this restriction helped to safeguard the independence of small and specialized thrifts, a valued goal from the standpoint of the principle of *community sovereignty*. On the other hand, it also served as a form of state interference with natural market competitive processes, violating the principle of *competition*. In this way, the debates over Regulation Q brought two of the most cherished American principles of order into direct conflict. This helps to explain why the American battles over the repeal of this restriction (and other restrictions with similar features) were so fraught and hard to resolve.

SPAIN: THE RESURGENCE OF THE PRINCIPLE OF STATE
SOVEREIGNTY IN THE 1970S

The economic troubles of the late 1960s marked the beginning of the end of
the privileged position of the Opus Dei technocrats within the Franco regime.
Out-of-control inflation and the return of a persistent and severe balance of
payments problem had revealed the limits of indicative planning. The 1969
eruption of the MATESA scandal, the Franco regime's "sole great politico-
economic scandal," provided the final nail in the coffin.[89]

MATESA was a textile machinery company owned by the Catalan industri-
alist (and prominent member of Opus Dei) Juan Vila Reyes. By the mid-1960s,
the company had become Spain's largest export firm and the recipient of more
than half of the total export credit granted by the Banco de Crédito Industrial
(a state-owned official credit institution established by the technocrats).[90]
When investigators uncovered evidence of extensive fraud at MATESA, its
creditors (which included the Banco de Crédito Industrial) suffered massive
losses, many of which were ultimately absorbed by the Treasury. This scandal
not only discredited the official credit institutions that were so crucial to the
execution of development plans, but it also offered ammunition to political
critics concerned about corruption within the Franco regime. In the words
of historians Gabriel Tortella and José Luis García Ruiz, the MATESA scandal
"uncovered for all to see the flimsiness and vulnerability of all of this financial
scaffolding . . . forc[ing] policy makers to review the entire network of state-
controlled financing."[91]

Franco responded by reshuffling his economic cabinet. The existing minister
of finance, the minister of industry, and the governor of the Bank of Spain were
forced to resign in 1969, and new actors with close ties to the central bank and
to academic economics were appointed in their place. Until this time, the Bank
of Spain, and especially its Research Services department, had served as a refuge
for economists who had contributed to the creation of the 1959 Stabilization Plan
but had been pushed to the sidelines with the ascendance of the technocratic
planning bureaucracy.[92] Key figures in the new regime included Enrique Fuentes
Quintana, a professor of economics at the Complutense University of Madrid
who was appointed to the Bank of Spain's Board of Governors in 1970, and Luis
Ángel Rojo, an economics professor at the same institution who was appointed
head of the Bank of Spain's Research Services department in 1971.

These actors, who straddled academia and government, were responsible
for training an entire generation of Spanish economists. Both Rojo and Quintana had trained at top economics departments in the UK and United States in
the 1950s and 1960s, including the London School of Economics and the University of Chicago, and continued this tradition with their proteges, sending
many economists at the Bank of Spain for additional training with actors (like

Harry Johnson and Milton Friedman) who were major luminaries of neoliber-alism.[93] Under the tutelage of Rojo in particular, the Research Services depart-ment at the Bank of Spain grew into the country's most prominent applied economic research institution. By the early 1970s, a position in the department had became a top ambition for young Spanish economists.[94]

One of the key features to distinguish this group of academics with close ties to the central bank (hereafter "the central bank reformers") from the tech-nocrats who had preceded them was relatively greater commitment to certain elements of a neoliberal agenda. The central bank reformers were especially enthralled by the promises of monetarism to resolve what they perceived as the greatest and most intractable threat to the Spanish economy: unchecked infla-tion. At the most basic level, monetarism seeks to create a better-functioning economy not through the exercise of fiscal policy but through the control of monetary aggregates. Gaining better central bank control over the money supply was an especially cherished goal for Bank of Spain Research Services head Ángel Rojo, perhaps the most prominent figure in Spanish economics at the time. This early interest in monetarism distinguished leading Spanish economists from their peers in many other countries in the late 1960s, when the embrace of monetarism and its goals was not yet a mainstream perspective. In Spain, however, economists' embrace of monetarism did not arrive as part of a larger package of efforts intended to restrain the state's hand in the economy and society, as it did in countries like the United States or UK. Spanish "neo-liberals" in the 1960s, including the actors who inhabited top positions in the central bank, remained committed to other elements of an interventionist agenda that was more closely associated with Keynesianism, which included support for progressive tax policy and the promotion of a "social economy."[95]

This background helps to explain why the central bank reformers' key criti-cism of indicative planning was not that it gave the state too much power in managing economic life per se, but that it was ineffective. The central bank reformers dismissed indicative planning as too conservative, arguing that real economic progress would require policy makers do more than simply reallocate resources to important users—there was a need to reform the structure of the economy itself.[96] And the key structural factor the reformers saw as standing in the way of progress was the extent to which "the great banks and their privileged groups of industries" remained free to use "their economic power to maintain their own advantage, not to advance development."[97] From their perspec-tive, the Spanish economy was not up to the task of modernization until this issue was resolved. As Fuentes Quintana argued in the late 1950s, "the high degree of monopolization and the underdevelopment problems of the Spanish economy," meant that any policy attempt to stimulate the economy "could only generate inflation"—the country's number one economic prob-lem in the 1960s and 1970s.[98]

This reconceptualization of the fundamental problem to be solved led the central bank reformers to advocate for the deregulation of the financial system. In keeping with familiar Spanish institutional traditions, challenger groups (in this case, the central bank reformers), faced with a system organized around the principle of *corporate harmony*, appealed to the principle of *state sovereignty* by arguing that the underlying problem with the current system was that public-minded experts (in this case, those in the central bank) had limited power to overcome private resistance and steer the economy toward the greater good. The intention with deregulation, then, was to allow the central bank to secure more effective control over monetary policy—and, by extension, the behavior of private banks and the persistent problem of uncontrollable inflation.

How was this supposed to work? The specific goal of the central bank reformers was to establish a true money market in Spain (which is to say, a market where banks and other financial intermediaries actively trade very short-term and liquid debt instruments) that would operate like the money markets in more developed financial systems like the United States and UK. The presence of a money market was expected to give the central bank reformers much more fine-grained control over economic dynamics, including inflation. It would do so by providing monetary policy makers with an additional tool that would allow them to inject liquidity into the monetary system in a more routine and discretionary fashion.[99]

This goal explains why the central bank reformers set their sights on dismantling the interest rate controls that governed Spanish bank deposits and loans from a very early point. These restrictions, which included a maximum rate on bank deposits and a minimum rate on bank loans, had been explicitly established by the CSB to minimize competition and ensure easy profits for incumbent banks in the 1930s.[100] The technocrats had not touched these restrictions in their reforms to the financial system. Instead, they had layered new initiatives (e.g., favorable interest rates for certain types of export financing and for medium-term credit) on top of this framework. Yet from the standpoint of the central bank reformers, this framework was the root of the problem. Any restriction that maintained the outsized market power of the banking oligopoly and reinforced the absence of price competition was not conducive to the creation of a money market (and, by extension, to the control over the money supply the central bank reformers so desperately wanted). These restrictions disincentivized banks from attempting to maximize operating margins by participating in a market for their cash surpluses.[101] Accordingly, the annual reports of the Bank of Spain called for the liberalization of interest rate controls as early as 1966, well before the central bank reformers rose to new positions of power within the state.

This opposition to the interest rate control regime placed the central bank reformers into direct conflict with the technocrats. These latter actors had been less concerned about the inflationary consequences of the interest rate control regime, since they were confident that bold state stimulation of internal demand via indicative planning would effectively address any problems.[102] Instead, they saw preexisting controls on bank lending rates as part of the broader infrastructure that allowed them to execute indicative planning: these restrictions acted as key levers that could be manipulated to direct credit toward favored sectors and penalize "unproductive" sectors.[103] In threatening the interest rate control regime, then, the central bank reformers also directly threatened the indicative planning agenda itself.[104]

For similar reasons, the technocrats also opposed efforts by the central bank reformers to dismantle the special rediscount line framework, which had served as the centerpiece of the technocrat-introduced regulatory reforms of 1962. The central bank reformers rightfully perceived a trade-off between the ample bank access to cheap liquidity this framework allowed and the Bank of Spain's capacity to effectively exert influence over monetary policy. If banks have ready access to other sources of funds, they are less susceptible to the machinations of the central bank. Accordingly, the central bank reformers also saw the special rediscount line framework, which acted as a channel of monetary expansion that operated outside of central bank control, as directly threatening their broader goals.[105]

This conflict between the technocrats and the central bank reformers reflected a familiar tension between the principles of *corporatist harmony* and *state sovereignty*. When the goal is to keep a corporatist system functioning effectively, as it is under the principle of *corporatist harmony*, respect for the established social hierarchy is not necessarily incompatible with order—in fact, it might even help to promote it. This was the view that the technocrats embraced in the 1950s and early 1960s, when they took care to appeal to the interests of the leading private banks to induce these institutions to redirect credit toward state-sanctioned users. However, when the goal is to enhance the state's legitimate power to organize and direct an unruly private sector, as it is from the standpoint of *state sovereignty*, allowing private interest groups to continue pursuing their own particularistic interests at the expense of the public good seems incompatible with order. It was this view that encouraged the central bank reformers to focus on strategies designed to force the powerful private banks to become more responsive to their dictates.

Of course, this was much easier said than done. At first, things seemed promising for the central bank reformers. They secured an early victory with a successful amendment to the interest rate control framework in 1969 that eliminated the regulatory floor on loan rates and linked the regulatory ceilings on loan and deposit rates (which had previously been arbitrarily set by the minister of finance) to the central bank rediscount rate by way of fixed differentials. Initially, this change accomplished what the central bank reformers had hoped: it gave the Bank of Spain more power to influence short-term interest rates, and by extension, slow the rate of credit expansion. However, this success was short-lived. The technocrats responded to this reform by further expanding the scope of the special rediscount framework, effectively negating the reform's effects. In 1971, the central bank reformers scored an additional victory by successfully dismantling the special rediscount line framework, replacing it with a new "compulsory investment ratio" that required banks to use a certain proportion of deposits to fund credits to state-specified users. Although this reform nominally continued to serve the goals of indicative planning, it also furthered the goals of the central bank reformers by severing one of the key channels that allowed monetary expansion to occur outside of central bank control. The scope of the Bank of Spain's regulatory authority also increased in 1971, when this institution received additional powers to regulate cajas and industrial banks (and not just commercial banks). Yet progress stalled here. The final and most important item on the central bank's reform agenda—completely dismantling the interest rate control framework that governed bank lending and deposit taking—took much longer to achieve. The key reason was that the powerful Big Seven banks had no interest in any reform that might subject them to price competition—and these banks held a tremendous amount of economic and political power. The central bank reformers recognized that they would need to tread carefully.

A very gradual and piecemeal approach to financial deregulation that made little economic sense followed.[106] In 1972, the central bank reformers took initial steps toward financial deregulation that did almost nothing to disrupt the established hierarchy or promote price competition within the banking system. They started by deregulating the commissions banks charged on their lending activities, a move that only enhanced the profitability of these institutions in an oligopolistic lending market. In 1974, the reformers also pushed through the deregulation of restrictions on the establishment of new bank branch offices, which also favored the interests of large banks who were already best poised to seize this opportunity. The hope among the central bank reformers was that starting with reforms that served large bank interests would make these powerful institutions more amenable to the broader project of financial deregulation.[107]

In 1974, Spanish policy makers successfully liberalized interest rates on loans or deposits with terms of more than two years. Since relatively few banks actually offered loans or solicited deposits with these longer terms, this was more of a symbolic than a substantive change. However, banks and policy makers alike recognized that it set a precedent for potential reforms to come. While this event was strongly endorsed by the Bank of Spain, the Ministry of Finance, and the Ministry of Commerce, it divided banks, with the Big Seven banks vehemently opposing any change to the interest rate ceiling framework and smaller and less established banks supporting it on the hopes that they might secure greater market share in a deregulated environment.[108]

Blocked by opposition from the leading banks, further efforts to reform the interest rate control framework stalled until 1977, when the central bank reformers suddenly found themselves in a more advantageous position to push through substantial reform. With Spain's transition to democracy in 1975 came the risk that other political actors might seize control over the financial reform process—and potentially actors who were less friendly to bank interests than the central bank reformers.[109] When leading central bank reformer Enrique Fuentes Quintana was appointed deputy prime minister in the first cabinet after the Francoist state (in 1977), he seized the political opportunity to push through the Bank of Spain's long-cherished goal of liberalizing bank deposit and loan interest rates with maturities of one year or longer. In keeping with the principle of *state sovereignty*, Fuentes Quintana justified this reform by arguing that it would enhance aggregate welfare by finally dismantling a key structural roadblock, thereby creating "a financial environment in which economic actors would be malleable to [the central bank's] interventions" via the creation of price competition.[110]

However, the pace of further change to the interest rate control framework slowed after the reforms of 1977. It took another five years before Spanish policy makers moved to completely phase out these restrictions, and an additional five years beyond that for this regime to be totally dismantled. This pattern suggests that once the central bank reformers obtained the outcome they desired most—some degree of price competition for banks in loan and deposit markets, which would motivate banks to participate in a money market—they eased off the promotion of other competition-boosting reforms.[111] Well into the 1980s, leading Spanish banks continued to be insulated from serious competition from foreign banks, from official credit institutions, and from the domestic stock market.

Conclusion

The events of the 1960s and 1970s linked the regulatory traditions of the past to those of the future. Each country entered this period with a different bank regulatory regime, which embodied a now-dominant principle of order from a limited choice set. Over the course of this period, these regulatory regimes started to change. But this change was at the level of the details of regulation, not in the general regulatory approach. Preexisting institutional arrangements deeply influenced the kinds of regulatory reforms that policy makers initially developed to address the problems associated with rising inflation in each country.

In the United States, policy makers operating in a regulatory regime that already underscored the benefits of *community sovereignty* perceived hazards in intensifying competition between banks and thrifts and blamed these dynamics for recent disruptions to credit markets. This understanding of the problem to be solved directly informed the kinds of regulatory solutions policy makers considered. They initially endorsed the expansion of bank-style regulatory restrictions (interest rate ceilings) to a new class of financial institutions (thrifts), even as they also preserved important regulatory advantages for these smaller and more specialized thrifts. In Canada, policy makers operating in a regulatory regime that emphasized the benefits of maintaining *elite autonomy* were attuned to the hazards of state interference with the choices of bank managers and directors. They believed that recent troubles in credit markets stemmed from restrictions (like interest rate ceilings) that hampered banks' ability to pursue activities of their choosing and sought to eliminate these restrictions. In Spain, policy makers in a regulatory regime organized around preserving *corporatist harmony* saw hazards in insufficient state-led coordination of the financial system. To ensure that limited financial resources were flowing to where they would do the greatest good, policy makers sought to work with the interests of powerful financial institutions to elicit desired behavior from the system as a whole. To achieve this goal, they relied on familiar quid pro quo patronage relationships with banks, this time in the form of the special rediscount line framework.

The divergent regulatory responses of the 1960s held important implications for how each country's financial system would develop moving forward. Although all three countries encountered more intense economic pressures in the 1970s, these pressures were felt more keenly in the United States and Spain than in Canada, in part because of differences in the structures of each country's financial system. In this decade, heated battles over financial regulatory reform followed in both the United States and Spain, but ended with different outcomes. In the United States, the push for substantial regulatory reform was largely unsuccessful, as advocates of deregulation faced strong resistance from advocates of preserving the Regulation Q framework. In Spain, the push for reform was more successful, as actors within the central bank obtained key positions of power and used their influence to push for financial deregulation, albeit in a gradual and piecemeal way. Crucially, in both cases—as well as in Canada in the 1960s—opposition to the regulatory status quo also took a predictable form. In each country, challenger groups resurrected the alternative principle of order that had lost in the reform debates of the 1920s and 1930s in making arguments for regulatory reform.

The next chapter, chapter 7, takes up where this one leaves off. Over the course of the 1980s, the prevailing model of banking regulation in each country changed course, often in dramatic ways. By the end of this decade, each country's regulatory regime bore little resemblance to the regulatory regime that had characterized each country at the start of it. To explain this process of dramatic regulatory change, chapter 7 will highlight the decisive influence of the devastating banking crises of the 1980s—or, more precisely, the very different ways in which the major events of these crises were interpreted and understood in each country.

7

The Rise of New Regulatory Models in the 1980s

The United States, Canada, and Spain entered the 1980s with clearly distinctive models of banking regulation in place. In the United States, policy makers had inched toward financial deregulation in the early 1980s, finally taking steps to phase out interest rate ceilings for both banks and thrifts and relaxing restrictions that limited the scope of permitted activities for thrifts. Yet even after these reforms were introduced, the US bank regulatory system continued to stand out in comparative perspective in its preservation of restrictions designed to keep financial institutions small, independent, or geographically and functionally specialized. Canada, by contrast, entered the 1980s with an unusually laissez-faire regulatory system; a few additional reforms in the early part of this decade only reinforced this tendency.[1] In Spain, a group of actors with close ties to the central bank had recently pushed through a new approach to financial regulation that was marked by a strong commitment to market liberalization. The expressed purpose of these Spanish reforms was to break up the entrenched market power of the leading commercial banks, something that the central bank reformers saw as a key impediment to their effective execution of monetary policy.

By the end of the 1980s, however, the prevailing regulatory model in each country had changed dramatically. In all three cases, legislators introduced sweeping reforms that ushered in a major shift in regulatory orientation. In the United States, banking regulation became oriented toward reinforcing market mechanisms at any cost—even when doing so came at the expense of protecting small and specialized financial institutions. In Canada, banking regulation came to feature a stronger, more proactive role for the state in regulating and supervising banks, breaking with a centuries-long tradition of industry self-regulation and state noninterference. In Spain, regulation also became much more interventionist, with the central bank reformers breaking with the heavy push for financial liberalization that had characterized the 1970s and assuming a much more direct and proactive role in regulating and supervising banks.

Seeds of discontent with existing regulatory models had been present in all three countries since at least the 1970s, but, as we shall see, it took a major financial crisis in each of them to tip the balance toward the widescale embrace of a new regulatory approach. The mechanics of how this process unfolded will not surprise most scholars of policy change. In each country, challenger groups seized the political opportunity created by a serious financial crisis to push through an alternative vision of effective regulation. Incumbent supporters of the regulatory status quo struggled to defend the existing regulatory model in the face of this growing pressure and saw their dominance fade. What is more surprising, however, is the specific path that these regulatory reforms took in each country. The major legislative reforms to financial regulation that defined the late 1980s and early 1990s—which signaled a sea change in regulatory orientation in each country—were not mere rational responses to the specifics of the crises that had preceded them. In each case, the events of the crisis were subject to multiple interpretations—yet the interpretation that took hold in each country bore the imprint of a familiar but *latent* principle of order.

In the United States, the prevailing explanation for the crisis of the 1980s drew from the principle of *competition*. Policy makers focused on the dangers of government protection, which was thought to have encouraged bankers to take excessive risks through its effects on market discipline, and on the failures of bureaucratic regulators to step in and combat this excessive risk taking until it was too late. In Canada, the prevailing explanation drew from the principle of *public rights*. Policy makers focused on the hazards of entrusting depositor protection to the professionalism and benevolence of elite bankers in a system that deregulation had recently opened to new groups. In Spain, the prevailing diagnosis drew primarily from the principle of *state sovereignty*. Here, policy makers also referenced the dangers of disrupting the established banking status quo, but they were especially attuned to the hazards of regulatory arrangements that gave too little power and authority to expert regulators, who had both the foresight and the requisite motives to prevent potential problems from spiraling into crisis. In short, the search for new regulatory solutions remained constrained by the kinds of alternative principles of order that were already embedded in each country's long-standing political-cultural institutions. The dynamics of this process offer the key to solving one of the major puzzles that motivated this book: why the national regulatory models of the 1990s and 2000s differed so significantly from the national regulatory models that had preceded them in the 1960s and 1970s, but also remained so distinctively (and predictably) different across countries.

This chapter considers each country's case in turn, with each section opening with a sketch of the transformative financial crises that rocked each country in the 1980s. Then, I discuss the prevailing diagnoses that emerged among policy makers to explain these crises, paying careful attention to the contestation that led up to these taken-for-granted understandings. Each section then concludes by showing how these prevailing understandings of the crisis informed the content of major legislative reforms to financial regulatory policy in the 1980s and 1990s.

Crisis and the Resurgence of Competition in the United States

The 1980s were hard for American financial institutions of all kinds. Rising interest rates in the 1970s, in tandem with new competitive pressures from domestic and international sources, placed severe pressure on the profit margins of banks and thrifts alike. These pressures only intensified after Paul Volcker, the recently appointed chairman of the Federal Reserve, attacked inflation in August 1979 by aggressively increasing interest rates. As interest rates remained in the double digits through the middle of 1981, borrowing costs skyrocketed, forcing financial institutions to seek out investment opportunities that might offer higher rates of return.

Although these market conditions were troubling for many banks, they were absolutely devastating for thrifts. Thrifts held the vast majority of their assets in the form of long-term loans, which meant that they faced particular trouble adjusting to the sharp increase in borrowing costs that accompanied the high interest rate environment. In a single year, between 1980 and 1981, thrift income fell from $781 million to negative $4.6 billion. By 1984, nearly a quarter of the industry was insolvent (on the basis of tangible net worth).[2]

Congress was well aware of these problems. It had recently passed two regulatory reforms, the 1980 Deposit Institutions Deregulation and Monetary Control Act (which established a schedule for phasing out the Regulation Q interest rate ceilings for banks and thrifts, reduced net worth requirements for thrifts, and increased deposit insurance coverage to $100,000 per account) and the 1982 Garn-St Germain Depository Institutions Act (which further broadened thrift powers by allowing these institutions to lend to riskier commercial real estate ventures and in new consumer markets), to relieve some of these pressures on banks and thrifts.[3] However, both reforms ultimately failed to stave off crisis—and, arguably, may have made the crisis worse when it finally arrived.

The 1980s were dominated by a series of progressively more serious financial crises that touched virtually every corner of the US financial system. In the early part of the decade, a "less developed country" (LDC) debt crisis dominated policy makers' concerns, but the impact was primarily confined to larger, internationally active commercial banks. As large banks had looked for new strategies to boost declining profit margins in the 1970s, many had expanded into lending to the governments and private sectors of LDCs. In August 1982, the Mexican government was on the verge of default and announced that it would no longer be able to meet its debt obligations. By the end of 1983, the governments of twenty-seven other LDC countries had followed suit. Over the six years that followed, these debtor nations repeatedly rescheduled and restructured their payments to US bank creditors. It eventually became clear that the entirety of this debt was unlikely to ever be repaid in full, and this chapter was finally brought to a close with a controversial US-orchestrated debt relief plan in 1989. Although policy makers managed to avert a systemic financial crisis, large US banks were forced to absorb losses that significantly deflated their reported profitability for several years.[4]

In the middle of the decade, banks with heavy exposure to the agricultural and energy sectors struggled to adjust to sharp declines in farm values and an oil and gas bust.[5] Bank failures were especially common among newer entrants to these lines of business. The 1982 failure of one small commercial bank in Oklahoma City, Penn Square Bank, brought the US banking system to the brink of crisis. Penn Square had been active in selling oil- and gas-related loans to other banks before it failed because of heavy losses from plummeting energy prices. One of Penn Square's top customers had been the Continental Illinois National Bank and Trust Company, then the country's seventh largest bank, which had purchased nearly $1 billion in speculative loans from the troubled small bank.[6] After Penn Square collapsed, nervous depositors turned on Continental Illinois as well. Worried that the failure of such a large financial institution might spark a systemic financial crisis, regulators at the FDIC made the controversial decision to extend financial support to the bank's uninsured creditors—which included depositors with accounts valued at more than $100,000. In the congressional hearings that followed in 1984, Comptroller of the Currency C. Todd Conover noted that federal banking regulators would likely act similarly to prevent the failures of the nation's eleven largest banks moving forward. This was the origin of the "too-big-to-fail" bank bailout framework.

While American policy makers found all these events deeply disquieting, the worst was yet to come. In 1987, record waves of failures started to occur among savings and loan (S&L) institutions, a subcategory of thrifts. The crisis only intensified in the years that followed. Between 1986 and 1995, more than a third of the entire thrift industry disappeared. The deposit insurance fund for these institutions went bankrupt relatively early in the crisis, requiring the American taxpayer to absorb the costs of an additional $132 billion thrift rescue package.[7] Although the early troubles for thrifts had stemmed from the severe asset/liability mismatch they faced in a high interest rate environment, new sources of trouble had also emerged in the deregulated environment of the 1980s. Entrepreneurial actors with a higher tolerance for risk started to enter the thrift industry in record numbers in the early 1980s, attracted by the combination of expanded powers and activities and lax accounting standards for thrifts. Between 1982 and 1985, thrifts' share of both assets and deposits rapidly increased; in the same period, evidence of mismanagement and excessive risk taking increased as well. Many of the new entrants had achieved rapid growth by engaging in risky or unsound banking practices, including risky investments in volatile commercial real estate ventures. To fuel this rapid growth, many thrifts had also resorted to paying above-market interest rates on deposits and often turned to costly deposit brokers to obtain these funds.[8] While these dynamics played out across the country, they were especially pronounced in the Sun Belt states and in states with more energy-dependent economies.

By the mid-1980s, regulators recognized that the thrift industry was teetering on the brink of disaster. The Federal Home Loan Bank Board (FHLBB), the regulator of federally chartered thrifts, began taking steps to restrict many of the most dangerous practices in 1985.[9] The damage, however, had been done. The extreme risk taking of the preceding five years had started to catch up with thrifts by 1987, especially among those most active in energy and commercial real estate markets. Net thrift industry income declined from −$7.8 billion in 1987, to −$13.4 billion in 1988, to −$17.6 billion in 1989. Hundreds of troubled thrifts began to fail, and the rising tide of failures was stemmed only by a massive government bailout of the industry in 1989.[10]

While banks may have fared better than thrifts in this period, they were not immune from the crisis. Many banks suffered from the late 1980s collapse of commercial real estate markets, with these effects felt especially keenly in urban areas in the Northeast, California, Alaska, and southwestern states.[11] Between 1980 and 1994, over sixteen hundred federally insured US banks failed or received FDIC financial assistance, far more than in any other period since the creation of the federal deposit insurance system. In 1991, the accumulated bank failures threatened to wipe out the reserves of the FDIC. At this point, the two crises (the S&L debacle and the real estate crisis in banking) of this era had become closely linked in the minds of policy makers.

In this period, American debates over financial regulatory reform took on a new sense of urgency. Perhaps the most striking feature of the debates of the late 1980s and early 1990s was the degree to which policy makers and interest groups across political lines agreed on the basic story of what had happened during the crisis. Even as policy makers debated what exactly should be done to fix the underlying problem, in other words, they were remarkably consistent in their shared understandings of what the underlying problem *was*.

The prevailing diagnosis of the crisis focused on one feature of the institutional environment in which the limited financial deregulation of the 1980s had unfolded. Instead of blaming deregulation itself for the disaster that had followed, policy makers and many concerned interest groups emphasized that this process had occurred in a context where the presence of *deposit insurance* blocked beneficial market discipline. As University of Chicago economist George G. Kaufman argued before Congress in 1989, "deregulation . . . does not mean no regulation. Rather, it means a transfer from government regulation to market regulation. . . . For this change-over to work, market regulation and market discipline must be allowed to work. If not, there is truly no regulation or discipline at all, a sure-fire recipe for financial disaster. And that is what happened with the thrifts."[12] The specific argument was that deposit insurance had caused, or at least greatly exacerbated, the crisis by creating *moral hazard*, or the tendency for protected organizations (in this case, banks and thrifts) to take on more risk when they are insulated from the consequences. Viewed through this lens, the central problem with deposit insurance—as a form of state intervention into the financial system—was that it interfered with the natural incentives of market actors (e.g., depositors, creditors, shareholders) to discipline excessively risky behavior among banks or thrifts. With the government now on the hook for the costs of bank failure, this logic went, why would market actors care to prevent the kind of risky behavior that might lead to failure?

This was an explanation of the crisis that we might expect to see from leading American economists in the 1980s, at a time when their discipline had been recently revolutionized by ideas about rational expectations, efficient markets, and a renewed commitment to laissez-faire.[13] Indeed, American economists and other advocates of the "economic style" in law and policy schools had been warning legislators about the incentive-distorting effects of deposit insurance since at least 1983. These concerns, of course, were nothing new. Recall that opponents of adopting deposit insurance in the first place had espoused similar worries back in the 1930s. However, recent policy changes, combined with new developments within financial economics, had given these old concerns new salience. The 1980 Depository Institutions Deregulation and Monetary Control Act, in phasing out the Regulation Q ceilings, also dismantled a regulatory restriction that had long been framed as a safeguard against the risk-boosting effects of deposit insurance. The same 1980 legislation had also expanded the generosity of deposit insurance coverage, increasing it from $40,000 per account to $100,000 per account in an attempt to bolster the stability of the financial system. Both developments likely contributed to economists' and policy makers' renewed attention to the incentive-distorting features of this policy framework.

The 1977 publication of a seminal paper by financial economist Robert Merton further redirected scholarly attention toward the risk-boosting incentives associated with deposit insurance. This paper made a case for conceptualizing deposit insurance as a put option on the value of a bank's assets, with a strike price equivalent to the value of bank debt. It formalized the notion that banks, as the beneficiaries of deposit insurance, had a strong incentive to maximize asset risk to exploit this underpriced put option.[14] The paper's argument also implied that, because banks paid premiums based on the size of their deposit holdings, and not the risk they presented to the system, deposit insurance was currently underpriced and included few incentives for bankers to limit risk. Financial economists and legal scholars articulated and built on this argument in testimony before Congress throughout the early 1980s. For example, Edward J. Kane, professor of economics and finance at Ohio State University, directly linked the presence of underpriced deposit insurance to the growing fragility of the US banking system in testimony at a 1983 Senate hearing.[15]

It is also not surprising that many members of the financial industry, including large banks, some investment firms, and financial consultants, subscribed to this diagnosis of the thrift crisis as a product of insufficient market discipline induced by government interference in the form of deposit insurance. As one financial consultant, Bert Ely, bluntly argued in 1990, "Government cannot insure in a safe and sound manner. . . . When you put Government in charge of insurance, the principles of insurance get trampled."[16] This general emphasis on the dangers of government overreach, and the expected negative impact on the operation of market mechanisms, served the preexisting interests of large banks in a less regulated financial system. Indeed, by the early to mid-1980s, representatives from large banks had already started to frame their arguments in favor of financial deregulation, and against expanded prudential regulation (e.g., regulation designed to protect financial institutions from risks that might jeopardize their financial health), by appealing to the perceived dangers of any form of government interference that interfered with market mechanisms. Consider, for example, the arguments that Citibank vice president Thomas F. Huertas offered against the imposition of more stringent risk-based capital requirements for banks in 1985:

> [These requirements] . . . can only dilute and distort market discipline, for they weaken the incentive of market participants to monitor and discipline banks independently. Society can either rely on the market or on the regulator to discipline banks, and the safer choice for depositors, for the FDIC and for the banking system as a whole is, in our view, to allow the market to discipline banks.[17]

Huertas's arguments imply that there is a trade-off between government regulation and market regulation: that expanding the government's regulatory footprint is undesirable and even dangerous precisely because it might interfere with the organic competitive mechanisms that keep order intact. In other words, this was the same "moral hazard" argument against government *protection* applied to forms of government *regulation* as well. Thus, when the banking and thrift crisis intensified at the end of the decade, it was only too easy for bankers to follow economists in attributing the crisis to the actions of government (specifically, to the government's creation of deposit insurance). Bankers understandably found an account of the crisis that blamed the government for the problems of the 1980s more appealing than an account that blamed the recently deregulated financial industry.

The feature of this episode that is most important for our purposes, however, is the degree to which this particular explanation for the crisis resurrected familiar themes associated with the principle of *competition*. The implication behind the arguments economists and bankers used throughout the 1980s—including the logic they used to diagnose the thrift and banking crisis at the end of this decade—was that competitive forces, left to their own devices, are the best possible guardians of order within the financial system. Any external factor that interferes with the operation of these competitive forces is, by definition, a source of disorder. By the end of the twentieth century, American bankers and economists were expressing this principle using highly technical language about the benefits of market discipline, the effects of mispricing deposit insurance, or the costs of moral hazard. Yet these arguments, in their most basic elements, were remarkably similar to the *competition*-based arguments used by the opponents of branching restrictions at the turn of the twentieth century and by the supporters of Andrew Jackson's crusade against the rechartering of the Second Bank more than 150 years earlier.

That economists and leading bankers endorsed a diagnosis of the crisis that focused on the dangers of interfering with market discipline is hardly surprising, given the preexisting worldviews and interests of these actors. What is much more surprising is the extent to which this diagnosis also became widely accepted by actors who had endorsed a very different vision of effective regulation only a few years earlier. The views of the federal banking and thrift regulators provide a case in point. Chapter 6 explained how these regulators combined forces with monetary policy makers, members of the Carter and Reagan administrations, economists, and large banks in the 1970s and early 1980s to push for the elimination of the Regulation Q interest rate ceilings and the limited expansion of permitted activities for thrifts. However, after successfully pushing through reforms that secured these outcomes (e.g., the Depository Institutions Deregulation and Monetary Control Act of 1980, the Garn-St Germain Act of 1982), this coalition split.

In the mid-1980s, the federal banking and thrift regulators had joined smaller banks and congressional Democrats in opposing additional, more substantial forms of financial deregulation, including expanded powers for banks to participate in financial activities like proprietary trading, principal investing, or commodity speculation. They also pushed for stronger prudential regulatory standards for banks, including strengthened risk-based capital requirements.

In both efforts, regulators were opposed by large financial institutions, most academic economists, and conservative politicians, who continued to draw from the principle of *competition* to justify support for further deregulation and opposition to additional regulation.

This raises an important question: why were the US banking regulators still resistant to reducing the government's regulatory footprint in the mid-1980s, when many other members of the coalition that had recently secured the deregulatory reforms of the early 1980s took a very different view on this point? To explain this stance among regulators, attention to the ongoing influence of the principle of *community sovereignty* in the bank regulatory system is warranted. In 1985, Fed Chairman Paul Volcker made his agency's position on effective regulation clear in his testimony before Congress. In a hearing on deposit insurance reform, he explicitly warned American policy makers about the dangers of depending too much on market discipline (versus government intervention) in regulating banks:

> Our financial history demonstrates unambiguously the dangers of relying on market discipline alone. Prior to the 1930s, market discipline did not prevent bank failures or systematically discourage excessive risk-taking— until after periodic crises had occurred, at great expense to the economy generally.[18]

Volcker not only argued that market forces had provided inadequate protection against excessive bank risk taking well before the financial safety net of the 1930s had been created. He also suggested that market forces themselves could amplify or exacerbate crisis—and must be restrained on this basis. As he put this point at the same 1985 hearing, "Market forces tend to impose a draconian form of discipline, often creating a crisis atmosphere that can complicate an orderly resolution of the problem and pose dangers of a greater or lesser degree, for other institutions and the banking system."[19] This skeptical view of market discipline, which frames unfettered competitive market forces as *disruptive* to financial order, aligned with the well-established principle of *community sovereignty*. It was also at the root of regulators' opposition to deregulatory reforms that threatened to further reduce the financial system's deconcentrated or specialized character.[20] This was true not just at the Fed, but at the FDIC and Office of the Comptroller of the Currency (OCC) as well.

To summarize: by the early 1980s, some limited financial deregulation had already occurred in the United States, promoted by actors (including, at the time, the federal banking and thrift regulators) that appealed to the principle of *competition*. But a closer look at the comments and the other policy choices of the American banking regulators in the mid-1980s suggests that regulators were not yet complete converts to a laissez-faire, market-oriented regulatory philosophy. Well into the mid-1980s, the US banking regulators were still underscoring their commitment to preserving a deconcentrated and specialized financial system structure—including by supporting policies that limited other forms of competition between banks and nonbanks—and to maintaining the kind of proactive government regulation and supervision needed to protect this structure.

It was only in the late 1980s, as the thrift crisis was reaching its peak, that there were clear indications that the tide was starting to shift at the regulatory agencies. In this period, regulatory explanations for crisis increasingly drew from themes associated with the principle of *competition*. As one example, an internal FDIC publication from 1987 attributes the thrift crisis to the absence of market discipline, following the same general line of reasoning that economists and bankers had recently used to justify further financial deregulation or to oppose stronger capital standards: "Recent experience with deposit insurance in both the banking and thrift industries indicates that . . . better supervision and market discipline are required. . . . Insured institutions can raise funds at risk-free rates regardless of the riskiness of their investments. This creates an incentive to invest in high-risk activities."[21] Similar interpretations of the crisis were also evident at the Federal Reserve, where Alan Greenspan had recently replaced Volcker as chairman of the Board of Governors.

This same diagnosis of the crisis as a product of inadequate market discipline also featured in the final report of the National Commission on Financial Institution Reform, Recovery and Enforcement, an independent advisory commission charged with examining and identifying the causes of the thrift crisis. This report described the existence of deposit insurance as "a fundamental condition necessary for the collapse [of the S&L industry]," further institutionalizing this understanding of what had gone wrong.[22]

As the cost and scope of the economic devastation associated with the thrift and banking crises mounted, even Democratic policy makers who had once strongly opposed additional deregulation on *community sovereignty* grounds started to question the desirability of a banking system organized around preserving a deconcentrated and specialized structure at any cost. By the late 1980s, most of these actors had also come to accept the general diagnosis of the crisis as a failure of market discipline. In 1989, Senator Donald Riegle (D-MI), the soon-to-be-chairman of the Senate Committee on Banking, Housing, and Urban Affairs, remarked, "There are concerns that flaws in the system of Federal deposit insurance . . . can actually encourage excessive risk taking."[23] Senator Jim Sasser (D-TN) also pointed to the familiar problem of "moral hazard" as one of central problems to be resolved through future regulatory reform: "Something must be done to address the issue of 'moral hazard.' All too often, it pays for federally insured institutions to gamble with depositor dollars by making risky investments. If the risk pays off, the owners win. If not, the Federal Government—the taxpayers, that is—are left on the hook."[24]

Accordingly, when Federal Reserve Chairman Alan Greenspan declared in 1990 that "the fundamental problems with our current deposit insurance program are clearly understood and are, I believe, subject to little debate among those with drastically different prescriptions for reform," he was offering an accurate depiction of the state of thought on this topic in the United States.[25] Most observers, regardless of their overall political stance, agreed that deposit insurance and its disruptions to market discipline had been at the root of the most recent crises.

In the same period, policy makers, regulators, industry actors, and economists similarly began to converge around a secondary explanation of the crisis, which focused on the perceived problems of regulatory forbearance. Regulatory forbearance can be loosely defined as the tendency for government actors to let problems in the banking system slide. This theory of disorder, too, had been initially resurrected by financial economists in the regulatory reform debates of the early to mid-1980s. These actors had pointed to what they saw as the intractable problem of regulatory forbearance to explain why deposit insurance must be eliminated or substantially reformed. Public servants, unlike more impartial market participants, were believed to lack the necessary political will to regulate their way out of the moral hazard problem that deposit insurance created. In the words of economics professor Edward Kane, government bureaucrats naturally had "short horizons and political constraints" that prevented them from following "strictly economic interests" in regulatory decision making.[26] Government regulation and supervision, in short, inevitably gave rise to regulatory forbearance.

Faced with the sticker shock of resolving this crisis at its height, American policy makers in the late 1980s started to ask pointed questions about why so many technically insolvent thrifts had not been shut down years earlier, before they could do more damage. The perceived problem of regulatory forbearance provided a ready answer. In February 1989, the members of the Shadow Financial Regulatory Committee, a lobbying group comprising economists and other financial market participants, concluded that the crisis had been made possible, at least in part, by "policies of regulatory forbearance and prolonged deferral of resolving problem cases."[27] The American Bankers Association, unsurprisingly, echoed similar arguments during congressional hearings in the early 1990s—better to blame regulators than financial institutions for the failures that had followed.[28]

This interpretation of the root cause of the crisis, like the focus on the moral hazard of deposit insurance, also cut across political lines. Even the legislators and regulators who were accused of providing this forbearance seemed to sign on to this understanding of what had gone wrong. As Republican congressman Jim Leach (R-IA) wrote in a scathing 1988 letter to the House Committee on Banking, Housing, and Public Affairs, "The dilemma we are confronted with is of our own making. Too loose laws have led to too loose regulation which in turn has led to too loose banking practices. . . . Multi-billion dollar obligations have been made by politicians refusing to stand up to special interest concerns and made larger by regulators preferring to buy time rather than spread ill winds through an industry strewn with ill will."[29] Similarly, Democratic senator Alan Dixon (D-IL) attributed the recent disaster in the thrift industry to the same cause, arguing that "regulators were slow to see the risks in the thrift industry and to address them promptly; indeed, some deregulatory steps were taken which made the situation worse."[30] Senator Jim Sasser (D-TN) echoed similar points: "This crisis—the S&L bailout—is largely a failure of the regulatory system."[31] From the American perspective, the regulatory failures of the 1980s did not stem from insufficient regulatory *powers* to address emerging problems—they stemmed from inadequate regulatory *will* to do something about these problems.

In summary, when US policy makers in the late 1980s and early 1990s searched for explanations for what had gone so wrong with thrifts and banks, they found ready answers in a well-established but latent principle of order: the principle of *competition*. The devastating thrift crisis, which arrived on the heels of multiple previous crises, seemed to highlight the inadequacy of a regulatory system founded on the principle of *community sovereignty* for the modern age. The interpretation of the crisis as a product of both incentive-distorting state interference with the competitive process (the moral hazard effects of deposit insurance) and the inherent insufficiency of government rule (regulatory forbearance) echoed arguments previously advanced by financial economists and financial institutions who had favored additional financial deregulation and lax prudential regulation in the early to mid-1980s. This crisis, and its prevailing diagnosis as the product of too little market discipline and excessive regulatory forbearance, directly informed the content of legislative reforms to financial regulation in the late 1980s and early 1990s.

In August 1989, President George H. W. Bush signed the massive Financial Institutions Reform, Recovery, and Enforcement Act (FIRREA) into law. The centerpiece of this reform was a $150 billion taxpayer-funded thrift industry bailout package. The legislation established the Resolution Trust Corporation (RTC) and charged this newly created organization with liquidating hundreds of insolvent thrifts and reimbursing their depositors. It also introduced emergency reforms to the regulatory system itself, including increases to capital requirements for thrifts (which signaled a clear break with the previous regulatory pattern of reducing requirements for smaller or struggling financial institutions).

As Senator Kennedy (D-MA) explained, this move toward more restrictive capital requirements was inspired by policy makers' newfound understanding of the folly of sacrificing solvency standards to protect the survival of small or specialized financial institutions: "Misplaced sympathy for the thrifts has led the Federal Government to relax capital and regulatory standards, and the resulting system has been abused by high-flying investors. In a sense, we have been killing the thrifts with kindness."[32] Policy makers and regulators now seemed to believe that giving thrifts special advantages had caused more problems than it had solved. To address this issue moving forward, thrifts must be forced to compete on an even footing with other kinds of financial institutions.[33] Armed with the general understanding that government interference with competitive market forces had been a key cause of the S&L crisis, policy makers now sought to avoid repeating the mistakes of the past—even in cases where the deconcentrated or specialized structure of the financial system might be at stake. This represented a clear break with past American regulatory practice.

The same legislation also addressed the perceived problem of regulatory forbearance by reducing the discretion of the thrift and banking regulators, forcing these regulators to abide by codified supervisory procedures and to document more of their actions.[34] As Representative Schumer (D-NY) explained, this reform was expected to limit the potential for forbearance: "One of the problems I think we face is having too much flexibility in the law with regulators. . . . Having lived through this hellish nightmare of what's happened here, [I] don't want to just leave things to the discretion of the regulators."[35] The new legislation further reduced regulatory discretion by restricting regulatory control over accounting standards. In the years leading up to the crisis, thrift net worth reported using regulatory accounting principles (RAP) had been higher than thrift net worth reported using generally accepted accounting principles (GAAP). To prevent a repeat of the events that had produced the crisis, policy makers sought to prevent regulators from establishing alternative accounting standards at all.[36] Overall, FIRREA received widespread political and interest group support and passed quickly with few amendments in 1989.[37]

In November 1991, a second major reform, the Federal Deposit Insurance Corporation Improvement Act (FDICIA), built on and extended many of these reforms. This legislation was framed as a natural follow-up to the emergency reforms introduced in FIRREA: having stabilized the financial system, Congress was now ready to "begin the practice of preventive medicine."[38] Its primary purpose was to restore order and prevent the return of a similar crisis by restructuring the nation's deposit insurance system. Operating under the foundational assumption that deposit insurance had encouraged excessive risk taking among thrifts and banks in the 1980s, the architects of FDICIA sought to mitigate the adverse effects of this framework via multiple reforms.

First, to address the risk insensitivity (and underpricing) of deposit insurance premiums, FDICIA directed the FDIC to adopt a more risk-sensitive approach to calculating insurance premiums for banks and thrifts, linking premiums to how banks and thrifts scored on a supervisory rating framework (the five-element CAMEL rating framework) instead of linking them to the size of the financial institution's insured deposit holdings.[39] The idea was that well-capitalized banks that received top scores should pay lower premiums, in line with the lower risk they presented to the deposit insurance system, while riskier banks should pay higher premiums.[40] The legislation also explicitly limited further increases to deposit insurance coverage and restricted coverage of brokered deposits as part of an effort to mitigate the moral hazard effects of this incentive-disrupting framework.

The FDICIA reform legislation also introduced changes to the bank regulatory and supervisory system along the lines of what had already been adopted for thrifts. Banks were forced to increase capital, and the federal banking regulators also lost their discretion to set accounting standards for banks. The new legislation also legally required banking supervisors at the Federal Reserve and the OCC to implement progressively more severe penalties if a bank's capital ratios fell below prescribed levels (the "prompt corrective action" framework), with the goal of combatting regulatory inaction.[41] Regulators at the FDIC also faced additional limits: they were now obligated to pursue a "least cost resolution" policy in cases of bank failure by choosing the failure resolution method with the lowest cost to taxpayers.

Prevailing accounts of these legislative changes have tended to present them as a continuation of the deregulatory trends that emerged in the United States with the reforms of the early 1980s. Once the deregulatory floodgates had been opened, in other words, the march toward ever more market friendly regulation was inevitable. But a closer look at the development of American financial regulation in this period suggests that the paths to FIRREA and FDICIA were actually much bumpier than this. Key interest groups—including the federal banking regulators and leading Democratic policy makers—continued to resist a wholesale shift in regulatory orientation well into the late 1980s, instead clinging to old elements of the principle of *community sovereignty* that had historically defined the US regulatory system. It took the shock of the thrift and banking crises of the late 1980s to finally cast sufficient doubt on this approach; this was the key event that ushered in a new regulatory commitment to reinforcing market discipline within the financial system.

Crisis and the Resurgence of Public Rights in Canada

The 1980s were also difficult for Canadian financial institutions. Although the problems in the financial system in Canada did not match the scale of those in the United States, they were nonetheless extremely serious. In the early 1980s, Canada's experience of record-setting inflation and skyrocketing short-term interest rates mirrored that of the United States. A sharp rise in oil prices in

1979 had pushed inflation to new heights in Canada. As in the United States, the central bank (Bank of Canada) was also in the midst of experimenting with monetarism, with a corresponding focus on controlling the money supply rather than interest rates. This approach to monetary policy led to eye-wateringly high interest rates in Canada in the early 1980s. In April 1980, the prime rate (the rate at which banks lend to their best customers) hit 17 percent for the first time, then rose in December to 18.25 percent. In August 1981, the prime rate rose to 22.75 percent, the highest it has ever been, before or since.[42] At the same time, in July 1981, the Canadian dollar also sank to a forty-eight-year low against the American dollar, and the country entered into a serious recession between 1981 and 1982.[43] Overall, Canada experienced higher inflation, interest rates, and unemployment than the United States in this period.

These economic trends also placed extreme pressure on the profit margins of domestic banks in Canada. Like their US counterparts, Canadian banks had also been heavily engaged in lending to "less developed" countries in the 1970s and struggled to absorb the losses that followed. Moreover, Canadian near banks, like American thrifts, struggled to adjust to the severe asset/liability mismatch that developed in this climate of high inflation and interest rates. In 1983, Ontario was forced to take control of three insolvent trust companies— Seaway Trust, Greymac Trust, and Crown Trust—which attempted to boost declining profitability by funding a pyramid scheme based on short-term property flips.[44] Additional near bank failures followed in 1985 and 1986, with ten institutions declaring bankruptcy. These events placed pressure on the Canada Deposit Insurance Corporation (CDIC) deposit insurance fund, which had covered both banks and near banks since 1967.

Yet the crisis that ultimately inspired a serious rethinking of financial regulation in Canada occurred among chartered banks, not near banks. In 1985, two small, regional banks in the western province of Alberta were declared insolvent and liquidated at a steep cost to taxpayers. At the time, Canada had not experienced a single bank failure for over sixty years. Although the combined assets of the two failed banks—the Canadian Commercial Bank (CCB), based in Edmonton, and Northland Bank, based in Calgary—represented less than 1 percent of total banking system assets, the crisis was still costly and extremely politically salient.[45] It struck at the heart of what Canadians believed to be true about their own banking system: maybe banks here were less competitive than their counterparts elsewhere, especially the United States, but at least they did not fail. Yet, apparently, they did.

The two failed banks shared multiple common features. Both banks were located in Alberta, had been founded during the oil and real estate booms of the mid-1970s, and had engaged in unusually aggressive and risky lending practices. Both also suffered heavy losses during the recession of the early 1980s. The majority of assets for both banks consisted of loans granted to small, western businesses operating in the energy, real estate, and construction sectors—exactly those businesses hardest hit by the recession.[46] Additionally, the CCB had been an aggressive lender to US energy companies, which suffered after a sudden drop in world oil prices in the early 1980s.

Faced with growing losses, the CCB turned to the federal government for help in March 1985. The government of Canada, the government of Alberta, and six chartered banks quickly arranged a $255 million bailout package to support the bank. However, it soon became apparent that the CCB had not accurately assessed the magnitude of its loan losses, and the government/bank coalition was forced to advance another $300 million. At this point, nervous depositors began to lose faith in the CCB, and the deposit withdrawals that followed led the Bank of Canada to extend additional liquidity support. By Labor Day weekend, outstanding loans from the Bank of Canada to the CCB totaled $1.3 billion, and more than half of the CCB's assets were pledged as collateral to the central bank.

In early September, it became clear that the CCB's problems were fatal. On September 1, the inspector general of banks issued a press release that stated that the CCB and Northland Bank (another troubled Albertan bank) were unable to meet liabilities as they came due. The Bank of Canada issued its own press release the same day, stating that neither bank was viable, leaving no basis for further liquidity support.[47] On September 3, the CCB ceased operations, and Northland Bank was placed under a curator. Although Northland Bank had less international exposure than the CCB, it too had struggled to absorb heavy losses on loans to the troubled energy and real estate sectors. Northland executives had responded to these mounting losses by attempting to grow their way out of the problem, both by pursuing increasingly risky investments and by engaging in borderline fraudulent practices. When Northland's cash reserves fell below required levels, it too was allowed to fail at the end of September.

These bank failures led to immediate uproar in the House of Commons. Early conversations centered around the need for additional government support to the troubled financial system; discussions only indirectly touched on the causes of the bank failures. To maintain depositor and investor confidence in other smaller regional banks, the Progressive Conservative government under Prime Minister Brian Mulroney (who had won by a landslide in the 1984 federal election) introduced Bill C-79, which proposed to extend deposit insurance coverage to all accounts at CCB or Northland over $60,000. At the time, Canadian deposit insurance coverage was limited to $60,000 per account. The Mulroney administration had recently made government support of smaller, regional financial institutions a central policy priority, because it viewed a strong and vibrant regional banking system as vital to breaking up the entrenched financial dominance of the elite eastern banks. This bailout of the CCB's and Northland's uninsured depositors would come with a $420 million price tag, but the Mulroney government justified the cost in terms of preserving the stability of regional banks.[48]

This Progressive Conservative push to compensate uninsured depositors at these banks was also rooted in a particular understanding of what had caused the crisis. Initially, these actors attributed the CCB and Northland failures to bad luck. The problem was not that the banks had been poorly managed, in other words—they had simply been victims of the severe recession of the early 1980s (which, many Progressive Conservatives argued, had stemmed from misguided Liberal energy policies in the 1970s), which left them with little chance to succeed. The Liberal Party, the official opposition party at the time, critiqued the government's handling of the crisis. They underscored the failure of the March 1985 rescue package, criticizing the government for wasting taxpayer resources and for failing to recognize the severity of the CCB's problems. They also opposed Bill C-79 on the grounds that depositors with accounts valued at over $60,000 were more likely to be sophisticated corporations and entrepreneurs, not ordinary hardworking Canadians (and thus not entitled to a bailout). Representatives from the far-left New Democratic Party (NDP), meanwhile, focused on the need to address the factors that had encouraged the two failed banks to engage in imprudent risk taking from the start. As Lynn McDonald, an NDP MP from Toronto, argued in 1985, the NDP viewed prevailing corporate governance arrangements at the banks—including a management team filled with Americans—as a key source of the problems that had followed, arguing that no one appeared to be "tending the shop" at CCB.[49]

For their part, the leading chartered banks agreed that bailing out depositors who had been attracted by higher interest rates at the two failed banks would set a bad precedent. As Robert Korthals, president of TD Bank, argued, expanding deposit insurance to these actors would send the signal "that people who have taken imprudent risks are smart and those who have taken lower rates are the fools."[50] These arguments echoed similar concerns about the incentive-distorting effects of deposit insurance that were becoming more prominent in the United States in the same period.

Almost immediately after the two Albertan banks failed, the Mulroney government asked Supreme Court justice Willard Z. Estey to oversee an inquiry into the causes of these events and to offer recommendations for regulatory reform. The publication of the Estey Commission's final report in August 1986 changed the course of Canadian debates over bank regulatory reform. After months of an investigation that included holding public hearings in three cities, questioning eighty-five witnesses, and collecting thousands of documents and pages of testimony, the inquiry uncovered widespread evidence of unsound banking practices, highly concentrated risk exposures, and gross mismanagement at both the CCB and Northland.[51] Managers at both banks had responded to a deepening economic recession by attempting to mask increasingly desperate financial positions, adopting "bizarre" banking practices and accounting standards with this objective in mind.[52] And in both cases, the directors of the banks had failed to fulfill their responsibilities by relying too heavily on guidance from management when setting strategy.

Although the Estey Commission report placed little blame on the Mulroney administration itself, it highlighted how the failures of both external auditors (in the private sector) and government regulators (in the public sector) had contributed to the crisis. The external auditors of the failed banks, who were from Canada's largest and most respected accounting firms, had signed off on financial statements that did not reflect the true financial condition of these institutions. These findings were especially shocking in the Canadian context, where regulatory institutions had been built on the assumption that banks could be governed most effectively by leaving bank managers and directors to their own devices. Making matters worse, the Office of the Inspector General of Banks (OIGB), the country's bank regulatory agency, not only had failed to independently assess the quality of the CCB and Northland's loan portfolios but had actually ignored the few external auditor reports that challenged management's representation of the banks' financial conditions.

If there had previously been any doubt that mismanagement had contributed to the banks' failures, the Estey Commission report removed that doubt. This changed the tenor of the discussions of regulatory reform that followed. The Progressive Conservatives dropped the claim that the bank failures had been products of bad luck and timing, while the Liberals seemed to embrace the NDP's account of these events as products of excessive bank risk taking and corporate governance arrangements that encouraged such behavior.[53] For their part, representatives from the NDP continued to expand on the same themes they had initially introduced in 1985. To explain the origins of the crisis, these actors underscored the effects of demographic changes within the banking system after the financial deregulation of the 1960s and 1970s. As barriers to entering the banking business had fallen, a new kind of banker had emerged, and regulators had failed to keep pace with this changing reality. Simon de Jong (NDP-Regina, Saskatchewan) described this transformation on the floor of Parliament in 1987:

> You see, our regulators sort of assumed that our banks were controlled by a group of Methodist managers. It wasn't the fear of the government or the regulators which forced them to be honorable gentleman in banking, but the fear of God. . . . We are now living in a new era. The smart boys on the street do not have the fear of God in them.[54]

This line of argument has a clear historical precedent in Canada. In an institutional context that had long emphasized the benefits of reserving key political and economic privileges for benevolent and talented elites, policy makers (even progressive policy makers) were already primed to see potential hazards in the expansion of valued privileges to new groups. These changed circumstances, the NDP argued, required more proactive participation in prudential regulation from the state.[55]

By the end of 1986, the understanding that regulatory and supervisory weakness and inaction had contributed to the crisis cut across political lines. Mike Cassidy (NDP-Ottawa) put the point bluntly: "We have had a surfeit of public policy studies of regulation of financial institutions. . . . All these reports concluded . . . that there was a major systemic weakness in the government's ability to spot and identify problems in unhealthy institutions and, further, to do something about those problems once they began to be identified."[56] Earlier comments from Minister of State for Finance Barbara McDougall (PC-Toronto) suggested the same general diagnosis: "It is clear that [supervisory] improvements can be made and must be made. . . . United States regulators have far more powers than our regulators. They can sweep into a bank on Friday, kick out the management, go through it on the weekend and open it Monday as a new bank."[57] Liberals, too, agreed that the crisis had demonstrated that Canada must "change as well as . . . strengthen [regulatory] controls."[58] In contrast to a half century of regulatory decisions that affirmed the merits of preserving *elite autonomy*, note that this diagnosis draws directly from the principle of *public rights*, with its emphasis on the need for the state to proactively protect vulnerable members of the banking public from exploitation by powerful banks.

The elements missing from the prevailing Canadian diagnosis of the banking crisis are just as interesting as the elements this diagnosis included. Unlike American policy makers, Canadian policy makers largely neglected to interpret these events as a failure of market discipline (including a failure generated by the presence of deposit insurance). While concerns about threats to market discipline were not entirely absent—William Mulholland, chairman of the Bank of Montreal, for example, opposed expanded state oversight of the banking system on the grounds that "regulatory supervision is not, and cannot ever be, a replacement for the disciplines imposed by the market"—Canadian policy makers did not take up the interpretation of the crisis as a product of state-created moral hazard in the same way as their American counterparts. In part, this was due to the different content of the regulatory regime each group of policy makers was reacting *against*. As of the early 1980s, the Canadian regulatory system was marked by the absence of the kinds of restrictive and interventionist regulation that then characterized the US financial system (the presence of deposit insurance in Canada was the exception to this rule). In this context, it would have been a significant stretch to diagnose the recent crisis as a product of too much government intervention in banking, given the government's comparatively limited role in regulating banks in Canada.

In 1987, Canadian policy makers introduced three major regulatory reforms to address what had been firmly established as a problem of insufficient regulatory and supervisory protection of depositor rights. The first reform, the Office of the Superintendent of Financial Institutions Act, created a new prudential regulatory agency, the Office of the Superintendent of Financial Institutions (OSFI), which received greater powers and authority than its predecessor. The OSFI amalgamated the former bank regulatory agency (the OIGB) with the Department of Insurance and received the authority to supervise and regulate all federally chartered banks and insurance companies. As Progressive Conservative MP Bill Attewell explained, the explicit goal of creating this "more assertive" and "proactive" agency with a broader regulatory purview was to correct for the decline of the traditional "gentleman's approach" in banking, which had faded away in the post-deregulation era.[59] For centuries, Canadian policy makers had resisted the temptation to step in and direct banks' choices of structures and activities, instead permitting a small and privileged group of elite incumbent firms to govern themselves. In creating a substantially expanded role for the state in supervising and regulating banks, then, Canadian policy makers in the 1980s broke with a long historical tradition.

The second reform, the Financial Institutions and Deposit Insurance System Amendment Act, introduced other changes to the Canadian bank regulatory, supervisory, and deposit insurance systems. It gave the Canadian Deposit Insurance Corporation (CDIC) greater authority to directly inspect its members (or to require OSFI to do so), to subject prospective members to review, and to impose new conditions on insurance coverage.[60] It also increased deposit insurance premiums for all member banks, to compensate for the recent decline in the deposit insurance fund. Importantly, however, Canadian policy makers avoided a US-style approach of limiting the authority and discretion of the deposit insurance agency. In reforming the deposit insurance system, the goal was to grant the CDIC new powers that would enable the agency to be more judicious in granting and overseeing insurance, not to take away power from regulators.

A third reform, which involved amendments to the Canadian Bank Act, combined two seemingly unrelated initiatives. First, it strengthened the state's role in prudential regulation by assigning additional powers to the recently created OSFI, including the power to issue cease-and-desist orders to banks and to revalue bank assets secured by real estate.[61] Second, it granted additional powers to commercial banks, removing limits on the ability of these institutions to invest in or own securities firms and expanding their capacity to underwrite corporate securities directly. That these two elements of the reform package seemed at odds did not escape the notice of policy makers like Mike Cassidy (NDP-Ottawa), who noted that "the government has come up with a legislative compromise in which it is trying to both deregulate and *re*regulate the system."[62]

The paradoxical content of these reforms start to make more sense, however, when we consider the dilemma Canadian policy makers faced in this period. The 1985 bank failures shook the confidence of policy makers and the public by revealing major flaws in a banking system that had been long governed by industry self-rule. To protect vulnerable depositors and maintain banking system stability, observers across political lines agreed that these flaws needed to be addressed. It was this goal that had spurred the expansion of OSFI's supervisory and enforcement powers: as Minister of State for Finance Thomas Hockin (PC–London West) explained, "In the past, regulators have indicated that even when they were aware that unsafe or unsound business practices were being followed they frequently lacked the legislative authority to order the institution to cease the questionable practices."[63] The new legislation provided regulators with much-needed authority to intervene when necessary.

Safety and stability were not, however, the only considerations that mattered to Canadian policy makers in this period. In the late 1980s, Canadian policy makers were also extremely concerned about the competitiveness of their domestic banks in a globalizing marketplace. In this period, prosperity, if not safety and stability, was still understood to derive from a familiar source: allowing managers and directors of banks to freely select the lines of action that would (in their view) optimize profitability. Policy makers assumed that Canadian banks would require additional powers if they were to keep pace with rapidly changing international developments.

One key implication of the crises of the 1980s was that Canadian policy makers increasingly came to see the factors associated with the promotion of safety and stability (greater state intervention to protect depositors and policyholders) and international competitiveness (free bank selection of desired activities) as being at odds. In this context, language about "balancing" or "reconciling" these competing objectives became much more common. As Minister Hockin explained in 1987, when introducing his proposed amendments to the Bank Act, "During the last 2 ½ years the federal government was faced with a formidable challenge. It had the responsibility of formulating a policy which would, first and foremost, protect the public interest and the safety of depositors. Second, we wanted to introduce a policy which would allow our Canadian financial institutions to compete in a rapidly changing global environment. . . . [The twin] objectives were to protect the system and the depositors while making it a modern, global system."[64] Hockin's intention, in other words, was to "strike an appropriate balance" between developing a stronger, more proactive regulatory system and also promoting a more "strong and viable Canadian presence" in a globalizing financial world.[65]

Comments from Aideen Nicholson (L-Toronto) suggest that this understanding of effective regulation was shared by more than just conservative policy makers in this period. She, too, referenced the need to "strike the right balance" between issues of consumer protection and competitiveness in regulation:

> The government's goal of greater integration of services can lead both to greater competitiveness and to greater concentration. It is very important to ensure that appropriate balance is struck. Greater integration also brings with it greater potential for abuse and conflict of interest, and that's a greater need for consistent and vigilant regulation.[66]

The 1987 reforms to the Bank Act thus simultaneously signaled Canada's ongoing commitment to enhancing banking system performance via financial deregulation but also the country's new commitment to ensuring that expanded powers for banks would be accompanied by stronger and more proactive prudential regulation. Banks may have received the freedom to enter new markets, but they were also expected to comply with a much more powerful and interventionist regulatory and supervisory regime.

Crisis and the Resurgence of State Sovereignty in Spain

Although Spain had enjoyed one of the highest growth rates in Europe in the early 1970s, its economy stalled after 1975, when a series of deeply rooted structural problems came to a head.[67] After a brief lull in the late 1960s, inflation began to climb again in the early 1970s, peaking at an unprecedented 24 percent in 1977. Spain's balance of payments problem also returned, and Spain's real exchange rate appreciated 35 percent between 1970 and 1975.[68] As a country that imported 70 percent of its energy, Spain was also especially hard-hit by the 1973 oil price shock, with the industrial and transportation sectors (the biggest consumers of crude oil) bearing the brunt of these rising energy prices.

It was apparent to most observers in the mid-1970s that the Spanish economy was facing significant problems. However, these dynamics did not translate into a loss of political power for the central bank reformers who had assumed greater control over economic policy. In part, this was because Spanish policy makers were preoccupied by other issues in this period, especially the task of creating a new political system. When Franco died in 1975, Spain embarked on a transition toward democracy, holding the first democratic elections in almost five decades in June 1977. These elections ended with the victory of the centrist Unión de Centro Democrático (UCD) Party, led by Adolfo Suárez González, over the left-wing/socialist party Partido Socialista Obrero Español (PSOE). The Suárez government's first priority was to create new political institutions that would be both effective and stable. Managing the economy came second. The privileged position of the central bank reformers was also reinforced by the tight networks these actors had created between the top academic economics and political science departments, the Research Service department at the Bank of Spain, and the Treasury and Finance (Hacienda) departments of the Spanish state.

By 1978, however, the mounting problems in the Spanish economy had grown too pressing for politicians to ignore. The industrial sector confronted a triple challenge of rising energy costs, growing competitive pressures in a newly liberalized economy, and double-digit inflation, and it was on the verge of collapse. Skyrocketing costs of credit only made these problems worse. In the mid-1970s, the government had allowed real wages to rise to better manage social unrest at a potentially volatile time. Now faced with rising costs on multiple fronts, industrial firms turned to Spanish banks for credit to stay afloat. Although the banks readily accommodated this rising demand, they did so at very high interest rates. Spanish firms soon found themselves saddled with unprecedented debt. Between 1975 and 1979, the debt-to-equity ratio of the average Spanish industrial firm rose from 60 percent to 300 percent.[69]

While this trend had multiple causes, policy makers agreed that one of the most important had been the Spanish banking industry's curious path to financial liberalization in the 1970s. The policy changes of this era had allowed new groups to enter the financial system, leading to a tripling in the number of bank offices in Spain between 1973 and 1983. The most extensive growth had occurred among new entrants to the banking system and among small-to-medium-sized banks. After the repeal of the special rediscount line framework in 1971 and the 1974 liberalization of bank branching restrictions, the operating costs of all banks also increased sharply. However, the ongoing dominance of the Big Seven banks in both credit and deposit markets continued to heavily restrict price competition. In such an oligopolistic banking system, banks found it relatively easy to shift their rising operating costs onto borrowers.[70] These dynamics set off a dangerous chain reaction. To recoup rising operating costs, banks charged higher interest rates on loans to industrial firms. As industrial firms became even more highly leveraged, more of them started to fail, leading to additional losses for the banks that financed them. Banks, in turn, passed along these rising costs to the surviving industrial firms.

In 1977, these dynamics led to a record number of failures among Spanish industrial firms. Banks were doubly exposed to these failures because, beyond acting as lenders to these firms, they were frequently shareholders in industrial concerns. By 1978, this crisis in the industrial sector had officially transformed into a banking crisis. Its first victims were the Banco de Navarra and Banco Cantábrico, two smaller regional banks that became insolvent in the first two months of 1978. After this initial shock, a wave of additional failures occurred among other small regional banks, especially banks established less than a decade earlier. Many of these failing banks initially classified their problems as temporary liquidity issues, but further investigation by the Bank of Spain revealed severe solvency problems. Excessive concentration of risk was a pervasive issue, with many failing institutions surpassing established limits on total exposure to related parties or single entities.[71]

In November 1977, Spanish policy makers attempted to stem the tide of failures by establishing a Deposit Guarantee Fund, overseen by the Bank of Spain, that offered limited deposit insurance coverage to all bank depositors. In March 1978, this fund received authorization to go beyond compensating the depositors of already-failed banks to offer liquidity support to distressed banks. As the number of failed banks continued to climb, additional reforms in the early 1980s gave the deposit guarantee fund the authority to forcibly acquire and dispose of nonperforming assets from insolvent institutions and expanded the supervisory and enforcement powers of the Bank of Spain.[72]

These initial policy changes failed to prevent a second, more severe wave of the crisis. In 1982, the socialist PSOE Party had just secured its first electoral victory over the centrist UCD Party, with the right-wing Alliance Popular (AP) Party serving as the official opposition. This shift in political leadership was a major boon for the central bank reformers and their allies. Under the PSOE government, both the governor of the central bank (Mariano Rubio) and its vice-governor (Luis Ángel Rojo) were affiliated with, or trained by, the Research Service at the Bank of Spain. The same was true of the heads of the Finance and Economy departments of the state (Miguel Boyer and Carlos Solchaga, respectively). One implication was that most key Spanish economic decision makers in this period assumed "that the central bank's view reflected virtually unquestionable expertise."[73]

As the new socialist government was taking office, a number of large banks began to fail. These banks had developed heavy exposure to firms in volatile industries over the course of the 1970s and struggled to absorb losses on these industrial portfolios. One of the most prominent failures of this period was that of the Banca Catalana, an industrial bank group created in the 1960s by Jordi Pujol (then leader of the Catalan regional government) that was forcibly taken over by the Deposit Guarantee Fund in November 1982. After an audit revealed that the bank could not prove that credits granted to real estate companies could be recovered, its assets were sold at a discount to a consortium of leading Spanish banks at a massive cost to the state.

In 1983, an even greater scandal followed, which had a significant impact on the development of Spanish financial regulation moving forward. In February of that year, the massive holding company RUMASA was declared insolvent and forcibly taken over by the government. RUMASA had started as a small wine-producing company in the early 1960s but had since grown into a massive conglomerate encompassing more than three hundred subsidiaries and twenty banks. Many of RUMASA's banks had been acquired through purchases of struggling industrial banks and *cajas* in the 1970s, and they specialized in financing the group's industrial concerns, which included shipping companies, construction firms, and hotels and department stores. RUMASA's banks collectively held around 4 percent of deposits in the Spanish banking system at the time of its collapse. The company represented the only newcomer that had seriously challenged the dominance of the Big Seven in the 1970s.

The Bank of Spain had been aware of potential problems at RUMASA for some time. As early as 1978, examiners at the central bank observed that the holding company (and by extension, its banks) seemed to be experiencing financial difficulties. Examiners attempted to carry out several audits, but they faced a major hurdle in obtaining clear and properly audited balance sheets from the holding company. At the time, RUMASA did not have a clear legal obligation to provide this information.[74] Yet even without access to detailed financial reports, actors at the Bank of Spain and the Ministry of Finance saw enough to be worried. In the late 1970s and early 1980s, they repeatedly warned RUMASA's executives about the hazards of the growing concentration of risk within its banks and industrial companies.[75]

These concerns turned out to be warranted. In February 1983, the frustrated PSOE minister of finance Miguel Boyer Salvador, himself a protégé of Rojo and the Research Service department at the Bank of Spain, sent inspectors from the Bank of Spain to audit RUMASA. At this point, the holding company's executives had successfully dodged a comprehensive audit by the private-sector accounting firm Arthur Andersen for almost a year. Boyer's efforts finally brought this game of cat-and-mouse to an end. After inspectors disclosed that RUMASA was technically insolvent, a wave of deposit withdrawals at RUMASA-linked banks followed. Within a week, the government stepped in to nationalize and take over the holding company. In the press conference that followed, Boyer explained how RUMASA had engaged in "measures contrary to the most elementary of banking procedures for concentrating risks," including a pyramid financing scheme in which "the company used its own banks to finance expansion and acquired new companies to pay for those already purchased."[76]

By the time that Spain's banking crisis finally came to an end in 1985, 63 of its 110 banks had been seriously affected.[77] No bank established between 1973 and 1978 survived the crisis as an independent institution. Resolving the 1977–85 crisis also proved extremely expensive, coming at a total cost of 1.215 trillion pesetas (equivalent to the entirety of Spain's public debt and 5 percent of GDP).[78] In the end, this episode represented one of the biggest banking crises in Spanish history, and certainly the most serious crisis of the twentieth century.[79]

As in the US and Canadian cases, there was remarkable consensus in Spain on the leading causes of the 1977–85 crisis, even as the debates over regulatory reform remained spirited and prolonged. Virtually all agreed that the financial deregulation of the 1970s had played a role. As Minister of Finance Boyer explained to his fellow legislators in 1983, deregulation had given rise to "disorderly expansion" by paving the way for less professional, informed, or skilled bankers to enter the financial system. As he argued, the crisis could be attributed, at least in part, to "the breakdown of the banking 'status quo' in 1972, which led to the creation of new banks whose authorization in some cases should not have occurred given their speculative orientation and lack of professionalism, and that, in any case, reached the crisis stage insufficiently established and not in an adequate financial condition to deal with it."[80] Boyer's political rival, right-leaning Alliance Popular Party leader Abel Matutes y Juan, echoed a similar diagnosis: "Here, the problem . . . was not that more banks were needed, but more and better bankers."[81]

Academic and media accounts endorsed this diagnosis of the crisis as a product of disorderly expansion as well. As the following excerpt from a 1981 editorial in the left-leaning newspaper *El País* suggests, the media also attributed the crisis to the unruly competitive forces deregulation had unleashed:

> Recently, banks have been forced to accept decisive changes that have introduced a greater degree of freedom and competition in the financial market. Banks have thus lost much of their corporate character and have been forced to face increasing foreign and domestic competition, a phenomenon unknown since 1921—and, coinciding with the current economic crisis, this has caused remuneration on deposits and the narrowing of operating margins to rise to reckless levels, problems which have also been exacerbated by the concentration of risk in . . . banking.[82]

Leading economists, policy makers, regulators, and media commentators all turned to the principle of *corporatist harmony* to explain the Spanish crisis. Even as most groups, including actors with close ties to the central bank, continued to acknowledge the benefits that had come with financial liberalization and deregulation, they also recognized the new dangers that had followed from the disruption of the established banking hierarchy.

However, the prevailing Spanish diagnosis for the crisis did not focus solely on the impact of the recent proliferation of new banks in a deregulated era. Just as concerning to policy makers was the state's obviously limited capacity to discover and address undesirable behavior among financial institutions. Much was made of the fact that the authorities (both regulators at the Bank of Spain and the tax agencies) had been largely unaware of the true scope of problems at RUMASA and other financial institutions.[83] In the RUMASA case, the problem had been twofold: the company's financial statements had been hard for authorities to obtain, and the information reflected on these financial statements had been extremely opaque. Even after the government took control of the holding company, it was embarrassingly hard to unravel its web of affiliate firms because of the heavy use of investment trusts and other accounting vehicles that obscured true ownership relationships.[84]

A general consensus emerged among policy makers and regulators alike: the RUMASA failure had bloomed into a nationwide crisis because banking supervisors at the Bank of Spain had lacked the full legal authority to sanction wayward banks. Policy makers agreed that this general issue extended beyond the RUMASA case. As first vice president of the PSOE and financial reform advocate Juan Muñoz García (PSOE—Segovia) explained, "It has also been agreed that the entire [bank] sanctioning system has been shown to be ineffective. The entire sanctioning system that existed around the banking credit system has been insufficient and has been largely insufficient from the 1920s onwards, despite some modifications introduced along the way."[85] Leading Spanish academics, including the influential economist Álvaro Cuervo García, also identified the state's regulatory weakness as a central cause of the crisis.

This account of the crisis drew from the alternative principle of *state sovereignty*. Ironically, the very same principle that the central bank reformers had mobilized to justify their deregulatory push in the 1970s was now being used (by the same actors, as well as by Spanish policy makers across political lines) to critique an insufficiently interventionist supervisory and regulatory framework. The events of 1977–85 had revealed that central bank control over monetary policy was not the only thing that mattered for economic stability. The quality of prudential regulation and regulatory oversight clearly mattered too. In the United States, this strengthened discipline of financial institutions was expected to come from the market, but in Spain, it was expected to come from the state—or more specifically, from expert government regulators at an independent, public-minded central bank.[86]

The major postcrisis legislative reforms to Spain's financial regulatory system, contained in the Discipline and Intervention of Credit Institutions Law of 1988 (Law 26/1988), were deeply influenced by this prevailing diagnosis of the 1977–85 crisis as the product of too-easy entry into the banking business, excessive competition between banks, and the inadequate regulatory and supervisory strength of the Bank of Spain. In a sharp departure from the diagnosis of the thrift crisis developing in the United States in the same period, the prevailing explanation for the Spanish banking crisis implied that market forces, including the market discipline exerted by the creditors and shareholders of banks, were fundamentally ill equipped to maintain the proper functioning of a system as important to the public interest as the banking system.[87] During the debates leading up to the passage of this bill, Vice President Muñoz García made this point explicitly, arguing that the natural limitations of market actors created a gap that required impartial experts at the Bank of Spain to undertake a more proactive role in regulation and supervision: "In general, shareholders normally do not follow and cannot follow the evolution of [financial institutions], given the complexity from the point of view of accounting, decisions, etc. This can only be done . . . on behalf of an entity such as the Bank of Spain."[88]

This understanding of the relative benefits of market versus state supervision informed the content of the specific reforms included in Law 26/1988, which were mostly oriented toward strengthening the oversight and regulatory control functions of the Bank of Spain. The new law gave the Bank of Spain greatly increased powers to legally sanction banks and much greater control over bank financial reporting and disclosure standards.[89] In line with these objectives, Law 26/1988 required all banks to submit their quarterly consolidated financial statements directly to the Bank of Spain and gave the Bank of Spain more substantial authority to set accounting standards for banks at regulators' discretion.

These specific reforms were indicative of a more general trend. To correct for the delayed regulatory response that Spanish policy makers saw as so central to the production of the crisis, multiple features of Law 26/1988 reflected an effort to expand (rather than restrict) the authority and discretion of regulators and supervisors at the Bank of Spain, giving them new powers to set regulatory requirements and additional discretion to determine when and how to intervene to resolve problem banks. Finally, Law 26/1998 also sought to prevent a return of the problems that had given rise to the crisis by closing perceived loopholes in the structure of financial regulation, which were believed to have emerged from the "enormous dispersion and variety of the instruments" that currently regulated financial institutions.[90] It also gave the Bank of Spain ultimate authority over a wide range of financial institutions, not just banks, as part of an effort to address the "attendant voids and lack of coordination" that were thought to have contributed to the failed regulation of conglomerates like RUMASA. To fix the regulatory system, in other words, policy makers sought to reorganize it under greater centralized control.

In short, the various reforms included in Law 26/1988 were primarily oriented toward restoring order to the financial system by enhancing the capacity of a centralized and public-minded regulatory agency (the Bank of Spain) to oversee and direct financial institutions—private-sector actors—in need of greater guidance. The entrenched power of the central bank reformers, combined with the diffusion of international norms toward central bank independence, helps to explain why it was actors within the central bank (versus actors elsewhere in the Spanish state) who received this expanded authority.

It is notable that nothing about the crisis itself made its diagnosis as a product of too little state direction and control inevitable. Indeed, when viewed in comparative perspective, we see striking commonalities between the experience of the banking crisis of 1977–85 in Spain and the thrift crisis of the late 1980s in the United States. Severe financial crises emerged in both countries in the aftermath of skyrocketing inflation and volatile energy or real estate prices. In both countries, there was general agreement that these crises had roots in financial deregulation, which had paved the way for new groups to enter the financial system, and that they had unfolded in the presence of deposit insurance and been exacerbated by the failures of regulators or supervisors to address troubled institutions quickly and effectively. Yet where US policy makers saw too much state intervention as the ultimate cause of these problems, Spanish policy makers perceived the cause as too much market rule. These different interpretations become easier to understand when viewed through the lens of the ascending principles of *state sovereignty* in Spain and *competition* in the United States.

Conclusion

Discontent with existing models of banking regulation was already brewing in the United States, Canada, and Spain at the start of the 1980s, but it took a major financial crisis to spark dramatic regulatory reform in each of them. Crucially, the direction of reform was shaped by features of the broader institutional landscape in each country, which made particular alternative principles of economic order more readily available and salient than others. To explain what had gone so wrong in the 1980s, policy makers in all three countries eventually returned to familiar yet latent principles of order.

In the United States, policy makers found ready answers for the S&L and banking crises of the late 1980s in an account that drew directly from the principle of *competition*, which highlighted the dangers associated with all forms of state intervention that interfered with the operation of competitive market forces. Although concerns about government interference in financial markets had long predated the crisis, shifts within the economics profession, combined with policy changes in the early 1980s and advocacy from regulated financial institutions, had recently heightened their salience. Although it took a serious financial crisis before this new understanding of effective regulation would dominate the US financial regulatory system, its seeds had been planted years earlier, in the unsuccessful debates over financial regulatory reform that had defined the 1970s and early 1980s.

In Canada, policy makers settled on an explanation for the troubling failures of two western banks that drew from the principle of *public rights*. Faced with a situation in which a comparatively hands-off regulatory and supervisory system in a deregulated environment had clearly failed to protect the interests of depositors or taxpayers, policy makers perceived a need for stronger regulatory

institutions to better safeguard the rights of vulnerable individuals from exploitation by powerful groups. This line of reasoning, too, had a well-established
historical legacy in Canada. As in the United States, however, it took a serious
crisis for this new understanding of effective regulation to overtake policy makers' prior commitment to maintaining *elite autonomy*. In Spain, policy makers
primarily drew lessons from the principle of *state sovereignty* in diagnosing
the major causes of the crisis, although tenets associated with the principle of
corporatist harmony appeared in some of their arguments as well. Faced with
havoc in a newly deregulated banking system, Spanish policy makers perceived
the need to restore order to this system by drastically strengthening the powers, capacity, and scope of oversight for the centralized, public-minded Bank
of Spain. The goal was to restore order to the financial system by centralizing a
fragmented regulatory regime and by giving this arm of the state greater power
and authority to oversee and direct the activities of private banks.

This chapter has illustrated how legislative reforms to financial policy were
deeply shaped by the prevailing diagnoses of these crises in each country,
each of which drew on long-established principles of order. The legislative
reforms of the late 1980s and early 1990s had the effect of institutionalizing—
that is, materially embodying—a newly dominant principle of regulatory order
in the United States, Canada, and Spain. Even at a time that is generally recognized as a key moment in international regulatory convergence, as well
as an important moment in the global ascendance of neoliberalism, the three
countries considered here pursued distinctively different approaches to regulatory reform. In both Canada and Spain, policy makers granted much greater
authority, power, and discretion to independent regulatory and supervisory
agencies. In the United States, we see the opposite pattern. This new model of
regulation sought to restrict the discretion of banking regulators and supervisors, both to fight against the perceived problem of regulatory forbearance and
to better mitigate the market-disrupting effects of all forms of government
intervention in the financial system.

The next chapter, chapter 8, explains how these prevailing interpretations of
the crises of the 1980s—now institutionalized in concrete legislative reforms—
shaped the development of distinctive regulatory worldviews among the American, Canadian, and Spanish banking regulators in the 1990s and 2000s.

8

New Regulatory Visions in the 1990s

In the two decades leading up to the global financial crisis, banking regulators in the United States, Canada, and Spain gave dozens of public speeches at industry conferences, meetings, and other events. They published hundreds of working papers and research studies, testified before legislators on matters of national importance, and spoke to the media about key challenges, decisions, and policies. Five years after the crisis, some of these same regulators spoke directly to me about choices they made in this period. Collectively, this body of evidence indicates that banking regulators in each country subscribed to fundamentally different principles of economic order in this crucial period, with implications for the kinds of regulatory goals and strategies they prioritized in their regulatory roles.

For a hint into the content of these distinctive regulatory worldviews, contrast the following excerpts from speeches given by US, Canadian, and Spanish banking regulators at some point between the late 1990s and early 2000s:

It is critically important to recognize that no market is ever truly unregulated. The self-interest of market participants generates private market regulation. Thus, the real question is not whether a market should be regulated. Rather, the real question is whether government intervention strengthens or weakens private regulation. If . . . private market regulation is effective, then government regulation is at best unnecessary. At worst, the introduction of government regulation may actually weaken the effectiveness of regulation if government regulation is itself ineffective or undermines incentives for private market regulation. (Alan Greenspan, chairman of the Federal Reserve in the United States, February 21, 1997)[1]

Financial regulation is ultimately about maintaining public confidence in a stable financial system, a very important linchpin for a healthy economy. Financial regulation is also about protecting consumers. . . . Promoting safety and soundness is about consumer protection in a very fundamental way. We know that any financial sector over history, left to itself, has been susceptible to instability. Financial systems don't in my view always work according to perfect financial economic models. . . . Prudential regulation is designed to be a counterweight to the potential for problems. Consumers want confidence they will get their money back. (Nicholas Le Pan, superintendent of the Office of the Superintendent of Financial Institutions in Canada, 2005)[2]

It must also be remembered that situations of intense changes in the environment are the least amenable to stagnation or complacency. For this reason, it is important [for regulators] to insist that credit institutions engage in prudent capital strategies, and operate with ample holdings of high-quality reserves, because this is the way to make transition[s] . . . proceed more smoothly and with a better chance of achieving competitive advantages in the face of changes. (D. Pedro Pablo Villasante, Bank of Spain director general of Banking Supervision, April 27, 2004)[3]

A side-by-side reading of these statements suggests that these regulators were preoccupied by distinctly different problems, and that these problem definitions share important similarities with the prevailing diagnosis that emerged to explain the crises of the 1980s in each country. American regulators, still reeling from a crisis attributed to the incentive-distorting effects of the government safety net and to regulatory forbearance, remained preoccupied by the perceived dangers of insufficient market discipline throughout the 1990s and 2000s. Although the specific strategies they pursued changed over time, their commitment to enhancing the influence of market discipline in banking never waned. Canadian regulators, who gained new powers and authority in the aftermath of a crisis attributed to the state's failure to protect the rights and interests of the banking public, remained preoccupied by the dangers of inadequate safeguards for depositors and policyholders, which undercut public confidence in the banking system. They experimented with different strategies of striking the right balance between protecting vulnerable users of financial services and respecting the autonomy of those "doing the business" (bank managers and directors).[4] Spanish regulators, still recovering from a crisis blamed on the combination of rising competitive pressures and insufficient regulatory powers to address the problem, remained preoccupied by the dangers of uncontrolled market forces in the 1990s and 2000s. They approached regulation with an eye toward enhancing the state oversight and direction of bank activities.

Using the speeches, writings, and comments of banking regulators themselves, this chapter describes the distinctive worldviews that defined regulatory policy making in each country, emphasizing the connection to the once-latent, now-dominant principles of regulatory order that emerged to prominence after the late 1980s. It explains how the prevailing interpretations of the crises of the 1980s—and the principles of order they reflected—carried forward to shape the goals and approaches of national banking regulators in the 1990s and 2000s.

This argument offers new insight into the sources of the distinctive national regulatory frameworks of the immediate precrisis era. Departing from conventional economic or political explanations, and even from explanations that emphasize the effects of broader changes in economic thought, I argue that fully understanding these divergent regulatory approaches requires understanding how national banking regulators interpreted the events of the recent past. As the guardians of order in the banking system, regulators are highly attuned to the lessons learned from recent episodes of disorder. Yet as the previous chapters have shown, these lessons were always a matter of interpretation—interpretations shaped, in all cases, by the principles of order embodied in established political and regulatory institutions. Banking regulators, then, are not just members of professional communities. They are also members of national societies and influenced by the distinctive historical experiences and institutions of these societies.

Banking Regulation in a Deregulated and Globalizing World

Thus far, I have mostly focused on the decisions and arguments of legislators: congressional policy makers in the United States, members of Parliament in Canada, and members of the Cortes Generales (or, during the Franco era, members of the administrative state) in Spain. This focus was appropriate when the goal was explaining developments in financial regulation prior to the 1990s. However, as financial deregulation lifted more and more statutory restrictions on bank structures and activities, domestic legislators also lost much of the control they had once enjoyed over financial policy making. By the mid-1990s, banking regulation had become the domain of civil servants housed within semi-independent regulatory agencies, which were often (though not always) located within politically independent central banks. From this point onward, the story will focus on developments in policy making at these regulatory agencies, specifically the Federal Reserve in the United States, the Office of the Superintendent of Financial Institutions (OSFI) in Canada, and the Bank of Spain in Spain.

Importantly, even as financial deregulation increased the power of domestic banking regulators vis-à-vis domestic legislators, other simultaneous trends at the international level were restricting the autonomy of these regulators. After 1988, regulators from all the world's major financial capitals agreed to abide by the terms of the Basel Capital Accord, a transnational regulatory framework developed by the Basel Committee for Banking Supervision, located at the Bank for International Settlements in Basel, Switzerland. The Basel Committee, which originally included representatives from the central banks of each of the G-10 countries, had formed to solve a common problem in the early 1970s. As financial markets became increasingly volatile after the collapse of the Bretton Woods system, national regulators were eager for banks to hold more capital to protect against unexpected losses. Yet they hesitated to unilaterally impose regulatory restrictions that might place domestic banks at a competitive disadvantage. The 1988 Basel Accord (later known as Basel I) solved this dilemma by establishing minimum standards for bank capital adequacy that applied to all internationally active banks.

Under the terms of Basel I, banks were required to hold at least 8 percent (or 8 cents on every dollar) in regulatory capital against their risk-weighted assets. "Risk weighting" involved assigning bank assets to one of four risk-weight categories or risk buckets, each with its own regulatory capital charge (of 0, 20, 50, or 100 percent). Loans or investments that presented serious credit risk to banks, like commercial real estate lending or loans to small businesses or non-OECD governments, generally carried the full (100 percent) regulatory capital charge. That meant that the bank would need to hold $8 in regulatory capital for each $100 of the loan or investment. Less risky assets, including bonds issued by the governments of other OECD countries, short-term loans to other banks, and residential mortgages, carried lower regulatory capital charges, in line with the lower risk they presented to bank solvency. For assets like these, the bank was only required to hold a smaller amount of regulatory capital (between $0 and $4 for each $100 of the loan or investment, depending on the capital charge). Basel I also established a standardized definition of regulatory capital that specified the range of resources that qualified as capital for regulatory purposes.[5]

The provisions of Basel I were gradually amended over the 1990s and 2000s. The most significant change occurred in January 2001, when the Basel Committee issued a formal proposal to develop a new Basel Capital Accord (Basel II) that would retain the same 8 percent regulatory capital standard but would incorporate new methods for risk weighting assets. Instead of assigning assets to four broad risk buckets, Basel II would rely more heavily on a bank's own internal assessments of credit risk in calculating capital charges.[6] In this way, regulatory capital requirements were expected to become more sensitive to variation in the specific risks a bank had assumed—or at least the risks the bank *reported* assuming. In 2004, the Basel Committee formally agreed to adopt the proposed Basel II framework; member countries were asked to implement the new provisions by the start of 2007. In practice, however, most Basel member countries had not yet finished implementing the Basel II framework when the global financial crisis struck.

The adoption of the Basel Capital Accord led to lasting changes in bank behavior and narrowed the scope of domestic regulatory authority. These changes were real and important and have been thoroughly discussed elsewhere.[7] However, scholarship has had much less to say about the causes of ongoing *divergence* in regulatory standards across Basel member countries, an equally important trend that occurred alongside the international regulatory convergence of the 1990s and 2000s.

Fully understanding how national regulatory standards could continue to diverge even across countries that complied with the Basel Accord requires getting a bit into the regulatory weeds. Like most other forms of transnational regulation, the Basel Accord was designed to appeal to policy makers across a range of national settings. In practice, this meant that many of its provisions were created to be flexible, to leave considerable room for local discretion in regulatory policy making. One important way that national standards could continue to diverge under the Basel Accord involved different national definitions of underlying regulatory concepts. As one example that would prove particularly important in the 2008 crisis, regulators in different Basel member countries varied in their definitions of the point at which the financial support banks offered to third-party securitization conduits should be considered a "liquidity enhancement" (e.g., a promise to help with cash flow issues, but not solvency issues) or a "credit enhancement" (e.g., a riskier form of support that actively protected investors in the event of insolvency). These different definitions of the underlying concept held implications for calculating regulatory capital. Under the terms of Basel I, liquidity enhancements carried a 0 percent regulatory capital charge, while credit enhancements carried much higher capital charges (often 50 percent or more). Depending on where regulators chose to draw the definitional line, then, banks in different Basel member countries might engage in similar activities yet face different capital requirements.

Regulators in different countries also differed in their approach to determining which firms were eligible for Basel-style regulation. Technically, the Basel standards were supposed to apply to all internationally active banks. But which financial institutions counted as a "bank" for regulatory purposes? Did this category cover only deposit-taking institutions, as in the United States, or should it also encompass the financial subsidiaries of banks and standalone investment banks, as in Spain? Regulatory standards could also diverge across countries because of the common practice of "gold-plating." Domestic regulators were always free to go above and beyond the minimum regulatory standards outlined in Basel I, and sometimes they chose to do exactly that, creating additional restrictions or imposing stricter capital requirements than required. Finally, Basel I covered only one dimension of banking practice (capital adequacy). Domestic regulators were free to adopt different standards for other banking practices (e.g., loan loss provisioning) that had the potential to affect both capital adequacy and safety and soundness through effects on the size and quality of other kinds of bank reserves.

Before getting into how principles of order shaped these different regulatory approaches, it is worth entertaining another possible explanation for the regulatory developments of this period: changes in economic thought. The economics discipline transformed over the course of the 1960s and 1970s, as neoliberal ideas associated with the Chicago school of economics outflanked Keynesianism to become the new dominant paradigm. A number of sociologists have suggested that this paradigmatic shift contributed to the rise of increasingly permissive, hands-off economic regulation. As sociologist Dustin Avent-Holt argues, it was this ideological revolution that "made possible the diffusion of an alternative cultural understanding of markets" that emphasized the benefits of unregulated competition and government noninterference.[8] And because economists and their allies were already embedded in regulatory agencies and political parties when this paradigm shift in economic thought took hold, sociologists Elizabeth Popp Berman and Stephanie Mudge argue, these actors were also uniquely well-positioned to translate this cultural understanding into concrete economic and social policy change.[9]

While this transformation within the economics discipline was likely a necessary foundation for the regulatory changes that followed, it was not sufficient to bring these changes about. Economists holding doctorate degrees held regulatory power in the banking sector in all three countries under discussion (though there were more regulators with PhDs in economics in the United States and Spain than in Canada). Recall that the Spanish banking regulators had, in many cases, trained alongside some of their American or British counterparts in top US and UK economics departments.[10] Regulators in each of these countries, in other words, were exposed to similar abstract economic ideas, yet still approached regulatory practice in different ways. It turns out that abstract economic theory did not offer a precise playbook for what exactly regulators should do to keep the banking system stable and prosperous. And banking regulators in all three countries, as we will see, filled in this gap by drawing from the perceived lessons learned from recent episodes of financial disorder.

An account of regulatory change that focuses exclusively on changes in economic thought also struggles to account for the timing of regulatory change within countries. In the United States, for example, the Chicago school revolution unfolded in the 1960s and 1970s, yet the decisive shift in the orientation of the American banking regulators did not occur until much later, in the late 1980s. As late as 1985, Paul Volcker was still speaking out against policy makers relying too heavily on market forces in regulating or supervising banks. Less than five years later, however, Alan Greenspan was actively championing enhanced market discipline as the solution to everything that ailed the banking system. Something must have happened within this narrow timeframe to generate such an abrupt about-face in regulatory orientation; I argue that the missing piece is regulators' institutionally structured interpretation of the thrift and banking crises of the late 1980s.

A final point before moving on to the details of this story. Important differences in the structure of each country's financial regulatory system in the 1990s and 2000s often make direct comparisons between countries difficult. For example, in both Canada and Spain, a single regulatory agency had exclusive authority over prudential regulation for commercial banks (this was OSFI and the Bank of Spain, respectively). Yet this same authority was subdivided across multiple regulatory agencies in the United States, including the Federal Reserve, the Office of the Comptroller of the Currency, the Federal Deposit Insurance Corporation, and state-level banking regulators. To allow for comparison across countries, my discussion of the US case will focus primarily on regulatory decisions made by the Federal Reserve. This was the American regulatory agency charged with regulating bank holding companies (the structural form that most large, internationally active US banks assumed) as well as an especially active member of the Basel Committee for Banking Supervision. In these respects, the Federal Reserve is the most direct analog to OSFI in Canada or the Bank of Spain in Spain. Additionally, these three countries also varied in the extent to which the central bank had the authority to establish prudential regulation for banks. In both the United States and Spain, the central bank (the Federal Reserve and the Bank of Spain, respectively) had this authority; in Canada, however, the prudential regulator (OSFI) was a separate institution from the central bank (the Bank of Canada).

As we will see in chapters 9 and 10, these structural differences in national banking systems also contributed to the divergent development of regulatory policy, typically by influencing the range of policy options that were open to banking regulators in different countries. Whenever this is the case, I make a point to acknowledge it in the narrative. Yet even as national banking regulators responded to different kinds of choice opportunities in this period, it is important to underscore that their responses were still broadly predictable. In each country, regulators followed a distinctive "style of play" that aligned with by-now familiar understandings of the sources of economic stability and prosperity.

Regulating to Enhance Market Discipline in the United States

By the start of the 1990s, US policy makers had settled on a clear diagnosis of the financial crises of the 1980s. Government protection, in the form of the government safety net in banking, had facilitated disorder by creating moral hazard. Since bank depositors, creditors, and shareholders no longer bore the full costs of bank failure with deposit insurance in place, these market actors had also lost their natural incentives to restrain imprudent bank behavior. In the face of this diminished market discipline, financial disaster had followed, as thrifts and banks had abused their freedom from market restraint by embracing excessively risky strategies. Compounding the problem, government regulators had lacked the political will to address these distorted bank incentives through strong regulation; instead, they had chosen to ease regulatory standards as troubled banks and thrifts sank even further into distress. Or so the story went.

It is apparent that banking regulators at the Federal Reserve in the 1990s and 2000s subscribed to the same understanding of the major causes of the crises of the 1980s. Consider how Federal Reserve Governor Alice Rivlin describes the key lessons learned from this experience in a 1996 speech:

> In the 1930s, Americans learned, expensively, about the hazards of not having a safety net in a crisis that almost wiped out the banking system. In the 1980s, they learned a lot about the hazards of having a safety net, especially about the moral hazard associated with deposit insurance. Deposit insurance, which had seemed so benign and so successful in building confidence and preventing runs on banks, suddenly revealed its downside for all to see. Some insured institutions, mostly thrifts, but also savings banks, and not a few commercial banks, were taking on risks with a "heads I win, tails you lose" attitude—sometimes collecting on high stakes bets but often leaving deposit insurance funds to pick up the pieces. At the same time, some regulators . . . were compounding the problem—and greatly increasing the ultimate cost of its resolution—by engaging in regulatory "forbearance" when faced with technically insolvent institutions.[11]

Here, Rivlin, like US legislators only a few years before, provides an account of the crisis that emphasizes the moral hazard effects of deposit insurance and regulatory forbearance as its primary causes. This general perspective was widely shared among banking regulators at the Federal Reserve. When Alan Greenspan, chairman of the Board of Governors at the Federal Reserve, argued in 1997 that "*without federal deposit insurance*, private markets presumably would never have permitted thrift institutions to purchase the portfolios that brought down the industry insurance fund and left future generations of taxpayers

responsible for huge losses," he was simply articulating the dominant regulatory view.[12]

This understanding of the most recent episode of financial disorder held
important implications for regulatory priorities at the Federal Reserve. If disorder emerges from too little market discipline, it follows that it is up to regulators to restore this missing factor. As Federal Reserve Governor Laurence
Meyer put the point in a 1999 speech: "I have noted that the safety net damp-
ens the incentive of the market to assess risks in banks. The solution is not to
ignore the potential for market discipline, but rather to find ways to enhance its
role in banking."[13] This overarching American emphasis on enhancing market
discipline manifested in three concrete regulatory strategies in the 1990s and
2000s: (1) mimicking market responses as much as possible; (2) scaling back
on existing government interventions and proactively blocking the creation
of new ones; and (3) increasing the quality and quantity of information banks
disclosed to market participants.

Greenspan, speaking in 1997, outlined the logic behind the Federal Reserve's
emphasis on ensuring that regulatory standards would mirror expected market
responses as closely as possible. Noting that the government safety net made
"necessary a degree of supervision and regulation [in banking] that would not
be necessary without the existence of the safety net," Greenspan suggested
that regulators and supervisors had no choice but "to act as a surrogate for
market discipline."[14] In regulating, however, these actors still had the duty
not to make the underlying problem (of absent market forces) even worse.
To avoid further disrupting the market mechanisms that facilitated order in
competitive systems, regulators should mimic market discipline as closely as
possible, or "endeavor to simulate the market responses that would occur if
there were no safety net."[15]

The specific strategies regulators used in pursuit of this goal changed
over time. In the early to mid-1990s, they focused on forcing banks to hold
more capital. As Greenspan explained this logic in a 1990 speech, because
the (government-safety-net-induced) absence of market discipline allowed
"too many banking organizations to travel down the road of operating with
modest capital levels," regulators were obligated to mimic what market actors
would have done in the absence of this safety net—that is, to introduce "capital
requirements that would, over time, be more consistent with what the market
would require if the safety net were more modest."[16] When viewed from this
perspective, strong regulatory capital requirements were entirely compatible
with the goal of enhancing market discipline in banking. However, as the 1990s
went on, the US banking regulators started to sour on high capital requirements as the solution to the problems the presence of the safety net had created. As Fed Governor Laurence Meyer explained in a 2000 speech, "After
the mid-1990s, [our] emphasis on high capital requirements as a corrective

to moral hazard began to change, as concerns that regulatory capital requirements had market-distorting effects of their own started to mount."[17]

Regulators at the Federal Reserve, always preoccupied with the dangers of inadequate market discipline and the moral hazard all government interventions created, began to worry that their own regulatory interventions (that is, capital requirements) were making these underlying problems worse. Their specific concern was that regulatory requirements to hold more capital had created powerful incentives for banks to game (or "arbitrage") existing regulatory standards, often to no productive purpose. Banks complying with the capital regulations of Basel I, for example, faced a powerful temptation to "cherry pick" assets, retaining those at the top of each Basel risk bucket while offloading those at the bottom of each bucket. This cherry-picking strategy appealed to banks because it allowed them to maximize risk (and potential rewards) for a given level of regulatory capital. Although regulators around the world saw problems in this practice, regulatory concerns about the incentive-distorting effects of capital requirements were especially acute in the United States. Banking regulators here already assumed that government interference with market forces was the leading cause of disorder in the financial system. Accordingly, any government intervention known to further distort the incentives of market players seemed especially incompatible with broader American regulatory goals—whatever the other benefits.

These concerns help to explain why regulators at the Federal Reserve were at the forefront of the international movement to reform the Basel framework after the late 1990s. They saw this effort as an extension of their broader strategy of bringing banking regulation more in line with the anticipated responses of market actors. The specific objective of the Basel II reform was to narrow the gap between a bank's regulatory capital (e.g., formal capital requirements outlined in Basel I) and its economic capital (e.g., the amount of capital banks voluntarily hold against the risks of particular assets, which reflects "the bank's own [internal] assessment of risk and capital needs"). The basic idea was that if capital requirements could be better aligned with what banks were already doing on the risk measurement and capital allocation fronts—that is, if they narrowed the gap between regulatory and economic capital—banks would naturally lose the incentive to participate in unproductive "regulatory capital arbitrage" schemes that only minimized regulatory compliance costs.[18]

Of course, as many contemporary observers pointed out, any regulatory approach that substitutes banks' own internal risk measures and capital allocation practices for the judgment of regulators might also result in banks holding substantially less capital. The US banking regulators had a clear stance on this trade-off. What mattered most to them was avoiding regulations that increased, rather than mitigated, market distortions—even if this goal came at the expense of the size of the buffers banks held against unexpected losses.

As Greenspan argued in a 2001 speech, the primary advantage of reforming Basel I was that the new Basel II approach would "better simulate . . . what an informed market and management would require for bank capital" through linking capital requirements more directly to the specific risks an individual bank had assumed (at least in the judgment of its managers).[19] Viewed from this perspective, the idea that "minimum regulatory equity capital might fall for some banks . . . on the basis of their portfolio risk profiles" seemed to be a helpful feature of this new regulatory system, not a bug.

The same commitment to boosting the influence of market forces in banking also motivated regulators at the Federal Reserve to scale back other kinds of government interventions and avoid the creation of new ones. Guided by the understanding that a key lesson from the crises of the 1980s was that "private market regulation can be quite effective, provided that government does not get in its way," regulators sought to create greater room for beneficial market forces by getting out of the market's way.[20] They started from the assumption that government regulation and market discipline were substitutes, and that supervision by the government was inherently inferior to supervision by an impartial, all-seeing competitive marketplace. As Alan Greenspan explained in 1990, "Rules, regulations, and supervision cannot substitute for market signals; they can only attempt to filter the worst mis-signals that seem to suggest to bank management that unusual risk-taking is permissible, if not desirable."[21]

The implications for regulatory strategy were clear. Throughout the 1990s and 2000s, regulators at the Federal Reserve actively opposed most attempts to expand the government's footprint in the banking system. Unsurprisingly, they were strong opponents of expanding the scope, generosity, or coverage of the government safety net (e.g., deposit insurance)—the primary villain of the crises of the 1980s—and supported multiple proposals to reform the deposit insurance system to make it more risk sensitive.[22] However, this opposition to government intervention extended beyond the safety net. As Greenspan explained in a 2001 speech, US regulators were also extremely reluctant to expand the scope of prudential regulation, on the grounds that increasing government regulation or supervision of banks might "intensify the perception of private parties that their responsibility for self-protecting diligence is reduced."[23] The underlying idea was that depositors, shareholders, and creditors (that is, the market) would fail to effectively supervise banks not just in the presence of a safety net, but also in the presence of strong (government) prudential supervision of banking organizations. If government actors were already monitoring and restraining risky bank practices, why would market actors assume a redundant role?

Of course, these government actors had been forced to step in and supervise banks in the first place because market actors, influenced by the government safety net, could not be trusted to keep risky banks in line. In the eyes of the

American banking regulators, these dynamics created a dangerous catch-22, or in Greenspan's words, "a kind of vicious circle of government replacement of market oversight," that regulators had a responsibility to prevent—or at least not exacerbate.[24] This understanding helps to explain why regulators at the Federal Reserve continually resisted expanding more intensive, bank-style regulatory restrictions to other types of financial institutions (like investment banks or the financial subsidiaries of commercial banks) and to novel financial innovations like securitization or derivatives.[25]

As a final strategy to boost the influence of market discipline, regulators at the Federal Reserve sought to proactively enhance the quantity and transparency of the information banks disclosed to financial markets. The idea was that if market actors were to effectively discipline banks, they needed accurate and abundant information on the activities and strategies banks were pursuing. As Greenspan remarked in a 1996 speech, "It is only through adequate disclosure that market discipline can effectively be brought to bear as an important complement to supervisory oversight."[26] As the US financial system became increasingly complex in the 2000s, this regulatory prioritization of information transparency and disclosure only became more pronounced.[27] The implication was that government intervention was warranted only in the rare cases in which it allowed market participants to discipline banks more effectively.

Striking the Right (Regulatory) Balance in Canada

By the start of the 1990s, Canadian policy makers had settled on a clear understanding of the causes of the crisis of the 1980s. Policy makers blamed the crisis on the combination of changes within the banking profession and the failure of government to keep pace with these changes. Industry self-regulation may have once been sufficient to protect vulnerable users of financial services, but those days were long gone. In the weak regulatory and supervisory environment that had defined the 1980s, it had only been too easy for risk-hungry banks to exploit the public's trust and destroy public confidence by pursuing imprudent strategies.

Regulators at the newly established Office of the Superintendent of Financial Institutions (OSFI) clearly subscribed to this diagnosis of recent events. Guided by the desire to avoid a repeat of the 1980s, Canadian regulators believed that their primary duty was to take a more proactive role in maintaining consumer confidence by actively protecting depositors and policyholders from bank exploitation.[28] As OSFI Superintendent John Palmer explained in a 1998 speech, OSFI's primary mission was "a prudential one: We work to safeguard depositors and policyholders from undue loss. And we contribute to public confidence in the financial system."[29] Compared to their American counterparts, then, the Canadian banking regulators saw a more legitimate role for government in supervising banks. As Nicholas Le Pan, who replaced Palmer as OSFI superintendent in 2001, argued in a 2005 speech, "We know that any financial sector over history, left to itself, has been susceptible to instability"[30]—a reality that, in the view of Canadian regulators, warranted some degree of government regulation and supervision, safety net or no safety net.

Yet from the start, Canadian regulators also worried about the competitive impact of unduly restricting the autonomy of bank managers and directors. In the same 1998 speech where he described OSFI's mission, Superintendent John Palmer also warned that it was essential for regulatory standard setters to maintain due regard for the ability of Canadian banks to "compete with much larger foreign competitors and unregulated institutions."[31] In this respect, regulators at OSFI, like Canadian legislators before them, were highly attuned to the need to strike the right "balance" between prudential and competitive considerations in regulation, a commitment enshrined in the formal mandate of this regulatory agency.[32] Canadian regulators perceived much more tension in efforts to promote prosperity and stability than either their American or their Spanish counterparts. In Canada, stability and prosperity were thought to derive from different sources: government intervention was necessary to protect consumers and keep the financial system safe and stable, as the recent crisis had shown, but prosperity still stemmed from leaving the managers and directors of banks to their own devices.

Canadian concerns about the potential for regulation to interfere with bank performance became increasingly salient in the 1990s, as financial markets became increasingly globalized. One regulator, describing the climate at OSFI in this period, thought "Canada was being left behind. Our banks weren't innovating like the major American banks, like the major money center banks in the UK. And our banks needed to do more of what was going on in the States. . . . There were people here that suggested that our whole financial system was going to be hollowed out . . . hollowed out and consumed by the U.S. and British banks."[33] Over the course of the decade that followed, regulatory effectiveness became even more synonymous with regulatory skill in striking this "critical balance" between preserving safety and soundness within an environment that still "benefit[ted] consumers through a range of competitive options and pricing."[34] This overarching goal of striking the right balance manifested in three concrete regulatory strategies: (1) focusing regulatory efforts on the buffers banks maintained against potential losses; (2) pursuing "harmonization" with international regulatory standards; and (3) maintaining a "principles-based" approach to regulation and supervision.

Regulators at OSFI in the 1990s and 2000s prioritized banks maintaining sizeable and high-quality buffers against losses. As OSFI Superintendent Le Pan explained in a 2005 speech, this regulatory approach was expected to serve prudential goals by acting as "a counterweight to the potential for problems.

Consumers want confidence they will get their money back."[35] Bank capital, "the main defense against insolvency in the event things turn out worse than expected," was regarded as an especially important counterweight.[36] This explains why the Canadian banking regulators viewed their proactive push for conservative capital buffers as "core to what we do as regulators and supervisors." This same regulatory strategy also served broader Canadian regulatory goals in a different way: if regulators could be confident that the *users* of financial services would be well protected from the fallout from bank risk taking (as they were when banks maintained sizeable capital buffers), regardless of the strategies the bank pursued, regulators could also justify taking a more hands-off approach to regulating the strategic activities of those "actually doing the business" (bank managers and directors).[37] From the perspective of the regulators at OSFI, this strong emphasis on the adequacy of bank reserves allowed them to have it all: regulators could both keep consumers safe and confident and at the same time avoid too much interference with the strategic choices of banks.

As concerns about the global competitive position of Canadian banks intensified in the 1990s, Canadian banking regulators increasingly viewed the pursuit of regulatory harmonization as crucial to striking the right balance in regulation. They became much more concerned with "regulatory efficiency" in this period, defined as the balance between the costs and benefits of prudential regulation.[38] How could regulators maximize these benefits while also minimizing the costs? From their view, at least part of the answer lay in adopting regulatory restrictions that were identical to those found in other countries whenever possible. As Superintendent John Palmer explained the dilemma, "While we need to maintain prudential walls around our institutions, those walls can't be higher than those which we see in our major trading partners."[39] Increasingly, the regulators at OSFI felt that the best way to secure high-quality regulation for Canadian financial institutions was to work to improve regulation for all global financial institutions within transnational standards-setting bodies (like the Basel Committee) or in partnerships with regulators in peer countries. Beyond this, striking the right balance required that Canadian departures from international regulatory standards remain the exception, not the rule. Superintendent Le Pan underscored this point in a 2002 speech, noting that "our regulatory regime must not disadvantage Canadian financial institutions. . . . Competitiveness in rule setting may require that we think about adopting the approaches of others and preserving our differences only in the relatively few areas where differences matter to us for policy reasons."[40]

Finally, OSFI regulators also endorsed a "principles-based" approach to regulation and supervision. At the most basic level, a principles-based approach outlines rough standards for appropriate bank behavior but leaves the specific details of compliance to the judgment of bank managers and directors.[41] Under this model, regulation is much more of an iterative conversation between the regulator and regulated than a checklist of predetermined and specific rules. As Le Pan described this approach in a 2001 speech to banking industry leaders, "OSFI sets general guidelines for [regulatory compliance] systems and lets you devise and run them, rather than us being rigid in details. We rely on governance at institutions, with selective verification that those processes are effective, rather than adopt a comprehensive checklist approach in our assessment."[42]

This principles-based approach was a point of pride at OSFI throughout the 1990s and 2000s, often cited by regulators as one of the key strengths of Canada's regulatory system. This approach to regulation was so highly valued, at least in part, because of the role it was believed to play in allowing regulators to strike the right balance between prudence and competitiveness in rule setting. This approach continued to rely heavily on the judgment of bank managers (still viewed as vital to financial system prosperity) but also allowed the government to exercise persuasive normative influence. Historically, Canadian policy makers had assumed that elite bankers' intrinsic sense of professionalism and duty would be enough to keep the banking industry in line. While the crises of the 1980s had shown that this assumption was no longer justified, the legacy of the principle of *elite autonomy* continued in the form of a belief that the most effective form of bank regulation would leave the specific details of compliance up to those actually "doing the business."[43]

This emphasis on a principles-based approach reflected a distinctively Canadian view of the role of bank managers in producing economic order. In Spain, regulators assumed that bank managers and market actors like shareholders and depositors suffered from natural biases that made it hard for them to maintain order without external regulatory help. Yet even regulators in the laissez-faire United States were much more skeptical than their Canadian counterparts about the capacity of bank managers (alone) to follow the right principles without detailed rules. It is hard to imagine a similar principles-based approach taking hold in the United States, where regulators assumed that bankers freed from the discipline of the market (or the discipline of government regulation as a grossly inferior substitute) would automatically attempt to bend the rules and take excessive risks. By contrast, even after the disruptions of the 1980s, the Canadian banking regulators were much more likely to see long-term interests of bank managers as entirely compatible with the public's interests. Although regulators at OSFI often described their regulatory motto as "trust, but verify,"[44] in comparative perspective, it was not the "verify" part that made the Canadian approach distinctive, but the "trust" part. Canadian bank executives and managers continued to enjoy unusual leeway in determining the specifics of regulatory compliance well into the 1990s and 2000s.

Facilitating Centralized Oversight and Direction in Spain

By the start of the 1990s, Spanish policy makers had also settled on a clear diagnosis of the financial crisis of 1977–85. This account implied that the crisis had emerged from both the collapse of the "banking status quo" in Spain, which had unleashed disruptive competitive pressures and paved the way for unqualified groups to enter the banking business, and the inability of regulators to effectively address these problems. From this perspective, it was not just that Spanish regulators had lacked sufficient awareness of problems in the banking system (although this was part of it). They had also lacked the power and authority to do something about the problems they identified.

Regulators at the Bank of Spain had played an active role in constructing the interpretation of the crisis of 1977–85, and they clearly continued to subscribe to this interpretation in the 1990s and 2000s. In a retrospective account, Bank of Spain Governor Jaime Caruana highlighted "macroeconomic factors, weak regulatory frameworks, and bank mismanagement" as the leading causes of the crisis, emphasizing the rapid expansion in bank credit that had accompanied financial liberalization as one especially salient cause.[45] He argued that the rising competitive pressures that had defined this era contributed to both "credit risk mistakes" and "over-optimistic perception[s] of low risk" among bankers.[46] As he put the point in a 2002 speech, "Competition is a key factor in explaining credit supply dynamics. . . . Most credit risk mistakes are actually made during the expansionary phase, when optimism is prevailing, although only in the downturn will they become evident."[47] However, Caruana and other regulators also clearly believed that this crisis had gotten out of hand primarily because regulators had lacked the power and tools to effectively address these natural market dynamics.[48]

This interpretation of the crisis could not have been more different from the interpretation developing in the same period in the United States. Rather than attributing the crisis to the absence of market forces, regulators at the Bank of Spain saw it as a product of disruptive market forces, left unchecked. Moreover, instead of assuming that banking regulators and supervisors inherently lacked the motivation to intervene until it was too late, Spanish regulators assumed that these actors were actually among the actors *least* likely to engage in "forbearance" during difficult times. Consider how Caruana depicted the actions of Spanish banking supervisors during the 1977–85 crisis:

> One thing that the examiners at the Bank of Spain liked to repeat many times about the lessons of the crisis was that the insolvent banks showed different levels of losses, depending on who assessed them: the lowest level is the losses assessed by the banker; the next is that of the external auditor; then the supervisor; and finally the restructuring institution (DGF)—the

one that is in charge of the intervention—provides the highest figure, and usually, this is the real one. The lesson here is the importance of the supervisors' proactive assessment of the health of the troubled banks.

This account of the crisis implies that the Spanish regulators, drawing from the principle of *state sovereignty*, perceived market participants (like bankers, private auditors, or shareholders) as fundamentally less well equipped to supervise and regulate banks than more impartial, clear-eyed, public-minded public servants. In regulatory speeches throughout the 1990s and 2000s, regulators at the Bank of Spain frequently depicted market participants (like bankers, shareholders, and depositors) as inherently myopic, overly quick to follow their peers into suboptimal strategies, excessively focused on the short-term, and prone to overreaction.[49] By contrast, banking regulators and supervisors—because of their expert training and impartial, public-serving mission—were cast as much less likely to fall prey to these biases. It was thus right and proper for regulators and supervisors to assume the leading role in governing banks; indeed, from the Spanish perspective, the crisis of 1977–85 would have never become one if these actors had been given sufficient powers.

These different diagnoses of the crises of the 1980s directly translated into different regulatory goals in the 1990s and 2000s. Where American regulators focused on boosting the influence of market discipline at any cost, Spanish regulators focused on enhancing the ability of the state (in the form of the Bank of Spain) to oversee and direct bank behavior. Like the Canadian banking regulators in the same period, the Spanish banking regulators also assumed that the state had a duty to proactively intervene and restrain bank behaviors that might lead to instability. Moreover, unlike their Canadian counterparts, regulators at the Bank of Spain assumed that this responsibility went beyond protecting consumers and strengthening the capacity of financial institutions to "deal with adverse events." From the Spanish perspective, regulators were also tasked with smoothing and enhancing the actual functioning of the financial system, by proactively "harmoniz[ing] the interests of all parties involved (banks, savers and investors) with general interests."[50]

This broader mandate, of course, also required the Spanish banking regulators to take a much more active role in directing bank strategy. As Caruana explained in a 2002 speech, the Spanish regulators believed that they had a duty to "*creat[e] the right incentives* for market participants to not react in excess in a given cyclical position and avoid excessive misalignments," which justified a heavier-handed regulatory approach.[51] Indeed, the Spanish banking regulators viewed the effectiveness of market discipline itself as contingent on the quality of regulation and supervision. We see this in how Bank of Spain Deputy Governor Gonzalo Gil attributed the 2001 collapse of US energy company Enron to a "weak supervisory environment" that had caused "the excessive complacency of investors, and ultimately, the relaxation of market discipline."[52]

In pursuit of this overarching goal of enhancing state oversight and direction in banking, regulators at the Bank of Spain prioritized three regulatory strategies in the 1990s and 2000s: (1) counteracting or counterbalancing particularly disruptive market forces; (2) consolidating supervision and regulation; and (3) maintaining control over bank accounting standards. For most of this period, the Spanish banking regulators were especially attuned to the dangers associated with one market force in particular: procyclicality. Procyclicality refers to the tendency for financial market dynamics to amplify or exacerbate broader swings within the economy.[53] During upswings in the business cycle, banks often become overly optimistic and extend credit too freely, leading to problems when economic conditions inevitably decline. Similarly, during downturns, banks often become excessively conservative, sharply curtailing credit provision at the moment that the economy needs it most. From the standpoint of Spanish banking regulators, the disruptive "boom and bust" cycles that procyclical dynamics created represented a very salient form of "excessive misalignment" in the economy—one that regulators were duty bound to correct. If financial market participants were prone "to overreact to changes in the environment," then regulators must proactively counteract this tendency by "introduc[ing] rules that do not promote short-term strategies, but rather encourage counter-cyclical behavior."[54]

Regulators at the Bank of Spain also sought to enhance state oversight and direction by insisting on a consolidated approach to supervision and regulation. One of the key lessons from the crises of the 1980s, from their perspective, was the importance of evaluating the activities of financial groups as a unified whole, instead of treating each component (e.g., the commercial bank, other financial affiliates, bank subsidiaries located in other countries, etc.) as separate entities. In a retrospective reflection, Caruana directly connected this commitment to consolidated supervision to the lessons learned from the earlier crisis:

> In terms of the lessons that marked the way supervision has been done at the Bank of Spain since [the crisis] . . . one is the need for comprehensive, consolidated supervision. It is more than emphasis; it is almost an obsession. Examiners analyze the banking group, the whole group, interpreting regulation very strictly to encompass as much as possible. The lesson from the crisis was that it is sometimes a subsidiary of a subsidiary that ruins a bank.[55]

In the Spanish view, the 1977–85 crisis had reached such great heights because prominent financial organizations (like RUMASA) had successfully hidden risk exposures inside complex webs of affiliate organizations that remained opaque to regulatory view. To address this perceived cause of the crisis, and to correct for this deficiency moving forward, regulators at the Bank of Spain prioritized supervisory approaches that offered an extremely clear picture of everything a financial group was doing.[56]

A final strategy that the Spanish banking regulators used to enhance state oversight and direction was fighting to maintain their control over accounting standards for banks. Elsewhere, the same professional associations that established generally accepted accounting principles (GAAP) for other types of firms also established financial reporting standards for banks. Not so in Spain, where regulators at the Bank of Spain held the sole authority to dictate accounting standards for banks. In the two decades leading up to the 2008 crisis, the Spanish banking regulators fought hard to retain this unique power in the face of considerable international opposition, spending valuable political capital on this effort. As Caruana explained in a 2001 speech, this commitment was motivated by regulators' strong belief that "the practical experience of banking supervision over the last twenty years . . . has shown that accounting regulation has been a fundamental element in achieving a solid and stable financial system and efficient supervision."[57] This view made sense in light of the prevailing Spanish interpretation of the events of the recent past. In a context where regulators believed that the last crisis had been driven by too little regulatory awareness of risk exposures, this power to establish how banks reported their risks seemed like a power especially worth protecting.

Conclusion

This chapter used banking regulators' own words and publications to sketch the overarching regulatory goals that motivated their actions in the 1990s and 2000s. In all three countries, regulators sought to preserve safety and stability in the banking system while also ensuring that domestic banks would remain competitive on a global scale. Within this shared purpose, however, national regulators also subscribed to different understandings about how best to accomplish these aims. In each case, these understandings were informed by their recent experience of banking crisis—or more specifically, by the nation-specific principles of order that shaped how policy makers interpreted these events.

In the United States, Canada, and Spain, banking regulators believed that the crises of the 1980s had uncovered the limitations of the previous regulatory regime, and they were eager to restore the factors that had been missing. In comparative perspective, what is most striking is the degree to which these understandings of regulatory needs aligned with a preexisting, prevailing diagnosis of the crisis in each country. In the immediate aftermath of the crises of the 1980s, national legislators had sprung into action, introducing reforms that drew from particular conceptions of the primary causes of these episodes. This chapter revealed how the same interpretations also informed the way that actors at the Federal Reserve, OSFI, and the Bank of Spain approached their regulatory tasks in the 1990s and 2000s.

This connection is important because it implies that banking regulators at the Federal Reserve developed their obsessive focus on enhancing market discipline in the decades leading up to the 2008 crisis because they—like American legislators only a few years earlier—attributed the most recent serious financial crisis to the absence of this factor. It also helps to explain why banking regulators in Canada and Spain moved to embrace more interventionist regulatory approaches at a time when their US counterparts were actively turning their backs on these approaches. Canadian and Spanish policy makers had diagnosed the crises of the 1980s as products of inadequate regulatory powers or authority, and these prevailing diagnoses also informed the kinds of initiatives regulators pursued in the decades that followed. Regulators at OSFI in Canada, following the same pattern established by Canadian legislators, sought to balance a new commitment to expanded regulatory oversight for consumer protection with the need to avoid undue interference with the strategic choices of banks. Regulators at the Bank of Spain, on the other hand, had fewer compunctions about interfering with managerial judgment. Skeptical that bankers could achieve societally optimal outcomes without expert help, Spanish regulators focused on imposing greater oversight and direction on the banking industry.

The two chapters that follow trace the concrete policy impact of these distinctive regulatory worldviews in the United States, Canada, and Spain by illustrating how they shaped specific decisions in two key domains of regulation. Chapter 9 focuses on the regulation of bank exposure to a particular form of asset securitization—asset-backed commercial paper programs—that served as a key source of loss for many banks during the crisis. Chapter 10 focuses on the regulation of bank loan loss provisioning practices, which impacted the quality and size of the reserves banks held against losses suffered on lending activities. I focus on these two domains as case studies because they held direct implications for how banks experienced the crisis and have the advantage of allowing for relatively direct comparisons across countries.

It is nevertheless important to underscore that the influence of these different regulatory worldviews extended well beyond these domains. The influence of the American commitment to enhancing market discipline, the Canadian commitment to striking a balance between consumer protection and bank autonomy, and the Spanish commitment to enhancing state oversight and direction is evident in many of the other key regulatory choices that defined this period. National banking regulators also varied in how they conceptualized and regulated financial conglomerates, including the nonbank financial affiliates or subsidiaries of banks. They varied in their regulation of derivatives markets (and bank participation in these markets), in their desire to use subordinated debt as a regulatory tool, and in their implementation of Basel II. In each of these domains, too, national regulatory choices also followed predictable patterns that aligned with these distinctive principles of order.

9

Regulating Asset Securitization in the Post-Basel Era

Asset securitization played a starring role in the global financial crisis of the late 2000s. Prior to this era, banks had held assets like mortgages, auto loans, credit card receivables, or corporate trade receivables to maturity, keeping these loans on their books until they were fully repaid with interest. The rise of securitization revolutionized the banking business by allowing banks to transform these previously illiquid assets into securities that could be sold and traded in financial markets. Investors had long been hesitant to assume the kinds of risks banks assumed in lending to individual mortgage, auto loan, or credit card borrowers. Asset securitization allowed banks to repackage and sell this credit risk in a form that was much more appealing to investors.

Securitization transactions typically begin when an asset originator (often, though not always, a bank) sells a pool of medium- to long-term assets to a conduit, that is, a legally separate company with a narrowly defined purpose. The conduit then issues different stakes in the cash flow associated with these pooled assets to investors in the form of asset-backed securities (ABS). The actors who control the conduit then typically use the proceeds from these sales to finance new asset purchases, which may in turn be securitized.

Multiple features of this process enhance investor confidence in assuming credit risk. In pooling many loans and repackaging them in the form of securities, asset securitization makes investors more like banks: investors could now hold stakes in the risk associated with an entire asset portfolio, where the failure of any single borrower was unlikely to have much of an impact on the performance of the whole. Moreover, the practice of transferring assets to a legally separate company (the conduit) also made it easier for investors to separate the credit risk of the assets from the credit risk of the originating bank itself. Assets transferred to a conduit through securitization were "bankruptcy remote," which meant that the bank or its creditors could not claw back assets transferred to a conduit from investors in the event of bankruptcy.

In 1990s and 2000s, the global securitization market reached unprecedented heights, a process that contributed to the production of the global financial crisis. Many scholars have argued that the inherent complexity of securitization transactions, which generally combine hundreds or thousands of individual loans, also obscured the associated risk to market participants, leading many investors in ABS to assume much more risk than they realized.[1] Others have argued that the rise of securitization contributed to instability by eroding incentives for banks to effectively monitor and screen borrowers, because banks originating loans that are ultimately sold to investors lose the incentive to be cautious and prudent in lending.[2] Yet as economist Viral Acharya and colleagues have convincingly argued, one of the key ways that securitization impacted the financial health of commercial banks in particular involved the banks' *continued* exposure to the risk of securitized assets.

A closer look at dynamics in one massive securitization market, the asset-backed commercial paper (ABCP) market, helps to illustrate this point. In the 1990s and 2000s, banks around the world established securitization programs that financed the purchase of medium- and long-term assets by issuing short-term debt securities known as "asset-backed commercial paper" (ABCP). To create lucrative ABCP programs, banks transferred medium- and long-term assets to conduits they sponsored. The conduits then sold ABCP to investors, with the proceeds used to purchase and service additional medium- and long-term assets. The products of these ABCP programs became the largest short-term debt instrument in the world by the mid-2000s, with the total ABCP market valued at more than $1.2 trillion, surpassing even the market for US Treasury bills.

In August 2007, however, the global ABCP market collapsed.[3] The troubles began as some ABCP investors grew wary of the quality of the medium- and long-term assets backing these securities as problems in the mortgage market became more apparent. When some of these investors responded by failing to "roll over" or renew their ABCP holdings in the summer of 2007, others panicked and sought to quickly unwind their own ABCP exposures as well. Facing an increasingly serious funding shortfall, many ABCP programs were forced to sell off long-term assets at very low (fire-sale) prices.[4] These dynamics should have produced heavy losses for ABCP investors, but as the crisis grew, it became apparent that banks—and not investors—were absorbing most of the associated losses. "Securitization without risk transfer" was the cause of this trend: many of the banks that had sponsored ABCP programs had technically transferred their assets to ABCP conduits but remained first in line to absorb the associated losses because of the additional services they had continued to provide to these programs.[5] Making matters worse, the majority of sponsoring banks held no or very little regulatory capital against these risk exposures. They struggled to absorb the losses that followed.[6]

Although the events described above were a global phenomenon, they produced different fallout across national contexts. Different regulatory choices in key areas held important implications for how the ABCP crisis unfolded across countries, including for the United States, Canada, and Spain. Policy decisions in a few fine-grained regulatory domains affected the overall size of the ABCP market across countries, the extent to which banks (versus investors) were forced to absorb the losses when it collapsed, and the extent to which banks held sufficient capital to counterbalance these losses.

This chapter describes and explains the development of these divergent regulatory policy choices, which held direct implications for bank performance when the crisis hit. Its key argument is that each country's specific policies governing bank exposures to ABCP programs depended on the distinctive regulatory goals and worldviews outlined in the previous chapter. These worldviews gave rise to fundamentally different perceptions of bank participation in the securitization process and its relationship to effective regulation. In the United States, regulators regarded securitization as a prudential practice—a practice that actively made the banking system safer—while regulators in Spain saw the same practice as a serious and active threat to regulatory order. Regulators in Canada fell between these extremes, seeing both benefits and risks in securitization. These different views, informed by divergent principles of regulatory order, shaped the way that regulators addressed this practice at a critical historical moment.

One implication of this argument is that the regulatory failures of this period are not reducible to either the inherent complexity of the financial instrument being regulated or exclusively to "cultural capture" from the regulated industry. Instead, national banking regulators made better or worse choices in this setting because they subscribed to different understandings about the causes of order and prosperity in the financial system, which informed their views on the relative merits and drawbacks of bank participation in the securitization process.

Securitization without Risk Transfer

Why would banks engage in "securitization without risk transfer" in the first place? Answering this question requires taking a step back to consider the many ways that participating in the securitization process could generate profits for banks. Banks could use the practice to instantly free up funds that could then be used to fund other investments. When banks sold assets (e.g., loans) to the market via securitization, they were compensated for the costs of the transferred assets. The proceeds of the deal could then be used to pursue potentially more lucrative investments elsewhere. Banks also earned fees by providing various services or supports to securitization conduits, some of which will be discussed in detail below. A third possibility was for banks to hold the end products of securitization transactions—asset-backed securities (ABS)—which could increase or decrease in value.

Finally, banks could use securitization to save on costly regulatory capital. Under the terms of the Basel Capital Accord, banks calculated regulatory capital as a ratio of risk-weighted assets. This gave banks seeking to minimize capital a big incentive to remove assets from the balance sheet. Off-balance-sheet assets typically carried no capital charge (or a very minimal capital charge), especially compared to assets remaining on the balance sheet. In theory, this made sense: assets that left a bank's balance sheet presumably presented less risk to the bank, so it was reasonable for banks to hold less capital against them. How, then, did assets leave a bank's balance sheet? If a bank *sold* an asset to another party, that asset would accordingly be removed from the bank's balance sheet. While the principle seems simple enough, securitization blurred the line between the kinds of transactions that should qualify as "true" asset sales and those that should not. When a bank transferred assets to a securitization conduit, it technically "sold" these assets to the conduit. Yet sponsoring banks often continued to retain some exposure to the risks or rewards of these assets, and sometimes even the majority of these risks or rewards. Should transactions like these qualify as a "true sale"?

The accounting principles in force through the late 1990s implied that they should. Under generally accepted accounting principles in most countries, banks were eligible to remove any assets they transferred to a "bankruptcy remote" conduit from their consolidated balance sheets—even if the bank continued to derive the majority of risks or rewards from the conduit's operations. Again, with fewer assets reported on the balance sheet, banks were also obligated to hold less regulatory capital against these assets. As banks around the world actively searched for ways to maintain a competitive edge in a globalizing financial system, this ability to shed regulatory capital via securitization was seen as a very important benefit.

In the late 1990s, however, accounting standards-setters began to revisit the accounting standards governing the "true sale" treatment of assets transferred to securitization conduits. In 1998, the International Accounting Standards Committee (IASC), a committee established by professional organizations for accountants in Australia, Canada, France, Germany, Ireland, Japan, Mexico, the Netherlands, the United Kingdom, and the United States, issued a new accounting interpretation (SIC-12) that tightened the conditions under which a sponsoring organization (like a bank) should be considered "in control" of a conduit. The IASC (which would later become the International Accounting Standards Board or IASB) was not a governmental body, but the accounting standards (International Financial Reporting Standards or IFRS) it issued carried considerable normative influence. The SIC-12 interpretation alarmed bank sponsors of ABCP programs because it would directly affect their ability to achieve regulatory capital savings through ABCP programs. According to the new standards, if a bank was "in control" of a securitization conduit, the conduit was no longer considered a legally separate third party. Instead, it would be classified as a subsidiary of the bank, and its assets would need to be reported on the consolidated balance sheet (as the securitization transaction would no longer be considered a "true sale"). Without off-balance-sheet treatment (and the regulatory capital savings that came with it), industry participants and regulators recognized that the ABCP market might disappear altogether.

In practice, this change in international accounting standards had little impact before 2002. In most countries in the late 1990s and early 2000s, banks were free to choose between preparing their financial statements in accordance with the terms of IFRS (the international standards established by the IASB) or those of national generally accepted accounting principles (GAAP). In most countries GAAP did not include this new interpretation of conduit consolidation standards, so banks with ABCP programs that prepared financial statements in accordance with GAAP could simply continue with business as usual.[7] This began to change, however, after the epic collapse of US energy company Enron in 2001, which highlighted the dangers of allowing firms to abuse off-balance-sheet special purpose entities (one type of conduit). With this example fresh in mind, national accounting standards setters began to crack down on conduit consolidation standards, adopting revised standards modeled on SIC-12. In Europe, including Spain, the architects of national GAAP agreed to adopt these changes as early as 2001 and 2002. In the United States and Canada, the organizations establishing GAAP for these countries (the Financial Accounting Standards Board, FASB, in the United States; and the Accounting Standards Board, AcSB, in Canada) issued similar interpretations (FIN-46R and AcG-15) in 2003 and 2004, respectively. In the end, the effect was similar across countries: the bank sponsors of ABCP programs suddenly had no choice but to report assets from conduits from which they derived the majority of risks or rewards on the balance sheet.

These changes to global accounting standards presented banking regulators around the world with a common dilemma. The new accounting interpretation of conduit consolidation standards required banks that sponsored ABCP programs to bring these program assets back onto their balance sheets. The Basel Capital Accord required banks to hold regulatory capital against on-balance-sheet assets. Yet regulators recognized that if banks were forced to hold more capital, their incentives for issuing ABCP would likely disappear—and the trillion-dollar market as a whole (which was dominated by banks) might no longer exist.

A second major way that banks gained exposure to ABCP programs involved the many additional services banks provided securitization conduits, particularly in the form of credit and liquidity enhancements. Banks understood that some investors remained skittish about investing in ABS; one technique they used to make ABCP even more attractive to investors was to offer additional forms of credit or liquidity support to conduits. Credit enhancements refer to a bank's explicit promise to absorb possible losses from the asset portfolio controlled by the conduit. These enhancements include techniques like overcollateralization, excess spread accounts, or explicit credit guarantees. Under the terms of the Basel Accord, this form of additional support to conduits carried a relatively high regulatory capital charge (between 50 to 100 percent), in line with the relatively high risk it presented to banks. In agreeing to absorb some potential conduit losses, in other words, the bank could put its own financial health in jeopardy.

The second type of support, liquidity enhancements, refers to temporary loans a bank might provide a conduit. This form of support was designed to allow otherwise creditworthy conduits to withstand temporary funding shortfalls. The purpose was to address cash flow issues, not to absorb the losses from potential asset defaults. It was not uncommon for an ABCP conduit (which invested in long-term assets but issued payments to investors on a relatively short-term basis—often every thirty days) to temporarily lack the cash needed to pay investors on a set schedule. Conduits looked to banks for liquidity support to make these payments on time. The conduit was then supposed to immediately repay the bank liquidity provider as soon as cash became available.

Under the terms of Basel I, liquidity enhancements carried a 0 percent regulatory capital charge, reflecting the minimal risk this form of support was thought to present to banks. In theory, liquidity support would be extended only to otherwise creditworthy conduits, but the problem was that a temporary loan could easily turn into a permanent one if the conduit became insolvent after receiving liquidity support. To guard against this possibility, banks that provided liquidity to conduits were supposed to draw up detailed contracts that specified the conditions (e.g., asset quality standards) under which liquidity support should no longer be expected. In some, but not all, countries, banking regulators attempted to formalize the terms of these contracts.

Banking regulators in different national contexts adopted different strategies in addressing these emerging regulatory challenges in the ABCP market. In the majority of Basel member countries—the United States and Canada included—regulators responded to the changes in the accounting standards that governed conduit consolidation by giving banks "regulatory capital relief" for ABCP program assets that returned to their balance sheets after account-ing standards changed. That is, banking regulators in these countries did not require banks to hold any regulatory capital against these on-balance-sheet assets, even though the terms of the Basel Capital Accord technically required them to do so. As financial economists have shown, this regulatory decision held direct implications for the ongoing growth and development of the global ABCP market.[8] In a handful of Basel member countries, however, like France, Portugal, and Spain, banking regulators made a different choice in this area. They chose not to offer banks regulatory capital relief, which had the effect of chilling domestic bank participation in the ABCP market. The Spanish banking regulators actually went a step beyond this, using their extensive authority over bank accounting standards to further tighten already strict criteria for achiev-ing off-balance-sheet treatment for assets transferred to a conduit.[9]

Second, national banking regulators also varied in their treatment of the liquidity enhancements banks provided to ABCP conduits. One option was to voluntary assign higher regulatory capital charges to liquidity enhancements, for example, capital charges that went above the minimum 0 percent capital charge outlined in Basel I. National regulators could also make different deci-sions about where to draw the line between a liquidity enhancement (which carried no regulatory capital charge) and a credit enhancement (which carried a higher capital charge). In many Basel member countries, the United States included, regulators initially left these decisions up to banks. It soon became apparent, however, that banks' liquidity enhancement contracts often featured excessively loose asset quality standards. Regulators in many countries revis-ited this issue in the mid-2000s, but the changes they made generally failed to go far enough. The loose terms under which banks around the world had extended liquidity support to conduits represented one of the key channels through which the collapse of the ABCP market transformed into a banking crisis. When the ABCP market collapsed in 2007, many banks were contractu-ally bound to continue providing liquidity support to troubled conduits, even after it became apparent that the conduits might not be able to repay these temporary loans.[10] In the United States, this process resulted in bank liquid-ity providers absorbing more than *97 percent* of all ABCP program losses, at an estimated total cost of between $68 and $204 billion.[11] Combined with the minimal amount of regulatory capital banks held against this form of risk exposure, these losses seriously threatened the solvency and stability of banks, not just in the United States, but in Germany, the Netherlands, the UK, and other countries as well.[12]

There were some exceptions to this trend, however. Banks in the few coun-tries where regulators went above the Basel minima to impose significantly higher regulatory capital charges for liquidity enhancements, or where regula-tors had insisted on tighter asset quality standards for a conduit to be eligible for liquidity support, were better prepared to withstand these events.[13] Because banks in Spain did not receive regulatory capital relief for consolidated ABCP programs, they tended not to sponsor ABCP programs at all, making the regulation of liquidity enhancements somewhat of a moot point. Yet Spanish banking regulators nevertheless formally assigned a 100 percent regulatory capital charge to all liquidity enhancements to securitization conduits, an act that only affirmed their intention to dissuade banks from offering this form of support.

In Canada, unlike Spain, banks did actively sponsor ABCP programs. Yet unlike their American counterparts, the Canadian banking regulators had insisted on narrow requirements for a conduit's eligibility for liquidity support. From a very early point, Canadian regulators determined that only "general market disruption" forms of liquidity enhancement should carry the 0 percent regulatory capital charge. A "general market disruption" liquidity line could be accessed only if trading in the ABCP market stopped for reasons completely unrelated to the underlying quality of the assets contained with conduit. Examples of something that could trigger this form of liquidity support included terrorist attacks or natural disasters. All other, less narrowly defined forms of liquidity support carried a much higher capital charge. Canadian banks, seeking to save on regulatory capital, largely responded to this regulatory regime by extending only "general market disruption" liquidity lines to the conduits they sponsored. As a result, when the ABCP conduits sponsored by Canadian banks ran into trouble during the crisis, these banks were technically not required to extend liquidity support to them and initially failed to do so (citing the lack of a general market disruption). Accordingly, Canadian ABCP investors, rather than banks, were on the hook for absorbing the losses of the failed ABCP programs.

Table 9.1 summarizes the major differences across these three countries in their regulatory approaches to bank exposure to ABCP programs. Overall, regulators at the Federal Reserve chose to maintain comparatively lax standards in this area, even after the homegrown Enron collapse underscored the potential for off-balance-sheet conduits to obscure risk. Specifically, the US banking regulators chose to offer banks regulatory capital relief for consolidated ABCP program assets, required banks to hold very little regulatory capital against liquidity enhancements provided to conduits, and failed to introduce strict asset quality standards for the extension of liquidity support. Regulators at OSFI in Canada followed American regulatory approaches in some of these areas: for example, they also granted banks regulatory capital relief for consolidated ABCP program assets. However, these regulators also maintained a uniquely strict definition of the kinds of liquidity enhancements that were eligible for a 0 percent regulatory capital charge, with important implications for the kinds of liquidity support Canadian banks offered to conduits. Regulators at the Bank of Spain took a very different approach to the regulation of bank

TABLE 9.1. Regulation of Bank Exposure to ABCP Programs in the United States, Canada, and Spain

	US: Permissive	Canada: Less Permissive	Spain: Strict
Regulatory capital relief for consolidated ABCP program assets	Yes	Yes	No
Regulatory definition of asset quality cut-off for liquidity support	<u>Before 2004</u>: None <u>After 2004</u>: 90 days nonperforming	Restrictive—support offered only in event of general market disruption (GMD)	Moot point (100% capital charge)
Regulatory capital charge for short-term liquidity lines	<u>Before 2004</u>: 0% <u>After 2004</u>: 10%	<u>Before 2004</u>: 0% for GMD lines; 100% for all others <u>After 2004</u>: 0% for GMD lines; 10% for other short-term liquidity lines	100%

securitization exposures, not only refusing to give bank regulatory capital relief for consolidated ABCP program assets, but actually using their own power over bank accounting standards to tighten standards for conduit consolidation even further, in ways that made off-balance-sheet status even harder for the sponsors of securitization programs to achieve. On its own, this policy choice stalled the development of an ABCP market in Spain, but regulators here also chose to shut any potential loophole by assigning a full 100 percent regulatory capital charge to liquidity enhancements (giving banks no regulatory incentive at all to offer liquidity support to conduits).

The sections that follow explain how the different overarching goals of banking regulators in each country—enhancing market discipline in the United States, striking a balance in Canada, and enhancing state oversight and guidance in Spain—informed the development of these divergent policy choices.

Securitization as the Key to Financial Stability in the United States

Banking regulators in the United States took a comparatively hands-off approach to regulating bank participation in the securitization process in the 1990s and 2000s, an approach with devastating consequences for US bank outcomes when the crisis hit. There are multiple reasons why this approach was somewhat unexpected. One reason we might have expected the regulatory policies governing securitization in the United States to be comparatively strict, not comparatively lax, was that the US banking regulators had recently been given a front-row seat to the disastrous effects of allowing firms to abuse off-balance-sheet conduits. Executives at the failed energy company Enron had used complex networks of off-balance-sheet vehicles (a type of conduit known as a "special purpose entity") to obscure the company's mounting financial problems from the view of regulators and market participants. In many respects, these special purpose entities were very similar to the conduits banks used in asset securitization transactions.

Enron's collapse in October 2001, and the wave of corporate accounting scandals that followed, did inspire multiple changes to American economic policy more broadly, including changes to the accounting standards governing conduit consolidations. They also inspired the most far-reaching overhaul of American corporate governance and corporate disclosure practices since the Great Depression, the expansive Sarbanes-Oxley Act of 2002. Given this, we might have also expected some changes to the bank regulatory regime as well—or at least the standards that governed bank exposure to securitization conduits. Yet regulators at the Federal Reserve were actually among the strongest opponents of tighter regulatory restrictions on bank exposure to securitization conduits. As Alan Greenspan explained in 2002, this was an opposition motivated, at least in part, by regulators' skepticism that more or tighter regulation would solve the problem: "We have to be careful . . . not to look to a significant expansion of regulation as the solution to current problems, especially as price-earnings ratios increasingly reflect the market's perception of the quality of accounting. Regulation has, over the years, proven only partially successful in dissuading individuals from playing with the rules of accounting."[14]

In other words, it wasn't that American regulators were *unaware* of the similarities between the off-balance-sheet vehicles that had featured in the Enron fraud and those that banks were currently employing in common securitization transactions. As financial journalist David Glass wrote in a 2002 *American Banker* article, industry participants (regulators presumably included) were well aware of the "uncomfortable resemblance" between these structures: "The company's abuse of special-purpose entities to give the appearance of removing liabilities from its balance sheet—while in fact retaining the associated risk in disguised form—has cast a pall over the securitization market and has led to calls for tighter regulation."[15] But even as banking regulators recognized the resemblance, they still avoided acting. Indeed, instead of cracking down, they took the opposite approach, urging policy makers to avoid overreacting to Enron's "aggressive interpretations of accounting rules and misuse of structured transactions."[16]

To understand this stance, it is important to understand how regulators at the Federal Reserve perceived the relationship between bank participation in the securitization process and their broader mission of enhancing market discipline in the financial system. Crucially, regulators viewed securitization as a prudential practice—a practice that actively made the banking system *safer*—which came with important implications for how they approached its regulation. The US banking regulators believed that three specific features of asset securitization served prudential goals. First, they saw benefits in the way that securitization theoretically encouraged banks to improve their own internal methods of measuring credit risk. The idea was that unless banks already had a strong understanding of the value of the assets (e.g., loans) they wished to sell to the market, they were unlikely to make money on a securitization transaction. The practice of buying and selling credit risk via securitization, then, served prudential goals by giving banks a natural (market-based) incentive to improve internal credit risk measurement and management practices. A better understanding of risk was expected to prevent banks from taking on too much of it: in Greenspan's words, "better and more quantifiable estimates of risk are tantamount to risk reduction."[17] The same feature of securitization was also expected to serve prudential goals by reducing the need for regulators to step in to correct undesirable bank behavior. If banks (through participating in securitization) became more careful about understanding and managing their risks, regulators would not have to play such an active (and potentially disruptive) role in supervising these financial institutions.

As the United States prepared to transition to Basel II, securitization's perceived role in organically facilitating better risk management and measurement at banks became even more salient to regulators. In 2002, regulators at the Federal Reserve had made an alarming discovery: existing internal credit risk measurement systems at many banks were actually much less sophisticated than regulators had anticipated.[18] This realization placed regulators in a difficult spot. They had just spent a great deal of political capital advocating for revisions to the Basel framework that depended on banks' internal abilities to accurately quantify and measure credit risk. But recent indications suggested that these internal bank systems were not yet as developed as they should be. Regulators obviously wanted banks to improve these systems, since the success of their new approach depended on them, but they were also hesitant to force banks to make these changes. After all, the whole point of the Basel II reform effort was to mitigate existing regulation-induced disruptions to market mechanisms, not create new ones.[19] Luckily, securitization seemed to offer a way out of this dilemma. Since participating in securitization markets was expected to provide a natural (or market-driven) "way to incorporate advances in . . . risk management . . . into the operations of our large complex banking organizations," regulators expected that expanded bank participation in securitization markets would bring about the improvements regulators hoped to see without further intervention.[20]

Securitization was thus expected to contribute to safety and soundness in two respects: by creating enhanced market-driven incentives for prudent risk management and by helping to keep the government out of the banking business. As Alan Greenspan argued in a 1996 speech, "We must be assured that with rare and circumscribed exceptions we do not substitute supervisory judgments for management decisions. That is the road to moral hazard and inefficient bank management. Fortunately, the same technology and innovation [securitization] that is driving supervisors to focus on [risk] management processes will, through the development of sophisticated market structures and responses, do much of our job of ensuring safety and soundness. We should be careful not to impede the process."[21]

United States regulators also looked approvingly on securitization's role in diffusing credit risk to actors outside of the regulated banking system. By definition, the securitization process allowed banks to transfer the credit risks they formerly held to maturity to other types of financial actors, which included less regulated nonbank financial institutions. This risk-transfer process was also expected to further the broader goal of enhancing market discipline in banking. Recall that the US banking regulators perceived a trade-off between market discipline and all forms of government intervention into markets (regulation included). One implication of this view was that the US banking regulators ironically conceptualized *less regulated* financial institutions (which also lacked access to the government safety net) as fundamentally *better-regulated* financial institutions.

This perspective held important implications for how regulators conceptualized the risks and benefits of a practice (securitization) that transferred risk outside of the regulated financial system. In a 2005 speech, Greenspan outlined its supposed safety and stability benefits:

> Some other concerns about the transfer of credit risk outside the banking system seem to be based on questionable assumptions. Some observers believe that credit risks will be managed more effectively by banks because they generally are more heavily regulated than the entities to which they are transferring credit risk. But those unregulated and less heavily regulated entities generally are subject to more-effective market discipline than banks. . . . Private regulation generally has proved far better at constraining excessive risk-taking than has government regulation.[22]

In other words, securitization enhanced financial stability by shifting credit risk to institutions viewed (by regulators) as better equipped to bear it. If less heavily regulated financial institutions were "subject to more-effective market discipline," it followed that they were also less likely to engage in undesirable, excessively risky behavior. This same risk-transfer feature of securitization was also thought to serve prudential goals by acting as a mechanism to break up dangerous concentrations of risk within bank portfolios. In allowing banks to sell credit risk to the market, in other words, securitization also discouraged financial institutions from remaining overexposed to particular types of risk.[23]

Finally, US regulators believed that securitization enhanced market discipline by facilitating regulatory capital arbitrage. It was well known that securitization made it much easier for banks to shed undesired assets from their balance sheets (including assets that carried a too-high capital charge, from a bank's perspective), and by extension, to "game" or "arbitrage" existing regulatory capital restrictions. Recall that in the 1990s and 2000s, regulators at the Federal Reserve had strongly pushed for new approaches to calculating regulatory capital requirements designed to bridge the gap between what regulators wanted (regulatory capital) and what banks were already doing (economic capital). Importantly, regulators expected that whenever banks considered the gap between economic capital and regulatory capital for a particular exposure to be too large, they would respond by securitizing the exposure—that is, selling off the asset in question to investors instead of keeping it on the books. Like their counterparts in other countries, the US banking regulators saw the actual practice of regulatory capital arbitrage (that is, bank undertaking certain strategies or lines of business just to save on regulatory capital) as unproductive and wasteful. But crucially, they also believed that banks would engage in this practice only when *government regulation was not finely tailored enough* (e.g., where the gap between economic and regulatory capital for a particular exposure was excessively large).[24]

This perspective explains why the US banking regulators saw a bank's choice to securitize a particular risk exposure as providing a valuable signal to regulators. As regulators explained in speeches and publications throughout the 1990s and 2000s, a bank's choice to securitize served prudential goals by alerting regulators to the presence of potential "regulatory mistakes," or areas where the gap between regulatory capital and economic capital was currently too large. As Greenspan explained in a 1997 speech, "Migration of activity from government-regulated to privately regulated markets sends a signal to government regulators that many transactors believe the costs of regulation exceed the benefits. When such migration occurs, government regulators should consider carefully whether less regulation or different regulation would provide a better cost-benefit tradeoff."[25] When viewed from this perspective, securitization seemed to serve the broader regulatory objective of enhancing market discipline by identifying domains where existing regulations were causing especially severe market distortions.

Yet securitization also served as more than a warning signal. When banks engaged in securitization to reduce regulatory capital, they were also, in effect, *actively evading* what they saw as inappropriately strict restrictions. While banking regulators around the world recognized that securitization could produce this regulation-dodging effect, the US banking regulators were distinctive in the degree to which they underscored the positive features of this practice. In a 2003 speech, Federal Reserve Vice Chairman Roger Ferguson described securitization as a beneficial "release valve" that helped to automatically correct for regulatory mistakes: "We have tried hard to set risk-based regulatory capital requirements . . . below economic capital measures so that regulatory requirements will not affect the allocation of capital within the bank. If we make a mistake and set the regulatory capital requirements too high relative to market-based economic capital, we can read the effect of our error right away in the securitization of the exposure; securitization is a *release valve* that relieves the pressure of our mistakes."[26] In other words, securitization also served prudential goals by allowing banks to correct for the market-disrupting effects of regulation *independently*, without waiting for regulators to make the needed changes. From the standpoint of actors seeking to enhance market discipline in banking, this was a feature to be celebrated.

United States regulators' conceptualization of securitization as a prudential practice informed key developments in how they approached the regulation of bank exposures to ABCP programs. This viewpoint left regulators at the Federal Reserve relatively less attuned to the dangers or risks of this practice. With bank participation in the securitization process already defined as a valuable prudential tool, American regulators were never likely to follow a Spanish-style approach of restricting bank exposure to off-balance-sheet securitization, even after the Enron scandal brought some of the associated dangers to light. The justification that the US federal bank regulatory agencies offered for why they gave banks regulatory capital relief for consolidated ABCP program assets also reflected this view of securitization as a risk-reducing, rather than risk-boosting, practice. As regulators wrote in a 2003 joint notice of proposed rule making, they believed that ABCP programs presented very little risk to bank sponsors: accordingly, if they did not provide regulatory capital relief, the result would be "risk-based capital requirements that do not appropriately reflect the risks faced by banking organizations involved with the programs."[27]

The one regulatory change that the Federal Reserve did introduce in response to Enron concerned minor reforms to the regulatory treatment of liquidity enhancements. A September 2003 notice of proposed rule making proposed to tighten asset quality standards for ABCP conduits eligible for liquidity support, introducing a mandatory requirement for banks to stop extending liquidity support to conduits with assets that were more than sixty days past due. The same initiative also proposed to increase regulatory capital charges for short-term liquidity enhancements from 0 to 20 percent. Regulators justified both reforms by noting that they would simply codify preexisting industry practices. Consider the rationale regulators provided for increasing the regulatory capital charge for short-term liquidity enhancements: "holding risk-based capital against liquidity facilities with an original maturity of one year or less . . . is consistent with the *industry's practice* of internally allocating economic capital against this risk associated with such facilities."[28] Similarly, the rationale for introducing a sixty-day-past-due asset quality cutoff for liquidity support read as follows: "Assets that are past due 60 days or more generally are considered ineligible for financing based upon *standard industry practice* and rating agency guidelines for trade receivables."[29] In a context where aligning regulation more closely with existing industry practice was already defined as a top priority, and where government regulation and market discipline were perceived as substitutes, it is telling that the only legitimate reason regulators perceived (or at least, articulated) to tighten regulatory standards was to bring these standards closer to what banks were already doing.

This method of justifying their actions also left the US banking regulators comparatively vulnerable to industry arguments against tighter regulation. After all, if banks were the experts on their own practices, it was only too easy to argue that regulators had drawn the wrong conclusions about industry standards. Indeed, this was exactly the line of argument industry participants used to oppose these reforms. In a 2003 letter to the federal banking regulators, the American Bankers Association argued against the proposed increase in the regulatory capital charge for liquidity enhancements (to 20 percent) by contending that such an increase was inconsistent with the amount of economic capital banks were already setting aside against these exposures: "ABA member bank . . . experiences with liquidity facilities strongly suggests that the 20 percent conversion factor is too high. Their own internal data suggests a conversion factor of no more than 10 percent, on the conservative side, down to 5 percent."[30] Grace Vogel, deputy comptroller for financial and regulatory reporting at Citigroup, used the same line of reasoning to oppose the sixty-day-past-due asset quality test, arguing that this standard was too stringent, inflexible, and "one-size-fits-all" to be consistent with prevailing industry practices. Instead, she encouraged regulators to allow banks to develop their own asset quality tests, on the grounds that this would be more in line with the "agencies' goal of applying greater risk-sensitivity to the assignment of regulatory capital."[31] In this way, industry participants skillfully turned regulators' own rhetoric against more stringent regulations.

Regulators at the Federal Reserve seemed persuaded by these arguments. The final rule published in July 2004 lowered the proposed regulatory capital charge for short-term liquidity enhancements to 10 percent, on the grounds that it was "more reflective of the amount of economic capital that banking organizations maintain internally for short-term liquidity facilities supporting ABCP."[32] They also agreed to loosen asset quality standards for conduits eligible for liquidity support from sixty days nonperforming to ninety days non-performing. Regulators clearly responded to industry calls for looser standards. But as the above examples suggest, they seemed to be more compelled by reasoning that aligned with their own predetermined goals than intimidated by displays of industry power. In the next chapter, which examines the regulation of loan loss provisioning, this pattern will become even more pronounced.

Securitization Holds Risks and Benefits in Canada

Although the Canadian banking regulators followed a US-style approach in regulating asset securitization in many respects, Canadian standards departed from US ones in crucial other respects. Regulators at OSFI did follow the Federal Reserve in offering "regulatory capital relief" to banks forced by accounting standards to consolidate their ABCP program assets, but they also insisted on a much tighter definition for liquidity enhancements provided to these programs, restricting the 0 percent regulatory capital charge to enhancements with very narrowly defined terms. In what follows, I explain how these trends were influenced by the broader Canadian commitment to striking the right balance between prudential and competitive considerations.

Like the US banking regulators, the Canadian banking regulators also recognized, and celebrated, the beneficial effects that participating in the securitization process had for banks' internal credit risk measurement and management systems. They also recognized that the diffusion of credit risk that securitization afforded came with potential benefits. However, in the Canadian context, these benefits were somewhat less salient, a point that was reflected in the relative absence of discussions of these benefits from most Canadian regulatory speeches and publications. Regulators at OSFI also rarely referenced securitization's role in facilitating regulatory capital arbitrage, a feature that was often discussed (positively) by regulators in the United States. The biggest difference, however, lay in how Canadian regulators conceptualized and discussed the potential risks of securitization. Although they acknowledged that securitization came with important prudential benefits, they were also much more attuned to the potential dangers or risks of this practice. Nick Le Pan, OSFI superintendent, underscored this tension in a 2004 speech, noting that "the ability to diversify and transfer portions of credit risk to others has been an important reason why financial institutions over the past few years have been able to weather economic and market downturns. But a number of these types of transactions are highly complex and it can be very difficult to accurately assess the risk involved. It is not easy for financial institutions to maintain the capacity to make those assessments. I am cautioning institutions to be careful in this area."[33]

In the eyes of Canadian regulators, the complexity of securitization set this practice apart from many of the other kinds of activities banks were pursuing in the same period. As sociologist Donald MacKenzie and others have shown in detail, the sheer number of individual assets involved in a typical securitization transaction makes it hard for market participants to investigate the quality of these assets or to estimate default correlations across asset classes.[34] For regulators at OSFI, who believed that they had a duty to intervene in "situations where risk assumed by institutions is not matched by the required capability to measure, monitor and manage those risks," this complexity raised concerns.[35] They recognized securitization as one of only a few potential areas in which managers might not fully appreciate the true long-tail risks that they were assuming, introducing tensions for regulators seeking to balance a commitment to bank autonomy with the need to safeguard the banking public.

Although the Canadian banking regulators may have subscribed to a less rosy view of the relative risks and benefits of securitization than the American regulators, they were still highly attuned to the potential competitive impact of allowing banks to engage in this practice. Canadian regulators recognized that securitization could be extremely lucrative for banks and continually referenced this point in speeches and publications throughout the 1990s and 2000s. As concerns about the international competitive position of Canadian banks grew more pressing after the late 1990s, these competitive benefits became even more salient. As one OSFI regulator explained in an interview, this desire to ensure that Canadian banks maintained a competitive position in globalizing financial markets motivated regulators to endorse bank participation in novel securitization transactions—even when some of these deals made them a little uncomfortable from a prudential standpoint:

> The Canadian regime [of securitization regulation] did come to look like the American regime. . . . I can remember consideration of some very seminal transactions that were also being looked at by the Fed in the whole asset-backed securitization world. And there was a conscious attempt [at OSFI] to say, "Okay, within this sort of kind of [bank] size range we're okay with that kind of [securitization] structure." Now, would that be absolutely our preference? Probably not, but I think [it was motivated by] the recognition of a whole bunch of, sort of, more competitive realities around certain aspects of the capital regime.[36]

This approach to permitting innovative securitization transactions also tied into the broader regulatory objective of actively pursuing harmonization in regulatory standards.

Yet the places where Canadian regulators elected to depart from a US-style approach are equally instructive. To strike the right balance between prudential and competitive considerations, Canadian regulators placed heavy emphasis on ensuring that banks maintained sizeable buffers against potential losses. This applied to their approach to regulating potential losses from securitization exposures as well. As Le Pan suggested in a 2005 speech, "When used improperly [risk transfer mechanisms like securitization] can be used to mislead investors or can pose financial risks to the firms involved. But we don't want to throw the baby out with the bathwater. Nor do we want to forget that vulnerabilities will always be in part a matter of surprise. So what matters is financial institutions' *contingency capability*, financial cushions such as capital and reserves (which are now generally pretty high) and ability to withstand surprises."[37]

This commitment to ensuring that banks maintained adequate financial cushions against potential losses helps to explain some of the specific policy choices OSFI regulators made in this area. Like the US banking regulators, the Canadian banking regulators were not ready to witness the destruction of the lucrative asset-backed commercial paper market after a change in accounting standards, which helps to explain why they, too, chose to offer banks regulatory capital relief for ABCP program assets that returned to their balance sheets. To justify this choice, OSFI regulators argued that "while the accounting treatment [of the ABCP program] has changed, the risks to the bank have not."[38]

Yet the comparatively strong Canadian emphasis on ensuring that banks were ready "to withstand surprises" helps to account for their unique regulation of liquidity enhancements to conduits.[39] As early as the early 1990s, when the asset-backed securitization market was in its infancy, Canadian regulators made it clear that they were uncomfortable about the prospect of banks extending liquidity support to conduits on loosely defined terms. They took the stance that banks would need to hold capital against any exposure they retained to the credit risks associated with a securitization program—which included the liquidity enhancements they offered to conduits.[40] Accordingly, OSFI regulators initially went far above the Basel minimum standards by assigning a 100 percent regulatory capital charge to all liquidity enhancements—with a single exception. Very narrowly defined "general market disruption" (GMD) liquidity lines were assigned a 0 percent regulatory capital charge. This provided a powerful incentive for banks to offer this form of liquidity support. Funds offered via a GMD liquidity line would be forthcoming only under very rare and extreme circumstances—and regulators at OSFI were well aware of this reality.[41]

Canadian regulators stood firm in this idiosyncratic treatment of liquidity enhancements, even after they encountered substantial market pressure to adjust this approach. For example, even after the Canadian banking regulators followed the US banking regulators in adjusting regulatory capital charges for other kinds of short-term liquidity lines in 2004, they still refused to amend the 0 percent regulatory capital charge for GMD liquidity lines. This decision displeased analysts at the major US credit ratings agencies, S&P and Moody's, who were concerned (correctly, it turns out) that the GMD lines Canadian banks preferred would not offer sufficient protection to ABCP investors. The ratings agencies threatened to stop rating ABCP programs backed by this form of liquidity support, and in 2004, they made good on this threat. After S&P and Moody's refused to rate Canadian ABCP, only one small Canadian credit rating agency—Dominion Bond Rating Services—continued to provide ratings for these debt securities.

These dynamics presented a relatively serious threat to the continuance of the Canadian ABCP market, yet regulators held firm in their insistence that GMD liquidity lines should continue to receive more favorable regulatory treatment. When I asked a leading regulator to explain this choice in an interview, the regulator told me that the decision had been motivated by a desire to ensure that banks would continue to offer liquidity support to conduits only under very narrowly defined terms.[42] Having identified liquidity enhancements as a potential threat to the adequacy of the safeguards banks held against potential losses (a key regulatory focus) from the start, OSFI chose to make a stand in this area, which touched on the quality and quantity of the prudential safeguards banks held against risk exposures. Accordingly, the regulatory treatment of liquidity lines represented one area in which "differences . . . [really] matter to us for policy reasons."

Securitization as a Threat to Order in Spain

Regulators at the Bank of Spain took a much more conservative approach to regulating bank participation in the securitization process. They refused to provide regulatory capital relief for assets that came back onto bank balance sheets after changes to international accounting standards. If anything, they took the opposite approach, further tightening domestic accounting standards to make achieving nonconsolidated treatment of conduits even harder for banks. They also took an unusually strict approach to regulating the liquidity enhancements banks offered to conduits, requiring banks to apply a full (100 percent) capital charge to these exposures. These policy choices were shaped by regulators' commitment to enhancing the state oversight and guidance of bank behavior.

Regulators at the Bank of Spain saw the same three key features of securitization that attracted notice in the United States and Canada—its role in incentivizing banks to improve internal risk measurement systems, in facilitating the transfer of credit risk to unregulated financial institutions, and in facilitating "regulatory capital arbitrage"—as either incidental to, or actively threatening to, regulatory order. In a context where the enhancement of state oversight and guidance to banks was defined as the top regulatory priority, a process that threatened to obscure bank risk exposures from regulatory view by allowing banks to remove securitized assets from the balance sheet seemed especially problematic. In a system that regarded bankers, and the market participants who governed them, more as shortsighted and excessively self-interested than far-seeing, public-minded regulators, regulators were more likely to discount one of the benefits of securitization that was so prized in the United States and even in Canada: its role in encouraging banks to improve internal risk measurement systems. Regulators at the Bank of Spain agreed that securitization could have this benefit, but it simply carried less salience in a context where regulators were already assumed to be relatively effective in monitoring and strengthening these systems.

Like American and Canadian regulators, the Spanish regulators also recognized potential benefits of diffusing credit risk across the financial system. They were, however, much more attuned to the potential downsides of this diffusion. Regulators at the Bank of Spain worried that the spread of credit risk outside the regulated banking system might block regulators' capacity to oversee (and therefore correct for) potential threats to financial stability. As Bank of Spain Deputy Governor Gonzalo Gil explained in a 2006 regulatory speech, "From the point of view of financial stability . . . problems may also arise . . . in transferring risk[;] it may end up in unregulated institutions, favoring the accumulation of [financial-sector] imbalances and hampering the search for a solution in crisis situations."[43] Contrast this view with the American stance on the prudential *benefits* of transferring credit risk to less regulated institutions.

Finally, unlike the US banking regulators, who regarded the capacity of securitization to uncover potential "regulatory mistakes" as one of the practice's key benefits, Spanish regulators saw the same feature as a serious threat to order. They remained highly suspicious of any practice that allowed banks to transfer assets to affiliated subsidiaries (in this case, securitization conduits) if the bank retained any of the associated risks.[44] This was uncomfortably similar to one of the practices that had featured in the financial crisis of 1977–85, in which banks and industrial holding companies had hidden risk exposures within networks of subsidiaries. Spanish regulators did not attempt to hide their desire to repeat the regulatory mistakes of 1977–85 by clamping down on similar practices. In an interview with journalists at the *Financial Times*, José Maria Roldán, the former director of regulation at the Bank of Spain, invoked this historical experience to explain why his agency had taken such a hard-line stance on the consolidated treatment of off-balance-sheet assets:

> The Bank of Spain . . . has prevented banks from holding any kind of special purpose vehicles off balance sheet. This conservative stance arose because Spain suffered a big banking crisis in the 1980s when financial groups that had built big industrial empires crashed under the weight of cross-shareholdings and intra-group lending. "We learned early and the hard way," Mr Roldán said. "Since then, we have always looked at risk from a consolidated perspective. Nowadays, this may sound like plain vanilla supervision, but before IFRS [was adopted in Europe in 2005], we were

the first regulators to insist on the need to bring special purpose entities within the consolidation perimeter."[45]

In speeches and publications throughout the 1990s and 2000s, the Spanish regulators clearly and repeatedly stated their opposition to allowing banks to use securitization to engage in regulatory capital arbitrage, which they viewed as behavior "not consistent with prudent risk management and solvency."[46] In a 2005 speech, Gil explicitly connected the Bank of Spain's restrictive stance on securitization to a desire to crack down on regulatory capital arbitrage: "Regarding the transfer of risks . . . a total transmission of risk is required for banks to avoid making corresponding provisions against the potential for insolvency. . . . This prevents the securitization transaction from being used as a way to arbitrage capital."[47] The same commitment to ensuring that risk exposures remained on a bank's consolidated balance sheet (and therefore within the view of regulators) also aligns with the decision to assign a 100 percent regulatory capital charge to liquidity enhancements.

As further confirmation that it was securitization's capacity to remove assets from bank balance sheets (even as banks retained some of the associated risk) that Spanish regulators found most alarming, they seemed much more comfortable with any credit risk transfer strategy that was fully disclosed on a bank's balance sheet. For example, Spanish banks had been free to issue covered bonds backed by mortgages (*participaciones hipotecaria*) since 1981, which was relatively early in international perspective. Covered bonds, like asset-backed securities, are debt securities backed by pools of assets. The key difference is that the assets that back a covered bond remain on the sponsoring bank's balance sheet, whereas the assets contained within an asset-backed security are removed from the sponsoring bank's balance sheet (via the transfer to a conduit). This suggests that it was not asset-backed securitization's inherent complexity or facilitation of credit risk transfer that primarily bothered regulators—it was the partial transfer of risk.[48]

This raises the question of why Spanish policy makers ever allowed banks to engage in off-balance-sheet securitization in the first place. Between 1998 (when asset-backed securitization was legalized in Spain) and 2004 (when regulators amended bank accounting standards to make the off-balance-sheet treatment of conduit assets virtually impossible to obtain), a small market for ABCP did develop in Spain. Interviews with industry participants active in this period suggest that the initial decision to allow off-balance-sheet asset securitization was motivated by pressing public policy considerations, however, not by changes in perceptions of the underlying risks of this practice.

In the late 1990s, it was not clear whether Spain would be among the first adopters of the single European currency when it was introduced in 1999. Spain had been a member of the European Union for well over a decade, but the country was struggling to meet the European Monetary Union's requirements, which included meeting certain inflation, interest rate, debt, exchange rate, and public deficit targets.[49] Interest rates in Spain were still hovering in double digits; it would be difficult to bring them down to desired levels.[50] Yet Spain ultimately met these targets by 1998, after several consecutive years of sustained economic growth, thanks in part to extensive efforts by the Bank of Spain.[51]

In interviews, actors with close ties to the Bank of Spain reported that the primary reason policy makers sought to legalize asset-backed securitization in 1998 was to facilitate Spain's entry into the EMU. The newly established European Central Bank provided credit only against bank collateral that consisted of cash or highly marketable assets. These assets could consist of government, corporate, or bank bonds—or, crucially, asset-backed securities. As one high-ranking bank executive explained, this desire to become one of the founding members of EMU helps to explain why Spanish regulators temporarily put aside their reservations about off-balance-sheet securitization:

> I remember exactly the day when the Bank of Spain called me. It was probably . . . 1997. . . . [A key figure at the Bank of Spain], he called me and said, you have to convince the banks to securitize. Why? Because we were going to enter the EU. . . . And we were a country, bankerized [bank based], not securitized [market based]. So we didn't have bonds, we had banking loans. . . . And the way in which the euro was going to inherit—the German way of providing liquidity by the Bundesbank—they were giving [accepting] ABS as collateral, so we needed collateral. So that's why the Bank of Spain said, "You have to convince the banks to produce bonds, so that they have the assets to participate in this."[52]

Yet even as Spain eased regulatory requirements for asset securitization in the late 1990s, regulators remained wary of the practice's potential risks—which helps to explain why they backpedaled only six years later. Both in interviews and in official regulatory publications, the Spanish regulators insisted that they had no choice but to issue Circular 4/2004 (which tightened bank accounting standards in ways that made many forms of asset securitization, including ABCP, uneconomic for banks) because new regional accounting standards demanded this change. It is true that a 2002 EU directive required all EU firms (banks included) to issue financial statements that complied with IFRS accounting standards, starting in 2005. Yet nothing about the content of these standards explains why Spanish regulators adhered to such a strict interpretation of them, why they elected to implement the reforms earlier than in other peer countries, or why they chose not to offer banks regulatory capital relief for ABCP program assets that returned to the balance sheet. In one regulatory speech, Gil seems to hint at the true purpose of Circular

4/2004: "Ultimately, Circular 4/2004 not only enables compliance with the regulations of the European Union, which, as you may guess, is an essential prerequisite, but also ensures that the Spanish accounting framework remains consistent with the *best practices in risk management*."[53]

In short, the looming regional implementation of the regional IFRS standards offered an excellent opportunity for regulators at the Bank of Spain to accomplish two goals at once: first, to signal their deep commitment to the broader project of regional economic and regulatory convergence (by adopting very strict versions of these regional standards and doing so much earlier than many other EU countries) and second, to crack down on a practice (off-balance-sheet securitization) that they had long seen as a potentially serious threat to regulatory order. As we will see in the next chapter, the specific Spanish regulatory commitment to regional convergence was less pronounced in areas where international standards were not compatible with cherished domestic regulatory goals.

Conclusion

By 2004, the United States, Canada, and Spain had developed distinctive approaches to regulating bank exposure to securitization programs. In each case, policy choices in this area held direct implications for how banks experienced the global financial crisis, particularly the devastating 2007 collapse of the global ABCP market. Although US banking regulators had multiple compelling reasons to tighten the regulation of bank exposure to securitization programs in the early to mid-2000s, they largely failed to do so. Instead, they publicly defended a hands-off regulatory approach in speeches and publications, provided banks with regulatory capital relief for ABCP program assets that returned to their balance sheets, and failed to require banks to adequately provision for the additional risk exposures associated with liquidity enhancements.

The Canadian banking regulators followed an American-style approach to securitization in many respects but departed from US standards in a few key areas. They also offered banks regulatory capital relief for on-balance-sheet ABCP program assets and did little to prevent banks from engaging in increasingly complex securitization transactions. They did hold firm, however, to a stringent approach to liquidity enhancements, an area they had long seen as exposing banks (and the consumers and depositors who depended on them) to the risk of undue loss. This had beneficial implications for bank performance during the crisis. The Spanish banking regulators took a uniquely strict approach to regulating securitization. They were notoriously reluctant to allow banks to engage in securitization transactions that removed assets from the balance sheet if the bank still retained the associated risks and rewards. Even after Spanish policy makers formally authorized banks to participate in asset-backed securitization in the late 1990s, regulators continued to maintain strict standards that prevented banks from receiving regulatory capital advantages from this activity. They assigned a 100 percent regulatory capital charge to liquidity enhancements offered to securitization programs and preemptively changed accounting standards in ways that made it nearly impossible for banks to receive off-balance-sheet treatment for assets transferred to ABCP programs.

Each regulatory approach reflected the influence of different regulatory goals in each country. In the United States, banking regulators viewed many of the defining features of securitization as features that served the broader objective of enhancing market discipline in banking, which helps to explain why regulators at the Federal Reserve were so comparatively attuned to the benefits of this practice and so inured to its risks. In Canada, where regulators pursued the broader objective of "striking the right balance" between prudential and competitive considerations, regulators were both relatively less attuned to the perceived prudential benefits of securitization and more attuned to the risks than were regulators in the United States. In Spain, regulators seeking to enhance state oversight and guidance saw many of the same defining features of securitization as fundamentally incompatible with regulatory order.

10

Regulating Loan Loss Provisions in the Post-Basel Era

A bank's stability depends on more than just the riskiness of its investments. It is also affected by the quality and size of the buffers the bank holds against potential losses. I have already devoted a great deal of attention to one component of these buffers—the regulatory capital banks hold against the possibility of unexpected financial shocks—but there are others. The reserves that banks set aside against potential bad loans are also vital to safety and soundness. To account for the reality that at least some borrowers will fail to fully repay the loans granted to them, banks set aside funds (known as the loan loss reserve or the allowance for loan and lease losses) to absorb the expenses associated with failed loans. If a bank's loan losses overwhelm these funds, its reported income—and potentially, its day-to-day operations—will be negatively affected. For this reason, excessively high loan losses combined with inadequate loan loss reserves have historically served as one of the primary causes of bank failures worldwide.

In the 1990s and 2000s, banking regulators were acutely aware of the dangers of banks making too few provisions against bad loans. Less than a decade earlier, large banks worldwide had experienced significant losses on loans in what became known as the less-developed-country (LDC) debt crisis. When the magnitude of the problem in this sector became clear, many financial institutions only narrowly averted catastrophe. This experience was common to many countries; however, the regulatory policies that developed to govern loan loss provisioning in its aftermath varied considerably across national borders. Unlike bank capital, which was subject to minimum requirements set at the international level through the Basel Accord, the regulation of bank loan loss provisioning was determined exclusively at the national level.

This chapter examines the development of loan loss provisioning regulation in the United States, Canada, and Spain in the 1990s and 2000s. In the United States, banking regulators did not encourage banks to enhance their loan loss reserves when credit risk was on the rise in the late 1990s and early 2000s. Even worse, they put up little resistance to a push by securities regulators to block bank engagement in "overly conservative" loan loss provisioning practices. As a result, US banks faced relatively greater pressure to reduce loan loss reserves in the lead-up to the crisis, an outcome that economist Eliana Balla and colleagues directly link to the substantial difficulties US banks experienced during the 2008 crisis.[1] As loan losses during the crisis quickly swamped the minimal reserves American banks had set aside to absorb them, many were forced to sharply increase their loan loss provisions (at great expense) at a time when they were already struggling to make ends meet.[2]

In Canada, the picture was less grim. Canadian banking regulators departed from their American counterparts in prioritizing conservative loan loss provisioning practices in the 1990s and 2000s and pursued regulatory efforts that aligned with this goal, even when these efforts came with a heavy political cost. As a result, although Canadian banks experienced fewer loan losses overall than either American or Spanish banks, they were also comparatively well positioned to withstand the losses they did experience. In Spain, regulators went beyond the conservativism of the Canadian approach by implementing a unique requirement for loan loss provisioning known as "dynamic provisioning." Instead of merely encouraging banks to err on the side of caution in setting aside reserves, this approach mandated the application of an additional (regulator-determined) "statistical provision" to banks' loan loss calculations. Bank managers were forced to set aside larger provisions than they otherwise would during economic boom times. Although high loan losses during the Great Recession eventually also swamped the balance sheets of Spanish banks, placing many of these institutions into jeopardy, their sizeable loan loss reserves allowed them to weather the storm for much longer than banks in peer countries.[3]

The central argument of this chapter is that these divergent regulatory policy choices were shaped by the same overarching goals that guided other elements of regulatory policy making in each country, including the regulation of asset securitization described in the previous chapter. These different regulatory worldviews were not the only factors that mattered for the development of regulatory policy in this area—but they did matter. Banking regulators in the United States, Canada, and Spain in the 1990s and 2000s often faced different choice opportunities in regulating loan loss provisioning because of the different structures of their respective financial regulatory systems. For example, regulators in each country differed in the degree of autonomy they had in setting bank accounting standards, which came with implications for the range of policy responses structurally available to them. Yet in cases where choice was possible, the content of their regulatory worldviews helps to explain why regulators chose particular paths over alternatives.

Regulating Loan Loss Provisions: Beyond the Basel Standards

As a general rule, banks favor minimizing loan loss provisions for the same reason they seek to minimize regulatory capital: funds that banks set aside to absorb potential losses are not funds that can be used to finance new, potentially profitable investments. When a bank makes a loan loss provision, the value is recorded as an expense directly deducted from the current earnings reported on a bank's balance sheet. An implication is that if a bank makes a high loan loss provision one quarter, its ability to meet the quarterly earnings targets established by securities analysts (and closely watched by other market participants) may be threatened—an outcome that banks are generally eager to avoid. Banking regulators, on the other hand, tend to view conservative loan loss provisioning practices favorably. From a prudential standpoint, substantial loan loss reserves serve as critical buffers that protect bank operations from the inevitable ups and downs of an investment-based business.

Regulatory concerns about the adequacy of bank loan loss reserves became more salient in the late 1990s, when the global economy was in the middle of an extended period of expansion. Bank lending tends to follow a highly cyclical pattern, with lending standards growing increasingly lax during periods of economic prosperity and tightening up during times of economic distress or recession. As this expansionary phase continued, banking regulators around the world started to worry that their institutions might forget the lessons of the past and set aside too few reserves to absorb the losses that would inevitably arrive with a downturn.

Indeed, the text of the original 1988 Basel Capital Accord acknowledged the importance of loan loss reserves as a critical aspect of a bank's overall financial health, with direct implications for the sufficiency of its regulatory capital holdings.[4] The Basel Committee's initial attempts to achieve international convergence in this area, however, were ultimately abandoned after encountering roadblocks. Even today, bank loan loss provisioning is regulated almost entirely at the national level.

Prudential banking regulators, however, were not the only regulators concerned with what banks were doing in this area. Banking regulators may have focused on the implications of loan loss provisioning for bank stability and solvency, but accounting regulators were also highly interested in whether reported loan loss provisions were or were not sending accurate signals about the quality of a bank's loans to external observers. Accountants seek to present a clear, timely, and accurate picture of a firm's financial condition, and this presentation of accurate information to investors is understood as a basic precondition for the effective functioning of markets. Starting in the late 1990s, the actors who regulated bank accounting practices, which included both the organizations that established accounting standards (accounting standards setters) and the regulatory bodies charged with enforcing accounting and disclosure standards for publicly traded companies (securities regulators), became increasingly interested in the question of how well current loan loss provisioning arrangements were functioning as market signals.

Actors interested in the accurate and transparent presentation of a bank's financial condition found the practice of loan loss provisioning particularly concerning for a few reasons. First, the size of a bank's loan loss reserve—and by extension, the value of provisions it adds to this reserve—is supposed to reflect management's best estimate of losses inherent in the bank's loan portfolio *at that particular moment in time*. But these estimates are ultimately a judgment call. Since loan repayments are generally received on a fixed schedule (e.g., once a month), and it can take time for borrowers to begin missing payments, there is always a temporal gap between a loan's issuance and the moment it becomes apparent that the loan will carry a loss. External circumstances can also change in ways that increase the chances that at least some loans will turn out to be impaired (e.g., oil prices could go down, impacting the stability and creditworthiness of firms in the oil business), and this up-to-date reality should also be reflected in estimates of losses inherent within the loan portfolio.[5] In practice, the judgment calls bank managers must make about the expected impact of events on a bank's loan portfolio (that is, the estimates that guide the calculation of loan loss provisions) involve not only specific qualitative and quantitative information but also managerial discretion. And the impressionistic or privileged nature of some of this information also makes it difficult for external observers to independently verify the appropriateness of managerial choices in this area.

Second, accounting regulators also noted that close connections between loan loss provisions and a bank's reported income made this practice potentially ripe for abuse by managers seeking to obscure the true financial position of their firms. The manipulation of loan loss provisions could be used to boost or reduce reported earnings, and earnings were the main quantity that attracted shareholders' notice.

Third, accounting regulators recognized that managerial estimates of loan losses could easily become forward looking: that is, anticipating losses that could happen in the future, versus reflecting losses already suffered (but not yet materialized) at the present moment. A basic accounting principle is that information reported on the financial statement must reflect only events that took place before the statement date, not events that have not yet occurred.

Taken together, these features of the practice of loan loss provisioning made accounting regulators uneasy. They understood these problems to be especially acute for "general" provisions, one particular category of loan loss provisions. "Specific" loan loss provisions are designed to cover losses associated with certain, documented events (such as past-due payments, or other default-like events) and were generally allocated against known losses on individually assessed loans. As economists Claudio Borio and Philip Lowe explain, specific provisions—which tend to be supported by "verifiable evidence" of a probable loss and "backward-looking"—present fewer problems from an accounting standpoint.[6] General provisions, by contrast, cover losses associated with less precise or less certain events and are often supported by less direct verifiable evidence. General provisions were often allocated by banks against losses expected to affect an entire portfolio or category of loans (versus an individual loan). For example, a bank might use observations of the proportion of loans that had defaulted within the previous year to allocate general provisions for the current year.[7]

This concern among accounting regulators that bank managers might abuse the discretion they enjoyed in establishing provisions, especially general provisions, became even more pronounced in the late 1990s, as the problem of earnings management (firms using creative accounting techniques to manipulate reported earnings) rose to the top of the global policy agenda for these regulators. Although these basic dynamics were common to all three countries considered in this book, these conflicts between the interests of banking regulators and accounting regulators were resolved differently in each of them.

Before moving on to the heart of this story, a quick orientation to the organization of accounting and securities regulation in each country is necessary. In most countries, the organization charged with establishing generally accepted accounting principles (GAAP) for firms—the accounting standards setter—differed from the organization that enforces accounting and disclosure standards for publicly traded firms—the securities regulator. In the United States and Canada, the accounting standards setter was an independent, private-sector body made up of accounting professionals. In the United States, this body was the Financial Accounting Standards Board (FASB), created by the professional association of the country's Certified Professional Accountants (American Institute of Certified Public Accountants or AICPA) in 1973. Technically, the Securities and Exchange Commission (SEC), the securities regulator in the United States, had the official authority to establish GAAP for firms. In practice, however, the SEC has always delegated this authority to FASB and has respected its autonomy in setting standards.[8]

In Canada, the accounting standards setter (and FASB equivalent) was the Accounting Standards Board (AcSB), established by the professional association for chartered accountants in Canada (the Canadian Institute of Chartered Accountants or CICA). The AcSB retains statutory authority to set accounting standards; multiple securities regulators enforce compliance with accounting

TABLE 10.1. Division of Authority over Accounting Standards Setting and Accounting Regulation in the United States, Canada, and Spain

	Type of Activity			
	Accounting Standards		Enforcement of Firm Accounting/Disclosure Practices	
	Banks	Firms	Banks	Firms
Spain	Bank of Spain	ICAC/IFRS	Bank of Spain	CNMV
Canada	CICA		Provincial Securities Administrators	
US	SEC (delegates to FASB and AICPA)		SEC	

and disclosure practices. In Canada, securities law was developed and enforced at the provincial or territorial (versus federal) level; therefore, Canada had no equivalent of the federal SEC but rather operated with multiple securities regulators overseeing firms registered within the relevant province or territory. The Ontario Securities Commission (OSC), the securities regulator for the province of Ontario, played a particularly prominent role in this system because the country's financial capital, Toronto, was located within the province.

In Spain, the accounting standards setter was a government body. After 1989, the Instituto de Contabilidad y Auditoría de Cuentas (ICAC), an agency within the Ministry of Economy (MoE), was responsible for developing Spanish GAAP for all nonbank institutions. Accounting standards for banks, however, remained under the control of the Bank of Spain. Spanish autonomy in establishing GAAP was reduced by an EU directive adopted in June 2002 that that required all EU-area firms to prepare financial statements in accordance with International Financial Reporting Standards (IFRS) published by an independent, international, private-sector accounting body, the International Accounting Standards Board (IASB).[9] Throughout the 1990s and 2000s, the Spanish securities regulator, the Comisión Nacional del Mercado de Valores (CNMV), enforced appropriate accounting and disclosure practices for all nonbank financial institutions; the Bank of Spain served a similar function for banks. Table 10.1 summarizes the division of responsibility for the development and enforcement of accounting standards in each country.

Loan Loss Provisioning as Threat to Market Discipline in the United States

In September 1998, SEC Chairman Arthur Levitt announced a nine-point plan to combat the emerging practice of "earnings management" at publicly traded firms, that is, using aggressive accounting tactics to intentionally mislead stakeholders about the true economic condition of the firm. In the same period, the SEC had grown increasingly concerned that publicly traded banks might attempt to use general loan loss provisions to manipulate earnings. The specific worry was that bank managers might try to use general provisions to smooth earnings, deducting overly large provisions when quarterly performance was stronger than typical (reducing reported earnings), but overly small provisions when performance was weaker (boosting reported earnings).

Soon after Levitt's announcement, the SEC started to crack down on bank loan loss provisioning arrangements. It issued formal letters to a number of large banks, questioning their practices in this area. At the same time, the agency undertook a highly publicized investigation of loan loss provisioning practices at one prominent bank, SunTrust Bank, that had a reputation for conservatism and prudence. SunTrust was then in the process of acquiring another financial institution (Crestar Financial Corporation) and had a common-stock registration statement pending before the SEC. Before agreeing to grant approval, the SEC required SunTrust to restate and *reduce* its reported loan loss provisions for the years 1994–96. Note that SunTrust's reported provisions were not too low, as we might expect from a bank seeking to deceive investors by presenting an overly rosy picture of its true financial condition (again, recall that *lower* loan loss provisions equate with *higher* reported earnings). The problem, in the SEC's eyes, was that reported provisions at SunTrust were too high—the bank's executives had set aside more provisions than necessary to absorb the losses materializing in its loan portfolio.

Industry participants and banking regulators alike were alarmed by these actions. The adjustment that the SEC sought from SunTrust was expected to lead to a material change in the bank's reported earnings, which would increase by over $100 million. Most of the US federal banking and thrift regulatory agencies, the Federal Reserve included, were uncomfortable with the precedent the SEC's actions set. As they saw it, the timing of this crackdown on conservative loan loss provisioning could not have been worse. The US economy was then in the ninth year of what is conventionally a seven-year business cycle, and regulators were growing increasingly concerned about the credit risk likely accumulating within the banking system. If anything, this was a time for banks to err on the side of caution in provisioning for loan losses—but the SEC, with its recent enforcement actions, was sending the exact opposite message.[10] Banks themselves also viewed the SEC's actions in a negative light. Bank executives resented threats to their autonomy in determining appropriate provisions, and they also worried about the costs of getting caught in the middle of a turf battle between banking regulators (seeking larger reserves) and the SEC (seeking greater precision and transparency in loan loss provisioning).[11]

In November 1998, the banking and thrift regulators took collective action to prevent this experience from being repeated. They persuaded the SEC to join them in developing clearer regulatory guidance for loan loss provisioning. Yet even after the parties issued a joint statement announcing their commitment to working together, the SEC privately continued its crusade. In the months that followed, the securities regulator continued to send letters to financial institutions questioning loan loss reserve disclosure practices, a practice that alarmed bank executives and exacerbated the overall climate of uncertainty. The US banking regulators made another attempt to address this issue in March 1999, persuading the SEC to issue yet another joint statement reiterating a commitment to working alongside prudential regulators to improve regulatory guidance in this area.

Yet only one month after this second joint statement, the SEC was back to old patterns. On April 12, 1999, the Financial Accounting Standards Board (FASB) published a controversial article in *Viewpoints*, an official FASB publication that features staff and board member views on accounting matters. This article "clarified" the existing interpretation of GAAP related to loan loss provisioning by reprinting FASB's interpretation of Statement of Financial Accounting Standards No. 5 (FAS 5) virtually word for word. Firms were instructed by FAS 5 to calculate loan loss provisions based on loan losses that had already occurred ("incurred losses"), not losses that are expected to occur ("future losses").[12] The *Viewpoints* article was controversial not because of its content (which, again, did not change at all), but its timing.[13] Reiterating an accounting interpretation that bank managers already believed they were complying with raised a question—why had FASB chosen to publish it at all? Rex Schuette, chief accounting officer at State Street Corporation, described the confusion in the industry in this period: "Bankers want to know: is there a problem with the current accounting? Does the SEC view the rules differently from bank regulators and industry? If so, what are the rules?"[14]

The SEC only encouraged this uncertainty when it followed up on the *Viewpoints* article with an announcement—given at a public meeting of FASB's Emerging Issues Task Force—that banks should use the guidance outlined in the article to calculate loan loss provisions. While the SEC claimed to be "neutral" on the question of whether banks would need to adjust their current loan loss provisioning practices, they announced that any bank that had previously misinterpreted GAAP had until the end of the second quarter of 1999 to make appropriate adjustments without penalty. The announcement of this formal transition period only heightened concerns that the SEC was looking for a change in behavior.

At this point, most of the federal banking and thrift regulators were fed up. Three regulatory agencies—the Office of the Comptroller of the Currency (OCC), the Office of Thrift Supervision (OTS), and the Federal Deposit Insurance Corporation (FDIC)—requested that Congress hold formal hearings on the issue of loan loss provisioning regulation. The hearings that followed helped to clarify the SEC's motivations in this area. On June 16, 1999, SEC representatives, which included SEC general counsel Harvey Goldschmid, testified before the Financial Institutions and Consumer Credit Subcommittee of the US House of Representatives. Goldschmid opened by defending the FASB and SEC's recent actions, arguing that the SEC had a duty to combat excessively conservative loan loss provisions because they interfered with the "signals of capitalism" that allow markets to function effectively: "Let me explain the dangers. . . . Putting extra reserves, as much as possible in a reserve, sounds like it is good, the more the better for that rainy day. One danger is for shareholders. They will not know the true value of the bank if there are greatly excessive reserves. . . . The signals of capitalism that tell the markets and tell the board when things begin to go bad will not be there and the ability to correct early, to change course, to do good things will not be there also."[15] In essence, the SEC viewed conservative bank loan loss provisioning practices as incompatible with investor protection and adequate disclosure, and by extension, with effective market functioning. Investors needed accurate information to make informed choices.

Regulators at the OCC, OTS, and the FDIC countered these arguments by reminding policy makers that an aggressive crackdown on bank loan loss provisioning practices risked systemic instability. They explained that banks had already reported that they planned to lower loan loss reserves in response to the SEC's most recent actions and urged Congress to take steps to prevent this outcome.[16] Yet regulators from the Federal Reserve were conspicuously absent from this group. Only a few weeks earlier, these regulators had surprised their colleagues by seeming to ratify the SEC's position on loan loss provisioning (as reflected in the *Viewpoints* article). After the article was published, the Federal Reserve issued its own new guidance on loan loss provisioning. Although this guidance explicitly noted that banks should feel free to increase loan loss reserves under the terms of American GAAP, this was not how the industry interpreted the matter.[17] As one financial journalist writing for the *Journal of Accountancy* explained, most bankers interpreted this guidance as dissuading banks from engaging in conservative loan loss provisioning practices: "The Fed's guidance led bankers and bank regulators to worry that [the Fed], albeit indirectly, was encouraging reductions in allowances for loan losses at a point in the business cycle when prudence dictates such reserves should be increasing."[18]

In a speech given only two weeks before the June 1999 hearing, Federal Reserve Deputy Governor Laurence Meyer offered some insight into the considerations that had motivated the issuance of the agency's new guidance. As he explained it, "Although we disagree with the need for banking organizations to revise previous financial statements, battling the SEC on many of these issues seems not the proper course. They have an obligation to enforce sound reporting and disclosure practices as best they can, and our financial markets have been well served in the process. . . . As bank supervisors, we should [also] welcome the market's help to identify and assess banking risks and to minimize the risk of moral hazard."[19] Thus regulators at the Federal Reserve chose not to oppose the SEC's push for greater transparency in loan loss provisioning precisely because they saw this effort as consistent with the *broader objective of enhancing market discipline* in banking. Faced with the choice between preserving a traditional tool of banking regulation (conservative loan loss provisioning) and improving existing accounting and disclosure practices in ways designed to serve investor interests, the US banking regulators opted for the latter.

When Meyer was formally called to testify before the House subcommittee in June 1999, he backpedaled on this stance. He agreed that the SEC's endorsement of the *Viewpoints* article violated the collaborative arrangement between the securities regulator and the federal banking and thrift regulators, and was, on this basis, undesirable. At this point, however, the damage had been done. Trade press coverage from this period indicates that publicly traded banks were more confused than ever about the kinds of behavior regulators expected to see.

Pushed to come to an agreement by policy makers in the House and (later) the Senate, the federal banking regulators and the SEC issued a final joint statement on July 12, 1999, that clarified their mutual commitment to working together on regulating loan loss provisioning. As part of this statement, the SEC explicitly agreed to consult with the appropriate banking or thrift regulator when determining whether to bring enforcement actions against a bank thought to be setting aside excessively conservative loan loss provisions. This was the first time the SEC had offered this concession; on its face, it seemed like prudential considerations had finally triumphed over investor interests.

It soon became clear, however, that the interagency deliberations on appropriate loan loss provisioning standards were taking longer than expected. A draft proposal from the interagency loan loss provision working group, originally slated for release in March 2000, was still not ready by July of that year. Although none of the regulatory agencies offered an official explanation for the delay, confidential regulator comments to the media suggest that at least some saw it as the product of incommensurate priorities at the bank regulatory agencies and at the SEC: "Regulators have different explanations for the delay. . . . Some say that [it] stems in large part from disagreements between the banking agencies and the SEC. The bank regulators would prefer that banks be allowed to exercise judgment in setting reserve levels, while the SEC wants reserves to be tied to specific losses."[20]

As negotiations between the SEC and the bank regulatory agencies dragged on, developments elsewhere sparked additional pressure for regulatory change. In July 2000, the stalemate between the SEC and the federal banking regulators ended when a separate Taskforce on Allowance for Loan Losses established by AICPA (the professional association of certified public accountants in the United States) published a controversial draft proposal that clarified guidance for applying GAAP to bank loan loss provisioning. The taskforce had been created to provide a formal forum to resolve this increasingly controversial issue. The new guidance would have prevented banks from setting aside any general loan loss provisions at all.[21] Instead, banks would be allowed to increase loan loss provisions only in cases where a specific expected loss on a particular loan could be fully documented.

Unsurprisingly, the new guidance came under immediate attack from banking regulators, including the Federal Reserve. Although banking regulators successfully prevented this attempt to eliminate the entire category of general loan loss provisions, the actions of the AICPA taskforce greatly weakened the bargaining position of the banking regulators vis-à-vis accounting regulators. As Bert Ely, president of consulting firm Ely and Associates in Alexandria, Virginia, complained, "Loan-loss reserves have been around as long as banking, and all [regulators] had to do was defend well-established standard practices. Their delay created a vacuum that [accounting standards setters have] stepped into."[22] The episode finally came to an end in 2001, when the SEC and the federal bank and thrift regulatory agencies issued identical statements confirming that banks would need to abide by a much stricter interpretation of GAAP when calculating general loan loss provisions. Banks would be required to provide more documentation to support the reasonableness of any loss estimate, including by making some reference to historical loss rates for particular groups of loans.

Commentators regarded this as a victory for the SEC and its interests in enhanced transparency and precision. The reform had important implications. As Comptroller of the Currency John C. Dugan noted in 2009, it actively discouraged US banks from building up loan loss reserves at a time when credit risk was on the rise: "Using historical loss rates to justify significant provisions becomes more difficult in a prolonged period of benign economic conditions when loss rates decline. Indeed, the longer the benign period, the harder it is to use acceptable documentation based on history and recent experience to justify significant provisioning. When bankers were unable to produce such acceptable historical documentation, auditors began to lean on them . . . to reduce provisions."[23] Financial economists Eliana Balla and Andrew McKenna show that these policy choices also held direct implications for US banks' ability to withstand the 2008 global financial crisis. As loan losses accumulated, US banks were poorly positioned to absorb them. One result was that many banks were forced to significantly increase loan loss provisions at a time when liquidity was already in short supply, a practice that only compounded their troubles and set off a vicious cycle.[24]

In comparative perspective, two key developments in US loan loss provisioning regulation are especially noteworthy. The first is that the US banking regulators in the 1990s and 2000s did not define the proactive enhancement of bank loan loss reserves as a top regulatory priority. In other words, they were largely reactive, not proactive, in this regulatory domain. This was a pattern that held not just for the Federal Reserve, but also for the other federal banking and thrift regulatory agencies. Second, regulators at the Federal Reserve caved to pressure from accounting regulators to amend regulation in ways that discouraged a conservative approach to bank loan loss provisioning. With a broader agenda of enhancing market discipline in banking, regulators at the Federal Reserve were vulnerable to a line of reasoning that suggested that allowing banks to increase their buffers against losses beyond what market actors demanded would be incompatible with best regulatory practice.[25]

Loan Loss Provisioning as a Key Prudential Safeguard in Canada

In April 1998, the Canadian banking regulators were growing increasingly concerned about the credit risk accumulating within the banking system at a time of unprecedented prosperity. In a 1998 speech, OSFI Superintendent John Palmer explained that he worried that bank managers might face powerful temptations "to take on additional risk [when the economic cycle matures], without understanding what they're taking on because everything looks so good."[26] Soon after Palmer voiced these concerns, OSFI moved to strengthen bank practices in the area of loan loss provisioning.

The regulatory agency issued formal letters to all Canadian deposit-taking institutions. The letters encouraged banks to increase general loan loss provisions on the theory that the economic climate of the late 1990s was growing increasingly risky for lenders, and that general loan loss provisions should reflect this changing economic reality. All the major Canadian banks grudgingly complied with this request, slightly increasing their general loan loss provisions. Canadian bank profits were already under siege from rising global competition, and bank executives were hesitant to do anything that might disappoint shareholders by reducing reported earnings in this period. Nevertheless, they complied.[27]

However, even after banks took this initial step, regulators at OSFI remained dissatisfied. Remembering the experiences of the 1980s, in which Canadian banks had suffered significant losses on lending to less developed countries that they later struggled to absorb, regulators worried that bank loan loss reserves might still be inadequate to accommodate the challenges to come. Yet they also hesitated to impose new policies that might threaten bank profits at a delicate time. It was at this point that regulators at OSFI tried an alternative strategy: tinkering with bank accounting rules. Since the early 1990s, OSFI had held the statutory authority to "override" Canadian GAAP, which meant that the agency was legally authorized to permit banks to issue financial statements that departed from generally accepted accounting principles. Canadian banking regulators had never before used this power, which had been granted on the assumption that it would be used only in extreme circumstances, where prudential considerations required it. Typically, OSFI preferred to issue guidance related to accounting in collaboration with the Canadian Institute of Chartered Accountants (CICA), the private-sector body that established accounting standards for Canadian firms, and the provincial securities regulators who enforced compliance with these standards.

In October 1998, however, OSFI used its GAAP override powers for the first time as part of an effort to incentivize Canadian banks to boost general loan loss provisions. The agency sent formal letters to all federally regulated financial institutions that reiterated the need for banks to increase loan loss reserves and outlined two pathways for achieving this objective. The first pathway was for banks to gradually increase loan loss provisions over time, deducting them as expenses in accordance with established accounting standards—in other words, business as usual. The second, more controversial, pathway allowed banks to take a "one-time adjustment" to the loan loss reserve, deducting the expense of additional loan loss provisions from retained instead of current earnings. This approach violated GAAP and came with major implications for a bank's reported income. While deductions from *current* earnings are reflected on the income statement, deductions from *retained* earnings are not. Accordingly, banks that chose to utilize this second pathway would be free to increase loan loss provisions (pleasing regulators) while also avoiding any hit to reported earnings (pleasing bank executives accountable to investors and securities analysts).

Unsurprisingly, Canadian accounting regulators found the second pathway deeply distressing. They worried that investors would be misled about the bank's true financial condition. As one anonymous bank analyst explained in a 1999 *Financial Post* article, market participants interpreted these actions as evidence of OSFI's extreme commitment to maintaining high prudential safeguards, even at the expense of investor protection: "all [OSFI] wants is a prudent balance sheet. So to encourage banks to build their general reserves aggressively, OSFI passed them this carrot" of deducting the expense from retained earnings.[28]

For their part, regulators at OSFI argued that they would have preferred not to use their GAAP override powers, but inaction by the accounting bodies had forced their hands.[29] OSFI had held a series of meetings with CICA throughout 1997 and 1998 in which the banking regulators had urged the standards setter to reform accounting standards to allow for greater recognition of potential losses from as yet still-unimpaired loans. It was only after CICA hesitated to move forward on this initiative that OSFI took the unprecedented option of overriding GAAP.[30] This episode sent a clear signal to banks: ensuring that banks maintained substantial loan loss reserves was a critical priority for regulators—one that they were willing to spend valuable political capital to preserve.

Although the option to deduct loan loss provisions from retained earnings was extended to all chartered banks, only two minor banks (Quebec-based National Bank of Canada and Laurentian Bank of Canada) initially took OSFI up on this offer. While the Big Five Canadian banks probably would have liked to have followed suit, four of the five (the Bank of Montreal, Royal Bank of Canada, Toronto-Dominion Bank, and Canadian Imperial Bank of Commerce) were listed as publicly traded companies on the New York Stock Exchange (NYSE). Maintaining their NYSE membership required the banks to comply with US GAAP. Given the SEC's recent attack on loan loss provisioning arrangements, Canadian bank executives recognized that there would be no way to deduct general loan loss provisions from retained earnings and still remain US GAAP compliant.

Scotiabank, Canada's fifth-largest bank, did not face similar constraints because it was not listed on the NYSE. In December 1999, executives at Scotiabank elected to exercise the one-time opportunity to deduct loan loss provisions from retained earnings. The smaller Quebec-based banks had ruffled a few feathers when they enacted the change, but Scotiabank's decision represented a true scandal. Scotiabank not only was much larger than the Quebec banks—it also deducted a much larger loan loss provision ($550 million), with massive consequences for the bank's reported income. With the OSFI-sanctioned adjustment, Scotiabank's reported performance shifted from the very bottom to the very top of the Big Five banks.[31] At the time, CICA and many of the provincial securities regulators protested this accounting maneuver, but they lacked the legal authority to block it.

The Scotiabank case carried serious implications for the relationship between banking regulators and accounting regulators in Canada. Even before OSFI exercised its GAAP override, CICA had resented these powers and actively lobbied Canadian policy makers to repeal them.[32] In the aftermath of the Scotiabank episode, CICA's efforts only intensified. After 1999, the Ontario Securities Commission (OSC) joined CICA's crusade to strip OSFI's GAAP override powers. The OSC was especially embarrassed by the Scotiabank affair. Even before this event, the US-based SEC had hinted that it might withdraw from a regulatory agreement that allowed Canadian companies to offer securities in the United States using a prospectus based on Canadian disclosure requirements. Cancelling the agreement would have a devastating effect on Canadian financial markets. Accordingly, the OSC was especially keen to demonstrate its commitment to strict and transparent accounting and disclosure standards—meaning that Scotiabank's flagrant disregard for GAAP could not have come at a worse time.[33]

Intense public battles between OSFI, CICA, and the provincial securities regulators (especially the OSC) followed throughout the early 2000s, culminating in a series of parliamentary hearings. During these hearings, regulators at OSFI repeatedly contended that the GAAP override had been necessary to protect the safety and soundness of the banking system. As OSFI Superintendent Nicholas Le Pan explained in an August 2002 letter to the OSC, OSFI had "engaged in that effort [GAAP override] because we believed that it was important for safety and soundness reasons, because we believed that current GAAP did not adequately account for loan losses inherent in portfolios, and after a considerable (but unsuccessful) attempt to get accounting standards setters to reconsider the issue. Subsequent events have shown that our position was correct."[34] Representatives from the OSC and CICA countered by suggesting that the Scotiabank episode had shown that OSFI had become too powerful and was using its considerable powers to infringe on investor rights. They argued that investor protection depended on accounting standards that impartially reflect a firm's true financial position at a single point in time, and deviations (even those that served prudential goals) could not be tolerated.[35]

The Canadian banking regulators ultimately emerged victorious from this battle, retaining the statutory authority to override GAAP in cases where prudential considerations required such an approach. The victory, however, came at a high cost. The relationship between accounting standards setters and securities regulators suffered a heavy blow, and as late as 2013, interviews with banking regulators and accounting standards setters suggested that each group continued to hold very different perspectives on the legitimacy of OSFI's actions in this area.[36]

The Canadian approach to regulating bank loan loss provisioning stands out in comparative perspective in two major respects. First, it is clear that OSFI identified the enhancement of bank reserves against potential loan losses as a vital regulatory priority. This helps to explain why the regulatory agency used a controversial power to promote this goal, and why regulators justified the exercise of this power in the terms that they did. Second, the approach that OSFI took to proactively strengthen bank loan loss reserves also differed from the more heavy-handed and interventionist approach employed by regulators elsewhere, including at the Bank of Spain. The agency provided banks with a regulatory carrot to voluntarily induce increased provisions; it did not mandate a specific increase. This approach thus walked the fine line of balance between prudential and competitive considerations that Canadian regulators were hoping to achieve in this period. Ensuring that banks maintained high-quality reserves was a crucial part of protecting consumers from "undue loss," yet regulators remained attuned to need to leave banks free to voluntarily select this line of action if possible.

Provisioning to Counterbalance Procyclicality in Spain

Spain's long-desired entry into the European Economic and Monetary Union (EMU) in the late 1990s came with some less desirable economic consequences alongside beneficial ones. With EMU membership, short-term interest rates in Spain declined from the double digits (13.3 percent) in 1992 to the single digits (3.0 percent) in 1999, dropping even further (to 2.2 percent) by 2005.[37] Predictably, this sharp reduction in interest rates led to greatly expanded investment and demand for credit by households and businesses. Spain's entry into the EMU had also sent positive signals to foreign investors, encouraging additional investment dollars to pour into the country. By the start of the new millennium, Spain was in the midst of a massive credit boom and unprecedented economic expansion—arguably an even stronger version of what the United States was experiencing in the same period.

Regulators at the Bank of Spain were attuned to the potential prudential dangers of this trend. In a 2000 working paper, they pointed to the rising ratio of total loans to loan loss provisions among Spanish banks as an especially worrying development from the standpoint of safety and soundness:

> It is very difficult to persuade bank managers to follow more prudent credit policies during an economic upturn, especially in a highly competitive environment. Even conservative managers might find market pressure for higher profits very difficult to overcome. This is compounded by the fact that for many countries loan loss provisions are cyclical, increasing during the downturn and reaching their lowest level at the peak. To a large extent, this reflects an inadequate ex post accounting of credit risk. . . . Many credit risk mistakes are made during the expansionary phase of the economic cycle although they only become apparent ex post in the downturn.[38]

In other words, the Spanish banking regulators assumed that bank managers were naturally prone to loosen credit standards during economic booms, like the extreme credit boom that Spain was currently experiencing. Making matters worse, prevailing loan loss provisioning practices generally reflected this same optimism, with bank managers blissfully overlooking potential risks accumulating in their loan portfolios until it was too late.

Like the Canadian banking regulators, then, the Spanish banking regulators were highly concerned about the adequacy of banks' loan loss reserves. However, they differed from their Canadian peers in the additional emphasis they placed on the specific dangers of procyclicality in loan loss provisioning. Banking regulators worldwide recognized that loan loss provisioning was a highly procyclical activity, because banks generally must increase provisions dramatically whenever economic performance declines (e.g., when more loans are likely to become impaired). These sharp jumps in necessary provisions tend to exacerbate the credit crunches that appear during recessions.[39] But this observation carried different weight or salience across national contexts. In Spain, where combatting procyclicality was at the very top of the regulatory agenda, this particular feature of loan loss provisioning was also more likely to be seen as an issue in need of an immediate regulatory solution.

The model of dynamic provisioning that the Spanish banking regulators introduced in July 2000 was explicitly marketed by these regulators as a corrective to the procyclical nature of loan loss provisioning.[40] It added a new class of loan loss provision, the statistical provision, to the traditional categories of general and specific provisions. The statistical provision weighted a bank's own estimate of specific and general provisions by a factor that varied with the economy's place within the credit cycle. This factor would be larger (forcing bank managers to set aside more provisions than they otherwise would have) when credit conditions were good, and smaller (encouraging bank managers to reduce provisions and lend more freely) when credit conditions were bad. The purpose was to proactively guide banks toward better budgeting for latent expected losses by counteracting market forces, that is, the known effects of procyclicality.[41]

Spanish banks had two options for calculating the statistical provision. First, they could use their own historical loss experience during different phases of the business cycle. Alternatively, they could apply a set of coefficients developed by regulators at the Bank of Spain. In both cases, the statistical provision involved imposing regulators' views of appropriate loan loss provisions over those of bank managers or shareholders.

To justify the adoption of dynamic provisioning, the Spanish banking regulators emphasized its prudential benefits. But, importantly, they also contended that this method of calculating provisions offered a more *accurate* depiction of the loan losses that were likely to materialize in the loan portfolio. In a context where bank managers and other market participants were believed to suffer from biases that distorted their perceptions of credit risk, a policy framework that allowed more far-seeing, public-minded regulators to adjust for these misguided perceptions was also expected to bring loan loss provisions closer to the "true value" of impaired loans.[42]

The Spanish banking regulators faced considerable opposition from accounting regulators over the issue of dynamic provisioning, although this opposition did not come from within the country. Instead, it came from accounting standards setters at the IASB, the international accounting standards-setting body. After the EU in 2002 agreed to require all firms to prepare financial statements in accordance with International Financial Reporting Standards (IFRS) on or before January 1, 2005, Spain's unique dynamic provisioning model came under threat. From the standpoint of the IASB, the key issue was that the statistical provision was forward looking rather than reflective of losses already contained within the bank's loan portfolio. One IFRS standard—IAS 39: Financial Instruments, Recognition and Measurement—addressed this issue explicitly, requiring all banks to use a backward-looking, incurred-loss method to determine loan loss provisions. It specifically clarified "that loan loss provisions should not anticipate future events."[43]

The requirement to transition to IFRS standards presented regulators at the Bank of Spain with a serious dilemma. It seemed obvious that dynamic provisioning would no longer pass muster under the terms of this new accounting framework (given IAS 39). And at a time when regulators at the Bank of Spain had recently worked very hard to signal Spain's commitment to joining international and regional economic communities, they found it uncomfortable to be noncompliant with international standards. At the same time, the Spanish banking regulators also regarded dynamic provisioning as one of their most important regulatory accomplishments. They were not ready to give up such an important prudential tool, and they fought hard to retain it.

In sharp contrast to the implementation of international accounting standards related to asset securitization, regulators at the Bank of Spain spent valuable political capital resisting the IASB's efforts to eliminate dynamic provisioning. They responded to the IASB's critiques with multiple arguments, most of which emphasized that the statistical provision offered a more accurate and precise reflection of a bank's true economic condition at a point in time.[44] Bankers, they argued, are too reluctant to recognize latent losses during periods of economic prosperity. Since loan losses actually exist from the moment a bad loan is granted, the statistical provision (which corrected for this bias) better represented a bank's *true economic reality*. Thus, regulators argued, there was no conflict between the goals of accountants and the goals of banking regulators on this front. As a group of regulators explained in a 2000 working paper:

> There is something wrong in the level of profits shown [in financial reports] if the latent credit risk in the loan portfolio is not properly taken into account. Every loan intrinsically has an expected (or potential) loss that should be recognised as a cost by means of an early provision. Otherwise, the picture of the true profitability and solvency of the bank over time could be distorted. . . . If the total cost of the loan is not properly recognised and accounted for, bank managers willing to gain market share may be tempted during economic expansions to underprice loans. More conservative managers will face strong incentives to follow this aggressive pricing. . . . All these facts . . . seem to point at the same direction: there is a need for a statistical provision that covers the expected loss inherent to the loan portfolio.[45]

In 2004, these banking regulators and the IASB finally reached a compromise. The Bank of Spain agreed to adopt an amended loan loss provisioning regime for banks that was at least nominally an "incurred-loss" model (in keeping with the requirements of IAS 39). Yet the practical impact was virtually identical to that of the dynamic provisioning regime. The key change was that the statistical provision was reclassified: instead of serving as its own category, it was collapsed under the broader heading of a general provision and regulated accordingly.[46]

In comparative perspective, then, the Spanish banking regulators made it extremely clear that their priority in the domain of loan loss provisioning was to preserve a valuable regulatory tool that combatted the dangerous effects of procyclicality, a key area of concern for regulators seeking to enhance state oversight and guidance in banking.

Conclusion

The case of setting rules for bank loan loss provisioning offers additional insight into the drivers of divergent regulatory policy choices in the United States, Canada, and Spain in the decades leading up to the global financial crisis of the late 2000s. This represented a regulatory domain, unlike the regulation of bank capital requirements, in which national policy makers enjoyed considerable freedom to set their own standards.

In the United States, banking regulators at the Federal Reserve failed to prioritize banks erring on the side of conservativism when establishing loan loss reserves in the 1990s and 2000s. In fact, they yielded to pressure from accounting standards setters to reduce the discretion of bank managers in this area, affirming SEC policy statements that discouraged banks from being too conservative. In Canada, regulators at OSFI used virtually every policy tool at their disposal to encourage banks to increase the size of their loan loss reserves in the 1990s and 2000s. In the late 1990s, they spent valuable political capital by invoking their controversial GAAP override powers, a strategy they defended even in the face of sharp opposition from accounting standards setters well into the 2000s. In Spain, regulators at the Bank of Spain went even further. They developed a unique loan loss provisioning regime that forced bank managers to set aside additional provisions when times were good, which was designed to reduce the disruptive effects of procyclical market forces. Like their Canadian peers, the Spanish regulators also spent valuable political capital defending this practice from international accounting standards setters when it came under attack in the mid-2000s.

These divergent policy choices came with implications for bank performance during the crisis. The volume of poor-performing loans varied substantially across the three countries: banks in the United States and Spain saw greater problems in this area than banks in Canada (see figure 10.1). Yet

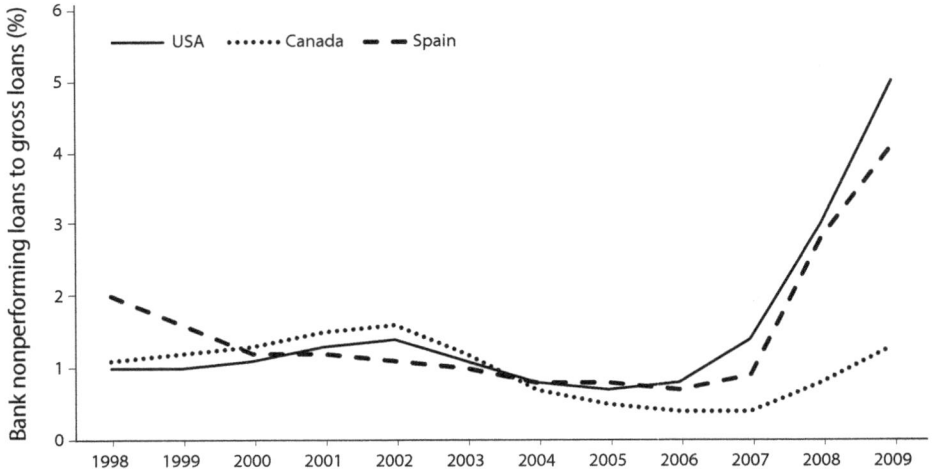

FIGURE 10.1. Bank nonperforming loans to total gross loans in the United States, Canada, and Spain, 1998–2009. *Source*: International Monetary Fund, Financial Soundness Indicators Database, fsi.imf.org (accessed June 1, 2017).

compared to the United States, both Canadian and Spanish banks were comparatively well provisioned against the loan losses they experienced.[47]

To explain the origins of these divergent policy choices, this chapter returned to a by-now familiar source: the principles of order reflected in the different worldviews of national banking regulators. The American banking regulators, obsessed with the benefits of enhancing market discipline and attuned to the dangers of its absence (in keeping with the principle of *competition*), were seemingly persuaded by the SEC's claims that forcing banks to reduce the size of their reserves against bad loans would improve the functioning of market mechanisms. This helps to explain their relative inaction in this important area, especially when compared their peers in other countries. By contrast, the Canadian banking regulators, consumed with striking the right balance between competitive considerations and prudential consumer protection (in keeping with the principle of *public rights*), viewed loan loss provisioning as an area where regulators had a duty to hold firm. The size of a bank's loan loss reserve, which directly impacted its ability to buffer loss, was framed as an important target for regulatory action on this basis. This helps explain why OSFI regulators took such a powerful and interventionist stance in this area when they failed to do so in many other regulatory domains. Finally, the Spanish banking regulators, focused on enhancing state oversight and guidance to the financial system (in keeping with the principle of *state sovereignty*), were much more concerned about the dangerous effects of procyclicality—which they saw as a natural outcome of unchecked market forces—than their American or Canadian peers. These concerns manifested in the unique regulatory treatment of loan loss provisioning, in which regulators attempted to counterbalance these effects by requiring bank managers to set aside more provisions than they otherwise would during times of economic prosperity. Once again, these different regulatory goals came with real implications for the development of different regulatory policies across countries at a critical time.

11

Visions of Financial Order

The 2008 financial crisis unfolded against the backdrop of different national regulatory regimes, which held important implications for how banks experienced these events. In the United States, banks famously enjoyed free reign to experiment with innovative financial instruments and faced little direct oversight of the risks they were taking. This lax regulatory regime led to predictable consequences when the excesses of the 1990s and early 2000s came to an end. In Canada, regulators also gave banks considerable freedom to pursue innovative activities, but they did more to insist that banks maintain conservative buffers against potential losses. While these regulatory choices represent only one piece of the broader Canadian success story during the crisis, they were relevant. In Spain, banks encountered much tighter restrictions on their abilities to partake in innovative activities and also faced a uniquely conservative regulatory regime in terms of setting aside reserves against potential losses. Stringent banking regulation did not stop the crisis from coming to Spain, but the troubles for Spanish banks would have been much worse without these standards in place.

In this book, I argue that different viewpoints among regulators, informed by nationally specific principles of order, offer a compelling explanation for the divergent regulatory outcomes that featured in the 2008 global financial crisis. By following the different regulatory paths taken in three countries—the United States, Canada, and Spain—in the decades leading up the crisis, I reveal how banking regulators in each country subscribed to different understandings of the causes of order and prosperity in the financial system, which encouraged different regulatory approaches in crucial areas. Too often, commentary on the financial system treats regulators as actors set apart from the rest of society, who operate in a world guided exclusively by scientific expertise and impartial mathematical modeling. This book counters that impression by revealing how often the actions of these regulators were guided by deeply rooted understandings about what makes a "good society" (or "good economy"). Regulators, like the rest of us, fill in gaps in their understanding by drawing from taken-for-granted assumptions about how the world works.

This account of regulatory policy making departs from the conceptualization of regulators currently found in most of the interdisciplinary scholarship on financial regulation. Dominant perspectives depict regulators as powerless to resist the many pressures associated with changing economic imperatives in a globalizing world, or alternatively, as neutral participants in a political process dominated by the regulated industry. My approach differs. I present financial regulators as autonomous social actors in their own right, with distinct worldviews that are not incidental to their choices but rather vital to them. Yes, as regulatory capture explanations have long suggested, regulated industries vary in their relative power and capacity to influence their regulators. But it is equally possible—yet not equally recognized—that national regulators may also be more or less receptive to industry arguments for reasons of their own. Attention to this additional source of influence on regulatory policy making allows for a deeper and better understanding of key trends in the evolution of financial regulatory systems.

In this respect, my perspective complements a small but growing literature on "cultural capture," which also suggests that regulators may be more or less vulnerable to industry influence for ideological and social reasons. The cultural capture account suggests that when regulators share common backgrounds, experiences, or network connections with those in regulated financial institutions, they are also more likely to be receptive toward industry arguments.[1] This account improves on standard regulatory capture explanations by going beyond purely material motivations (e.g., outright bribery, the promise of a job in the industry) to emphasize the "soft pressures" regulators encounter from the regulated industry. However, it still shares capture theory's emphasis on *industry pressure* as the central driver of policy making. Where I diverge from the cultural capture perspective is in my insistence that regulators are not simply the guardians of industry. They are also members of broader professional communities and (crucially!) of national societies. This multifaceted group membership opens regulators up to a much broader array of influences than even the most complex variant of the capture perspective considers. Regulation can be bad, in other words, even at times or in places where regulators are less beholden to the regulated industry. Indeed, financial regulators in different countries have often made different policy choices, I argue, because they inhabit different institutions that supply different visions of the causes of order and prosperity.

Institutional Change

The history of financial regulation in the last quarter of the twentieth century is undeniably a story of dramatic policy change. Between the 1960s and the 1990s, policy makers around the world cast off familiar models of banking regulation and embraced new ones that broke, often radically, with well-established national traditions. It is reasonable to think of financial policy making in this era, then, as an episode of *institutional change*.

The problem of institutional change has long presented a conceptual puzzle for sociologists, political scientists, and other scholars of institutions.[2] If institutions exert such powerful effects on policy making, and in ways that tend to fuel the reproduction of familiar policy approaches within countries over long stretches of time, then how do radical departures from the policy norm even become possible? Many of the scholars who have taken up this question have emphasized the role of crisis in encouraging departures from established paths.[3] Crises encourage change by raising questions about a formerly unchallenged status quo, widening political opportunities for challenger groups to promote new visions.

The process of crisis and reform also lies at the heart of the dramatic shifts in national approaches to financial regulation we observe in the 1980s and beyond. But attention to the disruptive power of crisis gets us only so far toward understanding why new regulatory models, when they arrive, take the distinctive forms that they do. Some scholars of institutional change have highlighted an additional influence that enables and constrains subsequent regulatory policy making: past historical experience, which shapes the range of options reformers consider when mobilizing for change. Focusing on the case of the American electricity industry in the 1920s and 1930s, for example, sociologist Marc Schneiberg shows how late nineteenth-century struggles over the emerging corporate order also left behind "organizational legacies" that later served as resources for groups seeking to challenge existing institutional arrangements.[4] The nature of these past "struggles, experiments with other possibilities and movements for alternatives" paved the way for the emergence of a very different, cooperative, and publicly based model of organizing electricity provision alongside the dominant model of large-firm corporate capitalism. The experiences of the past shaped the kinds of regulatory alternatives considered in the present.

When it came to the historical evolution of financial regulation, I find a very similar process at play. Here, actors within countries also drew from the legacies of the past to construct and advance new regulatory solutions in the aftermath of disruptive financial crises. Yet the content of these past struggles and experiments within countries were shaped themselves by larger social forces, and in ways that existing research has yet to fully realize. The organizational legacies that served as resources for regulatory reformers in the United States, Canada, and Spain—in the 1930s, yes, but also in the 1860s and the 1980s—reflected more than mere historical accident or chance. The conflicts of the past were institutionally patterned. Within the United States, for example, it was no accident that Thomas Jefferson and Alexander Hamilton fought over the same basic underlying principles of financial order as Paul Volcker and Ronald Reagan nearly two centuries later. It was also no accident that the principles underlying American regulatory debates were so persistently different from the principles that drove debate in Canada or Spain. Principles of order, embedded in national political and economic institutions, are broad enough to justify a range of policy stances; they also fluctuate in their relative dominance and latency within regulatory systems over time. Both processes help to explain why the specific content of financial regulation bounced back and forth between very different models over time—even as the pendulum's arc remained constrained by the principles of order that the broader institutional context made readily available and salient to national actors.

Attention to the *institutionally structured* nature of both past and present regulatory conflict, I argue, provides the key to solving one of the main puzzles that motivated this book: why regulatory standards remained so persistently different *across* countries even as they changed so dramatically *within* countries over time. Attempts to reduce these distinctive but evolving regulatory approaches to economic, political, or even purely structural considerations quickly run aground on empirical patterns that defy conventional expectations.[5]

Previous cultural accounts of economic policy making have been heavily criticized for their excessive determinism; for failing to recognize how specific cultural elements can travel across national borders, especially in the modern globalized era; and for neglecting or underplaying conflict, opposing views, or institutional alternatives within national settings.[6] All these critiques are valid, and it is important for modern scholars advancing culturally informed theories of policy making to avoid falling into the same traps. Yet it is equally important to recognize that the most recent generation of cultural-institutional theories of economic policy making, including those that describe countries in terms of their central institutional tendencies, are entirely compatible with accounts that emphasize heterogeneity and conflict within institutional orders. The answer to concerns about inadequate attention to agency or conflict in economic policy making is not to avoid cultural considerations altogether, as most of the existing scholarship on financial regulation has done. The answer is to make existing cultural explanations better.

Understanding the Ruptures of Post-1970s Capitalism

The 1970s represented a turning point in financial systems around the world. In this decade, the strong regulation and stability of the 1950s and 1960s started to give way to the permissiveness and economic instability that would come to define the neoliberal era. In the realm of social policy, governments pulled back on their former commitments to equality and rights, developing new approaches that individualized what were formerly collective risks and transferred the responsibility for supplying valued public goods from states to markets.[7] Similar dynamics played out in the realm of economic policy, as policy makers around the world scaled back on regulatory restraints in sectors from finance to transportation to telecommunications.

The policy changes of this period have already captured considerable attention from sociologists, primarily because they served as the starting point for many of the most significant economic and social transformations of the past three decades. Accounts of the precipitous rise in income inequality, the growing size and influence of financial markets, the growing power (and changing form) of corporations, and the increasing financialization of the economy all start with the neoliberal policy changes of the 1970s and 1980s.[8] Scholars have honed in on financial deregulation as a particularly influential shift.

My account adds to current understandings of the ruptures of post-1970s capitalism by revealing how these influential regulatory changes also depended on important but overlooked cultural and institutional dynamics. Most existing accounts of these policy changes were developed by analyzing the US case of regulatory transformation in isolation. They have emphasized, variously, the effects of rising inflation in the 1960s and 1970s, which led policy makers to seek to avoid blame for increasingly contentious choices about credit allocation; the effects of shifting paradigms within the economics discipline, which provided an intellectual justification for a turn toward market-oriented policy; the rising power of regulated financial institutions; and political dynamics within adversarial decision-making institutions or more credit-dependent political economies.[9]

Yet placing the US case of financial deregulation in comparative perspective reveals new and unexpected trends that earlier accounts struggle to explain. Perhaps the most striking trend is that the United States was comparatively slow, in international perspective, to embrace most forms of financial deregulation. This is not the outcome we expect from the country so often described as the paradigmatic neoliberal economy. Of course, nothing about this observation implies that the drivers of deregulation outlined above were not operating in this case. But it does change the nature of what these accounts are explaining. Each of the factors singled out by previous accounts—economic turmoil, paradigm shifts within the economics discipline, political contestation over credit, or the rising power of regulated firms—explains how American advocates of regulatory reform ultimately overcame resistance to push through a deregulatory vision. What they cannot explain, however, is why this resistance to financial deregulation in the United States was so pronounced in comparison to other countries. To explain this—an equally important feature of the puzzling American path to neoliberalism—we must turn to the broader cultural landscape that US regulatory reformers *and* their opponents were navigating in this and earlier periods.

An awareness of these cultural drivers of regulatory policy making clarifies certain aspects of the economic and social trends that followed. The United States currently stands out in global perspective in both its degree of financialization and its extremity of income and wealth inequality. Scholars have located the roots of both trends in the extensive US financial deregulation of the 1980s.[10] But placing the US case in comparative perspective introduces new questions about how, exactly, the policy developments of this era gave rise to these trends. Is it possible, for example, that the United States became so remarkably financialized *because* American policy makers dragged their heels on the kinds of deregulatory reforms that were then unfolding in other countries around the world? This interpretation seems especially likely in the context of recent studies that find that modern markets for securitization and other complex financial instruments emerged from the attempts of American legislators (or the members of the Johnson administration) to evade political pressures that emerged *in a highly regulated financial system* in the 1960s and 1970s.[11]

The Future of Banking Regulation—and What Can We Do about It?

What insights does this book have to offer to those interested in understanding the ongoing development of national financial regulatory systems—or changing these systems? One key lesson is that a full understanding of the regulatory policy-making process—both today and historically—requires closer attention to the broad principles of order that have guided the development of national systems of financial regulation for centuries.

The regulatory patterns that emerged across the three countries considered in the aftermath of the 2008 financial crisis offer a case in point. Although specific regulatory policies changed in both Canada and Spain after the crisis, the overarching orientation or goals of banking regulation in both countries has changed very little.[12] In the United States, regulatory change was more substantial, but even the most radical of these changes followed a predictable pattern. Consider the controversial Volcker rule, a centerpiece of the 2010 Dodd-Frank Act reform legislation. The Volcker rule prohibits commercial banks from engaging in proprietary trading or from investing in, or sponsoring, hedge funds or private equity funds. These new restrictions on bank activities signaled a clear departure from the hands-off regulatory approach that defined the United States in the 1990s and 2000s. At the same time, they also reflected a return to a by-now familiar American principle of order: *community sovereignty*, with its emphasis on the inherent benefits of specialization and fragmentation.[13] Even as the American regulatory system has changed considerably since the crisis, then, these seemingly radical changes have still unfolded in roughly predictable ways.

This observation raises questions about the potential for effective regulatory change. Are national policy makers doomed by institutions to repeat the regulatory mistakes of the past? Not necessarily. As the American case at the end of the twentieth century indicates, the institutions that are the focus of this study are flexible enough to accommodate a range of specific policy approaches. The same broader American institutional context, after all, was conducive to the development of one of the world's strictest systems of banking regulation (in the 1930s through the early 1980s) *and* one of its most permissive bank regulatory systems (in the 1990s and 2000s). Better or worse regulatory outcomes are possible in every institutional setting.

However, recognizing institutional influence in regulatory policy making does hold implications for where we should—and shouldn't—focus our efforts in attempting to bring about a more effective approach to financial regulation. Regulatory reforms designed to combat "regulatory capture" are still welcome. There are plenty of problems in this area to be solved. But it is important to recognize that this is likely to be only a partial fix. If the viewpoints of regulators themselves are also a source of more or less effective regulation, as I have argued in this book, attempts to limit industry influence in regulatory policy making are unlikely to catalyze substantial change on their own. Admittedly, recognizing that the situation is more complicated than the regulatory capture account suggests makes the problem of ineffective regulation much harder to solve. But denying this reality will not get us any closer to solving it.

Where should we focus our efforts instead? Americans today tend to see the stances of the political left and political right on financial regulation as being very different. The left worries about the capacity for large and diversified financial institutions to exploit their market power at the public's expense, and seeks to limit this power, either by subjecting systemically important institutions to stricter regulatory oversight or by forcing these institutions to become smaller or more specialized. The right worries about the hazards of government interference with beneficial competitive market forces, and seeks to minimize regulation because it might disrupt these market mechanisms. But placing these stances in comparative perspective reveals that they are actually flipsides of the same cultural coin.

As we move into a new, increasingly interconnected and complex era in the global financial system, I suggest that banking regulators—inside and outside the United States—must start thinking more broadly and creatively about potential regulatory solutions if they hope to keep pace with these changes. As recent episodes of crisis have made clear, large banks are not the only financial institutions that can get into trouble—or threaten to bring the rest of the financial system down with them. In the United States, the recent failures of smaller regional banks like Silicon Valley Bank, Signature Bank, or First Republic Bank are not easily explained by the usual American regulatory preoccupations with the hazards of concentrated power, functional diversification, or government overreach. To make greater sense of recent events, as well as better progress toward preventing the next crisis, American regulators might instead draw inspiration from some of the principles of order that have guided regulatory policy making in other countries—especially countries that did a better job of navigating the financial crisis the last time around. Regulators have more resources at their disposal than they realize; they can draw tools from other toolboxes.

The Spanish example may be particularly instructive. Spanish banking regulators have long been attuned to the potential downsides of rising competitive pressures, particularly their role in encouraging banks to take on greater risk. This view of a key and underrecognized factor that motivates banks to engage in undesirable behavior also happens to align with a large and growing body of scholarship in economic sociology that finds that organizations become more likely to cross the line into illegality, malfeasance, or excessive risk taking when they encounter more intense market pressures.[14] This pressure can come from greater exposure to profit-hungry shareholders, the need to respond to competitors, higher funding costs, or the threat of slow-growing profits. Regardless, the outcome is the same: banks facing greater market pressure are the most likely to get into trouble.

This alternative account of why banks take excessive risks implicates a very different kind of regulatory approach. Instead of seeking to reduce the size or the diversification of individual financial institutions, or alternatively, reducing the government's footprint in financial markets, American regulators might instead focus on blunting the intensity of the market pressures modern banks experience. In practice, this might come in the form of greater use of countercyclical capital or reserve buffers, following the general regulatory approach that the Spanish banking regulators pioneered in the early 2000s.[15] It could also come in the form of tighter regulatory limits on the types of funding sources banks are eligible to use, stricter liquidity requirements, or requirements to implement additional, risk-restraining corporate governance practices. One crucial point, however, is that these restrictions must apply to *all* financial institutions, not simply the largest ones or those that benefit from the greatest government protection. If market pressure itself drives undesirable organizational behavior, it follows that all financial institutions (and not just big or highly protected ones) are vulnerable to its effects. To avoid the regulatory mistakes of the past, the American financial regulatory framework must expand its scope to reflect this reality.

Of course, all of this is easier said than done. Even if American regulators embrace these alternative regulatory possibilities, they will face an uphill battle justifying them to policy makers and the public. Institutions place powerful limits on the kinds of arguments or justifications that make sense to actors, and many of the remedies outlined above will likely feel "unnatural" or "foreign" or "imported" to most Americans. Regulations designed to counterbalance or mitigate market forces violate the principle of *competition*, by allowing the judgment of regulators to override the collective judgment of market participants. And regulations that subject small financial institutions to the same standards as large ones violate the principle of *community sovereignty*, by undercutting the relative competitive position (and potentially, the independence and survival) of smaller, community banks.

These regulatory changes, then, will probably require considerable proactive justification from regulators to be accepted. Departing from the narrow array of regulatory models currently entertained in the US financial system is likely to be a challenge—but it is a challenge worth undertaking. If Americans want to continue with the market-oriented (or large-firm-focused) regulatory approaches of the past in other domains of the economy, then so be it. But the banking system, with its wide-ranging impact on the rest of society, is too important. As recent episodes of crisis have shown, when it comes to banking and finance, we no longer have the luxury of sticking with the same narrow regulatory scripts.

US Financial Deregulation in Comparative Perspective

The vast majority of scholarship on financial deregulation has focused on four events within the United States. These four defining events include:

- the 1980 Depository Institutions Deregulation and Monetary Control Act, which eliminated regulatory ceilings on the interest rates banks could offer on time or savings deposits
- the 1982 Garn-St Germain Depository Institutions Act, which broadened the range of permitted activities for nonbank savings institutions (thrifts)
- the 1994 Riegle-Neal Interstate Banking and Branching Efficiency Act, which repealed prohibitions on banks opening branch offices in other states
- the 1999 Gramm-Leach-Bliley Act, which repealed prohibitions on bank affiliation with organizations engaged in the underwriting, sale, or distribution of securities

Table A.1 compares the dates of each these deregulatory events in the United States with the dates of similar events in five of the world's other major financial capitals (Canada, Spain, Germany, France, and the UK). If a country lacked a similar regulatory restriction to begin with, this is denoted with "-".

Looking across all four domains of deregulation, we see that US policy makers were consistently the last or among the last to dismantle established regulatory restrictions in these key areas. Each deregulatory event is discussed in greater detail below.

Deregulation of Interest Rate Ceilings

In 1960, each of the six countries listed in table A.1 had some form of interest rate ceiling (restrictions on the maximum rates banks could offer on loans or deposits or both) in place. The US Banking Act of 1933 had granted the Federal

TABLE A.1. Patterns of Financial Deregulation in the United States, Canada, Spain, Germany, France, and the UK between 1960 and 1999

	Restriction to Be Deregulated			
	Interest Rate Ceilings	Bank Branching Restrictions	Prohibition on Securities Activities	Limits on Savings Bank Activities
US	1980	1994	1999	1982
Canada	1967	-	1987	1980
Spain	1974	1977	1974	1977
Germany	1967	-	-	-
France	1984	1966	1966	1966
UK	1971	-	1986	1986

Reserve the authority to limit the maximum rates commercial banks could offer on time, savings, or demand deposits. In 1980, US policy makers signaled their intention to eliminate these restrictions by passing the Depository Institutions Deregulation and Monetary Control Act. However, not until 1986 were deposit rate ceilings for American banks and thrifts completely phased out. Banks in certain US states also faced restrictions on the maximum interest rates they could charge on loans. The deregulation of these restrictions on loan rates began in 1978, when legislators in Delaware voted to eliminate them for in-state banks.[1] Banks in Germany, Spain, and France also faced interest rate ceilings on both deposits and loans; banks in Canada and the UK faced interest rate ceilings on loans only.[2]

Table A.1 shows that, by the time that US policy makers took their initial steps toward deregulating Regulation Q in 1980, four of the five other countries had already undertaken similar reforms. Canada completely liberalized loan rates and Germany completely liberalized loan and deposit rates in 1967.[3] British policy makers followed suit in 1971, and Spanish policy makers took gradual steps toward liberalizing loan and deposit rates in 1974, 1977, and 1981.[4] In Spain, policy makers liberalized the interbank rate, rates on loans with more than three-year terms, and long-term industrial bank deposit rates in 1969; rates on loans and deposits with terms of two years or greater in 1974; rates on loans and deposits with terms of one year or greater in 1977; and rates on loans and deposits with terms of six months or greater in 1981. All interest rate ceilings were completely dismantled by 1987. Only French policy makers began dismantling interest rate ceilings at a later date than did policy makers in the United States, although they did complete this process more quickly.[5]

Deregulation of Permitted Activities for Nonbank Savings Institutions

The financial systems of all six countries listed in table A.1 also included non-bank savings institutions that (1) specialized in serving narrower local or regional communities; (2) collected small savings from lower-income individuals, consumers, or workers; or (3) pursued a narrower range of financial activities (e.g., lending to the housing sector) than did commercial banks. These institutions were known as thrifts in the United States, near banks in Canada, building societies in the UK, *cajas* in Spain, *caisses d'épargne* in France, and *sparkassen* or *bausparkassen* in Germany. In the United States, the passage of the 1982 Garn-St Germain Depository Institutions Act substantially broadened permitted activities for thrifts. Previously, thrifts had been required to hold the vast majority of their assets in the form of residential mortgages, but this legislation permitted them to hold up to 40 percent of assets in commercial mortgages, up to 11 percent in secured or unsecured commercial loans, and up to 3 percent in direct equity investments in businesses.[6]

Depending on the exact definition of "expanded activities," the reform of thrift activities in the United States occurred either moderately late or very late in global perspective. The regulatory reforms of 1966–67 in France increased the flexibility of regulatory distinctions between commercial banks and nonbank savings institutions, broadening permitted activities for the latter group of institutions.[7] Spanish policy makers relaxed investment and reserve requirements for cajas in 1977, bringing the regulatory treatment of these institutions more in line with that of banks.[8] A 1980 revision to the Canadian Bank Act expanded permitted activities for mortgage loan companies and allowed these institutions to affiliate with banks.[9] The 1986 Building Societies Act in the UK expanded activities for building societies. In Germany, nonbank savings institutions had long operated under the same regulatory regime as private banks and were therefore already free to function as "universal banks by law and in practice."[10]

Deregulation of Restrictions on Bank Branching

Banks in three of the six countries listed in table A.1 faced restrictions on the ability to establish branch offices. The McFadden Act of 1927 prohibited US federally chartered banks from establishing branches if state law did not permit branching; the 1956 Bank Holding Company Act blocked US bank holding companies from acquiring banks in other states unless these acquisitions were permitted by the target bank's state. Change to this regulatory regime at the federal level arrived with the Riegle-Neal Interstate Banking and Branching Efficiency Act of 1994, which loosened prohibitions on branching by federally chartered banks. Some deregulation of bank branching had occurred earlier at the state level, but even these state-level changes came after comparable changes in France and Spain.[11] France repealed geographic restrictions on bank branching in 1966–67; Spain followed suit in 1977.[12] Banks in Germany, Canada, and the UK never faced similar restrictions.

Deregulation of Restrictions on Bank Participation in Securities Activities

Banks in five of the six countries listed in table A.1 also faced restrictions on participating in securities activities. The US Banking Act of 1933 formally prohibited banks from engaging in securities activities; the 1999 Gramm-Leach-Bliley Act repealed this prohibition, allowing deposit-taking institutions to deal in nongovernmental securities for customers, invest in securities for their own accounts, underwrite or distribute nongovernmental securities, or affiliate with companies involved in these activities. Regulators (like the US Federal Reserve) had made minor adjustments to this regulatory framework in 1987, reinterpreting section 20 of the Banking Act to permit affiliation with organizations earning up to 5 percent of total revenue from securities activities (this limit was increased to 10 percent in 1989 and 25 percent in 1997). However, even these minor modifications were late to arrive in comparative perspective. French policy makers repealed restrictions on bank securities activities in 1966, while Spanish policy makers removed legal distinctions between industrial and commercial banks in 1974.[13] The 1986 Big Bang financial reform in the UK freed British banks to underwrite securities. Changes to the Bank Act and Ontario securities regulation in 1987 eliminated comparable restrictions in Canada.[14] Germany had historically allowed commercial banks to operate as universal banks, precluding the need for deregulation in this area.

ACKNOWLEDGMENTS

This book took a long time to come to fruition, and I have many people to thank for helping me to get it across the finish line. This book started as my dissertation, and as the years have passed, I have grown increasingly grateful to my dissertation committee—Frank Dobbin, Michèle Lamont, Jason Beckfield, and David Scharfstein—for asking the right kinds of questions, and offering the hard feedback, that helped it get off to a solid start. Frank, especially, deserves a great deal of credit for not even blinking when a dissertation project that was supposed to begin in 1980 suddenly started in 1780. This book would not have been possible without his support, and it became much better from trying to meet his exacting standards for argumentation and effective writing. If any of the paragraphs in this book still lack topic sentences, I can assure you that it is not Frank's fault.

The majority of this manuscript was written while I was a member of the Sociology Department at the University of Toronto, and I greatly benefited from the vibrant intellectual and social community I found there. I presented on this project during my job talk, and my U of T colleagues will find that many of the insights and suggestions they offered at that event have found their way into these pages. I am especially grateful for the support and mentorship I received from Shyon Baumann, Yoonkyung Lee, Vanina Leschziner, Ron Levi, Melissa Milkie, Ito Peng, Scott Schieman, and Jack Veugelers, among others. Both my work and my social life were also enriched by the incredible community of (then) junior faculty I encountered there, especially Sharla Alegria, Irene Boeckmann, Christian Caron (and Jordan Fairbairn), Clayton Childress, Prentiss Dantzler, Fedor Dokshin, Alicia Eads, Fidan Elcioglu, Angelina Grigoryeva, Jonathan Horowitz, Neda Maghbouleh, Tahseen Shams, Chris Smith, and Geoff Wodtke. I also benefited from the feedback and friendship of the other economic sociologists in the G7 working group, including Laura Doering, András Tilcsik, Ryann Manning, Stefan Dimitriades, Santiago Campero, Sida Liu, and Anne Bowers.

In July 2022, I joined the Sociology Department at the University of Texas at Austin, which has served as an ideal intellectual home as I complete this book. Ken-Hou Lin was an early and active champion of this project, and I am deeply grateful for his support over the years. I am also grateful to my other colleagues at UT, including but not limited to Javier Auyero, Sarah Brayne, Jordan Conwell, Dagoberto Cortez, Christy Erving, Daniel Fridman, Jennifer Glass, Kathleen Griesbach, Mary Rose, Harel Shapira, Michael Sierra-Arévalo, Abby Weitzman, and Christine Williams, for offering support and insight as I make my way through the final stages of this process.

Outside of my department, I especially thank Heather Haveman, Laura Garbes, Dan Hirschman, and John Robinson III for taking valuable time away from their own work to offer extremely helpful feedback on mine. Sofía Pérez was kind enough to put me in contact with potential respondents in Spain; her work was also instrumental in developing my understanding of the Spanish case. Audiences at the University of Chicago and the American Sociological Association raised very helpful questions when this book was at a formative stage.

Two anonymous reviewers at Princeton University Press provided extremely perceptive comments that made this book much better, and I am very grateful for their thoughtful attention and insights. I also thank PUP editors Meagan Levinson and Eric Crahan and series editor Andreas Wimmer for seeing promise in this project and supporting its development. Kathleen Kageff provided excellent copyedits.

Audra Wolfe deserves her own paragraph for agreeing to read what was then a 175,000-word manuscript about banking regulation with such good cheer. Thank you, Audra—your careful edits helped me say what I wanted to say so much more effectively.

I am also grateful for the external funding that made this work possible. Various components of this project were funded by the Edmond J. Safra Center for Ethics at Harvard Law School, Harvard's Weatherhead Center for International Affairs, the National Science Foundation, the Tobin Project, and the Canada Research Chairs program. Funding from the Canada Research Chairs program directly supported the efforts of three outstanding research assistants: Claire Sieffert, Zhen Wang, and Anjali Roy.

I am also very grateful to the bankers, banking regulators, and accounting professionals in the United States, Canada, and Spain who took the time to speak with me about their work in 2013 and 2014. It is easy to second-guess regulation from the sidelines, but much harder to be the person making the decisions in real time. Writing this book has only increased my respect for the difficult and often thankless tasks regulators perform.

There were moments—many moments—where it felt like this book would not come together. A few friends and colleagues provided support at exactly the right time, and without them, I'm not sure the book would exist at all. Clayton Childress and Vanina Leschziner offered insightful feedback and (maybe even more importantly) extensive cheerleading as I worked my way through the many successive versions of this manuscript. Fidan Elcioglu,

András Tilcsik, Alicia Eads, and Ryann Manning (*especially* Ryann!) offered vital encouragement and sympathetic ears as I navigated the ups and downs of this process.

Other friends from graduate school, particularly Eleni Arzoglou, Jiwook Jung, Jeremy Levine, Kevin Lewis, Tracey Shollenberger Lloyd, Eunmi Mun, Ann Owens, Kristin Perkins, Eva Rosen, Dan Schrage, and Chana Teeger, saw me through the dissertation version of this project and have continued to provide support (and sometimes valuable distraction) as I worked through the book version. I thank Eva, especially, for her many kind and patient responses to panicked book-related texts.

I will always appreciate my amazing professors at Beloit College, especially Charles Westerberg, Kate Linnenberg, Carla Davis, and Emily Chamlee-Wright, who are the reasons why I started on this journey in the first place.

My greatest intellectual and personal debt is to the brilliant women of the FMF writing group: Laura Adler, Barbara Kiviat, and Carly Knight. They were there when this project started more than a decade ago, and they were there at the very end, reading an infinite number of chapter drafts in between. They somehow struck the perfect balance between offering the sharp and insightful feedback I needed to move forward while still providing the kind of encouragement that prevented me from totally giving up. Thank you, Laura, Carly, and Barbara, for always believing in this project, even when I had my doubts. I am in awe of your brilliance and so grateful for your friendship.

Outside of sociology, I am especially grateful for the friendship of Ruth Hamilton, Kelly Frazer, and Tom McHale, who helped me celebrate the successes and also got me through the roughest points. Eva Clark, Jess McCormack, Jenna Hartley, Lesley Craig, and Brenda Wylie have been my greatest cheerleaders for almost two decades. My sister, Mallory, has also been a constant source of love and encouragement as well as a great source of marketing advice. I also appreciate the perpetual support from my Lemke-Gallagher in-laws (Karen, Steve, Anna, Brian, Hugh, and Grace). Thank you for never asking why this book wasn't finished, even after six Thanksgivings of it being "almost there."

In the course of writing this book, I had my two wonderful children (Theo and Lucy) in the middle of a global pandemic. While their arrival has been my greatest joy, it was unfortunately not at all conducive to finishing this book. Many people made sacrifices to give me the time I needed to push this project forward in a difficult historical moment. I am particularly grateful to the child-care providers at the University of Toronto Early Learning Centre and the University of Texas Child Development Center, who cared for my children so ably during a time of great uncertainty and made it possible for me to do this work. My parents, Karen and Dave Pernell, also went far beyond any reasonable expectations, driving thousands of miles from Texas to Toronto (three times!) in the middle of the pandemic to provide the support and child care we desperately needed. In case they think their many contributions to this work have gone unnoticed, I have dedicated this book to them.

My final and greatest debt is to my partner, Jack Gallagher, who has made so many sacrifices to support this book that I will not even attempt to enumerate them here. Thank you, Jack, for your unfailing support of my work, and for the thousands of ways that you make my life outside of work more meaningful and fun.

NOTES

Chapter 1. Introduction

1. Merle 2018; Pfeffer, Danziger, and Schoeni 2013; Tooze 2018.

2. For different perspectives on these points, see Calomiris and Haber 2014; Acharya and Schnabl 2010; Fligstein 2021.

3. For examples, see Lin and Neely 2020; Quinn 2019; MacKenzie 2011; Fligstein and Roehrkasse 2016; Pernell et al. 2017.

4. Davis 2009; Pernell 2020; Dobbin and Jung 2010.

5. For more on cross-national variation in regulatory standards in this period, see Thiemann and Lepoutre 2017.

6. Some scholars argue that the Basel Capital Accord provided banks with new incentives to embrace complex financial instruments (as part of an effort to evade regulatory rules) or created new forms of systemic risk. See L. Allen 2004; J. Friedman and Kraus 2012. Others argue that the framework's design was too accommodating to banking industry interests (versus the public interest), or alternatively, that it did too little to combat systemic risk. See Petitjean 2013; G. Kaufman and Scott 2003; Dowd et al. 2011.

7. The financial crisis originated in the United States, and regulatory choices in this country (a financial hegemon) also carried an outsized impact for regulatory policy making in other countries. The US case, as the case of regulatory policy making that has attracted the greatest attention from other scholars of financial regulation, also offers a particularly direct link to existing conversations on this topic.

8. See, e.g., Acharya et al. 2013.

9. Balla and McKenna 2009; Admati and Hellwig 2013; Acharya et al. 2013; Financial Crisis Inquiry Commission 2011.

10. Arjani and Paulin 2013; see also Leblond 2011; Ratnovski and Huang 2009.

11. Fernández de Lis and Garcia Herrero 2009; Balla and Rose 2011.

12. Kodres 2023.

13. S. Johnson and Kwak 2011, 59.

14. Narter 2009; see also Pernell 2020; Lin and Neely 2020; Kroszner and Strahan 2014.

15. Pernell 2020, 289, fig. 2.

16. Krozner and Strahan 2014; Lin and Neely 2020, 61–66; Tomaskovic-Devey and Lin 2011; S. Johnson and Kwak 2011.

17. For a general description of the regulatory capture perspective, see Posner 2014; Wilson 1980; Peltzman 1976.

18. Stigler 1971; S. Johnson and Kwak 2011.

19. Kroszner and Strahan 2014; S. Johnson and Kwak 2011. The regulatory capture perspective was originally developed to explain the creation of regulatory restraints on free competition. However, its insights have been expanded to explain the turn toward financial deregulation. The basic idea remains that "as a rule, regulation is acquired by the industry and is designed and operated primarily for its benefit" (Stigler 1971, 3).

20. Stigler 1971; Wilson 1980.

21. "Award Winners" 2005.

22. "World's 100 Largest Banks" 1997. In that year, 1996, the top twenty largest banks also included three British banks, two French banks, and two German banks.

23. "Government Regulation and Derivative Contracts" 1997.

24. Palmer 2000.

25. Bank of Spain, n.d.

26. For a general discussion, see Hall and Taylor 1996; Steinmo 1989; Hacker et al. 2022.

27. Fourcade 2009, 20. Sociologists have been particularly attuned to the cultural dimensions of institutions, describing them as mutually supportive combinations of both "styles of reasoning"—taken-for-granted organizing principles or causal understandings that underlie social conventions—and "associated constellations of practices," or concrete material structures or arrangements (see Fourcade 2009, 15). On the phenomenological roots of institutions, see Berger and Luckmann 1966.

28. Fourcade 2009, 24.

29. Dobbin 1994; Fourcade 2009.

30. Lipset and Marks 2000; Dobbin 1994; Hall and Soskice 2001. But see Prasad 2012.

31. See, e.g., Lipset 1990.

32. See the appendix for more detail on this point.

33. See, for example, Thelen 2004; Fligstein and McAdam 2012.

34. Schneiberg 2007.

35. J. Kaufman 2009; Dobbin 1994; Fourcade 2009.

36. Quoted in Fourcade 2009, 35.

37. Covitz et al. 2013; Acharya et al. 2013.

Chapter 2. Conflicting Principles of Order within Political Institutions

1. For more on the concept of institutional constellations, see Fourcade (2009).

2. Trends in past scholarship inform my descriptions of the defining features of nineteenth-century Canadian and Spanish political institutions. Extant scholarship on the role of political-cultural traditions in shaping economic institutions has primarily focused on comparisons between the United States and two other countries: Britain and France. To maintain a connection to this established literature, I emphasize similarities between the Canadian and Spanish cases and these better-known British (Canada) and French (Spanish) cases before turning to the other distinguishing features of the Canadian and Spanish cases.

3. J. Kaufman 2009, 60.

4. J. Kaufman 2009, 56–79.

5. A. Hamilton 2003, 115.

6. Novak 2008.

7. Novak 2008, 763.

8. J. Kaufman 2009.

9. "Federalist Papers: No. 51" 1788.

10. For a discussion of these differences between British and American individualism, see Fourcade 2009.

11. On the evolution of voting rights, see Mintz 2004. On the dismantlement of aristocratic institutions, see the letter from John Adams to John Sullivan, May 26, 1776, Adams Papers, Founders Online, US National Archives, National Archives and Records Administration, https://founders.archives.gov/documents/Adams/06-04-02-0091. Even as Adams defended

property-related qualifications for voters, he also advocated for political institutions that would cultivate easy access to property for the "multitude."

12. DeMuth 2011.

13. There was no "Canada" to speak of until 1867, when the British colonies of the Province of Canada, Nova Scotia, and New Brunswick united into a single federation. This discussion of early nineteenth-century "Canadian" political institutions thus focuses on the political institutions that developed in the provinces of Upper and Lower Canada (1791–1841) and the Province of Canada (1841–67).

14. Lipset 1990, 1.

15. See Dobbin 1994; Fourcade 2009, 41.

16. Bagehot 1873, 175.

17. Fourcade 2009, 33, 41.

18. Churchill 1932, 23; see also Burke 1790. Citing the political disorder that had manifested after the French Revolution, Burke argued that societies that rejected time-tested inherited values and organizing principles in favor of untested alternatives were doomed to descend into chaos and dictatorship.

19. Well into the nineteenth century, the appointed upper house of Parliament enjoyed powers at least equal to those of the elected lower house. See UK 2000.

20. Political power in both Upper and Lower Canada was initially highly concentrated in the hands of the lieutenant governor and a small group of notable citizens (known as the Family Compact in Upper Canada and the Château Clique in Lower Canada).

21. Quoted in Ashcraft 2009, 123. The quote continues: "If man in the state of nature be so free, as has been said; if he be absolute lord of his own person and possessions, equal to the greatest, and subject to no body, why will he part with his freedom? Why will he give up this empire, and subject himself to the dominion and control of any other power? To which it is obvious to answer, that though in the state of nature he hath such a right, yet the enjoyment of it is very uncertain."

22. Fourcade 2009, 44.

23. Fourcade 2009, 26, 44.

24. J. Kaufman 2009.

25. See also Lipset 1990 for discussions of the historical salience of group rights in the Canadian political context. Even with these accommodations, however, British political traditions continued to reign supreme in Canada. The Constitutional Act of 1791 still required the inhabitants of Lower Canada to adopt the British-style Westminster parliamentary model of representative government and other key political institutions. When Upper and Lower Canada officially merged once again to form the Province of Canada in 1841, the new provincial assembly was also organized along similar institutional lines. And the Dominion of Canada, created when the colonies of Canada, Nova Scotia, and New Brunswick were formally united into a single federation in 1867, formally adopted these parliamentary institutions.

26. E.g., Lipset 1990; J. Kaufman 2009.

27. Calloway 2007; Pettipas 1994; Sprague 1995.

28. It is notable that, historically, marginalized groups in Canada frequently appealed to the principle of protecting public rights when arguing against forms of discrimination or advocating for respect for cultural traditions. For examples, see Borrows 1997; K. Smith 2014.

29. Eissa-Barroso and Vázquez Varela 2013.

30. McFarlane 2013, 181.

31. Dobbin 1994, 97.

32. P. Anderson 1974, 17; Dobbin 1994, 96–97. Characteristics of absolutism include the formation and national control of a standing army, the establishment of a bureaucratic model

of governance dependent solely on the ruler, the integration of the church into the state, and a mercantilist economic system. During the absolutist era in France, taxation was also administered at the national level.

33. In other words, local elites and independent landowners, who had previously enjoyed considerable autonomy within their own territories, were forced to put the interests of the Crown above their own particularistic interests. See Dobbin 1994, 96.

34. See Crozier 1973, 79; Hoffman 1963; Dobbin 1994, 98–99.

35. Dobbin 1994, 96, emphasis in original.

36. Fourcade 2009, 50. From the monarchist perspective, giving too much power to civil society (vis-à-vis the state) threatened to disrupt political order by encouraging revolution from below. From the republican perspective, the strong restraining hand of the state was necessary to avoid domination by societal elites (Dobbin 1994, 102).

37. As Dobbin (1994, 102) writes, one of the defining features of France's enduring institutions of government was the extent to which they "produced a vision of social order in which the state remained aloof from individual interests in order to direct the self-articulated actions of self-interested citizens toward public goals." Both Fourcade (2009, 51) and Dobbin (1994, 103) note the emphasis on state impartiality (and its perceived benefits) in explaining French support for rule by technocratic experts.

38. Like the French intendents, the Spanish intendants were tasked with improving local administration and linking it directly to the Crown rather than the (regional) viceroy. They enjoyed extensive executive, judicial, and military powers. See Lynch 1989.

39. Kern 1974, 30, 38; Esdaile 2000, 146.

40. Quoted in Shubert 2003, 169.

41. Hoffman 1963; Payne 1973.

42. These privileges included aristocratic control of large untilled estates and legally unalterable succession in the inheritance of landed property.

43. Payne 1973, 375; Lynch 1989.

44. Chen 2018.

45. McAlister 1963. As Wiarda (1996, 44) notes, "Spanish political culture was also defined by strong respect for authority, hierarchy, and acceptance of one's station in life."

46. Wiarda 1996, 47.

47. On *fueros*, see Strong 1893; Wiarda 1996, 81.

48. McAlister 1963, 352.

49. Chen 2018, 602.

50. Cánovas del Castillo 1888, 11, also quoted in Kern 1974, 31, emphasis added.

51. McAlister 1963.

52. Chen 2018.

53. Esdaile 2000, 144; see also Angel Smith 2016.

54. Angel Smith 2012, 117; Angel Smith 2016.

Chapter 3. Creating Chartered Banks in the United States, Canada, and Spain

1. See Carruthers 1996, 76–78.

2. Calomiris 2020, 1.

3. Calomiris 2020.

4. Calomiris 2020.

5. Bodenhorn 2002, 184.

6. Lewis 1882, 58.

7. Lewis 1882, 73.

8. Hill 2009; Hammond 1957, 115, 128.

9. Hammond 1957.

10. Quoted in Clarke and Hall 1832, 55.

11. Hill 2009.

12. Hill 2009.

13. The same group noted that the destruction of the federal bank would likely advantage the commercial northern states, with their more highly developed state banking systems, perhaps at the expense of the landed southern states. See Clarke and Hall 1832, 310.

14. Clarke and Hall 1832, 361, emphasis in original.

15. Rothbard 1962.

16. For more discussion of the economic conditions of this period, see Hinckey 2012, 233; Wilentz 2008, 205.

17. Hammond 1957, 251.

18. Hammond 1957, 237.

19. For a discussion of the basis of this opposition, see Hammond 1957, 238.

20. Support and opposition for the bill did not fall cleanly along interest group or party lines. It passed the House by a narrow margin, and the Senate by a wider margin. See Clarke and Hall 1832, 682; Hammond 1957, 240.

21. Hammond 1957, 251.

22. Hammond 1957, 371.

23. "President Jackson's Veto Message regarding the Bank of the United States" 1832.

24. *Boston Morning Post*, December 29, 1835, quoted in Lamoreaux 1994, 38.

25. Hammond 1936, 184.

26. Hammond 1936, 184.

27. Hammond 1957, 610–15.

28. Adam Smith 1804, 193.

29. Harris 1994, 611.

30. Plans for a chartered bank in Lower Canada were reinvigorated after the war of 1812, which was a boon for the Canadian economy. A group of Lower Canadian merchants petitioned the provincial assembly for permission to establish a chartered bank, advancing familiar arguments: a chartered bank would advance the public interest by creating a stable circulating medium, reduce the drain of specie to the United States, and aid commercial and agricultural pursuits. See Shortt [1896] 1986, 69.

31. Letter from Lieutenant-Governor Sir Peregrine Maitland, May 7, 1819, quoted in Shortt [1896] 1986, 91.

32. Breckenridge 1911, 16.

33. Breckenridge 1911, 34.

34. Breckenridge 1895, 77.

35. Breckenridge 1911, 22.

36. Shortt 1908, 326.

37. Davoud 1964, 104.

38. Breckenridge 1911, 46.

39. Easterbrook and Aitkin 1956, 456; see also Shortt [1896] 1986; Breckenridge 1911.

40. While members of the Liberal Party had more sympathy for the principles reflected in Lord Sydenham's plan, the majority of Canadian policy makers did not agree. See Shortt 1908, 330.

41. Shortt 1908, 135.

42. Andrew Smith 2012, 473.

43. Easterbrook and Aitkin 1956, 454.

44. Breckenridge 1911, 46–47; Easterbrook and Aitkin 1956, 453–54.

45. Shearer et al. 1984, 298.

46. Shortt 1964, 135–36; see also Shearer et al. 1984, 297.

47. Tortella 1977, 36–37. The discussion in this section draws heavily from the work of Spanish banking historians Gabriel Tortella Casares and José L. García Ruiz.

48. Tortella and García Ruiz 2013, 20.

49. Tortella and García Ruiz 2013, 21.

50. Tortella and García Ruiz 2013, 23.

51. Tortella and García Ruiz 2013, 23–25.

52. Tortella and García Ruiz 2013, 27, 34. The bank also often served as the government's fiscal agent, mediating other financial institutions, bankers, and suppliers, and discounting promissory notes on the government's behalf.

53. Martín-Aceña 2017.

54. Tortella and García Ruiz 2013, 42.

55. Spain 1849, 149.

56. Avecilla 1849, 100.

57. Bernal Lloréns 2004, 7, emphasis added.

58. Tortella and García Ruiz 2013, 49.

59. Tortella 1977, 14–15.

60. Only a single bank of issue was allowed to operate in each town, a policy that limited direct competition between Spanish banks.

61. Tortella and García Ruiz 2013, 50.

62. Martín-Aceña 2017, 23; Tortella and García Ruiz 2013, 44.

Chapter 4. Branching Regulatory Paths into the Twentieth Century

1. For a detailed discussion of this historical episode, see Greenberg 2020.

2. Menand and Ricks 2021.

3. The act also established minimum capital requirements, and at least half of the bank's capital needed to be paid in before the bank could open for business. West 2019, 22.

4. Letter from Hugh McCulloch to Morris Ketchum, May 11, 1863, quoted in Chapman and Westerfield 1942, 62.

5. Grossman 2008.

6. Board of Governors of the Federal Reserve System 1932.

7. Board of Governors of the Federal Reserve System 1932, 74–79.

8. "Strengthening the Public Credit" 1898, 30.

9. Ostrolenk 1930, emphasis added.

10. Board of Governors of the Federal Reserve System 1932, 82.

11. This is from the 1902 *Proceedings of the American Bankers Association*, quoted in Board of Governors of the Federal Reserve System 1932, 88–89.

12. Sullivan 2009, 285.

13. For a detailed discussion, see James and Weiman 2010.

14. James and Weiman 2010.

15. Moen and Tallman 1992.

16. Primm 1989; Wiebe 1962.

17. Barnett 2008, 93.

18. R. Johnson 2010.

19. See Barnett 2008, 96.

20. Andrew Smith 2012, 459, 465.

21. Breckenridge 1911, 67–70.

22. The discussion in this section draws heavily from Andrew Smith 2012.

23. Rose 1869, 10.

24. See Andrew Smith 2012.

25. Andrew Smith 2012.

26. Adam Smith 1905, 307.

27. Adam Smith 1905, 306.

28. This same principle of supporting intervention only in cases where the rights of vulnerable users of banking services were threatened also featured in other Canadian bank regulatory debates in the late nineteenth century, including the 1870 battle over usury restrictions. See Andrew Smith 2012 for an in-depth discussion of this debate.

29. Shearer et al. 1984, 300.

30. Breckenridge 1895, 290.

31. Breckenridge 1895, 291.

32. Breckenridge 1895, 291.

33. Easterbrook and Aitkin 1956, 467.

34. Pauly 2014, 146.

35. Tortella and García Ruiz 2013, 69.

36. Tortella and García Ruiz 2013, 73–75.

37. Tortella 2001, 30.

38. Tortella and García Ruiz 2013, 98.

39. Tortella and García Ruiz 2013, 99.

40. Tortella and García Ruiz 2013, 99; see also Paret 1921.

41. Pérez 1997.

42. Tortella and García Ruiz 2013, 92.

43. See De Riquer 1994.

44. Tortella and García Ruiz 2013, 90.

45. Martín-Aceña, Martinez Ruiz, and Nogues-Marco 2011.

46. Tortella and García Ruiz 2013, 97.

47. Tortella and García Ruiz 2013, 97.

48. Tortella and García Ruiz 2013, 97; see also Pérez 1997, 48.

49. Tortella and Palafox 1984.

50. Pérez 1997, 49.

Chapter 5. Debating Regulatory Reform in the 1920s and 1930s

1. Spain reported a 20 percent drop in economic activity in the early 1930s, on par with what was seen in Italy and Britain, but much less a drop than what was observed in the United States, France, Germany, or Canada. See Simpson 1995, 204. For more on comparative trends in national performance during the Depression, see Prasad 2012, fig. 8.1.

2. For illustrative examples, see Roe 1994; Prasad 2012; Calomiris and Haber 2014.

3. See, for example, Calomiris and Haber 2014; E. White 1982; Prasad 2012.

4. Board of Governors of the Federal Reserve System, n.d.

5. Bremer 1935, 40.

6. Rötheli 2013.

7. Mote 1979.

8. Mote 1979, 15–16.

9. Wicker 1980.

10. United States 1932b, 9908–16. This bill developed after a series of failed proposals, also sponsored by Glass, with similar provisions.

11. Kennedy 1973.

12. "Speeds Bank Bill by a Compromise" 1933.

13. For more details see also FDIC 1998.

14. FDIC 1998; United States 1933c, 2079.

15. Statewide branch banking was authorized only for those national banks and state member banks having capital of not less than $500,000. Lower capitalization was authorized in states having less than one million residents and without large cities. See Preston 1933, 593. The final reform also failed to remove the secretary of the Treasury from the Federal Reserve Board.

16. Bremer 1935, 54.

17. Board of Governors of the Federal Reserve System 1938, 92; Bremer 1935, 102; see also D. Hamilton 1985.

18. E.g., *To Provide a Guaranty Fund* 1932a, 26.

19. United States 1932c, 9985; see also the comments of Senator Duncan Upshaw Fletcher (D-FL) in United States 1932c, 9982.

20. United States 1932c, 9986.

21. *To Provide a Guaranty Fund* 1932a, 17.

22. *To Provide a Guaranty Fund* 1932a, 180.

23. *To Provide a Guaranty Fund* 1932a, 7.

24. Anderson's comments were entered into the record by Representative Robert Winthrop Kean (R-NJ), a former banker himself; see also United States 1932c, 10002; United States 1933e, 3956.

25. See also the comment from one New Jersey banker to the chairman of the House Banking Committee: "the unit bank is 'like the church . . . a community enterprise, its stock a community investment, its success a community pride. It is a community temple where the saver and the borrower meet in a home they call their own'" (Bremer 1935, 105).

26. United States 1932c, 9974.

27. United States 1933b, 2036.

28. United States 1932c, 9974–80. A final argument against branch banking focused on the hazards of establishing banks whose failure would devastate the economy. Even among opponents who accepted that branch banks were better able to withstand economic shocks than unit banks (and many did not), they remained concerned about the potential for a large bank failure to decimate the economy. See, e.g., *To Provide a Guaranty Fund* 1932b, 259.

29. Bremer 1935, 105.

30. United States 1933d, 5256.

31. *To Provide a Guaranty Fund* 1932a, 59.

32. *To Provide a Guaranty Fund* 1932b, 236.

33. United States 1933e, 3955–57.

34. United States 1933e, 3907.

35. United States 1933e. For many policy makers, the suitability of separating investment and commercial banking became even more apparent after a Senate investigation into the stock market crash of 1929 (the "Pecora hearings") uncovered additional examples of banks abusing the public's trust. See also United States 1933e, 3954.

36. United States 1933e, 3955.

37. Preston 1933.

38. Preston 1933; see also Gilbert 1986.

39. Prasad 2012, 221.

40. Calomiris and Haber 2014, 182–83.

41. Canada 1924a, 1187.

42. Plummer 2013.

43. See Canada 1923b, 4015–40.

44. Canada 1923c, 4091. For other examples of these arguments, see Canada 1923a, 1310; Canada 1923b, 4028.

45. Canada 1924a, 1199. Ten citizens were eventually arrested in connection with this event, including the bank's president and vice president, five directors, and an accountant; most of these actors were eventually convicted of fraud.

46. See the *MacLean's* editorial from Sir Frederick Williams-Taylor (1925).

47. Canada 1924b, 3917.

48. Canada 1924c, 3939–45; Canada 1924a, 1201, 1206.

49. Canada 1924c, 3960.

50. Canada Department of Finance 1924, cited in Carr, Mathewson, and Quigley 1995, 1152. To bolster this case, deposit insurance opponents also pointed to failed state-level experiments with deposit insurance in the United States. As one Liberal MP from Quebec put it, "There is not a single shred of evidence to show that any of these guarantees which took place in the United States were of any value whatever." Canada 1924a, 1206.

51. Canada 1924c, 3923.

52. Canada 1924d, 733.

53. Canada 1924d, 731.

54. Canada 1924c, 3948.

55. In other words, because the government would now be responsible for backing banknotes, note holders would no longer need the same security from chartered banks. See the comments of George Gibson Coote in Canada 1924c, 3935.

56. See the comments of Frederick Forsyth Pardee in Canada 1924e, 8–9.

57. Canada 1924d, 740.

58. E.g., Canada 1924a, 1186–87; Canada 1924f, 445; Canada 1924c, 3927.

59. See, e.g., Barkley 1931.

60. Bordo and Redish 1987.

61. See, e.g., McKenzie 1931.

62. Bordo and Redish 1987.

63. Crowle 1933.

64. Bordo and Redish 1987, 417.

65. Bordo and Redish 1987, 414.

66. Cabrera and del Rey 2007, 8.

67. Martín-Aceña, Pons, and Betrán 2009.

68. Martín-Aceña, Pons, and Betrán 2009.

69. Diario de Sesiones del Congreso de los Diputados 1918, 3468.

70. Gomez Ochoa 1991.

71. Malo de Molina and Martín-Aceña 2012, 77.

72. Malo de Molina and Martín-Aceña 2012, 78; Pérez 1997, 53.

73. "Banking Law of 1921" 1921, article 2, part 4, C, 6.

74. Malo de Molina and Martín-Aceña 2012, 77.

75. Gomez Ochoa 1991.

76. Cambó, quoted in López Muñoz 1981.

77. Cambó, quoted in López Muñoz 1981.

78. "Informaciones Mundiales" 1921, 13.

79. Cambó 1991, 738.

80. Speech by Francisco de A. Cambó, "Finance Minister, in the Congress of Deputies," reproduced in *Ordenación Bancaria en España*, Ministry of Finance, Madrid, 1921, part 3, pp. 5–31; also quoted in Martín-Aceña, Martinez Ruiz, and Nogues-Marco 2013, 40.

81. Diario de Sesiones del Congreso de los Diputados 1921, 3777.

82. Diario de Sesiones del Congreso de los Diputados 1921, 3776.

83. Gomez Ochoa 1991, 262.

84. Tortella and García Ruiz 2013; Paret 1921.

85. Olariaga 1921, 3 (translated).

86. Cambó 1991, 752.

87. Cambó 1991, 752.

88. Malo de Molina and Martín-Aceña 2012, 78.

89. Malo de Molina and Martín-Aceña 2012.

Chapter 6. Responding to New Dilemmas in the 1960s and 1970s

1. Krippner 2011; Goudarzi et al. 2022; Clayton and Pontusson 1998.

2. See, for example, Kroszner and Strahan 1999; Quinn 2017; Krippner 2011; Mudge 2019.

3. Board of Governors of the Federal Reserve System 1955.

4. For an excellent discussion of the tools of US monetary policy and how they were used in practice, see Krippner 2011, 109–14.

5. Krippner 2011.

6. For a detailed discussion, see Krippner 2011, 65.

7. Burger 1969.

8. MacDonald 1978, 61–63.

9. *Report of the Royal Commission on Banking and Finance* 1964, 562. See also MacDonald 1978, 64.

10. Quinn 2017.

11. L. Smith 1981; MacDonald 1978, 94, appendix 1.

12. In the United States, see, e.g., *Interest Rates and Mortgage Credit* 1966, 4–5. For Canada, see Azzi 1999.

13. In 1960, mortgages made up 80 percent of assets for the average US thrift and 75 percent of assets for the average Canadian near bank. See Brewer et al. 1993, 18; Poapst 1973, table A-8.

14. Mason 2004, 160–61; *Report of the Royal Commission on Banking and Finance* 1964, chap. 10.

15. C. Anderson 1970, 48; Pérez 1997, 58.

16. Prados de la Escosura and Sanz 1996.

17. Pérez 1997, 61.

18. Hardy 1968, 31.

19. Calvo-Gonzalez 2007.

20. Solsten and Meditz 1990.

21. Pérez 1997, 63.

22. Pérez 1997.

23. Ban 2011, 106.

24. Pérez 1997, 64.

25. C. Anderson 1970, 87.

26. C. Anderson 1970, 105.

27. Ban 2011, 107.

28. Hardy 1968, 34; Ban 2011, 107.

29. Pérez 1997, 86.

30. Burger 1969, 27.

31. *Interest Rates and Mortgage Credit* 1966, 2. All US congressional hearings referenced in this and succeeding chapters were obtained using the ProQuest congressional database.

32. *Interest Rates and Mortgage Credit* 1966.

33. *Interest Rates and Mortgage Credit* 1966, 35.

34. *Interest Rates and Mortgage Credit* 1966, 8.

35. *To Eliminate Unsound Competition* 1966a, 3.

36. *Housing and Financial Reform* 1974, 3, emphasis added.

37. *To Eliminate Unsound Competition* 1966b, 265.

38. *Interest Rates and Mortgage Credit* 1966, 26.

39. The National League of Savings and Loan Associations (the leading thrift industry lobbying group) had asked policy makers to provide greater direct financial support to the industry instead. *Interest Rates and Mortgage Credit* 1966, 60.

40. See Krippner 2011.

41. *Interest Rates and Mortgage Credit* 1966, 100.

42. Chant 1965, 170.

43. Thiessen 1999.

44. *Report of the Royal Commission on Banking and Finance* 1964, 365.

45. *Report of the Royal Commission on Banking and Finance* 1964.

46. Canada 1966a, 7234.

47. *Report of the Royal Commission on Banking and Finance* 1964, 78.

48. Canada 1967b, 3505–7.

49. Canada 1962, 41–46.

50. See Canada 1966b, 1192, 1200, 1320.

51. See Canada 1967a, 2670, 2762.

52. D. Smith 1973, 235–36.

53. MacDonald 1978.

54. In addition to this initial step toward deregulation, the 1967 reforms also included multiple other reforms designed to boost competition within the financial system. See Freedman 1998.

55. *Interest Rates and Mortgage Credit* 1966, 43; *Report of the Royal Commission on Banking and Finance* 1964, 274.

56. Pérez 1997, 72.

57. Nielsen 2008.

58. C. Anderson 1970, 105.

59. Pons Brias 2002, 59–60.

60. The hope was that creating new stand-alone banks to serve the needs of industrial borrowers seeking medium- to long-term credit (needs that the existing chartered banks then did little to fulfill) would enhance economic development.

61. Pérez 1997, 81. The provision allowing for the creation of stand-alone industrial banks also limited these institutions to establishing three or fewer branch offices, a serious competitive disadvantage in a context where the established Big Seven banks already controlled dozens of branch offices.

62. Pérez 1997, 83.

63. Although the official credit institutions did compete against banks in loan markets, they were also more vulnerable to political pressure to underwrite high-risk credits to struggling industries, weakening their competitive position. Pérez 1997, 83.

64. Pérez 1997, 84.

65. Pérez 1997, 84.

66. Pérez 1997, 84.

67. See Pérez 1997, 80.

68. Spain 1962.
69. Dymski 1999; Krippner 2011; Edwards and Mishkin 1995.
70. Krippner 2011.
71. Freedman 1998, 20.
72. Pérez 1997, 89.
73. See Luttrell 1972.
74. For a summary of the main conclusions of this report, see Heinemann 1972, 1.
75. Robinson 1972.
76. See C. Allen and Bartlett 1974.
77. Mason 2004, 208.
78. Krippner 2011, 81.
79. For a discussion of these arguments in other settings, see Berman 2022.
80. See the commentary in C. Allen 1973.
81. *Regulation Q and Related Measures* 1980, 831.
82. *Financial Structure and Regulation* 1973, 39.
83. *Depository Institutions Deregulation Act of 1979* 1979, 2.
84. *Now Accounts* 1977, 189–90.
85. *Financial Institutions and the Nation's Economy* 1976, 1635.
86. *Financial Institutions and the Nation's Economy* 1975, 1622.
87. United States 1975, 39949–51.
88. *Financial Institutions and the Nation's Economy* 1976, 1712.
89. Pérez 1997, 90.
90. Pérez 1997, 90–91; Eder 1971.
91. Tortella and García Ruiz 2013, 131.
92. Pérez 1997, 100.
93. Ban 2011, 253.
94. Ban 2011, 222–23.
95. Ban 2011, 237.
96. Ban 2016.
97. C. Anderson 1970, 102.
98. Ban 2011, 210.
99. Ban 2016, 43.
100. Pérez 1997, 102.
101. Pérez 1997, 103–4. The reformers' perspective on this matter aligned with the perspectives of leading international organizations, including the OECD, which also attributed the economic troubles in Spain to its rigid interest rate control framework.
102. Pérez 1998.
103. Pagoulatos 1999, 4.
104. Pérez (1997, esp. pp. 37–38) offers additional insight into how goals of the technocrats and the central bank reformers conflicted.
105. Pérez 1997, 94.
106. Pérez 1997, 105.
107. Pérez 1997.
108. Lukauskas 1997, 141.
109. Pérez 1997, 116–20.
110. Pérez 1997, 125.
111. Pérez 1997, 134.

Chapter 7. The Rise of New Regulatory Models in the 1980s

1. Revisions to the Bank Act in 1980 freed banks to directly own mortgage loan and venture capital subsidiaries and permitted them to offer new kinds of financial services.

2. FDIC 1997, 168, table 4.1; L. White 1991, 144.

3. FDIC 1997, 175–76. The Garn-St Germain Bill was cosponsored by Senator Jake Garn, Republican of Utah and the chairman of the Senate Banking, Housing, and Urban Affairs Committee, and Representative St Germain.

4. FDIC 1997, 199.

5. FDIC 1997, 313–14, 270, 275, 288.

6. FDIC 1997, 241; see also Haltom 2013.

7. Curry and Shibut 2000; FDIC 1997, 187.

8. FDIC 1997, 178.

9. FDIC 1997, 180.

10. FDIC 1997, 168.

11. FDIC 1997, 142, 153, 160, 321.

12. *Oversight Hearings on the Condition of the Banking System* 1989, 14.

13. For a detailed discussion of these changes within the academic discipline of economics, see Mudge 2019; Berman 2022.

14. The implication is that, since the value of a put option increases with the volatility of the underlying asset, profit-maximizing banks will naturally seek to increase asset risk in the presence of deposit insurance. See Merton 1977.

15. See *Financial Services Industry—Oversight* 1983, 900.

16. *Deposit Insurance Issues and Depositor Discipline* 1990, 135.

17. *Financial Condition of the Bank and Thrift Industries* 1985, 894.

18. *Deposit Insurance Reform and Related Supervisory Issues* 1985, 1264.

19. *Deposit Insurance Reform and Related Supervisory Issues* 1985, 1358.

20. For evidence that the US banking regulators continued to endorse multiple policies that were designed to protect the financial system's fragmented and specialized structure, see also *Deposit Insurance Reform and Related Supervisory Issues* 1985, 1333, 1363, 1141–42.

21. *Reform of the Nation's Banking and Financial Systems* 1987, 204–5.

22. National Commission on Financial Institution Reform, Recovery, and Enforcement 1993, 56.

23. *Oversight Hearings on the Condition of the Banking System* 1989, 2.

24. *Deposit Insurance and Financial Modernization* 1990, 270–71.

25. *Deposit Insurance Issues and Depositor Discipline* 1990, 17.

26. *Financial Services Industry—Oversight* 1983, 900.

27. *Oversight Hearings on the Condition of the Banking System* 1989, 24.

28. *Deposit Insurance Reform and Financial Modernization* 1990, 527.

29. *Condition of the Federal Deposit Insurance Funds* 1988, 163.

30. *Oversight Hearings on the Condition of the Banking System* 1989, 130.

31. *Deposit Insurance Reform and Financial Modernization* 1990, 88.

32. *Financial Institutions Reform, Recovery, and Enforcement Act* 1989, 174.

33. This same commitment to reinforcing free market processes informed other provisions of FIRREA, including the repeal of restrictions that blocked bank holding companies from purchasing thrifts. See, for example, *Financial Institutions Reform, Recovery, and Enforcement Act* 1989, 19.

34. *Financial Institutions Reform, Recovery, and Enforcement Act* 1989, 397.

35. *Financial Institutions Reform, Recovery, and Enforcement Act* 1989, 47.

36. *Deposit Insurance Issues and Depositor Discipline* 1990, 92.
37. *Financial Institutions Reform, Recovery, and Enforcement Act* 1989, 18, 1–2, 16–18, 26.
38. *Deposit Insurance Reform* 1990a, 1.
39. *Deposit Insurance Issues and Depositor Discipline* 1990, 162–63.
40. *Deposit Insurance Issues and Depositor Discipline* 1990, 67.
41. *Deposit Insurance Reform and Financial Modernization* 1990, 119.
42. Wright, 2018.
43. "Currency Markets; Canadian Dollar Falls to a 48-Year Low in the U.S." 1981.
44. Savage 2015.
45. Langan 1985; Dingle 2003.
46. Savage 2015, 224.
47. Dingle 2003.
48. Canada 1985a, 7509.
49. Canada 1985b, 7716–18.
50. Shortell 1985.
51. Clark 1986.
52. Clark 1986.
53. When Dan Heap, an NDP MP from Toronto, and Mike Cassidy, an NDP MP from Ottawa, restated on the floor of the House of Commons in 1987 that the crisis could be attributed to bad lending practices, these interpretations went unchallenged. See Canada 1987c, 6543; Canada 1987a, 5672.
54. Canada 1987a, 5696–97.
55. Canada 1987a, 5671, 5676.
56. Canada 1987a, 5672.
57. McDougall said this before the House of Commons Standing Committee on Finance in October 1985; see the coverage in Martin 1985.
58. Canada 1987a, 5700.
59. Canada 1987a, 5676; see also the comments of Mike Cassidy, in Canada 1987a, 5671.
60. Kyer 2017.
61. Canada 1987c, 6547; Canada 1987d, 7832.
62. Canada 1987c, 5671.
63. Canada 1987b, 6547.
64. Canada 1987a, 5666.
65. Canada 1987c, 6548–50.
66. Canada 1985c, 6551.
67. Sheng 1996, 88.
68. Sheng 1996, 88.
69. Pérez 1997.
70. Sheng 1996, 89–90; Pérez 1997, 113.
71. Sheng 1996, 87.
72. Sheng 1996, 90–91; Poveda 2012.
73. Pérez 1997, 139.
74. Burns 1983; Darnton 1983.
75. Burns 1983.
76. Darnton 1983. For more on RUMASA's fate, see Lukauskas 1992, 378.
77. Bertrán and Pons 2017.
78. Pérez 1997, 150.
79. Poveda 2012.
80. Cortes Generales 1983, 11, translated from Spanish.

81. Cortes Generales 1983, 46, translated from Spanish.

82. López Muñoz 1981.

83. Martín-Aceña 2018.

84. Sheng 1996, 93; Burns 1983.

85. Cortes Generales 1988a, 9625, translated from Spanish.

86. Support for expanded sanctioning powers for the Bank of Spain was not unanimous. Policy makers from the right-wing Alliance Popular Party worried about the hazards of assigning too much power to a regulatory body that operated with considerable independence from the legislature. Yet even these reform opponents did not reject the basic premise that restoring order to the financial system required the state to embrace a more proactive role in overseeing and directing the activities of financial institutions.

87. "Discipline and Intervention of Credit Institutions" 1988.

88. Cortes Generales 1988a, translated from Spanish.

89. Cortes Generales 1988b, 9772, translated from Spanish.

90. "Discipline and Intervention of Credit Institutions" 1988.

Chapter 8. New Regulatory Visions in the 1990s

1. "Government Regulation and Derivative Contracts" 1997.

2. "Economy and Efficiency in Financial Sector Regulation" 2005, 3.

3. "Encuentro del sector financiero 2004" 2004, 4.

4. Notes for an Address by Nicholas Le Pan 2002.

5. Regulatory capital was subdivided into two tiers. Tier 1 (core) capital included common stock, noncumulative perpetual preferred stock, and disclosed reserves. Tier 2 (supplementary) capital included other resources, including undisclosed reserves, real estate, and bonds. Banks were required to hold at least 4 percent in Tier 1 capital. The content of, and division between, Tier 1 and Tier 2 capital remained a somewhat contentious issue across countries.

6. The most advanced approach included in the Basel II framework allowed banks to use "their own internal measures" of factors like probability of default or loss given default for a given asset or portfolio of assets, and to incorporate this information as a "primary input . . . into the capital calculation." The Basel Committee supplied a function that banks could use to convert these internal estimates into risk weights. For more details on this framework, please see Basel Committee on Banking Supervision 2005.

7. See, for example, De Bondt and Prast 1999; Jablecki 2009; Jackson et al. 1999.

8. Avent-Holt 2012, 292; see also Moss 2011.

9. For an illustration of this process in the US case, see Berman 2022; Avent-Holt 2012. On the ascendance of finance-trained transnational economists on a global scale, see Mudge 2019.

10. For a detailed discussion of the academic training of regulators at the Bank of Spain, see Ban 2016.

11. "Supervision of Bank Risk-Taking" 1996.

12. "Evolution of Banking in a Market Economy" 1997, emphasis added. See also "Financial Modernization: The Issues" 1999.

13. "Agenda for Bank Supervision and Regulation" 1999.

14. "Central Banking and Global Finance" 1997.

15. "Government Regulation and Derivative Contracts" 1997; see also "Central Banking and Global Finance" 1997.

16. *Deposit Insurance Reform* 1990b, 191.

17. "Supervising LCBOs" 2000.

18. "Concerns and Considerations" 2003; see also "Financial Safety Net" 2001.

19. "Financial Safety Net" 2001.

20. "Evolution of Banking in a Market Economy" 1997.

21. "Subsidies and Powers in Commercial Banking" 1990, 8.

22. See, for example, "Financial Safety Net" 2001.

23. "Financial Safety Net" 2001.

24. For a detailed discussion of these points, see "Financial Safety Net" 2001. The same logic was also reflected in regulatory justifications for moving away from direct supervision of banks. See "Banking Supervision" 2000.

25. On expanding bank-style regulations to other financial institutions, see "Insurance Companies and Banks under the New Regulatory Law" 1999. On the regulation of financial innovations, see "Financial Engineering and Financial Stability" 2002.

26. "Banking in the Global Marketplace" 1996; see also "Controlling the Safety Net" 2001.

27. "Understanding Financial Consolidation" 2001.

28. See Palmer 2000, e.g.: "Building prudential protection [is] the heart of OSFI's job. . . . OSFI has not forgotten about the last recession and those that preceded it."

29. Palmer 1998.

30. "Economy and Efficiency in Financial Sector Regulation" 2005, 3.

31. Palmer 1998.

32. "Enhancing the Safety and Soundness of the Canadian Financial System" 1995, 6.

33. Personal interview 2013c.

34. Opening Statement by Nicholas Le Pan 2005, 3.

35. "Economy and Efficiency in Financial Sector Regulation" 2005, 3.

36. "Success and Relationships in Financial Sector Regulation" 2001; see also Palmer 2000.

37. Notes for an Address by Nicholas Le Pan 2002.

38. See, for example, Notes for an Address by Nicholas Le Pan 2002.

39. Palmer 2000.

40. "Financial Regulator's Perspective" 2002.

41. "Success and Relationships in Financial Sector Regulation" 2001; "Financial Regulatory Outlook" 2004.

42. "Success and Relationships in Financial Sector Regulation" 2001.

43. Notes for an Address by Nicholas Le Pan 2002.

44. OSFI 2007, 4; Shecter 2014.

45. Caruana 2009, 34.

46. "Asset Price Bubbles" 2002, 3.

47. "Asset Price Bubbles" 2002, 3.

48. See, for example, Caruana 2009, 34.

49. "Discurso de presentación del informe annual" 2001, translated from Spanish.

50. Bank of Spain, n.d.

51. "Asset Price Bubbles" 2002, emphasis added.

52. "Reflexiones sobre la estabilidad financiera" 2002, translated from Spanish.

53. "Asset Price Bubbles" 2002.

54. "Discurso de Presentación del Informe Annual" 2001.

55. Caruana 2009, 39.

56. "Supervision on a Consolidated Basis of International Spanish Banking Groups" 2002; see also Law 5/2005 2005.

57. "Discurso de Presentación del Informe Annual" 2001, 28.

Chapter 9. Regulating Asset Securitization in the Post-Basel Era

1. MacKenzie 2011; Judge 2012; Coval et al. 2009.
2. Purnanandam 2011; Immergluck 2009; Mayer, Pence, and Sherlund 2009.
3. Acharya and Schnabl 2010.
4. Acharya et al. 2013.
5. Acharya et al. 2013, 515.
6. Acharya and Schnabl 2010; Thiemann and Lepoutre 2017.
7. In European Union countries, this would change after 2005, when all firms were required to adhere to IFRS. But in the late 1990s and early 2000s, SIC-12 applied only to banks that prepared financial statements in compliance with International Financial Reporting Standards (IFRS), the accounting framework published by the IASC.
8. Acharya et al. 2013.
9. This choice was announced with the issuance of Bank of Spain regulatory *Circular* 4/2004 in April 2004.
10. Acharya and Schnabl 2010.
11. Acharya et al. 2013, 532.
12. Thiemann and Lepoutre 2017.
13. Acharya and Schnabl 2010.
14. "Corporate Governance" 2002.
15. Glass 2002.
16. "Gramm-Leach-Bliley Act and Corporate Misbehavior" 2003.
17. "Bank Supervision, Regulation, and Risk" 1996.
18. "Cyclicality and Banking Regulation" 2002.
19. "Finance: United States and Global" 2002.
20. "Cyclicality and Banking Regulation" 2002.
21. "Bank Supervision in a World Economy" 1996.
22. "Risk Transfer and Financial Stability" 2005.
23. "International Financial Risk Management" 2002.
24. "Recent Developments in Banking and Financial Markets" 1998.
25. "Government Regulation and Derivative Contracts" 1997.
26. "Basel II: Some Issues for Implementation" 2003, emphasis added.
27. Board of Governors of the Federal Reserve System 2003.
28. Board of Governors of the Federal Reserve System 2003, emphasis added.
29. Board of Governors of the Federal Reserve System 2003, emphasis added.
30. Letter from Paul Smith 2003.
31. Letter from Grace Vogel 2003.
32. Federal Register (United States) 2004.
33. "Address: Newsmaker Breakfast 2004.
34. MacKenzie 2011.
35. "Success and Relationships in Financial Sector Regulation" 2001, 2.
36. Personal interview 2013c.
37. "Economy and Efficiency in Financial Sector Regulation" 2005, 7, emphasis added.
38. OSFI 2004.
39. "Economy and Efficiency in Financial Sector Regulation" 2005, 7.
40. OSFI 2008, 3.
41. Personal interview 2013c.
42. Personal interview 2013c.
43. "El sistema bancario español" 2006, translated from Spanish.

44. "Titulización de activos" 2005.
45. Crawford and Tett 2008.
46. "El sistema bancario español" 2006, translated from Spanish.
47. "Titulización de activos" 2005, translated from Spanish.
48. Despite being early adopters of covered bonds, Spanish policy makers were relatively slow to amend legislation to allow for off-balance-sheet securitization: not until 1992 were Spanish banks legally allowed to issue mortgage-backed securities, and not until after 1998 were they legally allowed to issue other forms of asset-backed securities.
49. "Survey of Spain" 1995.
50. "Spain's Miracle" 1997.
51. Pérez 1997.
52. Personal interview 2013d.
53. "El sistema bancario español" 2006, emphasis added.

Chapter 10. Regulating Loan Loss Provisions in the Post-Basel Era

1. Balla and Rose 2015; see also Balla et al. 2012.
2. Balla and Rose 2015; Balla et al. 2012; see also Balla and McKenna 2009.
3. For evidence on this point, see Balla and McKenna 2009; see also Saurina 2009, 2.
4. Bank for International Settlements 1988, 2.
5. It can also be difficult to translate qualitative experiences (e.g., a regional economic shock) into precise quantitative estimates (e.g., 17 percent of loans are likely to default).
6. Borio and Lowe 2001, 37.
7. Borio and Lowe 2001.
8. Herdman 2002.
9. Ramos-Tallada 2010.
10. *Loan Loss Reserves* 1999.
11. *Loan Loss Reserves* 1999, 52–54.
12. For a copy of the *Viewpoints* article, see *Loan Loss Reserves* 1999, 122–33.
13. *Loan Loss Reserves* 1999, 41.
14. *Loan Loss Reserves* 1999, 53.
15. *Loan Loss Reserves* 1999, 18.
16. *Loan Loss Reserves* 1999, 37–49.
17. *Loan Loss Reserves* 1999, 34.
18. "Washington Furor over Loan Loss Reserves" 1999.
19. "Moving Forward into the 21st Century" 1999.
20. Garver 2000.
21. Garver 2000.
22. Garver 2000.
23. "Loan Loss Provisioning and Pro-cyclicality" 2009.
24. Balla and McKenna 2009.
25. *Loan Loss Reserves* 1999, 252.
26. Blackwell 1998.
27. Blackwell 1998.
28. Mathias 1999.
29. Palmer 1998.
30. Personal interview 2013b.
31. Reguly 1999.
32. "GAAP Departures Unsettle Investors" 1999.

33. Reguly 1999.
34. Letter from Nicholas Le Pan 2002.
35. Ontario Securities Commission 2003, 161–63.
36. Personal interview 2013b; Personal interview 2013a.
37. Royo 2020.
38. Fernández de Lis et al. 2000, 4.
39. Borio and Lowe 2001.
40. See Fernández de Lis et al. 2000, 9.
41. Fernández de Lis and García-Herrero 2009.
42. Fernández de Lis et al. 2000.
43. Gebhardt and Novotny-Farkas 2011, 300.
44. Personal interview 2013e.
45. Fernández de Lis et al. 2000, 11–12.
46. Saurina 2009.
47. For the US/Spain comparison, see Balla and McKenna 2009.

Chapter 11. Visions of Financial Order

1. Kwak 2014.
2. Clemens and Cook 1999; Schneiberg 2007; Fligstein and McAdam 2012.
3. See, e.g., Fligstein and McAdam 2012; see also Thelen 2004 for an alternative view.
4. Schneiberg 2007, 66.
5. Comparative trends in the relative permissiveness of financial regulation rarely aligned with the objective economic strain a country was experiencing. "Industry-friendly" regulation often emerged at times and places where the regulated industry was politically weak. Structural accounts that emphasize the fragmentation of the state or regulatory system struggle to explain how and why the content of banking regulation within countries changed so rapidly even as these broader structural conditions remained constant.
6. For in-depth critiques of standard cultural or cultural-institutional accounts of economic policy making, see Prasad 2012; Prasad 2006; Fligstein and McAdam 2012.
7. Berman 2022.
8. Hathaway 2020; Davis and Kim 2015; Krippner 2011.
9. On the effects of rising inflation, see Krippner 2011; Fourcade-Gourinchas and Babb 2002. On the effects of the neoliberal turn among economists, see Mudge 2019; Berman 2022. On the effects of adversarial institutions, see Prasad 2006. On the effects of a credit-dependent political economy, see Prasad 2012. On the effects of the rising political power of regulated banks, see Kroszner and Strahan 1999; Lin and Neely 2020; Prechel 2021.
10. Krippner 2011; Lin and Tomaskovic-Devey 2013.
11. See, for example, the accounts of the rise of securitization markets in Krippner 2011 and Quinn 2019.
12. In the decades since the crisis, Canadian regulators have embraced more dynamic approaches to assessing bank buffers against potential losses, but the basic features of the Canadian regulatory framework have remained largely unchanged. See, for example, "Canada's Domestic Stability Buffer" 2019. In Spain, the details of banking regulation are increasingly decided at the supranational (EU) level. However, within their capacity to act, regulators at the Bank of Spain have continued with familiar trends. The governor of the Bank of Spain (Pablo Hernández de Cos) has served as chair of the Basel Committee for Banking Supervision since 2018. In this role, he pushed for new international standards designed to combat procyclicality and reveal hidden risk exposures. Regulators at the Bank of Spain continue to publish articles supporting countercyclical regulation in leading economics journals. See Jiménez et al. 2017.

13. Other elements of the Dodd-Frank Act continue to affirm the principle of *competition* and its emphasis on the dangers of too much government interference in banking. The text of this legislation continues to emphasize the merits of enhancing market discipline in banking. It also emphasizes the perceived dangers of government interference in the form of limiting too-big-to-fail protections for banks and subjecting larger banks to tighter regulatory requirements. See the act's self-description in "Dodd-Frank Wall Street Reform and Consumer Protection Act" 2010, 1377.

14. See, for example, Fligstein and Roehrkasse 2016; Prechel and Morris 2010; Tomaskovic-Devey and Lin 2011; Pernell and Jung 2023; Eaton 2020.

15. The terms of Basel III have required American banking regulators to adopt some features of countercyclical regulation (e.g., a countercyclical capital buffer). However, these regulators have hesitated to make effective use of these powers (see McCoy 2015). The Federal Reserve Board has not raised the countercyclical capital buffer above zero since this buffer was established in 2016.

Appendix. US Financial Deregulation in Comparative Perspective

1. Sherman 2009.

2. Regulatory ceilings on deposits and loans generated similar practical effects. Existing research has often grouped controls on bank borrowing rates with controls on bank lending rates as aspects of a broader "interest rate control" framework (see Edey and Hviding 1995, 5–6).

3. Busch 2009, 89; Freedman 1998.

4. Needham 2012, 3–4; Salas and Saurina 2003, 1064–65; Pons Brias 2002, 6, 61.

5. Williamson and Mahar 1998, 14.

6. Mason 2004, 219.

7. Plessis 1994; Bulbul et al. 2013, 12.

8. Grifell-Tatjé and Lovell 1996, 1282.

9. Freedman 1998, 8.

10. Bulbul et al. 2013, 6.

11. These restrictions prevented interstate branching until 1978, when Maine passed legislation allowing banks or bank holding companies from states with a reciprocal policy to establish branch offices in the state. When Alaska and New York passed laws similar to Maine's in 1982, limited interstate branching became possible.

12. Plessis 1994; Pons Brias 2002, 61; Salas and Saurina 2003, 1064–65.

13. Pérez 1997, 106.

14. Freedman 1998, 9.

"Accounting for Loan Loss Reserves." 1999. US Senate. Hearing before the Committee on Banking, Housing, and Urban Affairs, Subcommittee on Securities. July 29.

Acharya, Viral V., and Philipp Schnabl. 2010. "Do Global Banks Spread Global Imbalances? Asset-Backed Commercial Paper during the Financial Crisis of 2007–09." *IMF Economic Review* 58, no. 1:37–73.

Acharya, Viral V., Philipp Schnabl, and Gustavo Suarez. 2013. "Securitization without Risk Transfer." *Journal of Financial Economics* 107:515–36.

"Address: Newsmaker Breakfast—National Press Gallery." 2004. Remarks by Nicholas Le Pan, Superintendent, Office of the Superintendent of Financial Institutions, Canada. October 7. Hard copies for all Canadian speeches 1998–2007, previously available on the OSFI website (http://www.osfi-bsif.gc.ca/osfi/index_e.aspx?DetailId=3607, accessed July 2012) are in the author's possession; they are also available from the Canadian government via Access to Information requests.

Admati, Anat, and Martin Hellwig. 2013. *The Bankers' New Clothes: What's Wrong with Banking and What to Do about It.* Princeton, NJ: Princeton University Press.

"An Agenda for Bank Supervision and Regulation." 1999. Remarks by Governor Laurence H. Meyer before the Institute of International Bankers Annual Breakfast Dialogue, Four Seasons Hotel, Washington, DC. September 27. https://www.federalreserve.gov/boarddocs/speeches/1999/19990927.htm.

Allen, Charles E. 1973. "The Hunt Commission Report: An Analysis of the Administration's Recommendations to Congress." *Federal Home Loan Bank Board Journal* 73:2–9.

Allen, Charles E., and Robert W. Bartlett. 1974. "The Hunt Commission Report." *Business Lawyer* 29, no. 2:497–523.

Allen, Linda. 2004. "The Basel Capital Accords and International Mortgage Markets: A Survey of the Literature." *Financial Markets, Institutions and Instruments* 13, no. 2:41–108.

Anderson, Charles W. 1970. *The Political Economy of Modern Spain.* Madison: University of Wisconsin Press.

Anderson, Perry. 1974. *Lineages of the Absolutist State.* London: New Left Books.

Arjani, Neville, and Graydon Paulin. 2013. "Lessons from the Financial Crisis: Bank Performance and Regulatory Reform." Staff Discussion Paper 2013–14. https://www.bankofcanada.ca/2013/12/discussion-paper-2013-4/.

Ashcraft, Richard. 2009. *Locke's Two Treatises of Government.* London: Routledge.

"Asset Price Bubbles: Implications for Monetary, Regulatory, and International Policies." 2002. Speech by the Governor of the Bank of Spain, Jaime Caruana. Presentation given at the Federal Reserve Bank of Chicago. April 24. https://www.bis.org/review/r020531d.pdf.

Avecilla, Pablo. 1849. *Diccionario de la legislación mercantil de España.* Madrid: Imp. de Severiano Omaña.

Avent-Holt, Dustin. 2012. "The Political Dynamics of Market Organization: Cultural Framing, Neoliberalism, and the Case of Airline Deregulation." *Sociological Theory* 30, no. 4:283–302.

"Award Winners: The World's Biggest Banks 2005." *Global Finance*, October 1, 2005. https://www.gfmag.com/magazine/october-2005/award-winners—the-worlds-biggest-banks-2005-.

Azzi, Stephen. 1999. *Walter Gordon and the Rise of Canadian Nationalism.* Montreal: McGill-Queens University Press.

Bagehot, Walter. 1873. *The English Constitution.* 2nd ed. Little, Brown.

Balla, Eliana, and Andrew B. McKenna. 2009. "Dynamic Provisioning: A Countercyclical Tool for Loan Loss Reserves." *FRB Richmond Economic Quarterly* 95, no. 4:383–418.

Balla, Eliana, and Morgan J. Rose. 2011. "Loan Loss Reserves, Accounting Constraints, and Bank Ownership Structure." Federal Reserve Bank of Richmond Working Paper 11-09.

———. 2015. "Loan Loss Provisions, Accounting Constraints, and Bank Ownership Structure." *Journal of Economics and Business* 78:92–117.

Balla, Eliana, Morgan J. Rose, and Jessie Romero. 2012. "Loan Loss Reserve Accounting and Bank Behavior." *Federal Reserve Bank of Richmond Economic Brief*, no. 12-03. March. https://www.richmondfed.org/~/media/richmondfedorg/publications/research/economic_brief/2012/pdf/eb_12-03.pdf.

Ban, Cornel. 2011. "Neoliberalism in Translation: Economic Ideas and Reforms in Spain and Romania." PhD diss., University of Maryland.

———. 2016. *Ruling Ideas: How Global Neoliberalism Goes Local.* New York: Oxford University Press.

Bank for International Settlements. 1988. "Basel Committee for Banking Supervision: International Convergence of Capital Measurement and Capital Standards." July. http://www.bis.org/publ/bcbs04a.pdf.

"Banking in the Global Marketplace." 1996. Remarks by Chairman Alan Greenspan at the Federation of Bankers Associations of Japan, Tokyo. November 18. https://www.federalreserve.gov/boarddocs/speeches/1996/19961118.htm.

"Banking Law of 1921." 1921. Spain. December 29.

"Banking Supervision." 2000. Remarks by Chairman Alan Greenspan before the American Bankers Association, Washington, DC. September 18. https://www.federalreserve.gov/boarddocs/speeches/2000/20000918.htm.

Bank of Spain. n.d. "Promoting the Stability of the Financial and Payment Systems." https://www.bde.es/wbe/en/sobre-banco/mision/funciones/promover_la_est_f67b52429f11281.html. Accessed August 31, 2023.

"Bank Supervision in a World Economy." 1996. Remarks by Chairman Alan Greenspan at the International Conference of Banking Supervisors, Stockholm, Sweden. June 13. https://www.federalreserve.gov/boarddocs/speeches/1996/19960613.htm.

"Bank Supervision, Regulation, and Risk." 1996. Remarks by Chairman Alan Greenspan at the Annual Convention of the American Bankers Association, Honolulu, Hawaii. October 5. https://www.federalreserve.gov/boarddocs/speeches/1996/19961005.htm.

Barkley, Frederick. 1931. "Bank Failures Common in U.S." *Maclean's Magazine*, May 1. https://archive.macleans.ca/.

Barnett, William P. 2008. *The Red Queen among Organizations: How Competitiveness Evolves.* Princeton, NJ: Princeton University Press.

"Basel II: Some Issues for Implementation." 2003. Remarks by Vice Chairman Roger W. Ferguson Jr. at the Basel Sessions, Institute of International Finance, New York. June 17. https://www.federalreserve.gov/boarddocs/speeches/2003/20030617/default.htm.

Basel Committee on Banking Supervision. 2005. "An Explanatory Note on the Basel II IRB Risk Weight Functions." Basel, Switzerland: Bank for International Settlements. June. https://www.bis.org/bcbs/irbriskweight.pdf.

Becker, Manuel, and Simon Linder. 2021. "The Unintended Consequences of Regulatory Import: The Basel Accord's Failure during the Financial Crisis." *Journal of European Public Policy* 28, no. 2:248–67.

Berger, Peter L., and Thomas Luckmann. 1966. *The Social Construction of Reality: A Treatise in the Sociology of Knowledge.* New York: Random House.

Berman, Elizabeth Popp. 2022. *Thinking Like an Economist: How Efficiency Replaced Equality in U.S. Public Policy.* Princeton, NJ: Princeton University Press.

Bernal Lloréns, Mercedes. 2004. "Financial Crises and the Publication of the Financial Statements of Banks in Spain, 1844–1868." *Accounting Historians Journal* 31, no. 2:1–26.

Bertrán, Concha, and María A. Pons. 2017. "Two Great Banking Crises and Their Economic Impact Compared: Spain 1976/1977 and 2008." *Journal of Iberian and Latin American Economic History* 35, no. 2:241–74.

Blackwell, Richard. 1998. "OSFI Backs Global Watchdog to Prevent Banking Crises." *Financial Post*, May 15. Accessed via Factiva database. https://www.dowjones.com/professional/factiva/.

Board of Governors of the Federal Reserve System. 1932. "Branch Banking in the United States." Material prepared for the information of the Federal Reserve System by the Federal Reserve Committee on Branch, Group, and Chain Banking. https://fraser.stlouisfed.org/title/686.

———. 1938. *Federal Reserve Bulletin* 24, no. 2:73–179. February. https://fraser.stlouisfed.org/files/docs/publications/FRB/1930s/frb_021938.pdf.

———. 1955. "Minutes of the Federal Open Market Committee." August 2. https://www.federalreserve.gov/monetarypolicy/files/FOMChistmin19550802.pdf.

———. 2003. Notice of Proposed Rulemaking. September 12. https://www.federalreserve.gov/boarddocs/press/bcreg/2003/20030912/attachment.pdf.

———. n.d. "Total Commercial Banks in the United States." https://fred.stlouisfed.org/series/COMBNKTTL. Retrieved from FRED, Federal Reserve Bank of St. Louis, December 16, 2023.

Bodenhorn, Howard. 2002. *State Banking in Early America: A New Economic History.* Oxford: Oxford University Press.

Bordo, Michael D., and Angela Redish. 1987. "Why Did the Bank of Canada Emerge in 1935?" *Journal of Economic History* 47, no. 2:405–17.

Borio, Claudio, and Philip Lowe. 2001. "To Provision or Not to Provision." *Bank for International Settlements Quarterly Review*, September, 36–48. https://www.bis.org/publ/r_qt0109e.pdf.

Borrows, John. 1997. "Wampum at Niagara: The Royal Proclamation, Canadian Legal History, and Self-Government." In *Aboriginal and Treaty Rights in Canada: Essays on Law, Equality, and Respect for Difference*, edited by Michael Asch, 155–72. Vancouver: University of British Columbia Press.

Breckenridge, Roeliff Morton. 1895. *The Canadian Banking System, 1817–1890.* New York: Macmillan.

———. 1911. *The History of Banking in Canada.* Washington, DC: Government Printing Office.

Bremer, C. D. 1935. "American Bank Failures." PhD diss., Columbia University.

Brewer, Elijah, III, Thomas H. Mondschean, and Philip E. Strahan. 1993. "Why the Life Insurance Industry Did Not Face an S&L-Type Crisis." *Economic Perspectives* 17, no. 5:12–24. https://www.chicagofed.org/publications/economic-perspectives/1993/13sepoct1993-part2-brewer.

Bulbul, Dilek, Reinhard H. Schmidt, and Ulrich Schuwer. 2013. "Savings Banks and Cooperative Banks in Europe." SAFE Policy White Paper Series, no. 5.

Burger, Albert E. 1969. "A Historical Analysis of the Credit Crunch of 1966." *Review, Federal Reserve Bank of St. Louis* 5:13–30.

Burke, Edmund. 1790. *Reflections on the Revolution in France, and on the Proceedings in Certain Societies in London Relative to That Event. In a Letter Intended to Have Been Sent to a Gentleman in Paris.* London: J. Dodsley in Pall Mall. Retrieved December 15, 2021 via Gallica.

Burns, Tom. 1983. "Spain Seizes Hold of Conglomerate." *Washington Post*, February 25. https://www.washingtonpost.com/archive/business/1983/02/25/spain-seizes-control-of -conglomerate/8b1591dc-f5a8-411d-80cb-ddb101661e39/.

Busch, Andreas. 2009. *Banking Regulation and Globalization*. Oxford: Oxford University Press.

Cabrera, Mercedes, and Fernando del Rey. 2007. *The Power of Entrepreneurs: Politics and Economy in Contemporary Spain*. New York: Berghahn Books.

Calloway, Colin G. 2007. *The Scratch of a Pen: 1763 and the Transformation of North America*. Oxford: Oxford University Press.

Calomiris, Charles. 2020. "The Evolution of Bank Chartering." December 7. https://www.occ.gov /publications-and-resources/publications/economics/moments-in-history/pub-moments-in -history-evolution-bank-chartering.pdf.

Calomiris, Charles W., and Stephen H. Haber. 2014. *Fragile by Design: The Political Origins of Banking Crises and Scarce Credit*. Princeton, NJ: Princeton University Press.

Calvo-Gonzalez, Oscar. 2007. "American Military Interests and Economic Confidence in Spain under the Franco Dictatorship." *Journal of Economic History* 67, no. 3:740–67.

Cambó, Francesc. 1991. *Francesc Cambó: Discursos Parlimentaris (1907–1935)*. Barcelona: Editorial Alpha.

Canada. 1923a. *Hansard*, House of Commons. March 20. https://parl.canadiana.ca/.

———. 1923b. *Hansard*, House of Commons, June 18. https://parl.canadiana.ca/.

———. 1923c. *Hansard*, House of Commons, June 19. https://parl.canadiana.ca/.

———. 1924a. *Hansard*, House of Commons, April 9. https://parl.canadiana.ca/.

———. 1924b. *Hansard*, House of Commons. July 1. https://parl.canadiana.ca/.

———. 1924c. *Hansard*, House of Commons. July 2. https://parl.canadiana.ca/.

———. 1924d. *Hansard*, House of Commons. March 27. https://parl.canadiana.ca/.

———. 1924e. *Hansard*, Senate. March 4. https://parl.canadiana.ca/.

———. 1924f. *Hansard*, House of Commons. March 18. https://parl.canadiana.ca/.

———. 1962. *Submission to the Royal Commission on Banking and Finance*. October 16.

———. 1966a. Parliament. House of Commons. July 5. https://parl.canadiana.ca/.

———. 1966b. Parliament. House of Commons. Standing Committee on Finance, Trade and Economic Affairs. November 8. https://parl.canadiana.ca/.

———. 1967a. Parliament. House of Commons. Standing Committee on Finance, Trade and Economic Affairs. January 26. https://parl.canadiana.ca/.

———. 1967b. Parliament. House of Commons. Standing Committee on Finance, Trade, and Economic Affairs. February 22. https://parl.canadiana.ca/.

———. 1985a. *Hansard*, House of Commons. October 9. https://parl.canadiana.ca/.

———. 1985b. *Hansard*. House of Commons. October 17. https://parl.canadiana.ca/.

———. 1985c. *Hansard*. House of Commons. May 29. https://parl.canadiana.ca/.

———. 1987a. *Hansard*, House of Commons, May 4. https://parl.canadiana.ca/.

———. 1987b. *Hansard*, House of Commons, May 27. https://parl.canadiana.ca/.

———. 1987c. *Hansard*, House of Commons, May 29. https://parl.canadiana.ca/

———. 1987d. *Hansard*, House of Commons, June 30. https://parl.canadiana.ca/.

Canada Department of Finance. 1924. "Memorandum on Canadian Banking System and the Home Bank Case," March 3. 22, NAC RGl9 file 488-61-23.

"Canada's Domestic Stability Buffer: Swimming against the Tide." 2019. Remarks by Assistant Superintendent Jamey Hubbs, Toronto. January 23. https://www.osfi-bsif.gc.ca/Eng/osfi -bsif/med/sp-ds/Pages/jh20190123.aspx.

Cánovas del Castillo, Antonio. 1888. *Problemas contemporáneos*. Vol. 3. Madrid: Pérez Dubrull.

Carr, Jack, Frank Mathewson, and Neil Quigley. 1995. "Stability in the Absence of Deposit Insurance: The Canadian Banking System, 1890–1966." *Journal of Money, Credit, and Banking* 27, no. 4:1137–58.

Carruthers, Bruce. 1996. *City of Capital: Politics and Markets in the English Financial Revolution.* Princeton, NJ: Princeton University Press.

Caruana, Jaime. 2009. "Bank Restructuring in Spain: The 1978–83 Banking Crisis." In *Lessons Learned from Previous Banking Crises: Sweden, Japan, Spain, and Mexico.* Occasional Paper 79, Group of Thirty Meeting, February 4–6.

"Central Banking and Global Finance." 1997. Remarks by Chairman Alan Greenspan at the Catholic University Leuven, Leuven, Belgium. January 14. https://www.federalreserve.gov/boarddocs /speeches/1997/19970114.htm.

Chant, John F. 1965. "The Porter Commission on Canadian Banking and Finance." *PSL Quarterly Review* 18, no. 73:168–90. https://rosa.uniroma1.it/rosa04/psl_quarterly_review/article/view /11627.

Chapman, John M., and Ray Bert Westerfield. 1942. *Branch Banking: Its Historical and Theoretical Position in America and Abroad.* New York: Harper.

Chen, Linda. 2018. "Corporatism Reconsidered: Howard J. Wiarda's Legacy." *Polity* 50, no. 4:601–11.

Churchill, Winston S. 1932. "Consistency in Politics." In *Thoughts and Adventures*, 23–48. London: Thornton Butterworth.

Clark, Mark. 1986. "The Anatomy of a Failure." *Maclean's*, November 3. https://archive.macleans.ca/.

Clarke, Matthew St. Clair, and David A. Hall. 1832. *Legislative and Documentary History of the Bank of the United States.* Washington, DC: Gales and Seaton.

Clayton, Richard, and Jonas Pontusson. 1998. "Welfare-State Retrenchment Revisited: Entitlement Cuts, Public Sector Restructuring, and Inegalitarian Trends in Advanced Capitalist Societies." *World Politics* 5, no. 1:67–98.

Clemens, Elisabeth S., and James M. Cook. 1999. "Politics and Institutionalism: Explaining Durability and Change." *Annual Review of Sociology* 25, no. 1:441–66.

"Concerns and Considerations for the Practical Implementation of the New Basel Accord." 2003. Remarks by Vice Chairman Roger W. Ferguson Jr. At the ICBI Risk Management Conference, Geneva, Switzerland. December 2. https://www.federalreserve.gov/boarddocs/speeches /2003/20031202/default.htm.

Condition of the Federal Deposit Insurance Funds. 1988. US House of Representatives Committee on Banking, Housing, and Public Affairs. July 7.

"Controlling the Safety Net." 2001. Remarks by Governor Laurence H. Meyer at the 37th Annual Conference on Bank Structure and Competition of the Federal Reserve Bank of Chicago. May 10. https://www.federalreserve.gov/boarddocs/speeches/2001/200105102/default.htm.

"Corporate Governance." 2002. Remarks by Chairman Alan Greenspan at the Stern School of Business, New York University, New York. March 26. https://www.federalreserve.gov/boarddocs /speeches/2002/200203262/default.htm.

Cortes Generales. 1983. Diario del Sesiones del Congreso de los Diputados. Sesiones informativas de Comisiones: Economia, Comercio, y Hacienda. February 18. Translated from Spanish. https://www.congreso.es/en/busqueda-de-publicaciones.

———. 1988a. Diario del Sesiones del Congreso de los Diputados. Comisiones: Economia, Comercio, y Hacienda. Sesión celebrada el miercoles, May 11. No. 279. Translated from Spanish. https://www.congreso.es/en/busqueda-de-publicaciones.

———. 1988b. Diario del Sesiones del Congreso de los Diputados. Comisiones: Economia, Comercio, y Hacienda. Sesión celebrada el martes, May 17. Translated from Spanish. https://www .congreso.es/en/busqueda-de-publicaciones.

Coval, J., J. Jurek, and E. Stafford. 2009. "The Economics of Structured Finance." *Journal of Economic Perspectives* 23, no. 1:3–25.

Covitz, Daniel, Nellie Liang, and Gustavo A. Suarez. 2013. "The Evolution of a Financial Crisis: Collapse of the Asset-Backed Commercial Paper Market." *Journal of Finance* 68, no. 3:815–48.

Crawford, Leslie, and Gillian Tett. 2008. "Spanish Bank Spared Huge Writedowns." *Financial Times*, February 4. https://www.gale.com/c/financial-times-historical-archive.

Crowle, Harold E. 1933. "Central Banking." *Maclean's*, July 1. https://archive.macleans.ca/.

Crozier, Michel. 1973. *The Stalled Society*. New York: Viking.

"Currency Markets; Canadian Dollar Falls to 48-Year Low in U.S." 1981. *New York Times*, July 24. https://www.nytimes.com/1981/07/24/business/currency-markets-canadian-dollar-falls-to -48-year-low-in-us.html.

Curry, Timothy J., and Lynn Shibut. 2000. "The Cost of the Savings and Loan Crisis: Truth and Consequences." *FDIC Banking Review* 13:26–35.

"Cyclicality and Banking Regulation." 2002. Remarks by Chairman Alan Greenspan at the Conference on Bank Structure and Competition, Federal Reserve Bank of Chicago. May 10. https:// www.federalreserve.gov/boarddocs/speeches/2002/20020510/default.htm.

Darnton, John. 1983. "Spain's Stunning Takeover." *New York Times*, February 25. https://www .nytimes.com/1983/02/25/business/spain-s-stunning-takeover.html.

Davis, Gerald F. 2009. *Managed by the Markets: How Finance Reshaped America*. Oxford: Oxford University Press.

Davis, Gerald F, and Suntae Kim. 2015. "Financialization of the Economy." *Annual Review of Sociology* 41:203–21.

Davoud, H. T. 1964. "Lord Sydenham's Proposal for a Provincial Bank of Issue." In *Money and Banking in Canada*, edited by E. P. Neufeld, 95–105. Montreal: McGill-Queen's University Press.

De Bondt, Gabe, and Henriette Prast. 2000. "Bank Capital Ratios in the 1990s: Cross-Country Evidence." *Banca Nazionale del Lavoro Quarterly Review* 212, no. 53:71–97.

DeMuth, Christopher. 2011. "Competition and the Constitution." *National Affairs*. https://www .nationalaffairs.com/publications/detail/competition-and-the-constitution.

Deposit Insurance and Financial Modernization. 1990. US Senate Committee on Banking, Housing, and Urban Affairs. May 3.

Deposit Insurance Issues and Depositor Discipline. 1990. US House of Representatives. Commerce, Consumer, and Monetary Affairs Subcommittee of the Committee on Government Operations. October 3.

Deposit Insurance Reform. 1990a. US House of Representatives, Committee on Banking, Finance, and Urban Affairs. February 21.

Deposit Insurance Reform. 1990b. US House of Representatives, Committee on Banking, Finance, and Urban Affairs. September 13.

Deposit Insurance Reform and Financial Modernization. 1990. US Senate Committee on Banking, Housing, and Urban Affairs. April 26.

Deposit Insurance Reform and Related Supervisory Issues. 1985. US Senate Committee on Banking, Housing and Urban Affairs. September 11.

Depository Institutions Deregulation Act of 1979. 1979. US Senate Committee on Banking, Housing, and Urban Affairs, Subcommittee on Financial Institutions. June 27.

De Riquer, B. 1994. "La débil nacionalización española del siglo XIX." *Historia Social* 20:97–114.

Diario de Sesiones del Congreso de los Diputados. 1918. *Serie Histórica: Legislatura 1918–19*, no. 105 (December 10): 3453–82. https://app.congreso.es/est_sesiones/.

Diario de Sesiones del Congreso de los Diputados. 1921. *Serie Histórica: Legislatura 1920–21*, no. 80 (October 26): 3775–807. https://app.congreso.es/est_sesiones/.

Dingle, James F. 2003. "The Bank Failures of September 1985." In *Planning an Evolution: The Story of the Canadian Payments Association, 1980–2002*, 1–62. Bank of Canada, Canadian Payments Association. https://www.bankofcanada.ca/wp-content/uploads/2010/07/dingle_book.pdf.

"Discipline and Intervention of Credit Institutions." 1988. Law 26/1988. July 29. https://www.bde .es/f/webbde/SJU/normativa/eng/ficheros/en/l2688.pdf.

"Discurso de presentación del informe annual, pronunciado por el gobernador ante El Consejo de Gobierno del Banco de España." 2001. Remarks by Jaime Caruana. June. Madrid. Translated from Spanish. https://repositorio.bde.es/handle/123456789/21953.

Dobbin, Frank. 1994. *Forging Industrial Policy: The United States, Britain, and France in the Railway Age*. Cambridge: Cambridge University Press.

Dobbin, Frank, and Jiwook Jung. 2010. "The Misapplication of Mr. Michael Jensen: How Agency Theory Brought Down the Economy and Why It Might Again." In *Markets on Trial: The Economic Sociology of the U.S. Financial Crisis: Part B* (Research in the Sociology of Organizations, Vol. 30 Part B), edited by Michael Lounsbury and Paul M. Hirsch, 29-64. Leeds, UK: Emerald Group Publishing Limited. "Dodd-Frank Wall Street Reform and Consumer Protection Act." 2010. July 21. https://www.govinfo.gov/content/pkg/PLAW-111publ203/pdf/PLAW-111publ203.pdf.

Dowd, Kevin, Martin O. Hutchinson, and Simon G. Ashby. 2011. "Capital Inadequacies: The Dismal Failure of the Basel Regime of Bank Capital Regulation." In *Cato Institute Policy Analysis*, no. 681. https://ssrn.com/abstract=1961708.

Dymski, Gary. 1999. *The Bank Merger Wave: The Economic Causes and Social Consequences of Financial Consolidation*. Armonk, NY: M. E. Sharpe.

Easterbrook, W. T., and Hugh G. Aitkin. 1956. *Canadian Economic History*. London: Macmillan.

Eaton, Charlie. 2020. "Agile Predators: Private Equity and the Spread of Shareholder Value Strategies to US For-Profit Colleges." *Socio-economic Review* 20:791-815.

"Economy and Efficiency in Financial Sector Regulation." 2005. Remarks by Nicholas Le Pan, Superintendent, Office of the Superintendent of Financial Institutions, Canada (OSFI). To the Ottawa Economics Association. Ottawa. April 12.

Edey, Malcolm, and Ketil Hviding. 1995. "An Assessment of Financial Reform in OECD Countries." OECD Economics Department Working Paper 154.

Eder, Richard 1971. "Spanish Court Ruling Curtails Effects of Scandal." *New York Times*, February 25, 17.

Edwards, Franklin R., and Frederic S. Mishkin. 1995. "The Decline of Traditional Banking: Implications for Financial Stability and Regulatory Policy." Working Paper w4993. National Bureau of Economic Research.

Eissa-Barroso, Fransisco A., and Ainara Vázquez Varela. 2013. *Early Bourbon Spanish America: Politics and Society in a Forgotten Era (1700-1759)*. Leiden: Brill.

"El sistema bancario español: Tendencias recientes y retos de future." 2006. Remarks by Bank of Spain Deputy Governor Gonzalo Gil at the Asociación de Periodistas de Información Económica (APIE)—Universidad Internacional Menéndez Pelayo (UIMP). Santander. June 23. Translated from Spanish. https://repositorio.bde.es/bitstream/123456789/22153/1/IIPP-2006-028.pdf.

"Encuentro del sector financiero 2004." 2004. Intervención de D. Pedro Pablo Villasante 27 de Abril de 2004. Translated from Spanish. https://repositorio.bde.es/bitstream/123456789/22031/1/IIPP-2004-013.pdf.

"Enhancing the Safety and Soundness of the Canadian Financial System." 1995. Report by the Department of Finance, Canada. February. https://publications.gc.ca/collections/collection_2016/fin/F2-103-1995-eng.pdf.

Esdaile, Charles J. 2000. *Spain in the Liberal Age: From Constitution to Civil War; 1808-1939*. Oxford: Blackwell.

"The Evolution of Banking in a Market Economy." 1997. Remarks by Chairman Alan Greenspan at the Annual Conference of the Association of Private Enterprise Education, Arlington, Virginia. April 12. https://www.federalreserve.gov/boarddocs/speeches/1997/19970412.htm.

FDIC (Federal Deposit Insurance Corporation). 1997. "History of the Eighties: An Examination of the Banking Crises of the 1980s and Early 1990s." http://www.fdic.gov/bank/historical /history/vol1.html.

———. 1998. "Chapter 3: Establishment of the FDIC." In *A Brief History of Deposit Insurance*. https://www.fdic.gov/bank/historical/brief/index.html.

"The Federalist Papers: No. 51" 1788. *The Avalon Project*. Yale Law School, Lillian Goldman Law Library. https://avalon.law.yale.edu/18th_century/fed51.asp.

Federal Register (United States). 2004. *Risk-Based Capital Guidelines: Capital Adequacy Guidelines; Capital Maintenance; Consolidation of Asset-Backed Commercial Paper Programs and Other Related Issues* 69, no. 144 (July 28): 44908–25. https://www.govinfo.gov/content/pkg /FR-2004-07-28/pdf/04-16818.pdf.

Fernández de Lis, Santiago, and Alicia García-Herrero. 2009. "The Spanish Approach: Dynamic Provisioning and Other Tools." In *BBVA Working Paper* 0903. https://www.bbvaresearch.com /wp-content/uploads/mult/WP_0903_tcm348-212919.pdf.

Fernández de Lis, Santiago, Jorge Martinez Pages, and Jesús Saurina. 2000. "Credit Growth, Problem Loans, and Credit Risk Provisioning in Spain" Banco de España Working Paper 0018.

"Finance: United States and Global." 2002. Remarks by Chairman Alan Greenspan at the Institute of International Finance, New York. April 22. https://www.federalreserve.gov/boarddocs /speeches/2002/20020422/default.htm.

Financial Condition of the Bank and Thrift Industries. 1985. US House of Representatives Committee on Banking, Finance, and Urban Affairs, Subcommittee on Financial Institutions Supervision, Regulation and Insurance. October 2.

Financial Crisis Inquiry Commission. 2011. "The Financial Crisis Inquiry Report: Final Report of the National Commission on the Causes of Financial and Economic Crisis in the United States." Washington, DC. January. http://fcic.law.stanford.edu.

"Financial Engineering and Financial Stability." 2002. Remarks by Vice Chairman Roger W. Ferguson Jr. at the Annual Conference on the Securities Industry, American Institute of Certified Public Accountants and the Financial Management Division of the Securities Industry Association, New York. November 20. https://www.federalreserve.gov/boarddocs/speeches /2002/20021120/default.htm.

Financial Institutions and the Nation's Economy (FINE) Discussion Principles. 1975. US House of Representatives, Subcommittee on Financial Institutions Supervision, Regulation, and Insurance. December 18.

Financial Institutions and the Nation's Economy (FINE) Discussion Principles. 1976. US House of Representatives, Subcommittee on Financial Institutions Supervision, Regulation, and Insurance. January 20.

Financial Institutions Reform, Recovery, and Enforcement Act of 1989. 1989. US House of Representatives, Subcommittee on Financial Institutions Supervision, Regulation, and Insurance of the Committee on Banking, Finance, and Urban Affairs. March 16.

"Financial Modernization: The Issues." 1999. Remarks by Governor Laurence H. Meyer at the 1999 F. Hodge O'Neal Corporate and Securities Law Symposium, Washington University School of Law, St. Louis. March 12. https://www.federalreserve.gov/boarddocs/speeches /1999/19990312.htm.

"A Financial Regulator's Perspective on Evolving North American Markets" 2002. Notes for a Speech by Nicholas Le Pan, Superintendent, Financial Services Institute Off-the-Record Breakfast, National Club, Toronto. May 21.

"Financial Regulatory Outlook." 2004. Remarks by Nicholas Le Pan, Superintendent, Office of the Superintendent of Financial Institutions, Canada (OSFI). To the Economic Club of Toronto at the Albany Club, Toronto. November 25.

"The Financial Safety Net." 2001. Remarks by Chairman Alan Greenspan at the 37th Annual Conference on Bank Structure and Competition of the Federal Reserve Bank of Chicago. May 10. https://www.federalreserve.gov/boarddocs/speeches/2001/20010510/default.htm.

Financial Services Industry—Oversight. 1983. US Senate Committee on Banking, Housing, and Urban Affairs. June 21.

Financial Structure and Regulation. 1973. US Senate Committee on Banking, Finance, and Urban Affairs. November 6.

Fligstein, Neil. 2021. *The Banks Did It: An Anatomy of the Financial Crisis.* Cambridge, MA: Harvard University Press.

Fligstein, Neil, and Doug McAdam. 2012. *A Theory of Fields.* Oxford: Oxford University Press.

Fligstein, Neil, and Alexander F. Roehrkasse. 2016. "The Causes of Fraud in the Financial Crisis of 2007 to 2009: Evidence from the Mortgage-Backed Securities Industry." *American Sociological Review* 81, no. 4:617–43.

Fourcade, Marion. 2009. *Economists and Societies: Discipline and Profession in the United States, Britain and France, 1890s–1990s.* Princeton, NJ: Princeton University Press.

Fourcade-Gourinchas, Marion, and Sarah L. Babb. 2002. "The Rebirth of the Liberal Creed: Paths to Neoliberalism in Four Countries." *American Journal of Sociology* 108, no. 3:533–79.

Freedman, Charles. 1998. "The Canadian Banking System." No. 81. Ottawa: Bank of Canada. https://www.banqueducanada.ca/wp-content/uploads/2010/01/tr81.pdf.

Friedman, Jeffrey, and Wladimir Kraus. 2012. *Engineering the Financial Crisis: Systemic Risk and the Failure of Regulation.* Philadelphia: University of Pennsylvania Press.

Friedman, Milton, and Anna Schwartz. 1963. *A Monetary History of the United States.* Princeton, NJ: Princeton University Press.

"GAAP Departures Unsettle Investors." 1999. *Accountant,* April 1. Accessed via Factiva database.

Garver, Rob. 2000. "Accountants' Move Trumped Banks on Loan-Loss Reserves." *American Banker,* July 24. Accessed via Factiva database.

Gebhardt, Gunther, and Zoltan Novotny-Farkas. 2011. "Mandatory IFRS Adoption and Accounting Quality of European Banks." *Journal of Business Finance and Accounting* 38, nos. 3–4:289–333.

Gilbert, R. Alton. 1986. "Requiem for Regulation Q: What It Did and Why It Passed Away." *Review, Federal Reserve Bank of St. Louis* 68, no. 2:22–37.

Glass, David. 2002. "Can Fed Strike a Post-Enron Regulatory Balance?" *American Banker,* June 20. Accessed via Factiva database.

Gomez Ochoa, Fidel. 1991. "Por una nueva interpretación de la crisis final de la restauración: El gobierno Maura de agosto de 1921 y la reforma económica de Cambó." *Investigaciones históricas: Época moderna y contemporánea,* no. 11:251–72.

Goudarzi, S., V. Badaan, and E. D. Knowles. 2022. "Neoliberalism and the Ideological Construction of Equity Beliefs." *Perspectives on Psychological Science* 17, no. 5:1431–51.

"Government Regulation and Derivative Contracts." 1997. Remarks by Fed Chairman Alan Greenspan at the Financial Markets Conference of the Federal Reserve Bank of Atlanta, Coral Gables, Florida. February 21. https://www.federalreserve.gov/boarddocs/speeches/1997/19970221.htm.

"The Gramm-Leach-Bliley Act and Corporate Misbehavior—Coincidence or Contributor?" 2003. Remarks by Governor Mark W. Olson at the Conference on the Implementation of the Gramm-Leach-Bliley Act, American Law Institute and the American Bar Association, Washington, DC. February 6. https://www.federalreserve.gov/boarddocs/speeches/2003/20030206/default.htm.

Greenberg, Joshua R. 2020. *Bank Notes and Shinplasters: The Rage for Paper Money in the Early Republic.* Philadelphia: University of Pennsylvania Press.

Grifell-Tatjé, E., and C.A.K. Lovell. 1996. "Deregulation and Productivity Decline: The Case of Spanish Savings Banks." *European Economic Review* 40, no. 6:1281–303.

Grossman, Richard. 2008. "US Banking History, Civil War to World War II." *In EH.Net Encyclopedia*, edited by Robert Whaples. March 16. http://eh.net/encyclopedia/us-banking-history-civil-war-to-world-war-ii/.

Hacker, Jacob S., Alexander Hertel-Fernandez, Paul Pierson, and Kathleen Thelen. 2022. "The American Political Economy: Markets, Power, and the Meta Politics of US Economic Governance." *Annual Review of Political Science* 25, no. 1:197–217.

Hall, Peter, and Rosemary C. R. Taylor. 1996. "Political Science and the Three New Institutionalisms." *Political Studies* 44, no. 5:936–57.

Hall, Peter A., and David Soskice, eds. 2001. *Varieties of Capitalism: The Institutional Foundations of Comparative Advantage*. Oxford: Oxford University Press.

Haltom, Renee. 2013. "Failure of Continental Illinois" Federal Reserve Bank of Richmond. https://www.federalreservehistory.org/essays/failure-of-continental-illinois.

Hamilton, Alexander. 2003. "Federalist No. 17." In *The Federalist Papers*, edited by Clinton Rossiter, 113–18. New York: Signet.

Hamilton, David E. 1985. "The Causes of the Banking Panic of 1930: Another View." *Journal of Southern History* 51, no. 4:581–608.

Hammond, Bray. 1936. "Free Banks and Corporations: The New York Free Banking Act of 1838." *Journal of Political Economy* 44, no. 2:184–209.

———. 1957. *Banks and Politics in America from the Revolution to the Civil War*. Princeton, NJ: Princeton University Press.

Hardy, Martin E. 1968. "Stabilizing an Economy: Spain." *Finance and Development March 1968* 5, no. 1:30–36. International Monetary Fund, External Relations Department.

Harris, Ron. 1994. "The Bubble Act: Its Passage and Its Effects on Business Organization." *Journal of Economic History* 54, no. 3:610–27.

Hathaway, Terry. 2020. "Neoliberalism as Corporate Power." *Competition and Change* 24:315–37.

Heinemann, Erich H. 1972. "A Tree Falls, but Who Hears?" *New York Times*, January 16, F-1. https://www.nytimes.com/1972/01/16/archives/a-tree-falls-but-who-hears-hunt-study-produces-almost-no-reaction-a.html.

Herdman, Robert K. 2002. Testimony concerning the Roles of the SEC and the FASB in Establishing GAAP before the House Subcommittee on Capital Markets, Insurance, and Government Sponsored Enterprises, Committee on Financial Services. May 14. https://www.sec.gov/news/testimony/051402tsrkh.htm.

Hill, Andrew T. 2009. "The First Bank of the United States." Federal Reserve Bank of Philadelphia. https://www.federalreservehistory.org/essays/first_bank_of_the_us.

Hinckey, Donald R. 2012. *The War of 1812: A Forgotten Conflict*. Urbana: University of Illinois Press.

Hoffman, Stanley. 1963. *In Search of France*. Cambridge, MA: Harvard University Press.

Housing and Financial Reform. 1974. US Senate Committee on Banking, Housing, and Urban Affairs, Subcommittee on Financial Institutions. December 11.

Immergluck, D. 2009. "Core of the Crisis: Deregulation, the Global Savings Glut, and Financial Innovation in the Subprime Debacle." *City and Community* 8, no. 3:341–45.

"Informaciones Mundiales." 1921. *La Vanguardia*, October 27, 13. https://hemeroteca.lavanguardia.com/preview/1921/10/27/pagina-13/33288067/pdf.html.

"Insurance Companies and Banks under the New Regulatory Law." 1999. Remarks by Chairman Alan Greenspan before the Annual Meeting of the American Council of Life Insurance, Washington, DC. November 15. https://www.federalreserve.gov/boarddocs/speeches/1999/19991115.htm.

Interest Rates and Mortgage Credit. 1966. US Senate Committee on Banking and Currency. August 4.

"International Financial Risk Management." 2002. Remarks by Chairman Alan Greenspan before the Council on Foreign Relations, Washington, DC. November 19. https://www.federalreserve.gov/boarddocs/speeches/2002/20021119/default.htm.

Jablecki, Juliusz. 2009. "The Impact of Basel I Capital Requirements on Bank Behavior and the Efficacy of Monetary Policy." *International Journal of Economic Sciences and Applied Research* 2, no. 1:16–35.

Jackson, Patricia, et al. 1999. "Capital Requirements and Bank Behaviour: The Impact of the Basle Accord." Basel Committee on Banking Supervision Working Papers. https://www.bis .org/publ/bcbs_wp1.pdf.

James, John A., and David F. Weiman. 2010. "From Drafts to Checks: The Evolution of Correspondent Banking Networks and the Formation of the Modern U.S. Payments System, 1850–1914." *Journal of Money, Credit, and Banking* 42, no. 2:237–65.

Jiménez, Gabriel, Steven Ongena, José-Luis Peydró, and Jesús Saurina. 2017. "Macroprudential Policy, Countercyclical Bank Capital Buffers, and Credit Supply: Evidence from the Spanish Dynamic Provisioning Experiments." *Journal of Political Economy*. 125, no. 6:2125–77.

Johnson, Roger T. 2010. *Historical Beginnings . . . the Federal Reserve*. Public and Community Affairs Department Federal Reserve Bank of Boston. February.

Johnson, Simon, and James Kwak. 2011. *13 Bankers: The Wall Street Takeover and the Next Financial Meltdown*. New York: Random House.

Judge, Kathryn. 2012. "Fragmentation Nodes: A Study in Financial Innovation, Complexity, and Systemic Risk." *Stanford Law Review* 64:657–726.

Kaufman, George G., and Kenneth E. Scott. 2003. "What Is Systemic Risk, and Do Bank Regulators Retard or Contribute to It?" *Independent Review* 7, no. 3:371–91.

Kaufman, Jason. 2009. *The Origins of Canadian and American Political Differences*. Cambridge, MA: Harvard University Press.

Kennedy, Susan Estabrook. 1973. *The Banking Crisis of 1933*. Lexington: University Press of Kentucky.

Kern, Robert W. 1974. *Liberals, Reformers, and Caciques in Restoration Spain, 1875–1909*. Albuquerque: University of New Mexico Press.

Kodres, Laura. 2023. "Shadow Banks: Out of the Eyes of Regulators." International Monetary Fund. https://www.imf.org/en/Publications/fandd/issues/Series/Back-to-Basics/Shadow-Banks.

Krippner, Greta R. 2011. *Capitalizing on Crisis: The Political Origins of the Rise of Finance*. Cambridge, MA: Harvard University Press.

Kroszner, Randall S., and Philip E. Strahan. 1999. "What Drives Deregulation? Economics and Politics of the Relaxation of Bank Branching Restrictions." *Quarterly Journal of Economics* 114, no. 4:1437–67.

———. 2014. "Regulation and Deregulation of the US Banking Industry: Causes, Consequences, and Implications for the Future." In *Economic Regulation and Its Reform: What Have We Learned?*, edited by Nancy L. Rose, 485–544. Chicago: University of Chicago Press.

Kwak, James. 2014. "Cultural Capture and the Financial Crisis." In *Preventing Regulatory Capture: Special Interest Influence and How to Limit It*, edited by D. Carpenter and D. Moss, 71–98. Cambridge: Cambridge University Press.

Kyer, C. Ian. 2017. *From Next Best to World Class: The People and Events That Have Shaped the Canada Deposit Insurance Corporation, 1967–2017*. Ottawa: Canada Deposit Insurance Corporation (CDIC).

Lall, Ranjit. 2012. "From Failure to Failure: The Politics of International Banking Regulation." *Review of International Political Economy* 19, no. 4:609–38.

Lamoreaux, Naomi R. 1994. *Insider Lending: Banks, Personal Connections, and Economic Development in Industrial New England* Cambridge: Cambridge University Press.

Langan, Fred. 1985. "Two Failed Alberta Banks Shake Canadians." *Christian Science Monitor*, September 4. https://www.csmonitor.com/1985/0904/fbanks.html.

Law 5/2005. 2005. On the Supervision of Financial Conglomerates. April 22. Official State Gazette of April 23. https://www.bde.es/f/webbde/SJU/normativa/eng/ficheros/en/l-5-2005-en.pdf.

Leblond, Patrick. 2011. "A Canadian Perspective on the EU's Financial Architecture." In *Europe, Canada and the Comprehensive Economic Partnership Agreement*, edited by Kurt Hubner, 165–79. New York: Taylor and Francis.

Letter from Grace Vogel, Deputy Controller, Citigroup. 2003. To the Federal Bank Regulatory Agencies. November 19. https://www.fdic.gov/resources/regulations/federal-register -publications/03ccitigroupAMORT.html.

Letter from Nicholas Le Pan, OSFI Superintendent. 2002. To Purdy Crawford, Chair of the OSC Five Year Review Committee. August 21. https://www.osc.ca/sites/default/files/2020-12/fyr _20020829_report_com_lepan.pdf.

Letter from Paul Smith, Senior Counsel of the American Bankers Association. 2003. To the Federal Bank Regulatory Agencies. November 17. https://www.fdic.gov/resources/regulations /federal-register-publications/03cabariskbased.html.

Lewis, Lawrence. 1882. *A History of the Bank of North America*. Philadelphia: J. B. Lippincott.

Lin, Ken-Hou, and Megan Tobias Neely. 2020. *Divested: Inequality in the Age of Finance*. Oxford: Oxford University Press.

Lin, Ken-Hou, and Donald Tomaskovic-Devey. 2013. "Financialization and U.S. Income Inequality, 1970–2008." *American Journal of Sociology* 118, no. 5:1284–329.

Lipset, Seymour Martin. 1990. *Continental Divide: The Values and Institutions of the United States and Canada*. London: Routledge.

Lipset, Seymour Martin, and Gary Marks. 2000. *It Didn't Happen Here: Why Socialism Failed in the United States*. New York: W. W. Norton.

"Loan Loss Provisioning and Pro-cyclicality." 2009. Remarks by John C. Dugan, Comptroller of the Currency, before the Institute of International Bankers, March 2. https://www.occ.treas .gov/news-issuances/speeches/2009/pub-speech-2009-16.pdf.

Loan Loss Reserves. 1999. US House of Representatives, Committee on Banking and Financial Services, Subcommittee on Financial Institutions and Consumer Credit. June 16.

López Muñoz, Arturo. 1981. "Cambó y las crisis bancarias." *El País*, December 28. https://elpais .com/diario/1981/12/29/economia/378428403_850215.html.

Lukauskas, Arvid John. 1992. "The Political Economy of Financial Deregulation: The Case of Spain." PhD diss., University of Pennsylvania.

———. 1997. *Regulating Finance: The Political Economy of Spanish Financial Policy from Franco to Democracy*. Ann Arbor: University of Michigan Press.

Luttrell, Clifton B. 1972. "The Hunt Commission Report—an Economic View." Remarks to the Management Group of the Federal Reserve Bank of St. Louis, April 14.

Lynch, John. 1989. *Bourbon Spain, 1700–1808 (History of Spain)*. Oxford: Basil Blackwell.

MacDonald, Brian J. H. 1978. "The Canadian Chartered Banks and the Federal Government: An Analysis of the 1954 and 1967 Bank Act Revisions." Master's thesis, University of British Columbia.

MacKenzie, Donald. 2011. "The Credit Crisis as a Problem in the Sociology of Knowledge." *American Journal of Sociology* 116, no. 6:1778–841.

Malo de Molina, José Luis, and Pablo Martín-Aceña. 2012. *The Spanish Financial System: Growth and Development since 1900*. London: Palgrave Macmillan.

Martin, Douglas. 1985. "Troubles at Canadian Banks." *New York Times*, October 4. https://www .nytimes.com/1985/10/04/business/troubles-at-canadian-banks.html.

Martín-Aceña, Pablo. 2017. "The Banco de España, 1782–2017: The History of a Central Bank." *Estudios de Historia Económica* (Banco de España), no. 73:1–81.

———. 2018. "The Bank of Spain, 1782–2017: A History." In *Sveriges Riksbank and the History of Central Banking*, edited by Rodney Edvinsson, Tor Jacobson, and Daniel Waldenström, 172–206. Cambridge: Cambridge University Press.

Martín-Aceña, Pablo, Angeles Pons, and Concepción Betrán. 2009. "Financial Crises and Financial Reforms in Spain: What Have We Learned." In *Financial Market Regulation in the Wake of Financial Crises: The Historical Experience*, edited by Alfredo Gigliobianco and Gianni Toniolo, 119–68. Rome: Printing Office of the Banca d'Italia.

Martín-Aceña, Pablo, Elena Martinez Ruiz, and Pilar Nogues-Marco. 2011. "Floating against the Tide: Spanish Monetary Policy, 1870–1931." *Working Papers in Economic History, Universidad Carlos III de Madrid* 11, no. 10:1–29. https://core.ac.uk/download/pdf/6425821.pdf.

———. 2013. "The Bank of Spain: A National Financial Institution." *Journal of European Economic History* 13, no. 1:11–45.

Mason, David L. 2004. *From Buildings and Loans to Bail-Outs: A History of the American Savings and Loan Industry, 1831–1995*. New York: Cambridge University Press.

Mathias, Philip. 1999. "Regulator Told 2 Banks to Use Offbeat Accounting: Protected Profits at Laurentian and National as They Increased Reserves." *Financial Post*, March 30. Accessed via Factiva database.

Mayer, Christopher, Karen Pence, and Shane M. Sherlund. 2009. "The Rise in Mortgage Defaults." *Journal of Economic Perspectives* 23, no. 1:27–50.

McAlister, Lyle N. 1963. "Social Structure and Social Change in New Spain." *Hispanic American Historical Review* 43, no. 3:349–70.

McCoy, Patricia. 2015. "Countercyclical Regulation and Its Challenges." *Arizona State Law Journal* 47, no. 5:1181–237.

McFarlane, Anthony. 2013. "The Bourbon Century." In *Early Bourbon Spanish America: Politics and Society in a Forgotten Era*, edited by Francisco A. Eissa-Barroso and Ainara Vázquez Varela, 181–98. Leiden: Brill.

McKenzie, Allan. 1931. "Are the Banks Refusing Farmer Loans?" *Maclean's Magazine*, May 15. https://archive.macleans.ca/.

Menand, Lev, and Morgan Ricks. 2021. "Federal Corporate Law and the Business of Banking." *University of Chicago Law Review* 88, no. 6:1361–418.

Merle, Renae. 2018. "A Guide to the Financial Crisis: 10 Years Later." *Washington Post*, September 10. https://www.washingtonpost.com/business/economy/a-guide-to-the-financial-crisis—10 -years-later/2018/09/10/114b76ba-af10-11e8-a20b-5f4f84429666_story.html.

Merton, Robert C. 1977. "An Analytic Derivation of the Cost of Deposit Insurance and Loan Guarantees: An Application of Modern Option Pricing Theory." *Journal of Banking & Finance* 1, no. 1:3–11.

Mintz, Steven. 2004. "Winning the Vote: A History of Voting Rights." *History Now* 1. https://www .gilderlehrman.org/history-resources/essays/winning-vote-history-voting-rights.

Moen, Jon, and Ellis W. Tallman. 1992. "The Bank Panic of 1907: The Role of Trust Companies." *Journal of Economic History* 52, no. 3:611–30.

Moss, David A. 2011. "Reversing the Null: Regulation, Deregulation, and the Power of Ideas." In *Challenges to Business in the Twenty-First Century*, edited by Gerald Rosenfeld, Jay W. Lorsch, and Rakesh Khurana, 35–49. Cambridge, MA: American Academy of Arts and Sciences.

Mote, Larry R. 1979. "Banks and the Securities Markets: The Controversy." *Economic Perspectives* 3, no. 8:14–20.

"Moving Forward into the 21st Century." 1999. Remarks by Governor Laurence H. Meyer at the Conference of State Bank Supervisors, Williamsburg, Virginia. June 3. https://www .federalreserve.gov/boarddocs/speeches/1999/19990603.htm.

Mudge, Stephanie L. 2019. *Leftism Reinvented: Western Parties from Socialism to Neoliberalism*. Cambridge, MA: Harvard University Press.

Narter, Bart. 2009. "It Takes More Than a Village: The Decline of the Community Bank." *Bank Accounting and Finance* 22, no. 4:49–52.

National Commission on Financial Institution Reform, Recovery, and Enforcement (US). 1993. *Origins and Causes of the S&L Debacle: A Blueprint for Reform; A Report to the President and Congress of the United States.* Washington, DC: Commission on Financial Institution Reform, Recovery, and Enforcement.

Needham, Duncan. 2012. "Britain's Money Supply Experiment, 1971–73." Working Papers in Economic and Social History 10. University of Cambridge. September.

Nielsen, Klaus. 2008. "Indicative Planning." In *The New Palgrave Dictionary of Economics*, edited by S. N. Durlauf and L. Blume. London: Palgrave Macmillan. https://doi.org/10.1057/978-1-349-95121-5_982-2.

Notes for an Address by Nicholas Le Pan, Superintendent of Financial Institutions. 2002. To the Empire Club of Canada, Fairmont Royal York Hotel, Toronto. February 7.

Novak, William J. 2008. "The Myth of the 'Weak' American State." *American Historical Review* 113, no. 3:752–72.

Now Accounts, Federal Reserve Membership, and Related Issues. 1977. US Senate Committee on Banking, Housing, and Urban Affairs, Subcommittee on Financial Institutions. June 21.

Olariaga, Luis. 1921. "La ordenación bancaria y la reforma del banco." *El Sol*, December 2, 3.

Ontario Securities Commission. 2003. *Five Year Review Committee Final Report: Reviewing the Securities Act.* Toronto: Queen's Printer for Ontario. March 21. https://www.osc.ca/sites/default/files/2020-12/fyr_20030529_5yr-final-report.pdf.

OSFI (Office of the Superintendent of Financial Institutions Canada). 2004. "Asset Securitization, Prudential Limits and Restrictions." Guideline B-5. Issued July 1994, revised November 2004. Obtained from OSFI via Access to Information Act request, July 30, 2012.

———. 2007. "OSFI Annual Report, 2006–7: Charting a Course." Ottawa: Office of the Superintendent of Financial Institutions. https://publications.gc.ca/site/eng/9.668969/publication.html.

———. 2008. "Backgrounder: OSFI's Role in the ABCP Market Issue." Ottawa. April 22. Obtained from OSFI via Access to Information Act request, July 30, 2012.

Opening Statement by Nicholas Le Pan, Superintendent of Financial Institutions Canada (OSFI). 2005. To the Standing Senate Committee on Banking, Trade and Commerce, in Relation to Its Study on Consumer Issues Arising in the Financial Services Sector. Ottawa. February 10.

Ostrolenk, Bernhard. 1930. "The Revolution in Banking Theory." *Atlantic Monthly*, February. https://www.theatlantic.com/magazine/archive/1930/02/the-revolution-in-banking-theory/307111/?utm_source=copy-link&utm_medium=social&utm_campaign=share.

Oversight Hearings on the Condition of the Banking System. 1989. US Senate Committee on Banking, Housing, and Urban Affairs. October 5.

Pagoulatos, George. 1999. "Financial Repression and Liberalization in Europe's Southern Periphery: From 'Growth State' to 'Stabilization State.'" *Archive of European Integration.* https://aei.pitt.edu/2357/.

Palmer, John. 1998. Remarks by John R. V. Palmer, Superintendent of Financial Institutions to the Financial Reporting for Financial Institutions '98 Conference, Toronto. September 28.

———. 2000. Remarks to the Empire Club of Canada, Royal York Hotel, Toronto. June 8. Replicated in John Palmer and Caroline Cerruti, "Is There a Need to Rethink the Supervisory Process?" Discussion Paper at International Conference "Reforming Financial Regulation and Supervision: Going Back to Basics," Madrid. June 15, 2009. https://documents1.worldbank.org/curated/en/552861468054544285/pdf/535250WP0P11691nd0Caroline0Cerruti1.pdf.

Paret, L. Victor. 1921. *El estado y el Banco de España.* Madrid: Libreria General de Victoriana Suarez.

Pauly, Louis W. 2014. "Canadian Autonomy and Systemic Financial Risk after the Crisis of 2008." In *Crisis and Reform: Canada and the International Financial System*, edited by Rohintan P. Medhora and Dane Rowlands, 139–58. Montreal: McGill-Queen's University Press.

Payne, Stanley G. 1973. *A History of Spain and Portugal.* Vol. 1. Madison: University of Wisconsin Press.

Peltzman, Sam. 1976. "Toward a More General Theory of Regulation." *Journal of Law and Economics* 19:211–40.

Pérez, Sofía A. 1997. *Banking on Privilege: The Politics of Spanish Financial Reform.* Ithaca, NY: Cornell University Press.

———. 1998. "Systemic Explanations, Divergent Outcomes: The Politics of Financial Liberalization in France and Spain." *International Studies Quarterly* 42, no. 4:755–84.

Pernell, Kim. 2020. "Market Governance, Financial Innovation, and Financial Instability: Lessons from Banks' Adoption of Shareholder Value Management." *Theory and Society* 49, no. 2:277–306.

Pernell, Kim, and Jiwook Jung. 2023. "Rethinking Moral Hazard: Government Protection and Bank Risk-Taking." *Socio-economic Review.* Advance access https://academic.oup.com/ser /advance-article/doi/10.1093/ser/mwad050/7280452.

Pernell, Kim, Jiwook Jung, and Frank Dobbin. 2017. "The Hazards of Expert Control: Chief Risk Officers and Risky Derivatives." *American Sociological Review* 82, no. 3:511–41.

Personal interview. 2013a. With Canadian accounting standards setter. Toronto. July.

Personal interview. 2013b. With OSFI regulator. Ottawa. July.

Personal interview. 2013c. With OSFI regulator. Ottawa. July.

Personal interview. 2013d. With securitization industry participant. Madrid. March.

Personal interview. 2013e. With Spanish banking regulator. Madrid. March.

Petitjean, Mikael. 2013. "Bank Failures and Regulation: A Critical Review." *Journal of Financial Regulation and Compliance* 21, no. 1:16–38.

Pettipas, Katherine. 1994. *Severing the Ties That Bind: Government Repression of Indigenous Religious Ceremonies on the Prairies.* Winnipeg: University of Manitoba Press.

Pfeffer, Fabian T., Sheldon Danziger, and Robert F. Schoeni. 2013. "Wealth Disparities before and after the Great Recession." *Annals of the American Academy of Political and Social Science* 650, no. 1:98–123.

Plessis, Alain. 1994. "The History of Banks in France." In *Handbook on the History of European Banks,* edited by Manfred Pohl and Sabine Freitag, 185–296. Brookfield, VT: Edward Elgar.

Plummer, Kevin. 2013. "Historicist: The Home Bank's House of Cards." *Torontoist,* August 24. https://torontoist.com/2013/08/historicist-the-home-banks-house-of-cards/.

Poapst, J. V. 1973. "Developing the Residential Mortgage Market." Report Prepared for Central Housing and Mortgage Corporation. https://publications.gc.ca/collections/collection_2016 /schl-cmhc/NH15-476-1973-3-eng.pdf.

Pons Brias, Maria Angeles. 2002. *Regulating Spanish Banking 1939–1975.* Aldershot: Ashgate.

Posner, Richard A. 2014. "The Concept of Regulatory Capture: A Short, Inglorious History." In *Preventing Regulatory Capture,* edited by Daniel Carpenter and David A. Moss, 49–56. Cambridge: Cambridge University Press.

Poveda, Raimundo. 2012. "Banking Supervision and Regulation over the Past 40 Years." In *The Spanish Financial System: Growth and Development since 1900,* edited by José Luís Malo de Molina and Pablo Martín-Aceña, 232–34. New York: Palgrave.

Prados de la Escosura, Leandro, and Jorge C. Sanz. 1996. "Growth and Macroeconomic Performance in Spain, 1939–93." In *Economic Growth in Europe since 1945,* edited by Nicholas Crafts and Gianni Toniolo, 355–87. Cambridge: Cambridge University Press.

Prasad, Monica. 2006. *The Politics of Free Markets: The Rise of Neoliberal Economic Policies in Britain, France, Germany and the United States.* Chicago: University of Chicago Press.

———. 2012. *The Land of Too Much: American Abundance and the Paradox of Poverty.* Cambridge, MA: Harvard University Press.

Prechel, Harland. 2021. *Normalized Financial Wrongdoing: How Re-regulating Markets Created Risks and Fostered Inequality.* Stanford, CA: Stanford University Press.

Prechel, Harland, and Teresa Morris. 2010. "The Effects of Organizational and Political Embeddedness on Financial Malfeasance in the Largest U.S. Corporations: Dependence, Incentives, and Opportunities." *American Sociological Review* 75:331–54.

"President Jackson's Veto Message regarding the Bank of the United States." 1832. In *A Compilation of the Messages and Papers of the Presidents*, vol. 2, part 3, *Andrew Jackson, March 4, 1829, to March 4, 1833*, edited by James D. Richardson. July 10. Project Gutenberg Release 10858. https://www.gutenberg.org/files/10858/10858.txt.

Preston, Howard H. 1933. "The Banking Act of 1933." *American Economic Review* 23, no. 4:585–607.

Primm, James Neal. 1989. *A Foregone Conclusion: The Founding of the Federal Reserve Bank of St. Louis.* St. Louis: Federal Reserve Bank.

Purnanandam, A. 2011. "Originate-to-Distribute Model and the Subprime Mortgage Crisis." *Review of Financial Studies* 24, no. 6:1881–915.

Quinn, Sarah. 2017. "The Miracles of Bookkeeping: How Budget Politics Link Fiscal Policies and Financial Markets." *American Journal of Sociology* 123, no. 1:48–85.

———. 2019. *American Bonds: How Credit Markets Shaped a Nation.* Princeton, NJ: Princeton University Press.

Ramos-Tallada, Julio. 2010. "Financial Distress and Banking Regulation: What Is Different about Spain?" *Journal of Innovation Economics* 2:49–76.

Ratnovski, Lev, and Rocco Huang. 2009. "Why Are Canadian Banks More Resilient?" IMF Working Paper 152.

"Recent Developments in Banking and Financial Markets: Implications for Bank Supervision and Regulation." 1998. Remarks by Governor Laurence H. Meyer at the Financial Institutions Center, University of Tennessee, Knoxville. September 18. https://fraser.stlouisfed.org/title/936/item/36423.

"Reflexiones sobre la estabilidad financiera." 2002. Remarks by Subgobernador Gonzalo Gil at Fundación Pedro Barrié de la Maza, La Coruña, October 16. Translated from Spanish. https://repositorio.bde.es/handle/123456789/21977.

Reform of the Nation's Banking and Financial Systems. 1987. US House of Representatives Committee on Banking, Finance, and Urban Affairs. October 28.

Regulation Q and Related Measures. 1980. US House of Representatives Committee on Banking, Finance, and Urban Affairs, Subcommittee on Financial Institutions Supervision, Regulation, and Insurance. February 20.

Reguly, Eric. 1999. "Eric Reguly Examines Scotiabank's Conjuring Act." *Globe and Mail* (Canada), December 7. Accessed via Factiva database.

Report of the Royal Commission on Banking and Finance. 1964. Ottawa: The Queen's Printer. https://publications.gc.ca/site/eng/471955/publication.html.

"Risk Transfer and Financial Stability." 2005. Remarks by Chairman Alan Greenspan to the Federal Reserve Bank of Chicago's Forty-First Annual Conference on Bank Structure. May 5. https://www.federalreserve.gov/boarddocs/speeches/2005/20050505/.

Robinson, Roland I. 1972. "The Hunt Commission Report: A Search for Politically Feasible Solutions to the Problems of Financial Structure." *Journal of Finance* 27, no. 4:765–77.

Roe, Mark. 1994. *Strong Managers, Weak Owners: The Political Roots of American Corporate Finance.* Princeton, NJ: Princeton University Press.

Rose, John. 1869. *Speech by the Honourable John Rose, Minister of Finance, Canada, on Introducing the Resolutions on Banking and Currency.* Ottawa: Hunter and Rose.

Rothbard, Murray. 1962. *The Panic of 1819.* New York: Columbia University Press.

Rötheli, Tobias. 2013. "Innovations in US Banking Practices and the Credit Boom of the 1920s." *Business History Review* 87, no. 2:309–27.

Royo, Sebastián. 2020. "From Boom to Bust: The Economic Crisis in Spain 2008–2013." In *Why Banks Fail: The Political Roots of Banking Crises in Spain*, 119–40. New York: Palgrave Macmillan.

Saurina, Jesús. 2009. "Dynamic Provisioning: The Experience of Spain." *Crisis Response Note* 7. World Bank, Washington, DC. https://documents1.worldbank.org/curated/en/526531468330917547/pdf/503490BRI0Box3lponse0Note701PUBLIC1.pdf.

Salas, Vicente, and Jesús Saurina. 2003. "Deregulation, Market Power, and Risk Behaviour in Spanish Banks." *European Economic Review* 47, no. 6:1061–75.

Savage, Lawrie. 2015. "From Trial to Triumph: How Canada's Past Financial Crises Helped Shape a Superior Regulatory System." *Journal of Governance and Regulation* 4, no. 1:213–48.

Schneiberg, Marc. 2007. "What's on the Path? Path Dependence, Organizational Diversity, and the Problem of Institutional Change in the US Economy, 1900–1950." *Socio-economic Review* 5:47–80.

Shearer, Ronald A., John F. Chant, and David E. Bond. 1984. *The Economics of the Canadian Financial System*. 2nd ed. Scarborough: Prentice-Hall Canada.

Shecter, Barbara. 2014. "OSFI's Jeremy Rudin Says Top Banking Regulator Won't Rely on Housing Market Predictions." *Financial Post*, September 30. https://financialpost.com/news/fp-street/osfis-jeremy-rudin-says-bank-regulator-will-avoid-detailed-prescriptive-rules.

Sheng, Andrew. 1996. *Bank Restructuring: Lessons from the 1980s*. Washington, DC: World Bank. http://documents.worldbank.org/curated/en/533291468766518413/Bank-restructuring-lessons-from-the-1980s.

Sherman, Matthew. 2009. "A Short History of Financial Deregulation in the United States." Center for Economic and Policy Research Working Paper.

Shortell, Ann. 1985. "Counting the Cost of Failure." *Maclean's*, September 16. https://archive.macleans.ca/.

Shortt, Adam. [1896] 1986. *The Early History of Canadian Banking*. Toronto: Canadian Bankers Association.

———. 1908. *Lord Sydenham*. Toronto: Morang.

———. 1964. "Currency and Banking, 1840–1867." In *Money and Banking in Canada*, edited by E. P. Neufeld, 132–48. Montreal: McGill-Queen's University Press.

Shubert, Adrian. 2003. "Identities." In *A Social History of Modern Spain*, 144–205. London: Routledge.

Simpson, James. 1995. *Spanish Agriculture: The Long Siesta, 1765–1965*. Cambridge: Cambridge University Press.

Smith, Adam. 1804. *An Inquiry Into the Nature and Causes of the Wealth of Nations*. Vol. 2. Hartford: Printed for Oliver D. Cooke. Lincoln and Gleason, Printers.

———. 1905. *An Inquiry into the Nature and Causes of the Wealth of Nations*. Book 2, chapter 2. Edited by Edwin Cannan. London: Methuen.

Smith, Andrew. 2012. "Continental Divide: The Canadian Banking and Currency Laws of 1871 in the Mirror of the United States." *Enterprise and Society* 13, no. 3:455–503.

Smith, Angel. 2012. "The Corporatist Threat and the Overthrow of the Spanish Second Republic." In *European Democratization since 1800*, edited by John Garrard, Vera Tolz, and Ralph White, 116–37. London: Palgrave Macmillan.

———. 2016. "The Rise and Fall of "Respectable" Spanish Liberalism, 1808–1923: An Explanatory Framework." *Journal of Iberian and Latin American Studies* 22, no. 1:55–73.

Smith, Denis. 1973. *Gentle Patriot: A Political Biography of Walter Gordon*. Edmonton: Hurtig.

Smith, Keith D. 2014. *Strange Visitors: Documents in Indigenous-Settler Relations in Canada from 1876*. Toronto: University of Toronto Press.

Smith, Lawrence B. 1981. "Housing Policy in the Seventies." *Land Economics* 57, no. 3:338–32.

Solsten, Eric, and Sandra Meditz. 1990. *Spain: A Country Study*. Washington, DC: Federal Research Division, Library of Congress. https://tile.loc.gov/storage-services/master/frd/frdcstdy/sp/spaincountrystud00sols_0/spaincountrystud00sols_0.pdf.

Spain. 1849. *Colección legislativa de España*. Primer Cuatramiste 40. Madrid. En La Imprinta Nacionale.

————. 1962. Preamble to Law 2/62 of April 14. Banking Law of 1962.

"Spain's Miracle." *Financial Times*, October 17, 1997. https://www.gale.com/c/financial-times-historical-archive.

"Speeds Bank Bill by a Compromise." 1933. *New York Times*, January 21, 1 and 14. https://timesmachine.nytimes.com/timesmachine/1933/01/22/99287017.html?pageNumber=1.

Sprague, D. N. 1995. "Canada's Treaties with Aboriginal Peoples." *Manitoba Law Journal* 23:341–51.

Steinmo, Sven. 1989. "Political Institutions and Tax Policy in the United States, Sweden, and Britain." *World Politics* 41, no. 4:500–535.

Stigler, George J. 1971. "The Theory of Economic Regulation." *Bell Journal of Economics and Management Science* 2, no. 1:3–21.

"Strengthening the Public Credit." 1898. US House of Representatives 55th, 2nd Session. H.R. Report 1575. June 15. https://www.govinfo.gov/app/details/SERIALSET-03722_00_00-155-1575-0000.

Strong, Wm. T. 1893. "The Fueros of Northern Spain." *Political Science Quarterly* 8, no. 2:317–34.

"Subsidies and Powers in Commercial Banking." 1990. Remarks by Alan Greenspan, Chairman. Annual Conference on Bank Structure and Competition. Federal Reserve Bank of Chicago. May 10. https://fraser.stlouisfed.org/files/docs/historical/greenspan/Greenspan_19900510.pdf?utm_source=direct_download.

"Success and Relationships in Financial Sector Regulation." 2001. Notes for a Speech by Nicholas Le Pan, Superintendent of Financial Institutions, to the Insurance Bureau of Canada's Regulatory Affairs Symposium, Toronto. November 2.

Sullivan, Richard J. 2009. "Regulatory Changes and the Development of the US Banking Market, 1870–1914." In *The Origins and Development of Financial Markets and Institutions: From the Seventeenth Century to the Present*, edited by J. Atack and L. Neal. 262–93. Cambridge: Cambridge University Press.

"Supervising LCBOs: Adapting to Change." 2000. Remarks by Governor Laurence H. Meyer before a National Bureau of Economic Research Conference, Cheeca Lodge, Islamorada, Florida. January 14. https://www.federalreserve.gov/boarddocs/speeches/2000/20000114.htm.

"Supervision of Bank Risk-Taking." 1996. Remarks by Vice Chair Alice M. Rivlin at the Brookings Institution National Issues Forum, Washington, DC. December 19. https://www.federalreserve.gov/boarddocs/speeches/1996/19961219.htm.

"Supervision on a Consolidated Basis of International Spanish Banking Groups." 2002. Bank of Spain. https://www.bde.es/f/webbde/COM/supervision/politica/SUPERVISION_ON_A_CONSOLIDATED_BASIS_OF_INTERNATIONAL.pdf.

"Survey of Spain—the Lessons Get Harder—the Gonzalez Government Is Less Secure." 1995. *Financial Times*, June 30. https://www.gale.com/c/financial-times-historical-archive.

Thelen, Kathleen. 2004. *How Institutions Evolve: The Political Economy of Skills in Germany, Britain, the United States, and Japan*. Cambridge: Cambridge University Press.

Thiemann, Matthias, and Jan Lepoutre. 2017. "Stitched on the Edge: Rule Evasion, Embedded Regulators, and the Evolution of Markets." *American Journal of Sociology* 122, no. 6:1617–2050.

Thiessen, Gordon. 1999. "Then and Now: The Change in Views on the Role of Monetary Policy since the Porter Commission." C. D. Howe Institute, Toronto. March 11.

"Titulización de activos: Perspectivas desde un Banco Central." 2005. Remarks by Bank of Spain Deputy Governor Gonzalo Gil. Primer Foro Español de Titulización. EBN Banco. Marrakech. November 11. https://repositorio.bde.es/handle/123456789/22121.

To Eliminate Unsound Competition for Savings and Time Deposits. 1966a. US House of Representatives Banking and Currency Committee. May 9.

To Eliminate Unsound Competition for Savings and Time Deposits. 1966b. US House of Representatives Banking and Currency Committee. June 1.

Tomaskovic-Devey, Donald, and Ken-Hou Lin. 2011. "Income Dynamics, Economic Rents, and the Financialization of the U.S. Economy." *American Sociological Review* 76:538–59.

Tooze, Adam. 2018. *Crashed: How a Decade of Financial Crises Changed the World*. New York: Viking.

To Provide a Guaranty Fund for Depositors in Banks. 1932a. US House Subcommittee of the Committee on Banking and Currency. March 14.

To Provide a Guaranty Fund for Depositors in Banks. 1932b. US House Subcommittee of the Committee on Banking and Currency. March 28.

Tortella, Gabriel Casares. 1977. *Banking, Railroads, and Industry in Spain, 1829–1874*. New York: Arno.

———. 2001. "Bank Mergers and Consolidation in Spanish History." In *A Century of Banking Consolidation in Europe: The History and Archives of Mergers and Acquisitions*, edited by Manfred Pohl, Teresa Tortella, and Herman Van Der Wee, 18–49. London: Routledge.

Tortella, Gabriel, and José L. García Ruiz. 2013. *Spanish Money and Banking: A History*. London: Palgrave Macmillan.

Tortella, Gabriel, and Jordi Palafox. 1984. "Banking and Industry in Spain, 1918–1936." *Journal of European Economic History* 13, no. 2:81–111.

UK. 2000. Parliament. "House of Lords: Briefing." March. https://publications.parliament.uk/pa /ld199798/holbrief/ldreform.htm.

"Understanding Financial Consolidation." 2001. Remarks by Vice Chairman Roger W. Ferguson Jr. at a Conference Sponsored by the Securities Industry Association and the University of North Carolina School of Law, New York. February 27. https://www.federalreserve.gov/boarddocs /speeches/2001/200104052/default.htm.

United States. 1932a. *Congressional Record*. Senate. January 17. Accessed via the Proquest congressional database.

———. 1932b. *Congressional Record*. Senate. May 10.

———. 1932c. *Congressional Record*. Senate. May 11.

———. 1933a. *Congressional Record*. Senate. January 17.

———. 1933b. *Congressional Record*. House. January 18.

———. 1933c. *Congressional Record*. January 19.

———. 1933d. *Congressional Record*. House. February 28.

———. 1933e. *Congressional Record*. House. May 22.

———. 1975. *Congressional Record*. December 11.

"Washington Furor over Loan Loss Reserves." 1999. *Journal of Accountancy*. https://www .journalofaccountancy.com/issues/1999/sep/news3.html.

West, Robert Craig. 2019. *Banking Reform and the Federal Reserve, 1863–1923*. Ithaca, NY: Cornell University Press.

White, Eugene. 1982. "The Political Economy of Banking Regulation, 1864–1933." *Journal of Economic History* 42, no. 1:33–40.

White, Lawrence J. 1991. *The S&L Debacle: Public Policy Lessons for Bank and Thrift Regulation*. Oxford: Oxford University Press.

Wiarda, Howard J. 1996. *Iberia and Latin America: New Democracies, New Policies, New Models*. Lanham, MD: Rowman and Littlefield.

Wicker, Elmus. 1980. "A Reconsideration of the Causes of the Banking Panic of 1930." *Journal of Economic History* 40, no. 3:571–83.

Wiebe, Robert H. 1962. *Businessmen and Reform: A Study of the Progressive Movement*. Cambridge, MA: Harvard University Press.

Wilentz, Sean. 2008. *The Rise of American Democracy: Jefferson to Lincoln*. New York: W. W. Norton.

Williams-Taylor, Sir Frederick. 1925. "Canadian Banking Is Sound." *Maclean's*, January 1. https://archive.macleans.ca/.

Williamson, John, and Molly Mahar. 1998. "A Survey of Financial Liberalization." *Essays in International Finance* 211 (November): 1–75. https://ies.princeton.edu/pdf/E211.pdf.

Wilson, James Q. 1980. "The Politics of Regulation." In *The Politics of Regulation*, edited by James Q. Wilson, 357–94. New York: Basic Books.

"The World's 100 Largest Banks." 1997. *Wall Street Journal*, September 18. https://www.wsj.com/articles/SB874506097534224000.

Wright, Robert. 2018. "Wright: Anxious about Interest Rates? Well, Welcome to the 1980s." *Ottawa Citizen*, December 5. https://ottawacitizen.com/opinion/columnists/wright-anxious-about-interest-rates-well-welcome-to-the-1980s.

INDEX

absolutism, 257–58n33

Accounting Standards Board (AcSB) (Canada), 197, 221–22

Acharya, Viral, 194

agriculture, 83, 85, 93–94, 145

Alcalá Zamora, Niceto, 101

Aldrich, Nelson W., 71

Alfonso XII (king), 33

Alliance Popular (AP) Party (Spain), 165, 167, 269n87

Amadeo of Savoy (king), 77

American Bankers Association (ABA) (United States), 152, 207

Anderson, Benjamin M., 90

Arthur Andersen, 166

asset-backed commercial paper (ABCP) market, 194–95, 198, 199–200, 206, 210–11, 213

asset-backed securities (ABS), 2, 196

assets, 196–98

asset securitization: asset-backed commercial paper (ABCP) market in, 194–95, 198, 199–200, 206, 210–11, 213; benefits of, 206, 208, 209; in Canada, 208–11, 215; complexity of, 208–9; defined, 193; global, 194; process of, 193–94; rise of, 194; risks of, 2, 208, 214; in Spain, 211–16; in the United States, 201–8, 215; without risk transfer, 195–201

Attewell, Bill, 161

autarky, 115

Avent-Holt, Dustin, 177

Bacon, Robert L., 92

Bagehot, Walter, 28

Balla, Eliana, 218, 227

Banca Catalana (Spain), 165

Banco Cantábrico (Spain), 164

Banco de Barcelona (Spain), 59

Banco de Crédito Industrial (Spain), 134

Banco de Isabel II (Spain), 59, 60

Banco de Navarra (Spain), 164

Banco de San Fernando (Spain), 59, 61, 62

Banco Nacional de San Carlos (Spain), 58–59

bank asset concentration index, 8–9

Bank Circulation Redemption Fund (Canada), 76

Bank Holding Company Act (United States), 249

banking: accounting principles of, 196; Basel II framework for, 175–76, 181–82, 269n6; deregulation of, in securities activities restrictions, 250; interstate branching and, 249–50, 274n11; loss buffers in, 209–10; natural evolution of, 97; risks within, 1, 4, 175, 219. *See also specific aspects; specific banks*

Banking Act of 1933 (United States), 88, 247–48, 250

Banking Law of 1870 (Canada), 74

Banking Law of 1921 (Spain), 105

Banking Law of 1962 (Spain), 125–26, 127

banknotes, 44, 67

Bank of Barcelona (Spain), 101

Bank of Boston (United States), 46

Bank of Canada (Canada), 100, 111, 178

Bank of England (United Kingdom), 41–42

Bank of Montreal (Canada), 54, 230

Bank of New York (United States), 46

Bank of North America (United States), 44–46

Bank of Spain (Spain): credit from, 80; crisis interpretation by, 187; loan loss provisioning and, 232–35; market participants of, 188; name change of, 62; nationalization of, 126–27; reforms regarding, 102–5; as refuge, 134; regulation authority of, 178; regulatory policy and, 77–79; regulatory strategies of, 189; RUMASA and, 166; securitization and, 211–15; supervision at, 189. *See also* Banco de San Fernando (Spain)

Bank of Terrassa (Spain), 100–101

Bank of the United States (first bank), 46–49

A NOTE ON THE TYPE

This book has been composed in Adobe Text and Gotham.
Adobe Text, designed by Robert Slimbach for Adobe,
bridges the gap between fifteenth- and sixteenth-century
calligraphic and eighteenth-century Modern styles.
Gotham, inspired by New York street signs, was designed
by Tobias Frere-Jones for Hoefler & Co.